THE NEW COMMUNICATIONS LANDSCAPE

The innovative and rapid growth of communication satellites and computer mediated technologies in the late 1980s and early 1990s, combined with the deregulation of broadcasting, led many media commentators to assume that the age of a national television medium had been lost. In an age of global communication, the world market was dominated by a few transnational media conglomerates.

But what has become clear is that while the transnational media groups are increasing visibly, their contribution to the formation of a global public sphere is doubtful, the response from audiences is limited and their impact on the local cultural industry has been mixed.

The New Communications Landscape explores the theories of media globalization and examines the culture of local television programming. Addressing the radical changes which have taken place in the world television markets, the contributors analyze the blurring of distinctions between the global and the local. Using examples of programming from Europe, Latin America and Asia, *The New Communications Landscape* focuses on the industry, program strategy and content, audience, media policy and the future of local television around the world.

Contributors: Joseph Man Chan, Sheue-Yun Chen, Miquel de Moragas Spà, Anura Goonasekera, Junhao Hong, Koichi Iwabuchi, Lin-lin Ku, Paul S.N. Lee, Rico Lie, Chun-chou Liu, Bernat López, Gérard Pogorel, Philip Schlesinger, Jan Servaes, John Sinclair, Ubonrat Siriyuvasak, Colin Sparks, Joseph D. Straubhaar, Herng Su, Yean Tsai, Georgette Wang, Jian Wang.

Georgette Wang is Dean of the College of Social Sciences, National Chung Cheng University in Chia-yi, Taiwan. **Jan Servaes** is the Dean of the Faculty of Social and Political Sciences and Professor of the Department of Communication, Katholieke Universiteit, Brussel. **Anura Goonasekera** is Head of Research at the Asian Media Information and Communication Centre.

ROUTLEDGE RESEARCH IN CULTURAL AND MEDIA STUDIES

Series advisors: David Morley and James Curran

THE NEW COMMUNICATIONS LANDSCAPE

Demystifying Media Globalization

Edited by
Georgette Wang, Jan Servaes
and Anura Goonasekera

London and New York

First published 2000
by Routledge
11 New Fetter Lane, London EC4P 4EE

Simultaneously published in the USA and Canada
by Routledge
29 West 35th Street, New York, NY 10001

Routledge is an imprint of the Taylor & Francis Group

© 2000 Georgette Wang, Jan Servaes and Anura Goonasekera

Typeset in Baskerville
by HWA Text and Data Management, Tunbridge Wells
Printed and bound in Great Britain
by St Edmundsbury Press, Bury St Edmunds, Suffolk

British Library Cataloguing in Publication Data
A catalogue record for this book is available
from the British Library

Library of Congress Cataloging in Publication Data
The new communications landscape : demystifying media
globalization / [editors] Georgette Wang, Jan Servaes
and Anura Goonaskera
p.   cm. – (Routledge research in cultural and media
studies ; 7)
Includes bibliographical references and index.
1. Television broadcasting–Social aspects. I. Wang, Georgette. II.
Servaes, Jan, 1952– III. Goonasekera, Anura, 1940– IV. Series.

PN 1992.6 .N49 2000
302.23'45–dc21   99-056814

ISBN 0-415-22325-3

CONTENTS

CONTENTS

CONTENTS

FIGURES

TABLES

LIST OF TABLES

CONTRIBUTORS

Joseph Man Chan is professor at the School of Journalism and Communication, the Chinese University of Hong Kong, where he was formerly director. His research interests include international communication, political communication, the social impact of information technology, as well as media development in Greater China. He was a Harvard-Yenching Scholar and is president of the Chinese Communication Association, 1998–2000.

Sheue-Yun Chen is associate professor of sociology, principally concerned with pedagogy, technology and globalization. She currently lectures research and qualitative methods, and cultural studies in the Department of Adult and Continuing Education at National Taiwan Normal University. She has published on media globalization, state-press relations, media literacy, and lifelong learning.

Miquel de Moragas Spà is professor of communications at the Autonomous University of Barcelona (UAB), formerly dean of the Faculty of Communication Science and vice-rector of the same University. He is the founder and director of the Institute of Communication and the Centre for the Olympic Studies, UAB.

Anura Goonasekera is the head of research at the Asian Media Information and Communication Centre (AMIC) and adjunct professor in the School of Communication Studies at the Nanyang Technological University in Singapore.

Junhao Hong is an assistant professor at the Department of Communication, State University of New York at Buffalo. His research areas include international communication, media and society, and new communication technology. He is the author of *The internationalization of television in China* (1998).

Koichi Iwabuchi teaches media and cultural studies at the International Christian University, Tokyo. He has recently completed his PhD at University of Western Sydney, Nepean. His articles have been published in a number of journals including *Media International*, Australia and *Sekai*.

Lin-lin Ku is associate professor and head of the Graduate School of Journalism, National Taiwan University, Taiwan. Dr. Ku has published widely on the development and uses of new media in Taiwan. One of her major research areas is competing strategies of foreign television programs.

Paul S.N. Lee is director of the School of Journalism and Communication at the Chinese University of Hong Kong. His research interests include international communication, telecommunications policy and development communication. He is the author of *International Communication*, editor of *Telecommunications and development in China* and co-editor of *TV without borders: Asia speaks out.*

Rico Lie is a social anthropologist working at the Research Centre, Communication for Social Change (CSC) which is based at the Katholieke Universiteit Brussel (KUB), Belgium. He previously worked at the Universities of Nijmegen and Leiden in the Netherlands. His research interests include the areas of culture and communication and the interlinked processes of localization and globalization.

Chun-chou Liu is associate professor, Institute of Telecommunications at National Chung Cheng University in Taiwan. His teaching and research interest focus on the impact and implications of the global trends of media convergence on the local media market and national communication policy.

Bernat López doctor in Communication Sciences, is assistant professor in the Department of Communications at the Autonomous University of Barcelona and academic secretary of the Institute of Communications at the same university. His research areas are communication policies and decentralization of television.

Gérard Pogorel is professor of Economics and director of the Department of Economic and Social Sciences, Ecole Nationale Superieure des Telecommunications, (ENST) at the Paris Graduate School of Communications Sciences. His activities have focused on government and business policies in the areas of international communications, information technology and technology management. He has served as a consultant to the Organization of Economic Cooperation and Development (OECD), the European Commission, and institutions involved in formulating public and business policy in France and Europe.

Philip Schlesinger is professor of Film and Media Studies at the University of Stirling, Scotland, director of the Stirling Media Research Institute, and visiting professor of Media and Communication at the University of Oslo. He is conducting research on political communication and national identity in the European Union, UK and Scotland.

Jan Servaes is dean of the Faculty of Social and Political Sciences, professor and chair of the Department of Communication, at the Katholieke Universiteit Brussel. He is director of the Research Centre, Communication for Social Change (CSC), and coordinator of the European Consortium for Communications Research (ECCR). He has been a professor of International

Communication and Development Communication at the Universities of Cornell, Nijmegen, Thammasat and Antwerp, and president of the Participatory Communication Research Section of the International Association of Media and Communication Research (IAMCR). His most recent books include: *Approaches to development communication; Participatory communication for social change; Media and politics in transition: cultural identity in the age of globalization; Communication for development: one world, multiple cultures;* and *Theoretical approaches to participatory communication.*

John Sinclair is professor in International Communication at Victoria University, Melbourne, Australia. His work on the globalisation of media industries includes the books *Images incorporated: Advertising as industry and ideology,* and *Latin American television: A global view,* and also the co-edited works, *New patterns in global television* and *Floating lives.*

Ubonrat Siriyuvasak is chairperson of the Faculty of Communication Arts and deputy director of the Institute of Social Science Research, Chulaongkorn University, Bangkok, where she lectures in media studies. Her particular areas of interest include media structures, the media industry, popular culture, women and the media, children and media and audience studies.

Colin Sparks is professor of Media Studies at the Centre for Communication and Information Studies of the University of Westminster. He has written on many aspects of the mass media, particularly of the printed press. His most recent book is *Communism, capitalism and the mass media.* It is a study of the transition to democracy in the former communist countries of Europe.

Joseph D. Straubhaar is Amon G. Carter professor of Communication at the University of Texas Radio-TV-Film Department. He previously taught at Michigan State University. He worked as a foreign service officer in Brazil and Washington. He has published extensively on international media studies.

Herng Su is associate professor, Department of Journalism, National Chengchi University in Taiwan. She is the author of *Cultural impacts under an open sky.* Her research interests include various aspects of Japanese cultural goods such as manga, animation, and their impact in Asia.

Yean Tsai is associate professor of radio and television at National Chengchi University, Taipei, Taiwan. She has published two books on television series. Her studies on genre and formula of television drama, news narrative and cybernetics have appeared in *Communication Research Monographs, Mass Communication Research, Journal of Radio and Television Studies,* and the *National Chengchi University Journal* (in Chinese).

Georgette Wang is currently dean, College of Social Sciences, National Chung Cheng University in Chia-yi, Taiwan. She has worked as research associate at the Communications Institute, East-West Center in Honolulu, Hawaii, and taught in Taiwan and Hong Kong. She has published widely in the area of communication technology and society. She co-authored *Information society: A retrospective view* and edited *Treading different paths: informatization in Asia.*

Jian Wang formerly an assistant professor at the school of Journalism and Communication, Chinese University of Hong Kong, Dr. Wang is currently with McKinsey & Company's Hong Kong office.

ABBREVIATIONS

ABU	Asian Broadcasting Union
ad	advertising
ads	advertisements
AMIC	Asian Media Information and Communication Centre
ASEAN	Association of South-East Asian Nations
ASPA	Association for Scottish Public Affairs
AWSJ	Asian Wall Street Journal
BAT	British American Tobacco
BJP	Bharatiya Janata Party
BSE	bovine spongiform encephalopathy
CCP	Chinese Communist Party
CEO	chief executive officer
CNC	Centre National de la Cinematographie
CSC	Communication for Social Change
DBS	direct broadcast satellite
DCMS	Department of Culture, Media and Sport
DTH	direct to home
ECCR	European Consortium for Communications Research
EMU	European Monetary Union
ENST	Ecole Nationale Supérieure des Telecommunications
ETV	Extra Terrestrial Vision
EU	European Union
EURORETV	Europe, Television, Regions
FCC	Federal Communications Commission
FEER	Far Eastern Economic Review
GATT	General Agreement of Trade and Tariff
GDP	gross domestic product
GNN	Global News Network
IAMCR	International Association of Media and Communication Research

ICA	Indian Cable Act
IHT	International Herald Tribune
IIC	International Institute of Communication
IMF	International Monetary Fund
IT	information technology
ITC	Independent Television Commission
ITN	Independent Television News
JET	Japan Entertainment Television
MCOT	Mass Communication Organization of Thailand
MP	member of parliament
MPEAA	Motion Picture Export Association of America
MSP	Member of the Scottish Parliament
NGO	non-governmental organization
NIC	New Industrializing Country
NICO	New Information and Communications Order
NVOD	Near Video on Demand
NWICO	New World Information and Communications Order
OECD	Organization of Economic Cooperation and Development
PC	personal computer
PIPs	people, institutions, products
PNG	Papua New Guinea
PTT	Petroleum Authority of Thailand
SCTV	Shanghai Cable Television
SMG	Scottish Media Group
SNP	Scottish National Party
SPPA	Scottish Political Press Association
STUC	Scottish Trades Union Congress
TCI	Tele-Communications Inc.
TdM	Macau TV
TNAA	transnational advertising agencies
TNC	transnational corporations
TRIPS	Trade-related aspects of International Property Rights
TTV	Taiwan Television Company
TV	television
UAB	Autonomous University of Barcelona
UK	United Kingdom
UNESCO	United Nations Educational, Scientific and Cultural Organization
US	United States
VCR	video casette recorder
WTO	World Trade Organization

1

INTRODUCTION

Georgette Wang and Jan Servaes

When communications satellites and computer networks took off in the early 1990s, the world found itself faced with a new generation of communications technology which not only undermined geographical distances but also national borders. Fueled by a wave of communications policy deregulation, changes in the communications industries soon led to the belief that the whole world was now linked by global media which transmit messages in split seconds to audiences everywhere, including those living in the most remote corners of the world. The era of "global" communications thus pronounced itself arrived.

While the expansion of transnational media is quite obvious for us to see, to many, media globalization remains a myth as a concept (Ferguson, 1992). Whether we should be satisfied with the growth of a few transnationals as sufficient evidence for globalization has been a question begging for answers.

As researchers are still grappling with the true meaning of globalization, the world television industries, generally perceived to be an important dimension of globalization, seem to have increasingly drifted away from the idea of a singular, united global marketplace, although globalization remains an important competitive strategy in the media business.

One runs the inherent danger of simplifying matters by making such statements. There is no telling whether what one can observe at this stage marks the beginning of, or the temporary transition to, a new era. In fact changes in the world communications industry in recent years have been so rapid and drastic that observing it is like observing a bullet train in motion – we all know it is going very fast, heading somewhere, but that is about all.

However, even bullet trains make stops. In recent years we have come to witness interesting, albeit somewhat puzzling, developments in the world of communications: the transnationalization of national, or even local, television in several parts of the world, local appeal as a success formula for television but not for cinema, and media globalization and localization as concurring phenomena. These developments have painted a communications landscape that is quite different from what we were familiar with. They pointed to new directions for changes and exposed significant inadequacies in the framework of analysis that was employed in the past. It is only with a good look at the industry, the audience and the policies that we may finally be able to demystify some of the theoretical clouds surrounding media globalization.

The meaning of global communication

The vision of an era of global communications seems especially pertinent when changes in other spheres of human societies are taken into consideration. The 1990s, with the fall of the Berlin Wall as a prelude, have been marked by the collapse of both the physical and institutional barriers which had kept people apart over the previous several decades. The ever closer trade relationships among nation-states, the growing number of transnational corporations, the emergence of global health and environmental issues and a common style of consumption of material and cultural products have all helped to bring about what is described as the "globalization" of our world.

As an idea, globalization is not a product of the 1990s, or even the twentieth century, as some researchers have been quick to point out (Robertson, 1990; Hall, 1995). However, over the years the word has increasingly been used to refer to a process through which the entire human population is bonded into a single society (Albrow, 1990), or "the concrete structuration of the world as a whole," as described by Robertson (1990: 50). This "single society" then forms the framework for individual activities and nation-state operations. It is conceived both as a journey and a destination – with arrival at the globalized state a finality (Giddens, 1990; Featherstone, 1990; Ferguson, 1992), which constitutes a unit of analysis in its own right.

While globalization as a trend of development has been recognized by many, whether it necessarily brings a unified, homogeneous global culture remains a contentious issue. From a neo-Marxist and functionalist point of view (Wallerstein, 1990; Chew and Denemark, 1996; Hirst and Thompson, 1996), globalization, a product of capitalists' drive to expand markets and maximize profits, only serves to perpetuate the hegemony of the few Western powers.

Others, especially those with a sociology and cultural studies background (Featherstone, 1995; Hall, 1992; Robertson, 1990, 1992; Said, 1978, 1993; Smith, 1990; Waters, 1995), have emphasized the plurality of cultural development as a result of the anti-colonialism movement. Instead of losing one's "sense of place" because of increasing global influences, the importance of locality was underlined in the constructing and deconstructing, embedding and disembedding of social forces.

As pointed out by Featherstone (1995), globalization suggests simultaneously two views of culture. The first, taking a monoculturalist point of view, treats globalization as the "extension outward of a particular culture to its limits, the globe," through a process of conquest, homogenization and unification brought about by the consumption of the same cultural and material products (Featherstone, 1995: 6). The second one, adopting a multiculturalist stand, perceive globalization as the "compression of cultures."

While the meaning of globalization remains ambiguous, "media globalization" or "global media" have quickly become clichés in communications studies. Two questions can be raised about the use of such terms, however. First, what is meant by a globalized communications industry, and secondly, can we assume that a genuine globalization of the industry has already taken place? More precisely, what is the direction of changes that we can observe now – globalization, localization, or something else?

All too frequently when the term "global" is used in conjunction with the communications media or industry, it refers primarily to the extent of coverage, with the popularity of satellite television and computer networks serving as evidence of the globalization of communications.

Indeed, never before in human history has a single television channel been available in over 150 nations, nor has there been any communications medium which managed to attract hundreds of million of users. However, as Ferguson (1992) has pointed out, the linkages brought about by the so-called globalization process are largely confined to OECD and G7 member countries, which constitute one-third of the world population. And even when a medium, e.g. CNN, can put over 150 countries on its map, the rate of penetration and actual consumption can present rather a different picture. As Street (1997: 77) has said, the fact that a product is available everywhere is no guarantee that it achieves the same level of popularity, let alone acquires the same significance, meaning or response (Featherstone, 1990: 10). It is no secret that CNN's audiences normally account for only a small fragment of a nation's population.

But even with its conceptual flaws corrected, coverage is merely one of the important dimensions of the communications industry. The meaning of a globalized industry would be seriously distorted if other dimensions were left out of the discussion. These dimensions, including the dynamics of the market, modes of production, the contents and messages transmitted, are closely related to the perception of the role and function of communications in the globalization process, the direction of change in the industry, and ultimately, the cultural images presented by the theories of globalization. What roles and changes, then, should we expect to see in the communications industries according to the monoculturalist, and, contrastively, the multiculturalist, point of view?

The "local" factor in the emerging communications landscape

The monoculturalists' interpretation of globalization is often noted for its resemblance to the modernization and media imperialism theories. Both focused on the economic and technological forces in change, and suggested a one-way unilinear impact of Western – or American, to be specific – media on their audiences.

Economic incentives and technological developments have also been believed to be the major driving forces for globalization (Featherstone, 1995: 7; Robertson, 1990: 22). For the communications industry, the purported globalization process was fueled by yet another factor: policy deregulation. Although many would argue that nation-states are still capable of keeping things under control, this control is undeniably much less than it used to be (Wang, 1997; Chan, 1994).

With a significant number of institutional barriers removed, there seems to be very little left to obstruct profit-seeking ventures now that technological development has rendered distant transmission of audio and visual signals affordable to entrepreneurs. The world of communications has become a perfect stage for the workings of capitalism, finally on its way to becoming a genuine "single system," to borrow Wallerstein's expression (1990, 1997). Once a single system, global division of labor – as seen in other industrial sectors – is expected to emerge (Mittelman, 1996a) in the global communications industry. No longer will there be a need for every nation to maintain its own communications industry, just as there is no need for each one to have an automobile industry. A similar point of view was adopted by several communications researchers, e.g. Ito (1990), Cantor and Cantor (1986), in examining the internationalization of television programs.

There is no denying that competitive pricing is a major reason for the availability of American and Japanese programs in most parts of the world. However, if prices were the single most important factor at work, those companies which produce the cheapest and most attractive products, with the most extensive global distribution networks and best promotional skills, would have become the sole suppliers for the global market, leaving very little to the smaller, less competitive national and local players.

To critical theorists, communications media can be viewed as industries which commercialize and standardize the production of culture (Kellner, 1989). This definition highlights an important property of the media: a business that produces, distributes and sells marketable products. But the recognition of this property is not to overlook the media's other equally important characteristic: its being cultural.

Cultural products, more than any others, reflect the cultural values of their producers and the social reality in which they were produced. Viewing a television program or listening to the radio, therefore, cannot be seen as a simple act of consumption; these acts involve a rather complex process of decoding cultural meanings. Although competing prices may contribute to the wide availability of certain cultural products, the purchase of cultural products differs from the purchase of typical consumer goods in that considerations such as product quality may bear little significance in the decision to watch, or not to watch, a television program.

The cultural products market, therefore, does not operate on economic forces alone. Following a similar logic, communications technologies, the other purported major force for globalization, also have their blind spots in explaining all changes – a conclusion which we can derive, without too much difficulty, from the discussion of the significance of "place" and "local cultures" in the literature on globalization.

Compressing, but not eliminating, time and space

According to neo-Marxists, who advocate a homogeneous world view, one of the major characteristics of globalization is that everyone has the feeling of being a member of one single society. The feeling, as described by Albrow (1990: 8–10), is the sense of "the whole earth as the physical environment," where all are citizens, consumers and producers, possessed of a "common sense interest in collective action to solve global problems."

The increasing interdependencies of nation-states has been cited as a major cause for nurturing such a feeling. Today the international community can no longer afford to ignore problems such as deforestation, economic crisis or the spread of AIDS; issues that used to concern only national governments. One's livelihood can easily be affected by events that occur thousands of miles away, and the sense of a shared, common destiny for human-kind has begun to affect the way people conduct their daily lives. As Giddens (1990) has argued, the comforts and assurances of local communal experience are now undermined by distant social forces.

A factor of equal or greater importance in the compression of time and space is believed to be communications media (Harvey, 1990; Giddens, 1990; Mittelman, 1996b) – television in particular – which constantly brings distant events and concerns to the homes and minds of people around the world as they happen. To Giddens, this constitutes an intrusion of distant events into everyday consciousness. Because of the media, we are now better acquainted with the president of the United States than we are with our next-door neighbor; it is the media which bring our "imagined," "phenomenal" global community to life.

This compression of time and space, however, is not without its limits. As pointed out by Mittelman (1996b: 229), flows of capital and technology must eventually "touch down" in distinct places. These places, in contrast to the global phenomenal world, are where everyone lives his or her "local life."

To human beings, wanting a place where one feels a sense of belonging is natural. However, such a "sense of place" is cultural, as has been pointed out by Hall (1995: 178). Despite the intrusion of distant social forces, our feelings and perception of places remain closely associated with the memories and personal ties we have, together with the social, cultural, and even geographical and climatic setting of these places. As described by Bourdieu (1977; Featherstone, 1995: 92), the emphasis on what we call a "local culture" is "the taken-for-granted, habitual and repetitive nature of the everyday culture of which individuals have a practical mastery." This and the cultural forms, the common language, shared knowledge and experiences associated with a place, are, according to Featherstone (1995), the essence of the concept of local culture.

The "local," or what is associated with a "place" where one feels a sense of belonging, therefore, is unique in its own right. In his study of localism and cosmopolitanism, Hannerz (1990) found that some people who travel widely are actually local at heart, often reluctant to leave home. We may, therefore, be led to attend to matters of global concern or to venture outside our local setting by a need to more efficiently and effectively achieve a task or to protect our own self-interest, a desire to learn, or just plain personal preference or curiosity. However, to a great majority of the world population, the importance, significance and relevance of the global do not come near to that of the local. As pointed out by Tomlinson (1994), the world may be the ultimate determinant of our local experiences, but it is certainly not the center of most people's everyday awareness.

Also different is the nature of our familiarity with distant and nearby events and personalities. McLuhan (McLuhan and Power, 1989) has said that the media are the extension of man; experiences acquired from these extensions, however, cannot be the same as those acquired by man her- or himself. Tomlinson (1994: 156–7), in a discussion of immediate and mediated experiences, made the following observation of "familiarity" with a media personality: "...the extension of individual lifeworlds offered by the television screen is categorically different from the extension provided by direct social interaction. ...people routinely distinguish between television and 'real life.'"

It is true, perhaps, that we 'know' a media figure better than our next-door neighbor, but the nature of this mediated knowledge is different; it is generated in a different way, in a different context, encompasses a different depth and scope, and carries a different meaning.

Global economic and political factors and communications technologies therefore do serve to compress, but not eliminate, time and space; and the sense of place, something associated with the essence of a local culture, has become a major determinant in the restructuring of the world communications industry. To suggest that media globalization is no more than a part of a process of domination by Western, or American, media, and ultimately of the Westernization, or Americanization, of world cultures not only conflicts with the ethno-nationalist revival in Europe (Schlesinger, 1993; Servaes and Lie, 1997) and the advocacy of Asian values in Asia (Wang, 1997), but is, in Ferguson's (1993) words, "reductionist and fails even on a continental North American basis."

To modify the monoculturalist image of culture, Featherstone (1995: 6) suggested that globalization may be better considered as a "form, a space or field, made possible through improved means of communication in which different cultures meet and clash," or simply "a stage for global differences." According to him, this conception points directly to the fragmented and de-centered aspects of the globalization of culture, and in the mean time suggests greater cultural exchanges and complexity.

For the study of changes in communication, this role of communications as a field or space for different cultures to meet and clash suggests media globalization, but also localization. In recent years the few transnational media which have been labeled "global", e.g. CNN and HBO, have made special efforts to localize their program content and presentation format. What remains to be seen is whether localization did make any significant differences in the content delivered by the transnationals. According to Street (1997), there may have been changes in the way to package the products, but their substance largely remained the same:

> While it is true that Anglo-American products are modified to appeal to their international audience, the product itself still retains the hallmarks of its origins. There may be concessions, ways of 'tailoring' an original design, to suit certain markets, but these are small compromises within the main framework.
>
> (Street, 1997: 80)

A similar criticism was directed at "global multiculturalism" in that the diverse cultures emerging into the global airwaves were selected according to marketing strategies (Frith, 1989).

The criticism raised a crucial question in the study of communication: can a genuine "association with a place" be achieved by localization of the global media content? Is it possible that the fact that a medium's being global has precluded, in the first place, the possibility of it also serving the needs of the vastly diverse local audiences?

One may argue that a multiculturalist view of globalization does not advocate the localization of transnational media as the only venue for communication as a platform for cultures to meet and clash. But powerful as the idea may be, this view does not offer a clear picture, nor an indication of, how the structure of the world cultural industries has, and will, change; how different it is from what we used to have, and how the ideals of "meeting/clashing points" may be achieved and professed.

In fact the picture would be highly incomplete if only the global media – regardless of how localized they may be – are considered in a discussion of global versus local communication. What has happened to the media which are "local," not "localized?" When Hollywood movies conquer the global market, when transnational media take up to seventy, or even eighty percent of the global trade in terms of volume in audiovisual products (Hoskins *et al.*, 1995; Barker, 1997), is there no longer a need for us to look at the cultural industries that are local?

According to cultural and media imperialism theories, the demise of local cultures and cultural industries was something predictable, as a consequence of the importation of television programs. By the 1990s it has become evident that the theories have suffered from a lack of evidence. However the non-American cultural industries, including the local, the national and also the regional cultural industries, continued to remain outside of the limelight, largely swept aside in the globalization debate, attracting little interest from the academic community.

The non-American, including many of the non-transnational, cultural industries, however, do constitute a vast and important area for the study of communication globalization. The audience's preference for local programs, the prospering local television industries, the rise of cultural-lingual markets, and the decline of the national film industries all point to the inadequacy of political and economic factors alone in explaining changes in the market place, let alone the implications of these changes on media strategies, policy formulations and other important dimensions of globalization, e.g. identity, public sphere and, ultimately, the role and nature of culture.

The world television industry: a shifting scene

Obviously there can be no answers to the above questions until we have a better understanding of the nature of change in global communications industries and the forces that are driving such change. In short, we need to find out how the world's communications industries have changed before we can determine the role they play in a globalization process such as that defined above.

Before the 1990s, the world media market was dominated primarily by national enterprises, public or private. This dominance was quickly eroded by transnational satellite television channels in the early 1990s. But it took the academic community a while to grasp both the direction and nature of the change, especially changes in the developing world.

Latin America, for example, is faced with a new way of thinking about the constitution of the mass society, according to Martín-Barbero (1993). He noted a profound influence from transnationalization, but also from the emerging new social actors and new cultural identities. Communication, in this light, has become "a strategic arena for the analysis of the obstacles and contradictions that move these societies, now at the crossroads between accelerated underdevelopment and compulsive modernisation (Martín-Barbero, 1993: 187)."

It is perhaps due to this interplay of transnational and cultural forces that led to the formation of geolinguistic markets which, as Sinclair noted, include small and dispersed diasporic communities as well as groups of nations such as those in the Middle East and Latin America. These communities and nations, linked by a common language and similar cultural background, soon became a new frontier where local and national television programs have prospered. In Latin America, Mexico and Brazil have been, but are no longer the only, "net exporters" of television programs. Venezuela and Argentina are "new exporters," and Colombia, Chile, and Peru are seeking to join their ranks.

The Latin American case demonstrates the strength of the cultural-linguistic factor in market changes. However, this is not to deny the power of the other factors. Sinclair (Chapter 2) saw the dominance of American programs in the 1960s and 1970s as the initial phase of television development, and the rise of cultural-linguistic markets as the second. But he suggested that this phase will also pass, for the comparative advantage of language may be threatened as more transnationals begin to dub their programs in different languages, or even produce programs for a particular audience group.

Latin America is unique in its language and cultural homogeneity; in Europe, where a diversity of languages is found, de Moragas-Spá and López (Chapter 3) noted not the rise of a single cultural-linguistic market nor the dominance of global media, but a decentralization of the television industry. Triggered by policy deregulation and the rediscovery of autonomy by communities within a state, e.g. the Welsh and Gaelics in the UK, and the Catalans and Basques in Spain, local and regional programs – which the authors described as "proximity television" – became increasingly popular.

8

Many of the proximity television programs are part of a public system. In the long run, market forces are expected to play a decisive role in their further development. But as it is only in those "nations without state" that proximity television has enjoyed the most powerful support, whether the market will work for, or against, the further development of proximity television will depend upon the strength of the cultural and linguistic factors.

Cultural and linguistic factors have helped to develop a market niche for local and national television programs from former "cultural colonies" and minority communities; Wang, Ku and Liu (Chapter 4) found the same competitive edge to have kept them prospering in their own turf despite growing competition from outside their borders. But to secure and expand markets, there is increasing hybridization in program production as the transnationals localize and the national and local globalize. A similar development has been observed with Hollywood production as it captures the global market.

Hybridization has led to increasingly blurred distinctions between the domestic and the foreign, the local and the global, which, the authors argue, may not have been clearly delineable since the inception of the television medium.

Public sphere, nation-state and cultural identity

Given the drastic changes in the media industry, one crucial issue in the discussion of media globalization is the existence of a public sphere, at the local, national or global level, and how it has been affected by the process of change.

Sparks (1998), who in his earlier works refuted the idea of a global public sphere, found evidence for a public sphere in state-based localities, but not in localities which were defined by ethnic identity and diasporic self-consciousness (Chapter 5). With the power of the state circumscribed by global forces, many believed the public sphere at the state level to have suffered. Sparks, on the contrary, suggested that the state still is the most powerful of social actors; the state-oriented public sphere remains crucial and defending it should be a central democratic task.

Sparks' notion echoed a recent re-recognition of the power of the state. However, the relationship among nation-states, cultural identity and media remains to be an open issue. In his book *Imagined communities* (1983) Benedict Anderson argued that: "Nation-ness is the most universally legitimate value in the political life of our time" (Anderson, 1983: 12). His notion of imagined communities emphasizes the centrality of the idea that nationhood exists as a system of cultural signification.

Imagining communities is a lengthy process of forging links between social groups, of inventing community and suppressing differences, of establishing the context in which the members of the community under construction can develop common experiences, and interpret past experiences in similar ways. It involves the organization of collective memory – and, thus, of collective forgetting – and of the rituals and institutions that support such projects. Therefore, the discourse of nationhood can best be understood in relation to boundedness, continuities and discontinuities, unity in plurality, the authority of the past, and the imperatives of the present.

Though the relationship between identity and nationalism is ridden with paradoxes, it is also at the heart of the narrative of cultural modernity. This means that any investigation into this topic situates us at the center of some of the vital and invigorating debates taking place within the domain of modern cultural studies.

In other words, such a search moves along two important axes: space and time. While there was a time not so long ago when the media landscape and cultural identity were congruent, today's electronic communication environment allows for disconnection of medium and geography. Various cultures manifest different and fragmented identities. There are at least two possible ways of conceiving cultural identity: one essentialist, narrow and closed, the other historical, encompassing and open. The former thinks of cultural identity as an already accomplished fact, as a "product." The latter conceives cultural identity as something which is being produced, always in "process." Furthermore, the term cultural identity refers to two complementary phenomena: on the one hand, an inward sense of association or identification with a specific culture or subculture; on the other hand, an outward tendency within a specific culture to share a sense of what it has in common with other cultures and of what distinguishes it from other cultures (for an elaboration, see Servaes and Lie, 1997; Servaes, 1999). The studies by Ubonrat (Chapter 6) and Schlesinger (Chapter 7) have both successfully demonstrated the complexity of the issues involved.

In Thailand, Ubonrat found consumerism, rather than democracy, to have become the new emphasis of communications media and also new forces in forging identities. The importation of foreign films, television programs and publications has brought down the revenues of the local communications industry and transformed their audiences into global consumers. The new electronic media map, while making and shaping the "imagined Thai state," is at the same time breaking it.

The contradiction is demonstrated by the simultaneous use of media to place citizens into an imagined public space by offering information, civic education and open democratic fora during elections, and advocate "un-Thainess" by featuring actors, singers and fashion models with Western names and appearances with stories and locations set in foreign lands.

Undoubtedly there are global factors at work in culture and communication, but Schlesinger also noted instances of "localism," which has become a more significant framework of meaning and identity for distinctive communities. In Scotland, it may be difficult to determine the extent to which the Scottish media have promoted a sense of Scottishness among the public, but a reciprocal relationship between media consumption patterns and Scottish identities could be assumed.

By examining the role of media after the 1997 referendum on Scottish devolution, Schlesinger found the reconfiguration of politics closely related to media and communication. On the other hand communication and political spaces are being shaped from above and from below, as increasingly communication and cultural policy debate are played out at three levels, instead of one: the EU, the UK, and the Scottish.

Content and strategy: localization, globalization or something else?

As communication becomes the meeting point of so many conflicting and integrating forces, the center of the debate "has shifted from media to mediation," as Martín-Barbero noted, especially "the articulation of different tempos of development with the plurality of cultural matrices" (1993:187). Martín-Barbero analysed this mediation process from a historical perspective and eloquently described the process by which the narrative discourse of media adapted to the popular narrative tradition of myth and melodrama, and the way audiences learned to recognize their collective cultural identity in media discourse. Similarly Dissanayake (1994) has nicely explored the relationship between nationalism and media in Asia, and between the genre of melodrama and the development of Asian film genres.

Tsai's study on Taiwanese prime-time soap operas was not designed as a study of media mediation (Chapter 10), however, the implications are strikingly similar. With the intention to find the content structure of popular local cultural products, Tsai discovered that certain themes and structural elements may be universally juxtaposed across cultures. However, the lifestyle, behavioral pattern, perception of the cosmos and human relations depicted in these soap operas are visibly traditional.

Tsai noted that, contrary to the propositions that international cultural industries would help promote an integrated culture across national boundaries, local tradition remains a major plot subject of Taiwanese soap operas.

Cultural lingual factors were shown to have helped the formulation of new market niches in different parts of the world; however, in some instances they may bring about a negative effect. According to Iwabuchi (Chapter 8), Japanese corporations, one of the major exporters in the international market, found success in globalizing, or more precisely, "de-Japanizing" their game and cartoon programs, for traces of Japanese culture may trigger unpleasant memories of the Second World War, especially in Asian nations. Another strategy that proved to have worked with Japanese corporations was localization in the form of hybridization and creolisation, a strategy which heavily involved local producers. A combination of globalization and localization, therefore, proved to be the best strategy for Japanese transnationals.

But however successful Japanese corporations may be, in order to expand their market, they often relied on transnationals from other countries – American or Australian – for distribution, or even production. The rise of non-Western transnational media corporations, therefore, has not so much countered West-centric power relations as co-solidified it by coopting it to join the alliance, according to Iwabuchi.

Also faced with the strategic question of "globalization" or "localization" are advertising companies, but here the decision seems to have become a natural outcome of the organizational structure. As pointed out by Wang (Chapter 9), the number of international media organizations – organizations which are characterized by international allocation of resources, management and ownership – is outgrowing that of transnational media – nationally-based organizations extending business overseas. With decentralized management, expatriates in these companies advize and supervize production of advertisements, but they need to rely on local staff to supply cultural information to produce messages that have resonance with their local consumers. During this process, Wang argued, the "export of meaning" is giving way to collective production of culture.

Wang suggested that "glocalization," a dialectic process between universalism and particularism, and homogenization and heterogenization, be a viable means of analysis to address the questions of the content and context of cultural hybridities, their personal and social impact, and process of formation, maintenance and transformation.

Consumption: different patterns of program diet

Markets may be sought, created and maneuvered by capital holders, however, it is consumer demand that holds the key to ultimate success. In recent years the image of audience has undergone drastic changes, from that of passive, fragmented individuals manipulated by media to that of autonomous social groups which select and interpret program content according to their own interest and cultural background.

Research findings from ethnographic studies on audience behavior, however, failed to dispel the fear that transnational media may foster a homogeneous global culture, while the availability of American cultural products everywhere continued to bring back the concerns over cultural imperialism. Although major changes in the television industries are evidence of the popularity of local and national programs, not much is known about the consumption pattern of foreign *vis-à-vis* domestic products, or the nature of the impact from transnational media.

In a survey of 602 teenagers in Taiwan, a former Japanese colony, Su and Chen (Chapter 13) found local variety shows to be the most popular programs, but Japanese cartoons, Taiwanese, Hong Kong and American films were also quite high on the viewing list – a hybrid consumption pattern that was found in Straubhaar's study in Latin America as well (1991).

The finding shows the importance of shared language and cultural background and supports the cultural proximity theory; however, other factors, including program genre, scheduling and parents' education, also accounted for differences in viewing behavior. Su and Chen warned that unless there is sufficient information regarding audiences' overall consumption of cultural products, it is dangerous to draw a conclusion by looking at just the origin of the program.

Straubhaar (Chapter 12), using Brazil as an example, took a closer look at how class and cultural capital may affect the viewing pattern of different social groups. The study found that middle and lower classes preferred cultural products closer to their local cultures, while the higher classes, those who also had access to the new and expensive television systems, tended to be open to products from industrialized nations.

While language, culture and class can both facilitate and provide barriers against cross-border flow of television programs, Straubhaar pointed to the fact that in both Brazil and the Dominican Republic, the two countries where empirical data were available, groups across the cultural spectrum watch national television programs. Brazilian elites tend to have multiple layers of taste for American and European cultural products, but unlike what was suggested by the cultural imperialism theory, they seem to heavily identify with Brazilian culture.

The chapter by Lee (Chapter 11) sought to answer the nature of the impact of transnational media by presenting a three-tiered model of television consumption. Despite negative values carried by global television, it was found to have positive impact by providing an opportunity for the audience to broaden their outlook, absorb foreign culture and tolerate difference in others.

As to the emergence of a global culture as a result of a common pattern of consuming material and cultural products, Lee argued that global television at best affects the material cultural realm by demonstrating and encouraging consumerism. The spiritual realm of indigenous culture would remain rather intact and autonomous because global television touches only superficial rather than entrenching values of society. Lee, therefore, suggests that "global identity" is a misnomer.

For too long we have seen culture as a kind of zero-sum game in which the arrival of the foreign was equated with the defeat of the local. The challenge now is to understand how people negotiate between these different levels to produce new kinds of identities for themselves.

Policy: at a crossroads still

Communication policies and regulations were met with serious challenges when transnational television and computer networks began sending signals across national borders. Although there has been little evidence supporting neither the cultural homogenization nor the cultural imperialism theories, deregulating domestic media was a realistic solution many national governments reluctantly settled with, rather than a reflection of a change of heart. Therefore, as communication technology and global forces continue to develop, the battle to defend cultural integrity and national sovereignty seems to keep on.

One major battleground is found at the international level. Pogorel in his chapter focused on the February 1997 agreement at the World Trade Organization (WTO), an agreement which included a set of liberalization principles to be implemented in domestic regulations on telecommunications (Chapter 14).

At heart is the issue of market dominance when vertical and horizontal convergence of computer, communication and telecommunication industry seems to be crashing through the gate. Focus of attention is placed on competitive dynamics, fairness and social and also cultural considerations, although media-related issues have been kept aside in the WTO agreement. Pogorel called for the articulation of the domestic, regional and international levels of institutions, as the trend towards globalism conceptually confronts cultural considerations.

The WTO agreement may have brought about a unique set of concerns and considerations to policy makers at the state level; however, it is not the first nor the last one to touch upon issues sensitive to national interests. As Goonasekera pointed out in his chapter (Chapter 16), market competition coupled with ethnic and communal conflicts has set the stage for conflicts: conflicts between political elites and transnational media, and also among national leaders when they fail to agree on issues of mutual concern, as evidenced in the North-South debate on the New World Information and Communications Order (NWICO).

To allow for objective research when different countries are pursuing different policies, each with cogent arguments, Goonasekera calls for the construction of an "Ideal Type," a model to understand social structures and processes from a sociological perspective.

An "Ideal Type" can be constructed, but as Goonasekera pointed out, it is not found in pure form in reality. Indeed there can be no "Ideal Type" for policy making, for the political, economic, social and cultural context of policy formulation may be vastly different from one instant to the next, not to mention from one nation to another. However, despite such differences, there are underlying attitudes and philosophies for policy making that can be examined, and the chapter by Chan questions one philosophy which is rather popular among policy makers nowadays: protectionism (Chapter 15).

While technological advancement has made protective measures extremely difficult to implement, it is standing on false ground. Chan's analysis showed that, protectionism presupposes powerful media effect, the ideological nature of cultural products and an elitist cultural perspective which does not expect the mass to have a good sense of cultural judgment. It is deeply rooted in the fear of influence from foreign culture and the loss of cultural identity. These premises, however, failed to hold when confronted with high ratings of domestic programs and the rise of cultural-lingual television markets.

Using Hong Kong as a case for open policy, Chan argued that the fear that an open cultural policy will result in radical transformation of a culture is not warranted; it will not lead to the domination by foreign media, and Western influence can be positive. Domestic competition, Chan suggested, will be the key to preparing media for global competition.

Perhaps very few nations could be more used to Western influences than Hong Kong, a Chinese society placed under British colonial rule for ninety-nine years. At the other extreme of the spectrum would be China, a country which was closed to the outside world until the early 1980s.

To Chinese policy makers, an open policy may be realistic if economic growth is to be achieved; however, it is implemented not without hesitations. According to Hong (Chapter 17), China began to marketize and corporatize its television industry in the early 1990s, and soon Chinese television found itself competing against foreign programs which "entered the country unofficially."

Until now direct operation of transnational television has not been allowed in China, but the loosening of satellite dish control posed a serious challenge to both the authorities and the industry. In an attempt to reconcile between the need to continue its open-door policy and resisting Western influence, the Chinese Communist Party (CCP) has adopted several measures, including the promotion of domestic production and expanding exports, setting a quota system for imported programs, and the further decentralization and depoliticization of television. Despite these efforts, Hong noted these new policies reflected little change in the CCP concept of media and culture as a political tool and ideological state apparatus.

Future research directions

The theories of globalization have been challenged, criticized and modified, but few would deny that they do offer a fertile ground for research. The chapter by Lie and Servaes (Chapter 18) adopted a convergent and integrated approach in studying the complex and intricate relations between globalization, consumption and identity. Such an approach, the authors argue, would allow problems to converge at key crossings or nodal points. Researchers then are rid of the burden of studying linear processes in totality, e.g. production and consumption of global products, and instead are allowed to focus on the nodal points where processes intersect.

Several such nodal points were identified by the authors, including production, regulation, representation, consumption, action and local points of entry into the communications flow.

The nodal points approach highlights the richness of globalization as an area of research; however, it is also important to note that all these dimensions do rest on certain axial principles. Similarly, chapters in this book discuss the emerging communications landscape from quite different perspectives and at times present seemingly contradictory findings. Nonetheless, they do point out important features of the world cultural industries and converge on several points.

In this purported era of global communications, culture remains an important factor, either facilitating the transnationalization of national or local cultural industries, or impeding further growth of global media. Global media may be largest in terms of coverage; however, their size shrinks significantly if measured in terms of viewing rate. In many regions of the world the most important development in the communications industry has not been the further dominance of global media, but the emerging cultural-linguistic television markets. As the influence of transnational television tends to rest on a quite superficial level of cultures, no global culture or global identity – not in the fullest sense of the words – has been fostered.

As Hall (1995) indicated, it is human nature to want a place to which one feels he or she belongs; however, it is perhaps also human nature to want to reach out to the strange unknown world outside of this "place." Audiences may prefer home programs, but these are not all they watch. While some national programs are successful because of their distinct cultural characteristics, others may achieve similar success by promoting foreign values. It is the capitalist nature of the industry that made American products available everywhere. But this capitalist character failed to make them accepted everywhere.

It is difficult still to determine if communications has helped to offer a "place," as suggested by Featherstone (1995), where cultures meet and clash, or has in fact enhanced the cultural context in which individuals find the "place" that they feel attached to. Perhaps a closer analysis will show that here again, communications serves as a double-edged sword; and which of the two roles becomes more prominent will be extremely variable, from situation to situation.

The danger here is treating culture and language as another set of powerful, determining factors in communications studies, thus undermining the importance of others, including global forces, which seem to have been downplayed in this volume. In fact, no single factor, nor a group of factors, can fully explain what has, is, or will, take place. Globalization may be inadequate to describe the current process of change, but neither would localization nor regionalization suffice. As co-production further blurs distinctions between the global and the local, it is important to note that the two are dialectically opposed conceptually, but not necessarily in reality.

During a dynamic process of change, it is the interaction of factors that brings about endless possibilities.

References

Albrow, M. (1990). Globalization, knowledge and society." In M. Albrow and A.D. King (Eds), *Globalization, Knowledge and Society*. London: Sage.

Anderson, B. (1983). *Imagined Communities: Reflections on the Origin and Spread of Nationalism*. London: Verso.

Barker, C. (1997). *Global Television*. Oxford: Blackwell Publishers.

Bourdieu, P. (1977). *La Distinction*. Paris: Minuit. (English translation *Distinctions*, London: Routledge, 1984.)

Cantor, M. and Cantor, J. (1986). "The internationalization of TV entertainment." In S. Thomas (Ed.), *Studies in Communication*. Norwood, NJ: Ablex Publications.

Chan, J.M. (1994). "National responses and accessibility to Star TV in Asia." *Journal of Communication*, 44(3), 70–88.

Chew, S.C. and Denemark, R.A. (Eds) (1996). *The Underdevelopment of Development: Essays in Honor of Andre Gunder Frank*. Newbury Park, CA: Sage.

Dissanayake, W. (Ed.) (1994). *Colonialism and Nationalism in Asian Cinema*. Bloomington: Indiana University Press.

Featherstone, M. (1990). "Global culture: An introduction." In M. Featherstone (Ed.), *Global Culture*, 1–14. London: Sage.

Featherstone, M. (1995). *Undoing Culture*. London: Sage.

Ferguson, M. (1992). "The mythology about globalization." *European Journal of Communication*, 7, 69–93.

Ferguson, M. (1993). "Invisible divides. Communications and identity in Canada and the U.S." *Journal of Communication*, 43(2), 42–57.

Frith, F. (Ed.) (1989). *World Music, Politics, and Social Change*. Manchester: Manchester University Press.

Giddens, A. (1990). *The Consequences of Modernity*. Stanford, CA: Stanford University Press.

Hall, S. (1992). "The question of cultural identity." In S. Hall, D. Held and T. McGrew (Eds), *Modernity and its Future*. Cambridge: Polity Press.

Hall, S. (1995). "New cultures for old." In D. Massey and P. Jess (Eds), *A Place in the World?* 176–211. Milton Keynes: England.

Hannerz, U. (1990). "Cosmopolitans and locals in world culture." In M. Featherstone (Ed.), *Global Culture*, 237–52. London: Sage.

Harvey, D. (1990). *The Condition of Postmodernity*. Cambridge, MA: Blackwell.

Hirst, P. and Thompson, G. (1996). *Globalization in Question: The International Economy and the Possibilities of Governance*. London: Polity Press.

Hoskins, C., McFadyen, S., Finn, A. and Jackel, A. (1995). "Film and television co-productions: Evidence from Canadian-European experience." *European Journal of Communication*, 10(2), 221–44.

Ito, Y. (1990). "Mass communication theories from a Japanese perspective." *Media, Culture and Society*, 12, 423–64.

Kellner, D. (1989). *Critical Theory, Marxism and Modernity*. Cambridge: Polity Press.

Martín-Barbero, J. (1993). *Communication, Culture and Hegemony. From the Media to Mediations*. London: Sage.

McLuhan, M. and Power, B.R. (1989). *The Global Village: Transformation in World Life and Media in the 21st Century*. New York: Oxford University Press.

Mittelman, J.H. (1996a). "The dynamics of globalization." In J.H. Mittelman (Ed.), *Globalization: Critical Reflections*, 1–19. London: Routledge.

Mittelman, J.H. (1996b). "How does globalization really work?" In J.H. Mittelman (Ed.), *Globalization: Critical Reflections*, 229–41. London: Routledge.

Robertson, R. (1990). "Mapping the global condition: Globalization as the central concept", In M. Featherstone (Ed.), *Global Culture: Nationalism, Globalism and Modernity*, 15–30. London: Sage.

Robertson, R. (1992). *Globalization: Social Theory and Global Culture*. London: Sage.

Said, E. (1978). *Orientalism*. Harmondsworth: Penguin.

Said, E. (1993). *Culture and Imperialism*. New York: Vintage.

Schlesinger, P. (1993). "Wishful thinking: Cultural politics, media and collective identities in Europe." *Journal of Communication*, 43(2), 6–17.

Servaes, J. (1999). *Communication for Development: One World, Multiple Cultures*. Creskill: Hampton Press.

Servaes, J. and Lie, R. (Eds) (1997). *Media and Politics in Transition: Cultural Identity in the Age of Globalization*. Leuven: Acco.

Smith, A. (1990). "Toward a global culture?" In M. Featherstone (Ed.), *Global Culture*. London: Sage.

Sparks, C. (1998). "Is there a global public sphere?" In Tussu, D. (Ed.), Electronic empires. London: Arnold. [From Chapter 5, p. 33; no page numbers were provided.]

Straubhaar, J. and Viscasillas, G. (1991). "Class, genre and the regionalization of the television market in Latin America." *Journal of Communication*, 41(1), 53–69.

Street, J. (1997). "Across the universe: the limits of global popular culture." In A. Scott (Ed.), *The Limits of Globalization*, 75–89. London: Routledge.

Tomlinson, J. (1994). "Phenomenology of globalization? Giddens on global modernity." *European Journal of Communication*, 9, 149–72.

Wallerstein, I. (1990) "Culture as the ideological battleground of the modern world-system." In M. Featherstone (Ed.), *Global Culture*. London: Sage.

Wallerstein, I. (1991). "Culture is the world-system: a reply to Boyne", In M. Featherstone (Ed.), *Global Culture: Nationalism, Globalization and Modernity*, 63–6. London: Sage.

Wallerstein, I. (1997). "The national and the universal: can there be such a thing as world culture?" In A.D. King (Ed.), *Culture, Globalization and the World-System*, 91–105. Minneapolis: University of Minnesota Press.

Wang, G. (1997). "Beyond media globalization." *Telematics and Informatics*, 14(4), 357–64.

Wang, G. (1998). "Protecting the local cultural industry: a regulatory myth in the global age." In A. Goonasekera and P.S.N. Lee (Eds), *TV Without Borders: Asia Speaks Out*, 259–73. Singapore: AMIC.

Waters, M. (1995). *Globalization*. New York: Routledge.

2

GEOLINGUISTIC REGION AS GLOBAL SPACE

The case of Latin America

John Sinclair

In order to understand how the globalization of television production and distribution has developed and assumed the ever more intensive and complex forms it has today, it is necessary, though not sufficient, to take language and culture into account as primary "market forces" which enable the major producers and distributors of television programs and services to gain access to markets outside their nations of origin. In this context, it becomes helpful to discard the metaphor of the "worlds" which share a common language in favor of the concept of "geolinguistic region." Such regions have been the initial basis for the globalization of the media, notably in television programs and services. It should be emphasized that a geolinguistic region is defined not necessarily by its geographical contours, but more in a virtual sense, by commonalities of language and culture. Most characteristically, these have have been established by historical relationships of colonization, as is the case with English, Spanish, and Portuguese. However, in the age of international satellites, not only do former colonies counterinvade their erstwhile masters with television entertainment, but geolinguistic regions also come to include perhaps quite small, remote and dispersed pockets of users of particular languages, most often where there have been great diasporic population flows out of their original countries, such as Indians now living in the Gulf States, Britain, and North America, or the unique case of the Spanish-speaking minorities of diverse origin who inhabit the US.

The paradigm case of a geolinguistic region is Spanish, which is the "mother tongue" of some twenty countries in Latin America. The Portuguese situation is different, in that all the speakers of Portuguese in Latin America are in the one country, Brazil. Just as the United States contains about four times as many native speakers of English as does the UK (Crystal, 1997: 30 and 60), Mexico's population of 96 million is more than twice that of Spain, with its 39.7 million, and Brazil has sixteen times as many people as Portugal. Yet as well as Spain, there is one other major Spanish-speaking nation outside of Latin America but in that geolinguistic region to be taken into account, even if it is one in which Spanish is not the dominant

19

language: if we take the current estimate of 26 million people of Hispanic origin living in the US, which is nearly ten per cent of its total population of 265.8 million, the US would be the fifth-largest Spanish-speaking country in the world (*El Estado del Mundo*, 1996: 614–9).

In the geolinguistic regions of Spanish and Portuguese, certain media corporations have arisen which have been able to exploit the massive size of the domestic markets for which they produce as the key to the opening up of foreign markets in other nations that speak the same language. These other countries have provided them with a "natural" constituency for their output, and in spite of the fact that all of them also import English-language television programming and other media products such as films, the crucial fact is that the most popular programs, indeed entire television genres such as the Latin American soap opera or *telenovela* in particular, are in the same language and cultural ambit of the countries which so avidly consume them as imports.

Latin America as postcolonial space

Mil cuatrocientos noventa y dos: 1492 was the year which marks the beginning of "a major extended and ruptural world-historical event ...the whole process of exploration, conquest, colonisation and imperial hegemonisation" (Hall, 1996: 249). The same year in which Christopher Columbus landed on the islands of Cuba and Hispaniola, and claimed them for the Spanish Crown, saw the beginnings of the creation of the "proto-modern" nation-state of Spain (Galeano, 1973: 22; Williamson, 1992: 61–3). Soon after, an agreement to regulate territorial rivalries with their neighboring kingdom of Portugal, the Treaty of Tordesillas in 1494, established a dividing line between the Spanish- and Portuguese-speaking nations of the Americas just as existed in Iberia (Schwaller, 1987: 69; Bakewell, 1991: 57–80).

While it is not the intention here to provide a potted history of the Iberian nations and their American colonies, it is important to establish the main features of their colonial relationships. In this regard, it is significant to note that, although Latin America is the oldest postcolonial region outside the Mediterranean and its nations have had their independence for the longest period of time, relative to Asia and Africa, it also had the longest period under colonization, for independence did not begin to happen until some 300 years after settlement.

However, the banishment of Spain from Latin America ushered in an era in which other European powers and then the US could set up neocolonial relationships with the new nations through trade and investment. This initial trade with Europe laid the basis for the indebtedness and dependency which have continued to characterize the region. René Chateaubriand, French foreign minister at the time, observed, "In the hour of emancipation the Spanish colonies turned into some sort of British colonies" (quoted in Galeano, 1973: 216), referring to the considerable investments which Britain was able to make throughout the region, once the main barrier to its unconcealed ambitions there had been removed. Yet within a few decades, France also was involved: indeed, Fernand Braudel records that the name "Latin America" was in fact first used by France in 1865, expressly to further its own interests at a time when the French emperor Napoleon III was attempting to establish a European monarchy in Mexico (1993: 427). Thus, although "Latin America" since has been adopted universally as a neutral cultural-linguistic descriptor referring to all those nations which share a "Latin" language, either Spanish or Portuguese, in a a region stretching from the US border with Mexico in North America to the tip of continental South America, as a concept it has highly politicized and tendentious origins in European colonial rivalries.

As to the present century, the US government has a long history of direct and indirect interventions; support for client states led by repressive dictatorships and juntas; and "covert operations" and "low intensity conflicts." These tactics have been motivated by a desire to protect the massive private investment by US corporations in Latin America, often denounced as "US imperialism," and its determination to maintain the "security" of the region against whatever forces the US government has perceived to be inimical to those interests. Proceeding with both force and diplomacy (as in the Good Neighbor Policy between the World Wars, or the Alliance for Progress in the 1960s), the US has clearly and consistently asserted its political as well as economic hegemony over the entire region in the postcolonial era (McClintock, 1992: 89–90; Williamson, 1992: 322–7).

Language: "the perfect instrument of empire"

The story is told that when, in 1492, Antonio de Nebrija presented Queen Isabel of Spain with his grammar of Castilian, the first of any modern European language, she asked him what such a work was good for. "Language," replied the scholar, "is the perfect instrument of empire" (Williamson, 1992: 62). Castilian is the language that we now recognize as "Spanish", which became a world language in the process of colonization, but the name serves as a reminder that although Spain was the first nation to have a national language (Klee, 1991: 1), even in Spain itself today, there are several other languages still widely spoken in distinct regions, not to mention a surviving range of native languages and imported linguistic influences in the Americas over which Spanish was imposed.

Relative to the other languages of the Iberian peninsula, Castilian was a "language-of-power" (Klee, 1991: 1), not just as the language of administration for a vast empire, but the language upon which a "national print-language" could become standardized, and so create the "imagined community," the cultural dimension of nationhood, in Benedict Anderson's influential formulation. In fact, Anderson sees the nation-states of the Americas as the first independent nations of their kind (1991: 45-6), models for the postcolonial world. He makes the point that all the new American nations established in the independence era, whether Spanish, Portuguese, or English-speaking, were "creole states," that is, the colonial-born shared the same language and cultural heritage as the metropolis from which they had to free themselves. At least for these creole elites, there was no issue of an alien language, as there would be later with the new nations of the twentieth century in Asia and Africa. The outcome is that, compared to the other postcolonial continents, Latin America exhibits a unique linguistic homogeneity, for the most part at the level of a first language, and at the very least at the level of a lingua franca, a common tongue, amongst native peoples. Even the differences between Spanish and Portuguese are not so great as those which exist between the different languages of most neighboring countries in Asia or Africa. However, this homo-geneity is tempered by some heterogeneity which should not be ignored.

English speakers are familiar with sometimes considerable national variations in English, such as between British, American, Australian, and Indian English, and furthermore, with regional variations within a nation, such as English as it is spoken in New York compared to Atlanta or Los Angeles. Such variations can be differences in grammar and vocabulary as well as of pronunciation and accent, some of which might be particularly difficult to understand, or carry a negative status. Just so are there the same kinds of variations in the Spanish-speaking world: the characteristic lisp of Iberian Spanish is not used in the Americas, for example. Similarly, national groups such as Argentinians and Mexicans can be sensitive about each other's accents, in the same way as an American accent might still grate when heard on British or Australian television. Yet, although not all English speakers are exposed to a wide range of variations, by and large English speakers the world over can understand each other. This is one of the factors which makes English the world's principal geolinguistic region, and the basis for its development as a global television market. The point here, however, is that this also has been true for the Spanish- and Portuguese-speaking geolinguistic regions, although the traditional predominance of Latin American companies is now challenged in the age of international satellite transmission and globalization by US-based services transmitted in the region's languages.

In such an era, we have to think of how viewers might relate in different ways to television programming from various sources at distinct levels. For example, at the local level, viewers get the local news and sport in their city or district and at the national level, networked news and entertainment programming produced in and for the national market. There are two transnational levels: the world-regional level, at which *telenovelas* and other entertainment from the major producers in Latin America circulate; and the global, which usually means subscriber services like CNN – all in Spanish or Portuguese, of course. So, viewers in Lima, for example, can enjoy watching a local league sporting match and then the national news, affirming their identities as Limans and Peruvians respectively. However, watching an Argentinian or Mexican *telenovela* reminds them of the similarities they share with neighboring countries in their region (and perhaps also the differences), while flipping over to CBS Telenoticias or a Hollywood film dubbed into Spanish might make them feel more like privileged citizens of the globe.

This is not the place to speculate on whether any of these levels is becoming dominant over the others, as theorists of cultural imperialism and globalization have tended to fear. Rather, the point is that even though viewers in other regions of the world have access to all these levels, including the world-regional, only in Latin America are audiences in a whole host of nations able to be addressed by virtue of their more or less common linguistic and cultural heritage as a kind of "imagined community" on a world-regional scale, a feature of the region which the larger television producers have been well-placed to exploit. Furthermore, we are talking here not just of the geographic region of Central and South America and the Spanish-speaking Caribbean, but of the whole geolinguistic entities created by Iberian colonization: that is, the nations of Spain and Portugal themselves have to be included as part of the region in which their respective languages are spoken.

In the absence of comparative audience studies, it is not possible to say how far viewers, and which kinds of viewers, might be drawn in by the idea of a common Hispanic (Spanish) or Lusitanian (Portuguese) identity, or alternatively, how far the submerged differences between and within the Latin nations might provide a counterweight of resistance against being addressed as a member of such an international imagined community (Waisbord, 1996: 24–5). What is clear is that there is a demand for local, national and regional programming, that Latin America has developed its own television programming and genres which are popular at all these levels, and that a small number of producers have been able to seize a strategic advantage out of emphasizing similarity at the expense of difference, and so build themselves hegemonic positions over the commercialization of cultural similarities within their respective geolinguistic regions.

Now that many countries have had almost fifty years of television, it appears that passing through an initial stage of dependence to a maturity of the national market is, if not universal, then certainly a common pattern, of which the Latin American experience is paradigmatic. Crucial in the transition is the growth not just of the audience size, but of domestic program production, the emergent consensus amongst observers being that audiences come to prefer television programming from their own country, and in their own vernacular, or if that is not available, from other countries which are culturally and linguistically similar. Joseph Straubhaar calls this "cultural proximity:" "audiences will tend to prefer that programming which is closest or most proximate to their own culture: national programming if it can be supported by the local economy, regional programming in genres that small countries cannot afford" (1992: 14).

The development of Latin American national markets for television programming bear out this hypothesis, including the pre-eminence of Mexico and Brazil as "net exporters" within the region, to follow Rafael Roncagliolo's (1995) classification. Venezuela and Argentina are "new exporters", with Colombia, Chile, and Peru seeking to join them, but coming from far behind, while the rest of the nations in the region, most of which are the smaller nations of Central America and the Caribbean, are "net importers" (1995, p. 337). However, the last decade has seen rapid growth in the number and variety of channels available, due to the expansion of cable and satellite modes of distribution, which has brought in new service and content providers, including US corporations. Indeed, the age of Westinghouse's CBS Telenoticias and Time-Warner's HBO Olé, and other such special Latin services provided by the major US cable channels, is already moving into a further stage defined by the advent of digital direct-to-home (DTH) satellite delivery. This new "postbroadcast" technology has encouraged the major Latin American producers and distributors to enter strategic alliances with US satellite and cable services. These alliances, with their plans extending to Europe as well as Latin America, mark the beginning of a phase which brings Latin American television into the mainstream of globalization.

The consumption of television is related in the globalization literature to questions of cultural identity. In counterpoint to the evident trend towards cultural homogenization, a trend towards heterogenization is also recognized: "Culture is a multi-layered phenomenon; the product of local, tribal, regional or national dimensions, which is anything but a single national culture" (Richards and French, 1996: 30). Rather too often, however, the "local" becomes a catch-all category set up in contrast to the global, and tends to become equated with the "national" (Sreberny-Mohammadi, 1991). It was argued earlier that we can usefully think of different kinds of television addressing audiences at local, national, world-regional, and global levels. In the debate about globalization, and cultural imperialism before it, there tends to be a static, zero-sum conception of culture, or at least, the assumption that global or other foreign cultural influence carried by the media somehow necessarily drives out the local, national, and regional identities, rather than just adding another level of identification which co-exists with them in any given individual. As Morley and Robins have observed,

> every culture has, in fact, ingested foreign elements from exogenous sources, with the various elements gradually becoming "naturalised" within it ... cultural hybridity is, increasingly, the normal state of affairs in the world, and in this context, any attempt to defend the integrity of indigenous or authentic cultures easily slips into the conservative defence of a nostalgic vision of the past.
>
> (Morley and Robins, 1995: 130)

It is in this context that the Latin American theorization of *mestizaje* or hybridity has much to contribute, a perspective in which cultural identity "is not simply an object that is acted upon by external forces, but rather has been rethought as a complex field of action" (Schlesinger and Morris, 1997: 8–9). Although rejecting the concept of postcolonialism as not applicable to Latin America, Nestor García Canclini is also explicit in his rejection of the dichotomies of dominator and dominated, center and periphery, and sender and receiver. This leads to a post-modernist view of identity as deterritorialized and decentered (1997: 23–4). Jesús Martín-Barbero also draws attention to the deterritorialization of identities, in particular, as attributable to international television. He argues that Latin American television production and distribution on a regional basis is deterritorializing to the extent that the local is lost, and that it subsumes the cultural differences between Latin American nations, at the same time as it shapes a commercialized Latin American imaginary (Schlesinger and Morris, 1997: 10–11).

Silvio Waisbord is more agnostic. While accepting Ien Ang's view that subjective identities are "dynamic, conflictive, unstable, and impure" (quoted in Waisbord, 1996: 27), he also argues that "Perhaps the death notices written for national identities were premature" (1998: 389). Apart from this reminder that nation-states are still legitimate and effective units of political, economic, and sociocultural organization in a globalising world, Waisbord poses the question of identities as an empirical one, a matter of audience research to ascertain "how citizens actively build a sense of national identity beyond the interpellation of authorities and the shared consumption of mass culture." Even if we accept that Latin America is one of the world's eight great "civilizations" (Huntington, 1997), just because Latin American nations share a similar linguistic and cultural heritage does not ensure that pan-Latin American television programming is going to be uniformly accepted and interpreted – a program might have the right language and commercial properties, but the wrong cultural resonance (1997: 24-25). Evidence from regional programming executives suggests that this is indeed the case: programming "must be flexible enough to accommodate quite distinct national market contexts" (Wilkinson, 1995: 207). It follows that the sensitivity of such differences would be heightened in program exchanges between Latin American and Iberian nations.

Television markets of the Latin world

In Mexico, the development of television has been very much formed by the entrepreneurship of two generations of patriarchs from the one family, the Azcárragas, and by the emergence of their company, Grupo Televisa, as a quasi-monopolistic, cross-media conglomerate which not only has dominated the Mexican television market, but has been actively pursuing its ambitions in most of the rest of the Spanish-speaking world. This international drive has been most consequential for the structures which television has assumed both in the Latin American region, and to a more restricted degree, within the US.

Historically, Televisa has been able to exploit the "competitive advantage" of its market dominance in the world's largest Spanish-speaking nation as the basis for this international expansion. The fact that Televisa itself produces most of what it broadcasts means that it has vast stocks of programming available for international distribution which has already proven and paid for itself in its domestic market. However, a recent downturn in its fortunes has seen Televisa in crisis: it is almost a billion US dollars in debt and has been desperately selling down prime assets; its management has become unstable; it is facing real competition in its domestic market for the first time, and it is being subordinated to foreign-based partners in its international ventures.

At the end of 1995, Rupert Murdoch's News Corporation Limited announced that it would lead a pan-regional DTH satellite subscription service consortium, DTH Sky, which included not only Grupo Televisa, but also its counterpart in Brazil, Organizações Globo, and the major US cable corporation TCI (Tele-Communications Inc). This was a response to the advent of Galaxy, an initiative announced the previous May by the US-based satellite division of General Motors,

Hughes Electronics Corporation, which incorporated Televisa's cable competitor in Mexico, Multivisión, along with TV Abril (Globo's main cable competitor in Brazil), and Grupo Cisneros, owners of Venevisión, a major television producer and distributor based in Venezuela, another key market of the region ("Country Profile: Mexico," 1996: 7). Both services had begun transmission by the end of 1996.

Ironically, Televisa had been instrumental in the establishment of PanAmSat, the world's first private international satellite television corporation, but the subsequent merger of PanAmSat with Hughes, in September, 1996, effectively meant that Hughes acquired most of Televisa's interest in the restructured company (Grupo Televisa, 1997: 73). However, the growth of DTH depends on the recovery of the Mexican economy as a whole, and if the market proves too small to be profitable for both competing services, the company which controls the distribution of both of them at a global level, the new PanAmSat owned by Hughes, can either close one or the other down, or oblige them to merge. Either way, Televisa has become most vulnerable to the strategies of both its global as well as its regional collaborators: it might be added that Venevisión is a partner of Televisa in the US, although its competitor in Latin American DTH.

Globo in Brazil shares a number of historical and structural similarities with Televisa, notably a high degree of vertical and also horizontal integration of their various media activities. Each of them is the largest producer and distributor of television programming not just in their respective domestic markets but their entire geolinguistic regions. In terms of broadcast television in their domestic markets, Televisa is facing commercial competition for the first time (with TV Azteca), while Globo is much more experienced at keeping rivals at bay (notably SBT). In cable television, where the exploitation of their own domestically-produced material is less of an advantage, Globo has found a more difficult competitor in TV Abril, just as Televisa has with Multivisión in Mexican cable. In their export activities, Televisa has found it much easier than Globo to penetrate national markets in the rest of Latin America, but Globo has been much more successful in gaining entry to the market in Portugal than Televisa has been in Spain. In fact, beginning as a supplier of programming to Portuguese television, Globo has been able to acquire an interest in one of the privatized channels, and drive it on to market leadership (Sousa, 1997). It also has assumed an influential position as the major investor in the development of cable television in Portugal (Lusomundo Joins TV Cabo, 1998). By contrast, not only has Televisa been unsuccessful in joining up subscribers to its Galavisión service in Spain, but it failed to acquire a

Table 2.1 Ownership of Latin American DTH consortia formed in 1995–96 (percentages)

DTH Sky Latin America		Galaxy Latin America (DirecTV)	
News Corporation	30	Hughes Electronics Corporation	60
Grupo Televisa (Mexico)	30	Multivisión (Mexico)	10
Organizações Globo (Brazil)	30	TV Abril (Brazil)	10
Tele-Communications Inc (US)	10	Grupo Cisneros (Venezuela)	20

share in any of the private broadcast channels which were created at the beginning of the 1990s (Martínez, 1996). However, it has been able to join Spanish broad-casting and telecommunications entities in the less successful of the two DTH ventures in Spain (Peralta, 1997).

Convergence and the challenge to geolinguistic monopolies

Like "globalization," one of the great buzz-words of the 1990s is "convergence." The communications satellite, in both symbolic and practical terms, is one of the most significant instances of this epoch-making fusion of broadcasting, telecommunications, and data transmission. Much of the discourse about convergence presents it as a technological phenomenon, but that needs to be kept in perspective: it is not the technologies as such, but the commercial infrastructure sustaining them which is so consequential (McAnany, 1984: 188–9).

That is, as well as at the technological level, convergence is also occurring within the structure of the communication and information industries themselves, as telecommunication companies take up strategic holdings in more entertainment-based cultural industries such as subscription television, and enter into joint ventures with national and regional companies to do so. Vertically-integrated structures for content production and distribution formerly were amongst the more distinctive features of the Latin American model of corporate organization, of which Televisa and Globo are the paradigm cases, but now this mode of integration is becoming globalized. As is apparent in the case of both the Murdoch and the Hughes' Galaxy DTH ventures in Latin America, these integrated structures can cross the former divide between hardware or "carriage" (in that case, satellite design, manufacture, and management), and software or "content" (television program production and distribution). This kind of convergence has also transformed the international television business from an import-export trade in programs as products, to a postbroadcast industry which provides not so much particular products but continuous transmission of services, whether delivered via cable or delivered direct to subscribers.

Such immense technological and structural transformation has consequences for how we understand communications theoretically, and this includes the implications for language and culture. Following the Spanish geographer Manuel Castells, Morley and Robins argue that what Harold Innis called the "space-binding" properties of communications media now are redefining space in terms of flows, rather than of places as such, although with key economic and cultural "nerve centers" in the network of flows (1995: 26–9). We can think of geolinguistic regions as prime examples of such virtual restructured spaces, in which new centers have emerged. These include not just Mexico City and Rio de Janeiro, the home bases of Televisa and Globo, but also Miami. More than a strategically-located center for television production and distribution to serve both Americas, Miami has assumed a mythical place in the Latin American "collective imagination" (Monsiváis, 1994: 124), a virtual "capital of Latin America" (Whitefield, 1997).

But while respatialization, understood in this way as a dimension of globalization facilitated by convergence, seems to be overflowing geographical barriers to create global markets, the barriers of language and culture seem more resistant. They have substance as "market forces," or as Collins observes:

> Although new communication technologies have reduced the costs of transmitting and distributing information over distance (space binding), distinct information markets remain; here the most important differentiating factors are those of language and culture.
>
> (Collins, 1994: 386)

Thus, while paradigmatic of global respatialization, the transcontinental niches which the Spanish- and Portuguese-speaking television markets have carved out for themselves are also emblematic of the reassertion of linguistic and cultural difference which is taking place in the face of globalization. Even within those geolinguistic regions, there is further linguistic and cultural differentiation. Just as in Asia, where Sony first elaborated its strategy of "global localization", and Murdoch's Star TV tailored its offerings to the major linguistic groups rather than seek a pan-Asian audience, some of the US-based cable channels in Latin America have found it necessary to adapt and differentiate their services to the local market. This is a significant trend because it shows how the drive for global economies of scale, a force towards homogenization, is attenuated by the heterogenising factors of language and culture, although as Morley and Robins note, "the local" is usually not more specific than national, regional, or even pan-regional differences (1995: 117).

The technical properties of the new digital compression on the current generation of satellites not only allow the satellites to transmit many more channels than ever before, whether from the US, Europe, or elsewhere, but facilitate the provision of multiple audio tracks. This means that one image, say a Hollywood film on HBO Olé, or a Discovery channel travelogue, can be made available to cable operators and DTH subscribers dubbed into Spanish or Portuguese, as well as in the original version. Clearly for the Latin American market, the provision of at least dual audio tracks is elemental, but there are now much more culturally-sensitive bases for differentiation, such as musical taste cultures. Viacom's MTV not only has a separate service for Latin America, and within that, one for Brazil, but has created special programming feeds for Mexico at one end of the Spanish-speaking zone, and Argentina at the other. Based in the mythical space of Miami, so as to be seen to be above national partisanship, the core international material is augmented with distinct Mexican and Argentinian segments for those respective feeds. As well as increasing its total subscribers in the region, this strategy has also attracted local advertisers, in addition to the global ones that one expects to find everywhere on MTV (Goldner, 1997). MTV Latin America represents the kind of challenge which Televisa, Globo, and the other major producers and distributors of the region now face on their home ground in the era of convergence.

Thus, the comparative advantage of language difference which the Latin American companies once enjoyed as a kind of natural monopoly is under threat. It is not only the new satellite technologies of digital compression and conditional-access DTH reception which have brought this about: several of the global channels have gained their experience in the US with the potential audience of over 26 million Spanish speakers there, and the move into Latin America represents immense opportunities for them to exploit. At the very least, it is well worth their while to dub programs which have been produced in English. It could even be said that the prospect of the 300 million or more Spanish speakers of Latin America gives US producers an incentive to develop programming for the Latino market in the first instance, with Latin America, and Spain, as aftermarkets.

The development of the CBS Telenoticias news channel from a US domestic to an international service is a good case in point. A CBS executive observes that Latin America is more attractive than Europe for such ventures because the whole region only requires channels in two languages, as against the several languages needed for Europe (Francis and Fernandez, 1997: 38–40). As Mexico City and Rio surrender their traditional monopoly as centers of dubbing from English to Spanish and Portuguese to Los Angeles and Miami (Wilkinson, 1995: 22), US capital flows into new channels: one US investment group has joined with the Cisneros Group "to create a pan-Ibero-American media network" based in Miami (Sutter, 1997/98: 34).

As well as CBS and MTV, there is Turner's CNN, the Time-Warner/Sony venture HBO Olé, Murdoch's Fox Latin America, Spelling's TeleUno, ESPN, Discovery, and other US-based global channels providing satellite and cable services in Spanish and/or Portuguese to Latin America, so it is not surprising that as of 1996, 90 percent of television services (that is, satellite and cable signals rather than programs) imported into the Iberoamerican region were found to be from the US (Media Research and Consultancy Spain, 1997: 14). The same study found that the export of such services from the region mainly (70 percent) came from Televisa and Multivisión in Mexico, especially by virtue of their involvement with the Murdoch Sky and Hughes Galaxy DTH ventures respectively. Even though 90 percent of the services exported from Iberoamerican countries went to other regional nations of the same language (the rest mainly to the Spanish-speaking networks in the US), evidence of the geolinguistic cohesion of the region's trade, it also shows that the US services have been able to cross the language barrier without much movement back in the other direction. This trend is likely to consolidate if, as the study predicts, the trade in services rather than programs soon becomes the major form of audiovisual exchange (1997: 17–18).

Given that the US-based and other global corporations such as Hughes not only have taken over the technological vanguard in the region once held by PanAmSat, but also faced up to the content issue by extending themselves into the provision of services in the regional languages, if postbroadcast services do come to eclipse programs as the core of the television trade, then much of the comparative advantage once enjoyed by the major Latin American companies would be undermined. This will depend greatly on the level of cost of the subscriber services, which at present are such as to keep DTH out of the reach of mass audiences in most Latin American countries. In the medium term, it is likely that the subscriber services will remain the preserve of the more affluent and already more cosmopolitan elites who can pay to receive the global programming, while the mass audiences for broadcast television will continue to form a loyal market for the national and regional producers and distributors (Sinclair, 1999: 166–70).

It has been argued in this paper that the era of cultural imperialism in the 1960s and 1970s, when television program imports from the US reached their high-tide mark, has proven to be just an initial phase of television development. It was overtaken by a phase in which audiences learned to have more appreciation for programs which came to them out of their own language and culture. Beginning in the late 1970s, this has been the era in which Televisa and Globo have exploited their advantages to become the market leaders in their respective geolinguistic regions, but the indications are that this stage also will pass. As McAnany predicted, the fact that a nation can develop a strong cultural industry "may be no guarantee that the threat of external influence will not surface at a later date" (1984: 196). By the same token, the reassertion of US corporate dominance should not be inter-preted teleologically, that is, as the always-already inevitable victory of American capitalism, but analytically, as the logic of a cultural industry in which the US has a unique set of advantages able to overcome those of its competitors, ultimately even in their own national and regional markets.

Acknowledgement

This chapter draws substantially from material published in the author's book, *Latin American Television: A Global View*, Oxford University Press, Oxford and New York, 1999.

References

Anderson, B. (1991). *Imagined Communities: Reflections on the Origin and Spread of Nationalism* (2nd edn). London: Verso.

Bakewell, P. (1991). "Colonial Latin America." In J. Knippers Black (Ed.), *Latin America: Its Problems and its Promise*, 57–66. Boulder, CO: Westview Press.

Braudel, F. (1993). *A History of Civilizations*. New York: Penguin Books.

Collins, R. (1994). "Trading in culture: the role of language." *Canadian Journal of Communication*, 19, 377–99.

"Country profile: Mexico" (1996). *TV International*, May 6, 5–8.

Crystal, D. (1997). *English as a Global Language*. Cambridge: Cambridge University Press.

El Estado del Mundo: Edición 1997. (1996). Madrid: Akal Ediciones.

Frances, G. and Fernandez, R. (1997). "Satellites south of the border." *Via Satellite*, February, 28–42.

Galeano, E. (1973). *Open Veins of Latin America: Five Centuries of the Pillage of a Continent.* New York: Monthly Review Press.

García Canclini, N. (1997). "Hybrid cultures and communicative strategies." *Media Development*, XLIV(1), 22–9.

Goldner, D. (1997). "MTV rocks to Latin beat." *Variety*, May 19–25, 22.

Grupo Televisa (1997). *Annual Report 1996.* Mexico DF: Author.

Hall, S. (1996). "When was 'The post-colonial'?: thinking at the limit." In I. Chambers and L. Curti (Eds), *The Post-Colonial Question: Common Skies, Divided Horizons*, 242–60. London: Routledge.

Huntington, S. (1997). "The clash of civilizations?" In Foreign Affairs Agenda (Ed.), *The New Shape of World Politics*, 67–91. New York: Norton.

Klee, C. (1991). "Introduction." In C. Klee and L. Ramos-García (Eds), *Sociolinguistics of the Spanish-Speaking World*, 1–8. Tempe, AZ: Bilingual Press.

Lusomundo Joins TV Cabo (1998). *Cable and Satellite Europe*, January, 10.

Martínez, S. (1996). "Televisa se asocia a Radio Televisión Española, con la bendición de Aznar." *Proceso*, September, 8, 48–50.

McAnany, E. (1984). "The logic of the cultural industries in Latin America: the television industry in Brazil." In V. Mosco and J. Wasko (Eds), *The Critical Communications Review Volume II: Changing Patterns of Communications Control*, 185–208. Norwood, NJ: Ablex.

McClintock, A. (1992). "The angel of progress: pitfalls of the term 'post-colonialism'." *Social Text*, 10(2/3), 84–98.

Media Research and Consultancy Spain (1997). "*La Industria Audiovisual Iberoamericana: Datos de sus Principales Mercados 1997.*" Report prepared for the Federación de Asociaciones de Productores Audiovisuales Españoles and Agencia Española de Cooperación Internacional. Madrid.

Monsiváis, C. (1994). "Globalisation means never having to say you're sorry." *Journal of International Communication*, 1(2), 120–4.

Morley, D. and Robins, K. (1995). *Spaces of Identity: Global Media, Electronic Landsapes and Cultural Boundaries.* London: Routledge.

Peralta, B. (1997). "España: autorizan a Televisa para participar en la televisión digital." *La Jornada*, March 9, 53.

Richards, M. and French, D. (1996). "From global development to global culture?" In D. French and M. Richards (Eds), *Contemporary Television: Eastern Perspectives*, 22–48. New Delhi: Sage.

Roncagliolo, R. (1995). "Trade integration and communication networks in Latin America." *Canadian Journal of Communication*, 20(3), 335–42.

Schlesinger, P. and Morris, N. (1997). "Cultural boundaries: identity and communication in Latin America." *Media Development*, XLIV(1), 5–17.

Schwaller, J. (1987). "Discovery and conquest." In J. Hopkins (Ed.), *Latin America: Perspectives on a Region*, 57–70. New York: Holmes and Meier.

Sinclair, J. (1999). *Latin American Television: A Global View.* Oxford: Oxford University Press.

Sousa, H. (1997). "Crossing the Atlantic: Globo's wager in Portugal." Paper presented to the conference of the International Association for Mass Communication Research, Oaxaca, July.

Sreberny-Mohammadi, A. (1991). "The global and the local in international communications." In J. Curran and M. Gurevitch (Eds), *Mass Media and Society*, 118–38. New York and London: Edward Arnold.

Straubhaar, J. (1992). "Assymetrical interdependence and cultural proximity: a critical review of the international flow of television programs." Paper presented to the conference of the Asociación Latinoamericana de Investigadores de la Comunicación, São Paulo, August.

Sutter, M. (1997, 1998). "Hicks sets $500 mil Latin fund." *Variety*, December 22–January 4, 34.

Waisbord, S. (1996). "Latin American television and national identities." Paper presented to the conference of the International Communication Association, Chicago, May.

Waisbord, S. (1998). "The ties that still bind: media and national cultures in Latin America." *Canadian Journal of Communication*, 23(2), 381–401.

Williamson, E. (1992). *The Penguin History of Latin America*. London: Penguin Books.

Wilkinson, K. (1995). "When culture, language and communication converge: the Latin American cultural-linguistic television market." PhD dissertation. University of Texas at Austin.

3

DECENTRALIZATION PROCESSES AND "PROXIMATE TELEVISION" IN EUROPE

Miquel de Moragas Spà and Bernat López

In this chapter we intend to present some interim results of the research on "Proximate television and the information society in the European Union," carried out by a team of European researchers under the coordination of the Institute of Communications of the UAB (InCom).[1] It was finished in July 1999 and published in late 1999 (Moragas, Garitaonandía and López, 1999).

This text also incorporates some of the main conclusions of our earlier research on "Television and the regions in the European Union," finished in 1994 and fully published in the volume *Decentralization in the Global Era* (Moragas and Garitaonandía, 1995).

Both studies have been possible thanks to the participation of an extensive team of European experts, to whom we owe some of the data provided in this chapter. Our gratitude to all of them.[2]

Thus the focus of this chapter is on the processes which have lead to the present situation of the proliferation of regional and urban television stations in almost every European Union (EU) country.[3] Not only the processes and their causes are reviewed, but also the results of those processes – this takes the form of a tentative typology of "proximate" television stations in Europe – the financial viability of those small- and medium-scale broadcasters and its future in the light of the so called "digital revolution."

The unification process and the solid image the European Union offers nowadays to the world (strengthened by the process of adoption of a single currency, which will run from now to the year 2002) shouldn't make us think about it as a homogeneous entity, with little internal cultural and linguistic variations: on the contrary, not only is it constituted by fifteen sovereign countries, with a long history behind it and the respective cultures and languages (there are not less than eleven official languages in the EU institutions), but by a much wider diversity of "regional" cultures and languages (not less than 30 different languages are spoken today in the EU).

Certainly, only a few of those cultures and languages are the "dominant" ones, those which have succeeded to become official in the respective contries. During more than 200 years, those cultures have expanded at the expense of the neighboring cultures, linking themselves with the emergent nation-states, a relationship of which France and the French language are often quoted as a paradigmatic example. In this expansion, broadcasting played a central role in the decades following World War II, when the waves brought the dominant culture to every corner of each country.

Nonetheless, the crisis of the centralized nation-state and the generalization of political regionalization in Western Europe in the 1970s and the 1980s, side by side with the deep economical and technological changes in broadcasting and the cultural industries, have led to the rebirth of the "minority" languages and cultures. Many once "peripherical" communities, like the Welsh and the Gaelics in the United Kingdom, the Catalans and the Basques in Spain, the Frisians in The Netherlands, the Bretons in France, and many more, enjoy nowadays a recovery and "normalization" process, to which television, as we will see, crucially contributes.

In addition to this regional vitality, Europe also hosts a myriad of cities and medium-sized towns, many of which enjoy their own local or urban television station.

Conceptual tools: "decentralization," "television in the regions," "proximate television"

In our research we use some concepts, which may need clarification. First of all, we talk about *decentralization as a process*, which means that in almost all the EU countries there has been a switch from unitarian, state-wide and highly centralistic public service broadcasting structures to a more decentralized organization, in the geographical sense.

Another important concept is *regional television*, a term widely spread and used in English academic literature on the media, or the preferred term, *television in the regions*. It refers to the television activities of specific and deliberated regional coverage (lower than state-wide and higher than local), both in the geographical and journalistic (contents) sense. In the European recent tradition, "regional television" refers to the off-the-network and minoritarian broadcasts of the regional centers belonging to the national broadcasting corporations. Nonetheless, in the 1980s and the 1990s there has been a proliferation of independent television stations with specific and exclusive regional coverage, which themselves reject the term "regional television" as a description of their activities, because they consider it derogatory. Therefore, the more descriptive "television in the regions" seems to fit better with the wide diversity of experiences in this field, ranging from the urban televisions with regional spill-overs (the case of Barcelona Televisió, Rete 7 in Bologna, Italy, Paris Première in Paris, TLT in Toulouse, France...) and the regional centers of the nation-wide stations (France 3, BBC, TVE, RAI, RTP...), to the relatively huge broadcasting corporations of the Spanish regions of Catalonia or Andalusia (with a higher turnover than corporations of some small European countries).

It is worth pointing out that we make a distinction between the local and the regional levels, according to the empirical situation in Europe. Local television is mainly urban, because it is aimed at and only covers the city in which it works.[4] Television of regional scope covers a wider area, including several cities and its hinterlands, which constitute a "unit" in the administrative, historical, cultural, linguistic and geographic senses, in any combination. Nonetheless, our research has showed that this distinction is not so clear-cut as it seems, as we can identify many European TV stations which would primarily fit into the category of "local television," but which extend their (journalistic as well as geographic) coverage beyond the limits of the city. There is even the case of a TV station born locally, but which at present has reached an international coverage because it is distributed by satellite (Paris Première, the TV station of the French capital city).

These and other considerations have led us to coin the new (and problematic in its English version[5]) term "proximate television," first used in France ("télévision de proximité") in the late 1980s to name the new urban disconnections of the nation-wide public channel France 3. This is probably the main conceptual innovation we propose in our research, and it is aimed at overcoming the contradictions posed by the previous distinction between local and regional, so as to provide the communications policy makers with a new analytical tool.

Communication spaces

Indeed, research on television and communication policies is showing that the concepts used during the "broadcasting era" to analyze the various television models are becoming more and more worthless in the new era of diversity, fragmentation and decentralization of television.

In order to analyze the "old" era, the concept of "communication spaces" seems quite useful (Moragas, 1988). This term has allowed us to interpret the various television models according to their area of coverage, beginning with the most evident and simplest typology, the one which categorizes the different channels according to their transnational, national, regional or local-municipal coverage.

However, it was soon discovered that this typology contains several gaps and contradictions, such as the one identified above for the regional-local distinction, or the one expressed in the case of some European regions with a strong identity which claim the title of "historical nationalities" and promote new models of TV stations more relevant to the nation-states than to the old "regional television" model (these would be the Spanish cases, for instance, of Televisió de Catalunya in Catalonia and Euskal Telebista in the Basque Country).

This complexity of the typology of the "communication spaces" will be broadened due to the influence of the communication technologies in the creation or reshaping of those spaces. In the Internet era, local communication can be not only "local," and becomes global due to the worldwide reach of the Net.

Thus, the concept of "communication space" is a good starting point, but does not suffice in giving account of the extreme diversity of television experiences from the geo-cultural point of view, and needs to be enriched with other criteria which refer more directly to the uses, functions and contents of the different television models. The answer to this consideration is addressed in our proposal of "proximate television."

This proposal is not exactly aimed at naming a new kind of television, but more properly a new form of thinking about the issue. Our goal is not to set criteria which allow us to define which are and which are not "proximate television stations," but to ask ourselves about the new forms of television which try to give answers to the new links among broadcasters (or "narrowcasters"), geographical spaces and communication demands arising from the concrete experience of the citizens.

Producing and experiencing "proximate television"

The concept of "proximity" applied to television has to do with the idea that between the station and the recipients a "scene of shared experiences" can exist which, in the end, is reflected in the programming contents.

The main and more evident example of this proximity, of this "shared landscape," is reflected in the case of the news programs of the regional and local stations which refer to the close environment, available in the day-to-day experience of the viewers. Thus, for instance, the case of a snowfall in Barcelona, which very seldom occurs, seems to be a perfect subject for a "proximate" news program, as, in addition to the novelty and spectacular factors it embeds, it has direct effects in the core of this "scene of shared experiences." Not by chance, one of the most popular programs of the "proximate" TV stations is, precisely, its news programs.

Nonetheless, the demand for "proximate programs" is not limited to news, but, in a more complex way, spill over into other genres offering different interpretations and perspectives of reality: sports, talk shows, debates and, more recently, even fiction.[6]

With the multiplication of channels and the decentralization processes, television begins to be able to do what, until now, only other forms of media (the press, radio) were able to do: to interpret the reality from a set of cultural values shared by a small community.

Political factors in the decentralization of television

It is clear that the analysis of changes in communication should take into account the internal causes peculiar to each system, with special reference to technologies and their implications. But these circumstances are not enough to completely explain all of these changes: we have to consider as well the political and economic causes that support, or hinder, them. These are external factors to the television system in itself with a powerful, although indirect, influence.

Indeed, the development of the decentralization processes of television in Europe is the consequence of a more general process of decentralization, that has affected so many levels of European societies in the last twenty to twenty-five years. The process of European "unification" has also meant – to the surprise of some experts – the recovery of the autonomy for many regions and cities. In the modern Europe, regions have never been talked about as much as now, and the regional institutions are more present than ever in the political field or in the resources management. The united Europe has meant, in fact and historically, the political and economical emergence of regions. So, for example, the Maastricht Treaty (1992) created an institutional figure called Committee of the Regions, a consultative assembly integrated in the institutional body of the EU in which the regions and municipal powers of the EU countries are represented. Apart from the EU, some organizations of regions and cities of Europe have emerged or have been reinforced in the last ten years, such as the Regions of Europe Assembly or the Council of the Municipalities and Regions of Europe, which constitute powerful lobbies in Brussels.

The initiatives of television decentralization are parallel to numerous legal initiatives of political-administrative decentralizations undertaken by many European states in the last twenty years: Spain (1978–84), Italy (1972–77), France (1982–85), Greece (1994), Portugal (1974–78, 1998), Belgium (different times), United Kingdom (1997–98)…

In fact, the "proximate television" projects which are more competitive, those which reach a cultural and communicative presence that is more influential, even in terms of audience, have been produced in those regions which enjoy powerful supports – political and social – to their autonomy and specially in those communities that can be called, not without internal and external conflicts, "nations without states," as Wales (2.8 million habitants), Scotland (5 million), Catalonia (6 million) or the Basque Country (2.5 million). The federal German *Länder* have also ample competences in audio-visual matter, due to their high grade of political autonomy. The new regional political elites have been in many cases the main supporters of TV decentralization, seeing in the new stations a powerful platform for political communication.

But this political logic also has another side: the states are distrustful about the transfer of competences to the regional and local levels, and as a result, often create barriers and difficulties to the development of regional and local televisions inside their territory, even reimposing hurdles that have dissapeared among the countries due to the internal liberalization resulting from the directive "Television without frontiers."

Among these restrictions it is necessary to speak, for instance, about the strict obligations imposed on local and regional television in some national regulations, the precariousness and short duration of the licences given, the restrictions, or even the prohibition, of local and regional advertising on tv, the imposition of severe conditions for program planning or for the origin of productions.

Media deregulation: decentralization processes in the redefinition of the regulatory role of the state

Not only politics has to be dealt with when analysing the causes of TV decentralization. One also has to look at the processes which have heavily affected media systems in the last twenty years, and very specially, deregulation.

This is a process which has been widely documented and discussed in media research and media policy literature of recent times. It refers mainly to the changes in the role of the state and public administration in the regulation, operation and control of the electronic media and telecommunications during the last fifteen to twenty years. Even though those changes don't mean a complete loss of influence and control of the states over the media systems and communication policies, it is clear that their dynamics and logics of intervention have greatly changed and that they are no longer the single actors of the scene: they have to share now their protagonism. This loss of influence of the states has four main "leaks:"

- Privatization and commercialization of television
- The transfer of competences to the supranational level, mainly to the European Union
- Decentralization, with the regions and the local institutions emerging as main actors in the communication and television policies
- The rise of huge and worldwide telecoms operators which, thanks to the technological convergence allowed by the digitalization, overcome their traditional role as mere carriers to become true multimedia and global enterprises.

In the classical analysis on deregulation the role of liberalization and privatization aspects is usually stressed, even the impact of technology, but very seldom is decentralization seen as a phenomenon which integrates the whole deregulation process, at the same time as a cause and as being a consequence of it.

Those different dimensions of deregulation interact in a very complex way. Sometimes they complement each other, reaching synergies and strenthening its joint effects, as is clearly the case of liberalization/privatization and internationalization. In other occasions they can oppose each other, giving rise to tensions and contradictions. This may be the case of the relationships between privatization and decentralization.

The private sector still shows little interest in "proximate television"

Nowadays, names such as Springer, Bertelsmann, CLT, Mediaset, Hachette, Kirch, Murdoch or Canal Plus are as important in the European communication arena as the BBC, RAI, RTVE, ORTF, etc. could have been in the past. This presence of the private sector leads to new logics in the production and control of information and culture. The participation of the financial sector, the utilities enterprises (distribution of water, gas, electricity...), the big construction conglomerates, in the new communication businesses provokes a move of the communication systems' core from the political arena towards the commercial and financial ones.

Nevertheless, the majority of the initiatives in the field of "proximate television" have been launched and supported by the public sector. The private initiative has been until now quite shy in participating in "proximate television" ventures at a regional level, as they are much more interested in competing with public television for the national and international spaces.

To this consideration we should add the fact that the regulations standing in many countries have posed multiple hurdles to the presence of the private sector in "proximate television," as they impose several forms of centralized regulation which have prevented the access of private initiatives to local and regional television. For instance, the Spanish Private Television Act doesn't allow the creation of private TV channels with regional coverage. In France, the launching of private local TV stations is subject to a strict centralized control by the Conseil Supérieur de l'Audiovisuel.

Instead, the private initiative has been more active in local and urban television. There are two different reasons for two cases: the TV stations of the big metropolitan areas, and those of the small and medium-sized towns. The interest of the private initiative in TV stations aimed at the big cities is due to the concentration of audiences and the possibility of distribution through cheap infrastructures (over the air or cable networks). A paradigmatic case could be Paris Première, a channel broadcasting only to the French capital city in the first stages, but which became international (through the satellite) due to its success and the worldwide appeal of the "Ville des lumières." Another important cause of the involvement of the private capital in local (metropolitan) television is the fact that national television is yet "occupied" by public and private conglomerates, and the local space is the only "niche" left to find a place in the audiovisual landscape from which to prepare the "jump" to the national and international market (this could be the case of some German or French metropolitan channels).

Instead, the case of the TV stations of the small and medium-sized towns involves the participation of commercial initiatives which are also local, whose "social" benefits compensate the financial investments in the station, even if "small" local television is still a predominantly non-profit venture (supported by the municipalities and other local institutions, or by the most diverse organizations of the civil society).

Transfer of competences towards the European supranational organizations

A second and important loss of power of the states in the audiovisual sector is towards the supranational institutions, mainly the European Union.[8]

The communication policy of the European Union has assumed an extraordinary leading role in the last ten years, integrating the member states in a new and bigger regulatory setting that involves a transfer of sovereignty from the states to the Union in such a delicate field as is communication.

In this new context, the emergent idea has been the necessity to create a common market of production, distribution and audiovisual goods consumption, capable of guaranteeing, simultaneously, the survival of the European cultural identity and its industrial competitiveness (Vasconcelos *et al.*, 1994). The EU audiovisual policies have been defined as a form of resistance against the "audiovisual powers" (USA, Japan) whose industries not only question the supremacy and cultural identity of Europe, but also impoverish its economy and limit the possibility to create new jobs in this important sector (European Commission, 1993).

According to the data provided by Vasconcelos *et al.* (1994),

> the exports of the American industry to Europe have increased exponentially in the last decade: from $330,000m in 1984 to $3,600,000m in 1992. In 1991, the European Community represented 60 percent of the exports of the American audiovisual programs; the commercial deficit of the EU with the US has been calculated as approximately $3,500,000m per year.
>
> (Vasconcelos *et al.*, 1994: 16)

But at the same time, the EU media policies placed a bet on the liberalization of the internal market and the rupture of the national monopolies. There has been talk of two main ideologies in the EU broadcasting policymaking: the protectionist-interventionist against the neoliberal (Collins, 1994).

After this first phase of community audiovisual policies, defined by the desire to create and promote an "European audiovisual space" to support the rise of a common cultural identity, step by step it seems to impose the idea that, from the cultural and communication point of view, the real European patrimony is based on its diversity and the values of coexistence among cultures, developed as a result of a necessary (and many times troubled) coexistance among different peoples. For that reason, the debate about the "common" in Europe seems to be opened to a third way in favour of decentralization and the transfer of competences from the states to the regions in the field of communication. The creation of a common audiovisual arena allows the rise and consolidation of other different audiovisual spaces in addition to European and state ones: the regions and cities.

Decentralization coincides with the changes in telecommunications

The processes of television decentralization coincide with the phase of deregulation and privatization of television, but also with a significant change in telecommunications that involves numerous consequences: generalization of the use of communication satellites, implantation of the new cable networks with a large capacity, expansion of the number of conventional channels by ether, new forms of webcasting, etc.

The main technological cause of these changes is digitalization (Negroponte, 1995; Majó, 1997), which probably constitutes the origin and the essence of the rest of the changes, because it has altered the autonomy of the different phases of the manipulation of information, linking them much more closely: from production and transmission to reception and archive of information.

One of the clearest consequences of this process is the multiplication of channels and offers of communication, that extend the possibilities and competences of local communication.

Digitalization is determining the end of the "broadcasting era," to pass to a new phase of communication in which – although it seems paradoxical – there is a revalorization of the "local," not only in the "classic" audiovisual space, but also in the new setting of technological and communicative convergences of the "cyberspace" (Internet). In this sense, some experts have spoken of the "glocal" communication era: with local production and contents, but with a global diffusion.

Decentralization of television in Europe: historical evolution and main stages

Even though television in Europe in its first stages was a clearly centralized and state-wide venture, the early manifestations of decentralized activities can be traced back to the 1960s, and even to the 1950s in the case of the United Kingdom, in the form of regional centers which start to broadcast off-the-network short regional news bulletins. Nonetheless, those activities are clearly secondary, as the declared goal of the public television stations is to "re-nationalize" the severely damaged postwar European countries. In this sense, it is highly significant that the Allies imposed on the defeated Germany an extremely decentralized state structure, which had its correspondence in a completely regionalized broadcasting system (Klein-steuber and Thomass, 1995, 1999).

The historical development of decentralization processes of television in Europe can be divided roughly into three main stages (sometimes overlapping) to which we could add a fourth one which seems to emerge in recent times.

In the 1960s and the first half of the 1970s, some of the big public corporations (BBC in the United Kingdom, RTF-ORTF in France, RTVE in Spain) created their regional structures. It was what could be seen as a "natural" process, in the sense that those broadcasting corporations, which enjoyed a monopolistic situation, developed regional centers without any external pressure, only following the dynamics of a strategy of expanding their coverage "from the center to the periphery." Once they had attained an entrepreneurial solidity and had expanded their coverage to the entire country with one or two channels, and often coinciding with those processes, created centers outside the capital cities, where the headquarters of those corporations were always located. The monopolistic situation and the sustained increase in income (as the coverage and thus the licence fee extended to more and more people) allowed them to plan long-term investment.

41

Nevertheless, as pointed out above, those regional centers performed a second-ary role, acting as newsgatherers for the national channels and broadcasting only some minutes per week of off-the-network local news programming. Only slowly did they gain minutes of disconnection and expand the genres of the local programs, and in some cases began to act as producers for the network, although without questioning the hegemony of the central headquarters. As pointed out above, only Germany counted on a truly decentralized audiovisual system (in the German case, it is more appropriate to talk about "centralization processes," instead of "decentralization"), and in the United Kingdom, who were pioneers in the introduction of commercial television in Europe in 1954 with a formula based on a regionalized organization (Cormack, 1995, 1999).

The second stage can be placed between the mid-1970s and the mid-1980s. During this period, the issue of decentralization was placed in the forefront of the media policy agendas and public debates, in the frame of a more general debate about the reform of the public broadcasters, which suffered from the financial and ideological crisis of the 1970s. The new techniques of production and diffusion, which decreased the costs of broadcasting and made it more and more available for smaller communities and enterprises, stimulated this debate. During those years, the leftists made pleas for a decentralization of the existing television systems, both in the political (taking them away from the executive power) and territorial (opening-up to the territorial peripheries) senses. This debate is specially lively in France, Spain and Italy, but applies as well to the United Kingdom, Germany, The Netherlands, Denmark, Belgium... During this period, many important decentralizing experiences were carried out, from the open public access channels in Germany and The Netherlands, to the regional corporations in Spain (Jankowski, 1995; López and Corominas, 1995).

From the mid-1980s and the mid-1990s the debate concerning the decentraliza-tion and democratization of the public corporations was overriden by the emerging and much more tense debate on deregulation and, more recently, digitalization and globalization of television. The new private channels were interested in reaching the biggest audiences possible, to optimize their commercial incomes, thus rejecting decentralization, unless they were obliged to do it by law (like in Germany). On the other hand, the "old" public corporations, which had developed expensive and complex regional structures in the previous stages, tended to concentrate on the national level to compete with the new private channels. The presence of the regional element as a whole in the televisive systems lost visibility, faced with the avalanche of commercial channels and "popular" programs.

Nonetheless, amidst this panorama some initiatives seem to point at a fourth stage in the evolution of television in the regions, in which there can be seen symptoms of recovery and even of consolidation of local and regional television in the multichannel and fragmented audiovisual landscape of the near future. For instance, some public channels have relied increasingly on their regional structures and on "proximate programming" as a competitive strategy (as could be the case of France 3). On the other hand, many local televisive ventures have been launched in recent years, with the support in many cases of private initiative, even if public support stemming from the local political elites seems to be a never-ending engine for new "proximate television" initatives, as can be seen in the last five years in countries as The Netherlands (Jankowski and Schoorlemmer, 1999) and Denmark (Tufte, 1999).

From the market point of view, the existence of a real demand (and a growing one) for "proximate television" is clearly documented in the majority of the researched countries. Thus, in Spain the nine regional channels have increased their market share in Spain from 15 percent to 17 percent between 1995 and 1997, a specially meritory performance, taking into account that they don't cover the entire Spanish territory and that this has happened in a period of consolidation of private and satellite television. In France, the regional and local news in France 3 usually command more than 40 percent of the market share in their time slot, and up to 60–70 percent in some specially successful cases. In Germany, the seven regional public channels, produced by the regional public corporations, have resisted competition from private television much better in terms of market share than the two nationwide public channels.

In short, as we should see below, the "digital era" does not seem to necessarily convey the end of local and regional broadcasting: to the contrary, proliferation of channels and communication spaces seem to strengthen the competitive position of "proximate television."

A typology of "proximate television"

In contrast to what happened with national television during the early television epochs, of the 1950s and 1960s, local and regional television is far from being homogeneous or uniform. On the contrary, what is observed nowadays in Europe is a panorama of multiple forms and models of stations trying to adapt themselves and give an answer to the existent diversity (cultural, linguistic, political, demographic, geographic).

"Proximate television" is, by its own nature, the television of diversity. For this reason, in our comparative study we have elaborated a new typology of television models that could provide an answer to this diversity.

It should be taken into account that regions in Europe are not only the result of simple geographical or administrative divisions, but in many cases are the result of long historical processes, of the inheritance of feudal structures, of the romanization or even of earlier periods, which have resulted in important and deep cultural and linguistic differences in the continent.

The last 200 years of the history of Europe have seen a strong process of centralization that now, with the arrival of the twenty-first century, seems to give ground to the decentralization and the revival of local and regional cultures and languages, which become apparent in communications and in the European television. The typology of "proximate television," logically, will reflect this complexity.

Various classifications by typology can be proposed,[9] based on the criteria adopted: according to legal-organizational criteria, to the regime of ownership, to their dependence or independence in relation to superior territorial structures ("mirror" television versus "window" television) and according to the language used (minority or not).

A basic first distinction, useful for future analysis, sets the difference between "mirror" televisions and "window" televisions, according to the terminology proposed by Musso *et al.* (1991):

"Window" television refers to the classic disconnection from the national broadcast schedule, regional-specific programming offered in different territories simultaneously. These are produced by the organism regional delegations of the national broadcasting, or by independent regional corporations that collaborate to produce them. These disconnections are normally quantitatively short (between half an hour and one hour and a half per day) and they are focused on the information and current affairs macro genre (so, they can include hard news, current affairs, debate, documentary, talk shows...). Some of the examples of this type are the regional broadcasts of the BBC (UK), RAI (Italy), TVE (Spain), France 3 (France), ARD (Germany), ITV (UK), Antena 3 TV (Spain), RTL (Germany), TV2 (Denmark), and ORF (Austria).

"Mirror" television refers to complete schedules of the channels specifically addressed to concrete regions, made by television organizations of regional or local-metropolitan implant, independent from national broadcasting corporations. Often these channels attempt to imitate schedule models from the large national and international generalistic channels, even in the broadcast of programs of external production or imported material (telefilms, documentary, features, serials...). They fundamentally differ by having a concrete region as primary reference territory, although in practice they may broadcast beyond that territory (even extending internationally due to satellite). Moreover, with regard to content, "mirror" television schedules are constituted by an important contingent of "proximate" programs, that is programs specifically addressed to attending the tastes and the needs of audiences with contents close to their everyday experience.

In this category are included the nine regional channels, corresponding to the autonomous communities of Spain; Sianel Pedwar Cymru in Wales (UK), the regional channels of the German *Länder*'s corporations and a plethora of local channels with regional intention in almost all the EU states.

At a deeper level of analysis, the most useful typology for the study of "proximate television" experiences considers the legal personality of the television station, its level of institutional independence, its involvement with television institutions of a superior territorial range.

In this classification we can distinguish between:

Delegations or centers belonging to a national corporation   In this type we can make the distinction between regional centers of public corporations (BBC in the UK, TVE in Spain, RAI in Italy...) and delegations of private broadcasters.

In the first case they are always delegations without their own legal personality and with limited autonomy in budgetary and decision-making processes. In the second case, the "associated center" model is normally used, a company that has its own legal personality and that can incorporate in its shareholding shares external to the national broadcaster they work for (this is the preferred model by German private channels RTL and SAT.1; in Spain there are also some similar cases, as in Antena 3 TV).

Another substantial difference is that regional centers are part of the public channel basic structure, and they divide the territory in a more or less uniform way, following the division of the country in political-administrative regions. Instead, private television centers have a more contingent character, in the sense that they respond more to legal duties imposed on the channel (RTL and SAT.1 in Germany) or to tactical approaches in order to penetrate the territory (Antena 3 TV in Spain), so they are not created in all the regions, but in some important cities and corresponding hinterlands that can provide significant audiences to their disconnected broadcasts.

Nevertheless, the broadcasting activity of these centers or delegations, public or private television, is always "window" type. Moreover, they can produce programs for national diffusion, and generally act as correspondents for the news programs of the national corporation they are part of.

Independent organism of regional implant   There are television organisms with their own legal personality, officially independent, that operate in a regional reference territory. This doesn't mean, however, that their main activity consists only and mainly of the production and broadcast for their geographical scope. In fact, in this category we can find "window" broadcasting stations (as the regional companies of ITV in the UK) and "mirror" broadcasting stations (as the "autonomic" stations in Spain) and "mirror-window" broadcasting stations (the corporations of the German federated states, that at the same time jointly produce a national channel, named ARD, in which they insert their own disconnected programs, as well as regionally specific channels).

In this category we can also distinguish between public and private organisms. Of particular interest is the Welsh fourth channel (S4C): organically and legally it is an entity independent from a national channel, with its own legal personality and with a strictly regional implant. However, 75 percent of its schedule consists of programs in English, taken from the schedule of the national English Channel 4, with whom they have important institutional and technical bonds (S4C broadcasts for Wales through the same frequency as Channel 4 for the rest of the English territory). On the other hand, the Welsh channel does not legally depend on Welsh political institutions (non-existent until very recently), it depends on the central government, through the Welsh Fourth Channel Authority, a collegiated organism appointed by the central government in London. Therefore, it can be considered a broadcasting station "mirror" and "window" at the same time.

Television entity of a "small state" that extends its coverage to one or more regions from a neighbouring state This modality, which has almost disappeared, was developed during the first half of the 1980s in special circumstances (taking advantage of the situation with public monopoly in France to broadcast a "popular" schedule with substantial amounts of commercial advertising). This regional character was not intentional and derived from the hertzian spill-over from the country of origin, and is almost untraceable in the contents of the broadcasts (most of them being imported entertainment).

Due to the deregulation of the audiovisual spaces of the large states, they have lost their *raison d'être*, and now they look for the internationalization of their broadcasts through cable and satellite.

The clearest examples of this were RTL TV (generated in Luxembourg but watched in the French region of Lorraine) and TeleMontecarlo (generated in Monaco but watched in the East of France).

Local television with regional outreach (metropolitan television) It is the case of TV stations of local-urban character, but which extend their coverage beyond the strict borders of the urban center, in the technical sense (hertzian coverage) as well as from the journalistic point of view (interest in all the realities surrounding the city). They are mainly "mirror" televisions, in the sense that they produce and broadcast complete schedules of local-regional scope, but we can also find cases, specially in Italy, of "window" local TV stations, associated to networks and broadcasting network programs for most of the time of the schedule, relegating the programs specifically local to punctual disconnections.

This category is difficult to quantify, because borders between local and regional in the audiovisual sphere are not clearly defined and are moving all the time. However, with the progressive implant of cable networks, "local" channels with extralocal diffusion are more common, and sometimes become even international, as is the case of Paris Première.

"Small" local television It is the biggest category in quantitative terms, as it includes thousands of small local channels from Italy, Spain, Belgium, the Netherlands, Denmark, Germany... They are broadcasting stations of local scope, from small and medium cities, even boroughs and small villages.

Since 1974, when the first local stations appeared in Italy, this sector has grown steeply, but is permanently unstable due to the general precariousness of means and to the voluntary character of many initiatives.

These televisions can be subdivided into two groups, according to means of diffusion utilized: hertzian channels and cable channels. The first are generally the most succesful, because they can reach almost 100 percent of the population and they do not need to compete with the broader offers of cable networks. For a more detailed analysis, see Jankowski, Prehn and Stappers, 1992.

The difficult question of viability in the "digital era:" the tendency to a public-private mixed model

We can conclude from the above that all of the analyzed changes seem to favor a new flowering of "proximate television," but they are so quick and involve factors so diverse that it would be wiser to speak, for the moment, about tendencies. It is certain that in the future we could see the failure of some initiatives that today seem solid, and on the contrary, we could see how other initiatives will be consolidated that today seem precarious. In any case, these forecasts would not be possible with the viability criteria of the old "broadcasting era."

The most important fact is that these new processes of decentralization could not be considered as "marginal" phenomena, because they are produced – although in a different way and with many variants and versions – in nearly all the countries of the EU. Neither could they be qualified as a phenomenon of "minorities," because the concept "minority" for the audiences of "proximate television" is an anachronism. The idea that television audiences have to be massive, such as water or electricity consumption in the homes of big cities, should be rejected in the new era of audience fragmentation.

In this new "ecology" of communication, contrary to the first forecasts, the demand of "proximate" communication is manifested as an emergent demand, not marginal, and especially competitive with the offers and programs of the national and international channels each time moving further from the immediate experience of the viewers.

Nevertheless, the existence of a market for "proximate television" and its economic viability constitutes, logically, a factor that becomes everyday more decisive for the consolidation of this television model.

Although in the future the support of the public sector is still maintained, it won't be possible to imagine exclusive financing from this sector. At best, the public sector only seems to be in the position to guarantee the co-financing of television, in any of its levels.

With regards to this situation, the European communication policy has an important "methodical doubt" caused by the necessity of promoting a common market, also for the audiovisual industry, and the fact that one of the main assets of this cultural industry could be, precisely, its diversity.

The unification principle of the market is applicable, of course, to numerous communication areas, above all to the technology areas in which homogenization of standards is vital for European competitiveness. The *desideratum* consists in amortizing the production costs in broad interior markets, in the new big Common European Market. But this need for homogenization and harnessing the synergy of a new big common market does not seem so evident in the cases of cultural sectors and of television.

For example, must we keep seeing the multiplicity of languages existent in Europe as a handicap or can we start seeing it as a potentiality of its cultural and communication industry? Does speaking Catalan, for example, as in our case, constitute a problem or rather an advantage for our cultural industry?

From our point of view and thinking in the long term, there can only be one correct answer: diversity is wealth, not only cultural but economic. In the "post-broadcasting area" diversity should not be considered as an economic handicap, but as a market good, especially if all the possible synergies between different sectors and communication services are used.

Decentralization should stop being considered as a handicap or as a minor flaw needed for the defence of identity, and should start to be considered as a new opportunity of the audiovisual European market. To articulate the binomial "space of identity" and "cultural market" now constitutes the principal challenge of communication policies in Europe, in all its dimensions.

In this sense, the European experience demonstrates that the survival of these forms of television – basic for the global development of all communication systems – depends on a mixed support system: of its financing from the public sector and of its implantation in the market. Various examples exist that illustrate the benefits of a balance between public and private financing: the cases of Televisió de Catalunya (Catalonia, Spain), of Sianel Pedwar Cymru-S4C (Wales, in the UK), the multiple local and urban channels...

Finally, the analysis of the functions and the conditions of viability of television in the regions cannot be done without consideration of the important changes that the communication systems are undergoing in the transition to what is know as "information society" or "digital society."

The extensive influence of those changes stands out, affecting not only politics, culture and education, as it is known, but also other new sectors such as finances, industrial production, work, science, social welfare, health, etc.

Modern communication policies should promote the relationships between the sectors involved in the development of the "information society:" the audiovisual sector, cultural sector, management and economic organization, education, health and social welfare programs.

This process not only affects the European Union and its states in an general sense, but also affects, more concretely, its regions and cities. Its economic development depends of this interrelation (communication, culture and tele-communications). New communication technologies, far from eliminating spaces, increase its differentiation.

Notes

1 Under the direction of Prof. Miquel de Moragas Spà and the codirection of Prof. Carmelo Garitaonandía (University of the Basque Country).
2 The team is constituted by national correspondents: **Austria**: Hans Heinz Fabris and Gabrielle Siegert, Universität Salzburg; **Belgium and Luxembourg**: J.-M. Nobre-Correia, Université Libre de Bruxelles; **Denmark**: Thomas Tufte, University of Copenhagen; **Finland**: Tapio Varis, University of Helsinki; **France**: Isabelle Pailliart and Sylvie Bardou-Boisnier, Institut de la Communication et des Médias, Univ. Stendhal, Grenoble; **Germany**: Hans J. Kleinsteuber and Barbara Thomass, Universität Hamburg; **Greece**: Roy Panagiotopoulou, National and Capodistrian University of Athens; **Ireland**: Ellen Hazelkorn, Faculty of Applied Arts, Dublin;

Italy: Giuseppe Richeri, Centro di Studi San Salvatore, Venice; Renato Porro († 1998), Università degli Studi di Trento; **The Netherlands**: Nick Jankowski, University of Nijmegen; **Portugal**: Francisco Rui Cádima and Pedro Jorge Braumann, Universidade Nova de Lisboa; **Spain**: Maria Corominas and Bernat López, Autonomous University of Barcelona; **Sweden**: Peter Dahlgren, University of Lund; **United Kingdom**: Mike Cormack, University of Stirling. Secretariat and documentation: Marta Civil and Jaume Risquete, Institut de la Comunicació de la UAB.

3 At present: Austria, Belgium, Denmark, Finland, France, Germany, Greece, Ireland, Italy, Luxembourg, The Netherlands, Portugal, Spain, Sweden and the United Kingdom.

4 Inside this category, we could even distinguish between the proper local stations (corresponding to small and medium-sized towns) and the urban or metropolitan stations, broadcasting to big cities or capitals. Coinciding with the conference in Chia-Yi, Taiwan, was being held in Barcelona the "First European Conference of Televisions of Large Cities," hosted by Barcelona Televisió, June 1998.

5 It could be said that, strangely enough, we face a term referring to communications which has a difficult English translation, being the case usually the contrary, as the world has recently experienced with the Internet and all its associated terminology: words originally in English with more or less difficult local translations (or simply without translation).

6 For instance, the main success of the Catalan broadcaster Televisió de Catalunya in 1997–98, 14 years after its creation, has been a drama series broadcast in weekday's afternoons called *Nissaga de Poder*, which is a kind of local version of the famous American *Falcon Crest*.

7 Mergers and takeovers in this new privatized panorama poses important problems and dangers to the pluralism (Charon, 1991; Miguel, 1993; Sánchez Tabernero, 1994). In spite of the repeated recommendations of the European Parliament, the European Commission (http://europa.eu.int) hasn't succeeded in proposing a Directive to regulate this issue, certainly under the pressure of the big multimedia conglomerates and the dynamism of the facts, in permanent change (see European Commission, 1992 and 1994).

8 There is another European institution, the Council of Europe, but it is an intergovernmental institution which adopts recommendations and treaties with no binding power, unless incorporated into the national legislations.

9 What follows is an evaluation of our early typological proposal. See Moragas and Garitaonandía, 1995.

References

Charon, J.-M. (1991). *L'état des Medias*. Paris: La Decouverte-Mediaspouvoirs.

Collins, R. (1994). *Broadcasting and Audio-Visual Policy in the European Single Market*. London: John Libbey.

Cormack, M. (1995). "United Kingdom: more centralization than meets the eye." In M. de Moragas and C. Garitaonandía (Eds), *Decentralization in the Global Era*. London: John Libbey.

Cormack, M. (1999). "United Kingdom: political devolution and TV decentralization." In M. de Moragas, C. Garitaonandía and B. López (Eds), *Television on Your Doorstep. Decentralization Experiences in the European Union*. Luton: University of Luton Press.

European Commission (1992). *Green Paper on Media Pluralism and Concentration in the Internal Market*. COM (92)0480. Luxembourg: Office des Publications Officielles des Communautés Européennes.

European Commission (1993). *White Book on Growth, Competitiveness, Employment.* Luxembourg: Office des Publications Officielles des Communautés Européennes.

European Commission (1994). *Posible Evolución de las Consultas en Torno al Libro Verde "Pluralismo y concentración de los medios de comunicación en el mercado interior."* Valoración de la necesidad de una acción comunitaria.* COM (94)353 final. Luxembourg: Office des Publications Officielles des Communautés Européennes.

Garitaonandía, C. (1993). "Regional television in Europe." *European Journal of Communication* 8, 3.

Jankowski, N. (1995): "The Netherlands: in search of a niche for regional television." In M.de Moragas and C. Garitaonandía (Eds), *Decentralization in the Global Era.* London: John Libbey.

Jankowski, N., Prehn, O. and Stappers, J. (Eds) (1992). *The People's Voice: Local Radio and Television in Europe.* London: John Libbey.

Jankowski, N. and Schoorlemmer, M. (1999). "The Netherlands: regional television comes of age." In M. de Moragas, C. Garitaonandía and B. López (Eds), *Television on Your Doorstep. Decentralization Experiences in the European Union.* Luton: University of Luton Press.

Kleinsteuber, H. and Thomass, B. (1995). "Germany: the initiative in the hands of the *Länder.*" In M. de Moragas and C. Garitaonandía, *Decentralization in the Global Era.* London: John Libbey.

Kleinsteuber, H. and Thomass, B. (1999). "Germany: continuity of the Länder system and the rise of urban television." In M. de Moragas, C. Garitaonandía and B. López (Eds), *Television on Your Doorstep. Decentralization Experiences in the European Union.* Luton: University of Luton Press.

López, B. and Corominas, M. (1995). "Spain: the contradictions of the autonomous model." In M. de Moragas and C. Garitaonandía (Eds), *Decentralization in the Global Era.* London: John Libbey.

Majó, J. (1997). *Chips, Cables y Poder.* Barcelona: Planeta.

Miguel, J.C. (1993). *Los Grupos Multimedia.* Barcelona: Bosch.

Moragas Spà, M. de (1988). *Espais de Comunicació.* Barcelona: Edicions 62.

Moragas Spà, M. de and Garitaonandía, C. (1995). *Decentralization in the Global Era.* London: John Libbey.

Moragas Spà, M. de, Garitaonandía, C. and López, B. (1999). *Television on Your Doorstep. Decentralization Experiences in the European Union.* Luton: University of Luton Press.

Musso, P.H. (Dir.) (1991). *Régions d'Europe et Télévisions.* Paris: Miroirs.

Negroponte, N. (1995). *Being Digital.* London: Hodder and Stoughton.

Sánchez Tabernero, A., Denton, A., Lochon, P.-Y., Mounier, P. and Woldt, R. (1994). *Concentración de la Comunicación en Europa. Empresa Comercial e Interés Publico.* Barcelona: Centre d'Investigació de la Comunicació.

Tufte, T. (1999). "Denmark: new legislation, last minute rescue?" In M. de Moragas, C. Garitaonandía and B. López (Eds), *Television on Your Doorstep. Decentralization Experiences in the European Union.* Luton: University of Luton Press.

Vasconcelos, A.P. (1994). *Rapport de la Cellule de Réflexion sur la Politique Audiovisuelle dans l'Union Européenne.* Luxembourg: Office des Publications Officielles des Communautés Européennes.

Table 3.1 "Proximate television in the European Union:" A quantitative approach

Country	Square km	Population 1995 (thousands)	Regional centres or delegations of national organizations[a]	Setting up of the first delegations	Independent regional TV-stations	Period of creation	Local TV-stations with regional outreach (metropolitan)	Small and medium-sized local TV-stations
Germany	356,755	81,869	12–14 private W	Late 1980s	11 public corp. (W) with 8 channels (M)	1940s and 1950s (early 1990s in ex-GDR)	2–4	20–25
United Kingdom	244,046	58,533	13 public W	1950s	14 private W	1954–63		Negligible
France	547,026	58,060	25 public W 10 private (local) W	1960s 1990s	None	–	4–5	20–25
Italy	301,225	57,204	21 public W	1976–79	None	–		≈750
Spain	504,782	39,199	17 public W 7 private W	1969–71 1993	6 public corporations with 9 channels (M)	1982–89	4–5	400–500
The Netherlands	40,844	15,460	None		4–6 public M	Early 1990s		10–15
Greece	131,944	10,467	None					≈170
Belgium	30,513	10,146	None	1960s	2 public M[c] 2 private M[c]	1960s 2nd half of 1980s	2–3	20–25
Portugal	92,082	9,927	3 public W	1974–76	None	–		Negligible
Sweden	449,964	8,830	n.a.	n.a.	n.a.	n.a.	n.a.	n.a.
Austria	83,849	8,054	9 public W	1960s	None	–		Negligible
Denmark	43,069	5,220	None		8 public W	1983–88	1–2	≈50
Finland	337,009	5,110	None		None	–		Negligible
Ireland	70,283	3,586	None		None	–		Negligible

W: "Window". M: "Mirror". n.a.: not available.
a With regional output.
b Due to the very complex landscape of local tv in Italy, it is quite difficult to distinguish between "big" and "small" stations.
c They are aimed at one of the two cultural and linguistic regions of the country, although they can be seen in the whole country.

Source: Contributors to the research on "Proximate television and the Information Society in the European Union" (quoted in Note 3) and own research.

4

LOCAL AND NATIONAL
CULTURAL INDUSTRIES

Is there life after globalization?

Georgette Wang, Lin-lin Ku and Chun-chou Liu

"How local is local?" In an attempt to describe the emergence of a global civil society, Sreberny-Mohammadi (1996: 18) raised this question. Obviously there can be no readily available answer to it; for the same reason nor can there be a readily available answer to a perhaps more fundamental question: "What is local?"

What is worthy of notice here is not the fact that there are no quick answers to these two questions. Although "globalization" is becoming one of the most popular terms being used in intellectual, business, media and other circles since the late 1980s (Robertson, 1992), until this day academics are still struggling with the task of defining the term. Worthy of notice is how little attention questions on local and national industries have managed to attract. As Sreberny-Mohammadi (1996: 18) pointed out, "if defining globalization is difficult, at least theoretical energy is spent on the problem."

The discriminatory treatment of the global vs. the national and local reflects an imbalance of research interest that seems to have existed since the early days of communication studies. Marveled by the technological wonders and alarmed by the potential political, economic, and cultural influences brought by such wonders, academics and policy makers have paid much closer attention to the foreign, transnational, and global than they have to the domestic, national and local dimensions of communication industries when the flow of information has been examined. Even when raised in the theoretical debate of media imperialism and postmodernism, they have remained peripheral concerns.

From a global perspective, this negligence perhaps was understandable, but is no longer justifiable. Deregulation and technological growth have brought significant impact to the communications industry, and this impact is by no means limited to the few transnational media in the Western world. While policy makers are scrambling to keep satellite signals and computer network messages from freely flowing in and out of their national territories, national and local media are juggling for position in a market that has suddenly doubled, or even tripled, in size. The end result is a communication ecology in which the role of the local and national

52

vis-à-vis the transnational and global media is being redefined. To focus research attention on just the globalization aspect of change, therefore, is to miss half the picture.

It is the purpose of this chapter [1] to examine the development of the national and the local cultural industries in various parts of the world as transnational media became part of the globalization process. Are national and local cultural industries withering and dying as some feared, or are they rising to meet the opportunities offered by regulatory changes and new technologies? And what are the theoretical implications of these developments?

Local, national, regional, transnational and global: clouded meanings

Before the advent of the communications satellite, the world of communication was ruled by national media, public or private, which dominate the communication system within a sovereign state. Although national media tended to be urban-centered, local media, if they existed at all, were relatively unimportant due to their limited size and influence. This was especially true for television because the smaller the market size, the more difficult it was to justify the huge investment in personnel and facilities.

The situation, however, underwent drastic changes from the late 1980s onward; not only did the dominance by national media meet serious challenges, also challenged were the definitions of terms that were used to describe various types of old and new players in the market.

First the term "transnational television" was used to characterize media conglomerates such as CNN, HBO, and Disney that sold packaged programs across national borders. "Transnational television," therefore, seems to denote any television service with significant coverage beyond a single nation. But as the coverage of these services quickly expanded to include a great majority of the nations in the world, they were seen as something more than just "transnational;" they were "global," although few could tell how large an audience a medium needs to reach before it qualifies for the label (Ferguson, 1992).

Another significant development brought about by deregulation and technologies is the emergence of regional television. A region, defined as "a large tract of land" in the Webster Dictionary (1986 edition), usually denotes a geographical area bigger than a locality. But is it smaller or larger than a nation? In the existing body of literature, the term has been used in both ways. To some, "regional television" means television service covering several localities within a sovereign state, such as France's FR3 (Canova-Lamarque, Perrot and Lopez, 1995), but to others it refers to transnational television serving a geographical area that may encompass several nations, e.g. Star TV in Asia.

In addition to the ambiguities in the meaning of the term "regional," the emergence of regional television also led to the need to distinguish the "regional" from the "local;" if "regional television" serves more than one locality, then how does one define "local?" In other words, "how local is local?" In Belgium, it was found that the French-speaking community refers to its television as "local," but the Flemish calls its "regional," while the two are quite similar in size (Moragas and Garitaonandía, 1995: 31). In a similar vein, one also needs to ask "how national is national," especially when "local television" has frequently been used to mean "national television" as opposed to "global television" (Sinclair *et al.*, 1996).

It is not the intention of this paper to provide universally acceptable definitions for the above-mentioned terms so frequently used in the literature. However, some clarifications are necessary in order to conduct a meaningful discussion. In this paper the terms local and national cultural industries are used to describe mainly films and television services – including regional services such as FR3 – which are originated, operated, and targeted at audiences, within a sovereign state. They are different from the transnational, regional and global industries as the latter group of services target at audiences in more than one nation. While both regional and global cultural industries are transnational, regional industries normally have a more distinct audience group defined by language, ethnicity or religion, e.g. the Islamic world or Greater China.

Theoretical conception

When American programs were found to have dominated television schedules in developing nations in the 1960s and the 1970s, immediate concerns were raised over the political-economic ramifications of such dominance and its influences over the integrity of the local culture. According to the dependency theory, this spread of Western cultural products helps to consolidate and perpetuate a center-periphery relationship (Golding and Harris, 1997).

In comparison, there was not much concern about the influence such dominance may have over the development of local and national cultural industries, nor was there a serious attempt to understand how national and local cultural industries fared under the situation and its implications. Although there were calls for a more balanced international flow of information, it seemed generally assumed that unless protective policy measures were implemented, national and local media – hampered by a lack of capital, talent, and up-to-date facilities – would have little choice but to accept this invasion of their turf, a choice which might prove to be economically viable anyway since purchasing programs was much more affordable than producing programs of their own.

In the 1990s primary concerns of communication researchers were shifted to the loss of cultural identity and the decline of nation-states with the emergence of a global culture. In this argument local cultures were given a prominent place because they set the possibilities and limits for the global economy (Du Gay, 1997), or serve "as a resistance, as the source of particularities and variety, and as the ground of meaning for individuals and communities (Braman, 1996: 28). According to Giddens (Tomlinson, 1996: 86), the local and the global are opposing tendencies which engage in dialectical push and pull, disembedding and reembedding. Globalized socioeconomic systems formulate the context within which we conduct our local lives. Local cultures, therefore, are conceptualized as both the basis and the framework for the development of a global culture.

While local cultures had their place in the globalization argument, that of the local cultural industries was much less clear than that of the communications media in general. Despite warnings against a media-centric approach (Mohammadi, 1997), media – or more precisely transnational media – were perceived as vehicles of globalization. As one level of a global culture, the communication system was expected to form the material base for all other levels (Smith, 1990). According to Barker (1997: 13), television is inherently global for it is "an institution of capitalist modernity;" like other Western-originating institutions of modernity, it is dynamic and globalizing (Giddens, 1990: 16–17). While the diversity of audience needs in different local cultures were recognized, such needs could be satisfied by localizing global media. Local cultural industries, once again, were left out of the spotlight.

Postmodernists, as Smith (1990) and Featherstone (1990) pointed out, intended to stay away from determinism and the idea of a single, homogeneous global culture, and looked at globalization more in terms of processes. The question is how did the process begin, and where is it leading to, especially where communication is concerned? This lack of concern for local and national cultural industries leads one to suspect that, like dependency theory and the earlier modernization theory, the globalization argument is essentially repeating the one-way, unilinear model of change led by technology and capitalist interest. The major function of the media is to bring about, and to accommodate, the global-local dialectic process.

According to this model, the relationship between the local/national and the global is one of competition and tension, in which the success of one will inevitably bring failure to the other. Barker (1997: 93), for example, took the success and failure of soap operas as evidence of the local versus global tension. Although little was said about local and national cultural industries in this process, they have generally been treated as weaker opponents which will sooner or later be driven out of the market. Collins (1993), for example, regarded the internationalization of television program production as a form of "international division of labor" which helps to secure supply of the whole range of products by each producing what it produces best. In consequence, the death of a local or national cultural industry is no more alarming than the death of any other industry.

Several questions can be addressed at such a model. What is the nature of the relationship between the local and the global? Is it a zero-sum game that the local, national, regional and global cultural industries are engaged in? More importantly, with what level of confidence can we predict the fate of many Davids in the war against a handful Goliaths?

Answers to the above questions can only be found in the local and national cultural industries themselves.

Local and national cultural industries: dying or thriving?

Although local and national cultural industries failed to attract much attention from communication researchers, to many the cultural industry is not just any industry. Aside from the concern over the loss of cultural sovereignty and business opportunities, there is a need for cultural expression that a cultural industry addresses. Barker (1997: 12) points out:

> Television programs are not simple reflections of the world. Within a postmodern epistemology neither television's truth claim nor its aesthetic judgments can be held universally, they are inevitably culture and interest bound.

This statement is echoed by the constitution of Te Manu Aute, the organization of Maori Communicators in New Zealand (Dowmunt, 1993: 7):

> Every culture has a right and a responsibility to present its own culture to its own people. That responsibility is so fundamental it cannot be left in the hands of out-siders, nor be usurped by them.

Ideals, unfortunately, do not seem to reflect reality. In recent years the dominance of US products in international trade, a phenomenon which has been well documented in past research (Varis, 1974, 1984; Barker, 1997), has been further strengthened as the world enters the age of multi-channel broadcasting. According to the US Department of Commerce, net exports for the motion picture and television programming industry recorded a nearly twofold increase from 1987 to 1991 (US Department of Commerce, undated). While Varis (1974) found US products to have accounted for over 40 percent of all program hours exported worldwide in 1974, it was claiming 75 percent of the worldwide television programming exports in 1995 (Hoskins *et al.*, 1995; Barker, 1997). Hollywood majors alone were reaping US$3 billion in revenues from international television. These figures were contrasted with the insignificant amount of money spent by US television in purchasing foreign programs: not more than 2 percent in 1974 (Varis, 1974). In 1997, Britain, the only European nation with a sizable export, sold US$85 million worth of products to all of North America (Minton-Beddoes, 1997).

Another significant development was that in some countries, the increase was not merely in the amount of revenues, but also in the proportion of money spent on purchasing programs out of the total spending on programs. A study of fourteen European countries showed that from 1991 to 1996, the proportion of spending on purchased programs increased by nearly 5 percent (Figure 4.1 and see also study results in Table 4.6). On the other hand, the ratio of the cost of purchasing programs to that of producing programs remained significant in many countries (Table 4.1).

Table 4.1 Cost ratio of producing versus purchasing programs

Country	TV Station	1991	1996
Austria	ORF	1.90	1.34
Belgium (N)	BRTN	2.03	2.34
Belgium (S)	RTBF	2.20	1.76
Denmark	DR	5.25	5.26
	TV2	3.12	4.04
Finland	YLE	4.50	4.28
	MTV	2.30	1.21
France	France 2	2.22	2.01
	France 3	3.14	3.17
Germany	ARD	5.53	5.62
	ZDF	2.98	3.56
Greece	ERT	1.79	2.23
Ireland	RTE	6.58	6.86
Italy	RAI	2.90	4.34
Netherlands	NOS	3.26	2.92
Norway	NRK	9.31	7.35
	TV2	–	1.79
Portugal	RTP	2.04	1.94
Spain	RTVE	2.34	1.94
Sweden	SVT	6.47	3.98
Switzerland	SSR	1.84	1.52
UK	BBC	–	2.97
	ITV	1.95	3.56
	Channel 4	3.37	2.52
	BSky 8	–	0.94

Source: Screen Digest, April 1997

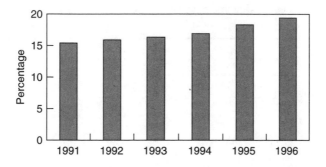

Figure 4.1 Cost of purchased programs as a proportion of all program spending in fourteen European countries

Source: Screen Digest, April 1997.

Trade statistics paint a grim picture of American domination. However, the situation can look rather different from another angle, especially when the development of local and national television in various parts of the world is more closely examined.

Local and national television industries

One major development in the audiovisual industry in recent years is the rapid expansion of the television market and the decrease of costs in transnational program distribution, thanks to the continued advance of technology. In 1997, the number of television-owning households in Asia was estimated to be around 400 million. By 2005 this number is expected to grow to 405 million, with a market value of US$29.4 billion. A similar growth was forecast in Europe (Barker, 1997: 48) where broadcast hours were expected to double in four years from 1996 to 2000, and the market for television programs has already increased by US$10.6 billion during the ten years from 1988 to 1998.

It may be natural for policy makers to be concerned about the penetration of American products into these lucrative markets (Barker, 1997:48); however, this drastic surge in television program supply capacity did not seem to have diverted the audiences' attention from local and national products. A survey of the top twenty programs in eight Asian nations showed that only a small percentage were foreign (Table 4.2), a rating record which was echoed in other parts of the world, including Europe and Latin America.

This popularity of domestically produced programs means that US producers were not the only ones to benefit from market expansion. Although over 40 percent of all imported television hours in Western Europe were American, Sepstrup (1989a) found that 73 percent of the total national supply in the continent was domestically produced. In Asian nations such as India and Korea, the percentage of foreign programs on national channels was negligible (Table 4.3). Even when

Table 4.2 Share of local production in the top twenty programs in Asian nations (1994) (percentage)

Country	Locally produced	Overseas acquired
Hong Kong	75	25
Indonesia	85	15
Malaysia	85	15
Philippines	95	5
Singapore	n.a.	n.a.
South Korea	90	10
Thailand (Bangkok)	90	10
Taiwan	100	0

Source: SRG Group

Table 4.3 Share of supply and consumption of foreign programs in selected nations

Nation	Percentage of total supply	Percentage of total consumption
Australia	54.2	37.0
India	8.3	1.9
Philippines	32.7	39.2
Korea	8.9	12.0
Bulgaria[a]	44.0	43.0
Hungary[a]	76.0	51.0
Italy[a]	42.0	32.0
The Netherlands[a]	92.0	64.0
Sweden[a]	75.0	28.0

a   Figures represent foreign programs in all channels, including national, satellite and spill-over channels, while the others represent figures of national channels only.

Source: Adapted from Goonasekera (1997) for Australia, India, Philippines and Korea; the rest adapted from Sepstrup (1990, 1994)

the percentage of supply is high, it was not necessarily matched by the consumption level, as was found in Sweden.

As pointed out by Morley and Robins (1995: 1–2), "deterritorialization" of audiovisual production, elaboration of the transnational system of delivery and development towards local and regional production complexes were taking place simultaneously. When more channels were made available, the need was for programs of a combination of origins and genres, not just one or two. According to Vic de Rosario, chairman of Viva Group, a major entertainment company in the Philippines, the future of his business lies in three types of audiovisual products: local television programs, good local movies, and international movies (Groves and Espiritu, 1997).

The situation in Taiwan may be a good example of the above observation. During the ten years from the late 1980s to the late 1990s, the total number of channels available to average viewers in Taiwan has grown twenty to thirty times. While the percentage of imported programs over major terrestrial television networks remained at around twenty in the past thirty years, all of a sudden the television market – cable and satellite included – was flooded by major trans-nationals. It was estimated, for example, that about US$11.6 million per year was

Table 4.4 Terrestrial television advertising revenue and growth rate (percentage)

Channel	1991–92	1992–93	1993–94	1994–95	1995–96
TTV	26.39	4.43	3.2	−0.41	−3.95
CTV	26.30	9.37	2.2	−5.40	6.25
CTS	27.47	0.29	−2.2	6.55	2.81

Source: Advertising Magazine, various issues

spent to acquire the broadcast rights for just five international channels: CNN, ESPN, Discovery, HBO and Star Movie (Feng and Su, 1994).

However, competition from transnationals has not threatened the livelihood of the terrestrial television networks. Despite a drastic fall in revenue growth rates from over 20 percent to single-digit, or even negative, growth rates (Table 4.4) since the early 1990s, the amount of advertising revenues has changed little over the past few years. In fact a couple of the networks have recently begun to show signs of recovery from the initial setback in growth rates.

Also unchanged for terrestrial television was the percentage of imported programs, which remained around 20 percent (Table 4.5). Despite fierce competition in the form of a much greater supply of imported programs from cable and satellite channels, terrestrial networks seemed determined to make locally produced programs their major attraction, and this persistence with local products does have its rationale.

In Taiwan cable networks are major carriers of transnational channels; however, these channels do not necessarily make up the core of cable programming. Number one on the list of the 1996 Estimate for Cable Advertising Revenue ("Advertising Statistics," 1997) was TVBS, a satellite service with Hong Kong investment but 100 percent local management. Most of the other top-ranking channels were also of a local or regional background, including Super Television, San-li, and Star TV. Even puppet shows which were once popular on broadcast television are making sizable profits again over satellite channels. According to the manager of a major cable conglomerate, although the amount of money paid to transnationals may be impressive, the most expensive program remains local – baseball games.[2]

Obviously it would be difficult for terrestrial television networks in Taiwan to go back to the notorious[3] profit margins they used to enjoy in the past few decades. However it is also obvious that local products have not only kept their turf in terrestrial television broadcast, but are prospering over cable and satellite channels as well.

By the mid-1990s, program production in various parts of the world was making significant progress with perhaps Africa the only exception, with only three nations

Table 4.5 Terrestrial television rates of imported programs

Year	Locally produced	Imported programs
1962 (TTV[a] only)	68.57	31.34
1972 (TTV only)	79.00	21.00
1982 (TTV only)	86.34	13.66
1991 (TTV only)	82.21	17.79
1998 (TTV only)	84.29	15.71
1998 5.11–17 (all terrestrial network TV)	79.68	20.32

a   TTV: Taiwan Television Company, the first terrestrial television network in Taiwan.

Source: TTV 30 Years (1992: 324–41), quoted in Feng and Su (1994: 77)

60

Table 4.6 Percentage growth in production spending in selected European nations

Country	Total ($)		Purchased ($)		Growth(%)	Produced($)		Growth(%)
	1991	1996	1991	1996		1991	1996	
Austria	252	335	53	92	73.58	199	243	22.11
Belgium	183	227	45	152	237.77	138	75	−45.65
Switzerland	296	443	92	169	83.69	204	274	34.31
Germany	2695	5432	450	1018	126.22	2245	4414	96.61
Denmark	155	221	16	24	50.00	139	197	41.72
Spain	831	1170	187	276	47.59	644	894	38.81
Finland	172	274	22	51	131.81	150	223	48.66
France	2025	2946	496	709	42.94	1529	2237	46.30
UK	3396	4139	352	802	127.84	3044	3337	9.62
Greece	171	195	55	68	23.63	116	127	9.48
Ireland	108	159	9	13	44.44	99	146	47.47
Italy	2548	2257	282	286	1.39	2266	1971	−13.01
Netherlands	354	437	35	44	25.71	319	393	23.19
Norway	94	159	5	18	260.00	89	141	58.42
Portugal	124	152	33	47	42.42	91	105	15.38
Sweden	326	579	28	54	92.85	298	525	76.17

Source: Adapted from *European Audiovisual Observatory* (1997)

producing their own programs (Gross, 1995: 226). While a greater percentage of programming expenditure may have been spent on purchasing programs, the amount spent on producing programs also increased as total spending increased. In Europe, where a significant percentage of the American exports were consumed, there has also been a significant growth in production spending. As shown in Table 4.6, except for Belgium and Italy, the growth in money spent on program production from 1991 to 1996 in sixteen European nations ranged from a low of nine percent in the United Kingdom and Greece to highs of 96 percent in Germany and 76 percent in Sweden.

Although statistics were sporadic, growth in program production was reported elsewhere, including West Canada, New Zealand, Brazil and several Asian nations. In Indonesia, for example, the number of domestically produced telepictures, miniseries and series grew from 730 in 1994 to 3,244 in 1996, while in Singapore the investment in audiovisual production in 1995 scored a record US$114 million, nearly quadrupling that of the previous year. In some nations local and national production was so vigorous that programs that were originally targeted at audiences at home began to reach into the regional market and became transnationals themselves, a development which will be discussed in greater detail in this paper.

National film industries

In contrast to thriving local and national television industries, film industries around the world have suffered in recent years. First, the dominance of American products seems especially visible in the international film market which, unlike the television

Table 4.7 American share of the European cinema market

	Features films produced[a]	Screens	Admissions (millions)	Average admissions per capita	Market share of national films (%)	Market share of American films(%)
1986[b]	457	19,200	658	2.0	28.0	57.0
1987	484	18,340	608	1.9	24.0	56.0
1988	466	17,600	559	1.7	25.0	60.0
1989	419	17,060	569	1.7	19.0	67.0
1990	421	16,730	564	1.7	19.5	70.0
1991[c]	499	16,900	579	1.7	17.0	73.0
1992	468	17,330	558	1.6	17.0	73.0
1993	502	17,330	636	1.8	15.0	75.0
1994	466	17,630	640	1.8	15.0	74.0
1995[d]	510	20,140	660	1.8	16.0	72.0

a Excluding Franco-European minority co-productions;
b From 1986: a 12-member EU;
c From 1991: including a unified Germany;
d From 1995: a 15-member EU.

Source: CNC (1997)

market, has been shrinking. In the Philippines, local films accounted for 40 to 50 percent of box office revenues in 1996, a significant drop from the 60 percent recorded in the previous year. Europe experienced a similar decline when the American share of the cinema market went from 57 percent in 1986 to 72 percent in 1995 (Table 4.7), while the non-American share of the US box office revenues was a mere 2 percent (Morley and Robins, 1995). In Scandinavia, American feature films constituted 75 to 80 percent of all box office revenues. In Norway, less than 3 percent of revenues came from local films, while in Finland it was less than two percent.

With rising costs and declining revenues, film production has become an investment that only the major companies are able to afford. This is reflected in smaller output in the majority of the nations in the world – with the US as an unusual exception. In Europe for example, the number of feature films produced went from 999 in 1983 to 804 in 1993, while in the US, this number increased from 336 to 450 during the same period (Table 4.8).

No good news was reported elsewhere in the world. In Taiwan, for example, a shrinking market coupled with the failure to integrate production and distribution have led to a steady decline in the number of locally produced films, from 163 in 1988 to 18 in 1996. In a comprehensive study of the Taiwan film industry, Lu (1997) found that in 1994 locally produced films constituted less than 5 percent of all the films shown in movie theaters. In the same year, the number of Hong Kong films shown in local theaters was seven times more than that of local films, and foreign (predominantly Hollywood) films eleven times more. The gross revenue of local films accounted for only 2 percent of the total box office revenue.

Table 4.8 Ten years of European film production

		1983	1985	1989	1990	1991	1992	1993
BE	Belgium	12	7	10	20	6	12	8
DE	Germany	77	64	68	48	72	63	67
DK	Denmark	11	9	18	13	11	15	14
ES	Spain	99	77	47	42	64	48	53
FR	France	131	151	136	146	156	155	152
GB	United Kingdom	38	47	27	47	46	42	60
GR	Greece	47	27	8	–	15	12	18
IR	Ireland	3	2	3	3	1	4	6
IT	Italy	110	89	117	119	129	127	106
LU	Luxembourg	0	1	3	1	2	3	4
NL	Netherlands	15	13	13	13	14	13	16
PT	Portugal	4	9	7	9	9	8	16
Total	**EU**	**547**	**496**	**457**	**461**	**525**	**502**	**520**
AT	Austria	12	12	11	14	11	10	–
CH	Switzerland	17	34	16	19	25	18	16
FI	Finland	13	15	10	13	12	11	13
IS	Iceland	4	5	2	2	4	6	2
NO	Norway	8	12	10	12	9	7	–
SE	Sweden	15	17	26	85	88	72	58
Total	non-EU	69	95	75	85	88	72	58
Total	**Western Europe**	**616**	**591**	**532**	**546**	**613**	**574**	**578**
AL	Albania	–	14	11	–	–	–	–
BG	Bulgaria	32	40	20	19	22	3	8
CS	Czechoslovakia	66	66	70	62	17	–	–
CZ	Czech Republic	44	53	55	53	15	11	18
DDR	German Dem.Rep.	16	19	–	–	–	–	–
EE	Estonia	–	–	–	–	5	5	–
HR	Croatia	–	–	–	–	–	3	–
HU	Hungary	25	21	37	23	20	22	25
PL	Poland	32	27	23	9	19	18	15
RO	Romania	32	27	23	9	19	18	15
RU	Russian Federation	–	–	–	–	–	65	137
SB	Serbia	–	–	–	–	6	3	–
SK	Slovakia	22	13	15	9	2	4	2
SU	USSR/CIS	148	156	160	600	300	400	–
UA	Ukraine	–	–	–	–	13	–	–
YU	Yugoslavia	29	24	29	21	–	–	–
Central and **Eastern Europe**		**383**	**406**	**372**	**465**	**502**	**151**	**226**
All	**Europe**	**999**	**997**	**904**	**1,011**	**1,115**	**725**	**804**
US	United States	336	356	356	477	583	519	450

Source: Screen Digest, July 1994

In view of the situation, it is not surprising that Cirio Santiago, Chief Executive Officer (CEO) of Premiere, one of the major entertainment companies in the Philippines, should openly admit that "the [local] film industry might go." And he would not be the only person to be concerned.

Pressured by the need to keep a film industry, a number of governments and international institutions have engaged in programs and projects designed to boost its growth. Canada was one of the first nations which launched such programs (Dowmunt, 1993: 16 and 22; Sinclair *et al.*, 1996: 27), followed by others including Indonesia, Taiwan, Iceland and France. Two notable examples of international agencies' involvement were Nordic Film and TV Fund which had an annual budget of US$10 million, and the European Community which has provided loans and support through its MEDIA program to small production companies since the late 1980s (Morley and Robins, 1995: 18).

Some of the projects achieved a certain degree of success in bringing life to indigenous film production. France was one of the very few nations which still has a vigorous national film industry. In Iceland, films supported by the nation's Film Fund scored box office revenues comparable to that of Hollywood films.

But not all of the endeavors brought significant improvement to the situation. It was not until recently that Canadian programs were found to be sufficiently attractive to audiences at home (Sinclair *et al.*, 1996: 27). In Indonesia, two of the fifteen government-funded films failed to even get local theatrical release in 1996. Subsidized Taiwan films managed to win major international awards, but few succeeded on the domestic market. Critics of the government policy contend that the judges' emphasis on personal, artistic expressions in funding decisions has led subsidized films to alienate themselves from the average viewer.

Aside from the drastically different performance of local and national television and film industries, at least two other trends of development are worthy of some attention here: increasing hybridization of local and national cultural products, and the emergence of cultural markets.

The pureblooded: increasingly difficult to find

It may be fair to say that "modeling, imitating and mutual learning" have always been part of the audiovisual business (Mattelart, 1976: 161; Wang, 1997). But the distinction between a local or national program and a transnational or global program may become increasingly blurred as hybridization of products takes place at both the local/national and the global level.

Among the first to try some form of hybridization were the global media. Globalization, as pointed out by Lull (1995), cannot do without interacting with diverse local conditions. To investors the pressure to engage in such interaction comes from the sheer fact that revenue from the overseas market has grown to such an extent that it no longer is a "fringe benefit" of the domestic market. To take Twentieth-Century Fox, one major transnational US film conglomerate, as an example, its revenue from overseas markets had reached 40 percent of its total revenue by the mid-1990s. With a forecast of 50 percent overseas revenues, the company CEO Strauss Zelnick once acknowledged that overseas market needs had had, and would continue to have, an influence on production decisions (Ohmann, 1996: 21).

The need to localize became more pressing as audiences were found to have shown little interest in the standardized, "canned" programs offered by transnational media. Despite the US's overwhelming dominance in world exports of audiovisual products, a study by Waterman (1988) found that during the 1980s, 80 percent of US overseas distribution went to seven countries: Australia, Canada, France, Germany, Italy, Japan and the UK – mostly nations of a socioeconomic background relatively similar to that of the US. Outside of these few nations, the market performance of global media was far less dazzling than had been thought.

In Asia, for example, of the nineteen transnationals which either set up headquarters in or up-link (send signals from a terrestrial station to satellite) from Singapore, HBO was the only one making a profit, and the rest were not expected to break even until five to six years later. One other major failure on the Asia casualty list was Murdoch's Pan-Asia channels (Minton-Beddoes, 1997), which had soon given way to programming catering to local tastes.

In Taiwan, ratings of an NBA game grew by more than ten times when broadcast over a terrestrial network, compared to the same match on a transnational channel. A local host was all it took to make the difference. Although Taiwan Cable Systems paid a rather handsome sum for the broadcast rights to transnational channels as mentioned earlier in this paper, on the list of 1996 estimates of cable advertising revenues, ESPN ranked twenty-two, Discovery thirty-five, and CNN not even on the list. In 1998 CNN was pressured to launch a promotion campaign in order to save its place in Taiwan's cable systems.

Before long it was clear that global television needs local repackaging to attract audiences. In China, Shanghai TV produced its own version of Sesame Street (Minton-Beddoes, 1997). Others tried franchising ideas (Gross, 1995: 10) or formats (Iwabuchi, 1997). In Indonesia, a local crew produced an Indonesian version of the Jackie Gleason show "The Honeymooners," while Japanese companies were busy selling local popular song contests to Asian audiences.

In addition to the effort to localize, there has been a visible growth of interest in co-production. To many national and local cultural industries, co-production has at least two advantages: it helps to overcome the shortage of capital and talent in program and film production, and at the same time facilitates access to overseas markets.

In France, one of the first nations to sponsor co-production projects, the proportion of co-produced films rose from 10 percent of total output in 1980 to 36 percent in 1995 (CNC, 1997). Similar trends were observed among European nations (Figure 4.2) and in other areas in the world.

Co-production is one – but not the only – way to reach markets beyond national borders. According to To and Lau (1998), the expansion strategies adopted by Hong Kong-based TVBS, a new transnational corporation in the region, can be

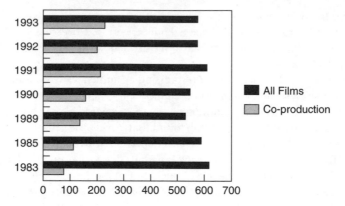

Figure 4.2 Ten years of film cooperation in Europe

Source: Screen Digest, July 1994

put in four categories: cooperation, capital investment, barter trade and consultancy contracts. Cooperation helped TVBS to capture the Taiwan market with a highly competitive local partner, while barter trade and consultancy allowed it to enter places where it would otherwise have little chance of doing business, e.g. Indonesia and India. To a successful enterprise such as TVBS, regionalization and globalization seem to be a natural development as the need to maintain growth pressures producers to seek opportunities overseas.

Elsewhere in Asia, there were plans for large-scale co-production centers besides cooperation projects undertaken by individual companies. For example, in 1996 Malaysia launched its US$2 billion Multimedia Super Corridor project to attract foreign investment. With the launch of Mesat, the project was designed as a home for co-production and also a springboard to regional and world markets.

Taylor (1995) has pointed out that cooperation among audiovisual producers will soon redefine the global market. What we have observed so far is increasing cooperation among those at all levels of the audiovisual business, including investment, management, production, distribution and promotion. Hybridization, therefore, is no longer limited to production.

When local products are sold overseas: the formation of cultural-lingual television markets

While media globalization attracted a great deal of attention from communication researchers and policy makers, an equally, if not more, important development for television in the 1990s took place when local and national cultural products began to find rather attractive business opportunities outside of their intended (domestic) market. The success of Telenovas in the Spanish-speaking world and Chinese serial dramas based on classic novels such as Judge Bao were but two of the examples.

Table 4.9 TVE International; number of subscribers as of January 1996

Europe Country	Subscribers	Latin America Country	Subscribers
Belgium	2,420,000	Argentina	4,650,000
Bulgaria	175,000	Bolivia	9,280
Finland	880,000	Brazil	688,472
France	1,280,000	Chile	425,000
UK	675,000	Columbia	56,375
Netherlands	480,000	Costa Rica	45,000
Ireland	45,000	Ecuador	46,000
Israel	800,000	El Salvador	22,000
Norway	558,000	Guatemala	6,786
Poland	275,000	Honduras	15,572
Portugal	20,000	Mexico	710,000
Rumania	75,000	Nicaragua	12,000
Sweden	280,000	Panama	13,703
Switzerland	2,350,000	Paraguay	65,000
		Peru	50,000
		Puerto Rico	157,400
		Dominican Republic	20,000
		Uruguay	63,000
		Venezuela	101,700
Total	10,313,000		7,157,350

Source: RTVE Variety, 1996, September 23–29: 110

Compared with programs offered by global television, regional programs have the advantage of a common language and shared cultural and/or religious background, which soon became the basis for the emergence of new television markets. In Asia, for example, segmentation of audiences has resulted in four cultural markets: Chinese, Hindi, Islamic and English (Lee and Wang, 1995). Other such markets include the Spanish-speaking population which reaches beyond Latin America into Europe (Table 4.9); the Arab world, Europe and diasporic or ethnic communities scattered in various corners of the world. These markets which had either been beyond the reach of national media or too small and spread out to be served by mainstream media, now provided new pastures as the cost of transnational delivery dropped.

Some of the major players now thriving in these regional markets include India, Hong Kong, Brazil and Egypt (Lee and Wang, 1995; Goonasekera, 1997; Sinclair, 1996; Barker, 1997; US Department of Commerce, undated).

The emergence of these new transnational players not only redefined the global television market structure, but has had significant influence on the development of local cultural industries. With abilities to cater to local needs and tastes yet sometimes featuring a fresher, more liberal programming format, regional exporters have become far more threatening competitors to local and national cultural industries than the US-based global conglomerates. Judge Bao, for example, managed to achieve high ratings in Taiwan, China, Singapore and Hong Kong be it a Hong Kong, or a Taiwanese production. Similar successes were reported of a number of serial drama produced in China, e.g. *Liu Luo-guo* and All Men Are Brothers (*Shui Hu Zhuan*), a record that no US-based global television player has been able to challenge so far.

Implications

From the above analyses we can make observations concerning at least three issues: the future of local and national television industries vs. that of the film industries, the nature of the relationships between global and regional, national and local cultural industries; and the implications of increasing hybridization of cultural products.

First, worthy of notice are the differences between the film and the television industries in responding to fierce competition from the transnationals. While the local and national television industries seem to be profiting from the change brought by deregulation and technology, the film industries are struggling for survival. The same abilities to cater to local needs and tastes do not seem to have given the film industries a competitive edge against Hollywood. Why?

Both film and television programs are audiovisual products; however, the human needs that they appeal to, and the world they construct, have become quite different since television gained wide popularity. Television, with its easy accessibility (from home), availability (up to twenty-four hours a day) and varied content, has in effect formed a part of the audience's everyday life, a presence which films are unable to achieve. As pointed out by Chiu Fu-sheng, CEO of Taiwan Era Video Enterprise, television, with its news, weather, and entertainment, caters to audiences' needs by reflecting, and also responding to, the cultural and social contexts in which they live. To attract audiences, films, therefore, must resort to other means, i.e. to appeal to fantasies by building a world detached from reality.[4]

This division of labor seems to have been further enhanced by the need for film makers to produce high drama with special effects which work best in movie theaters, thus giving them a competitive edge against the free-from-home television entertainment. Many of the Hollywood productions which achieved global success, including E.T., Titanic, and Jurassic Park, were among the best examples of such fantasy worlds built on the wide screen. With videotape rental, movie channels, and video-on-demand all competing for audiences, films will no longer be able to attract viewers to movie theaters if they – with or without an appeal to the audiences' social and cultural needs – cannot distinguish themselves from what is available at home.

Unfortunately for the local film industry, this "division of labor" is not in its best interest. All too frequently short of talent and financial resources, it is almost impossible for local film studios to reach the same level of technical and/or artistic sophistication as their Hollywood competitors. As a result, their attraction wanes when their advantage in cultural and social proximity ceases to be important. This loss of attraction of local films to viewers has been highly visible in Taiwan in recent years. Box office records showed that major losses in moviegoers were found mostly with local films. From 1990 to 1994 the number of local film viewers suffered a decline of over 80 percent when viewers of Hollywood and Hong Kong films began to return to theater houses (Lu, 1997).

Undoubtedly the "winning strategy" developed by Hollywood film makers, a strategy which is in essence similar to what is found in American television dramas such as Dallas and The X-Files, have also contributed to their market success. As Sepstrup (1990: 85) pointed out, US television producers have developed "a flair for creating popular fiction programs built on a cross-cultural common denominator with a much broader cultural approach..." In other words, it is what Dowmunt (1993: 21) described as "universal programming" that made Dallas a world success; hence those built within a more specific cultural context were less likely to achieve global popularity. Seinfeld, for example, fared miserably in several Asian nations, including Singapore and Taiwan. Similarly, for a film to be globally successful it has to come from universal situations.

A closer look at Hollywood shows that the "universal situation" that has helped so many films to succede, may have been a product of transnationalizing the industry itself, a process which started with the introduction of the preselling strategy in the 1970s (Wasser, 1995). According to Wasser (1995: 31), the most important feature of the strategy, one which allows producers to seek funding before the film begins shooting, is to encourage foreign producers to go to Hollywood and make Hollywood pictures "independent of the American companies and of American financing." Indeed in recent years in Hollywood there have not only been an increasing number of foreign producers, directors, actors and actresses – including familiar names such as Luc Besson, John Wu and Jean Renu – also on the list are foreign sources of capital. If Hollywood is a symbol of American cultural imperialism, today this "imperialist" is no longer purely American as some of the major film production companies are owned by Japanese corporations such as Sony Entertainment Inc. (Iwabuchi, 1997). It is therefore no surprise that to some critics, Hollywood not only fails to address the American audience in a profound way, the "American-ness" of its products is also in question under the economic circumstances of production (Wasser, 1995).

It would be interesting to see if Hollywood will become the ultimate embodiment of a genuinely "global" cultural industry, thoroughly "deterritorialized," both in outlook and spirit; so far the television industry has produced little evidence to support the claims and ideals of global media.

What, then, is left for the national film industries? To survive in the face of competition from Hollywood, some have crossed over into television production. Already film producers are getting the majority of their revenues from sources other than movie theaters, including videotape rentals, cable broadcasting and other video services. In a few years, convergence of media technology and the development of digital technology will bring sweeping changes which will minimize the differences in film and television production.

In Taiwan, the Central Film Production Corporation, one of the island's largest film companies, has managed to remain self-sufficient by producing television films, and others have tried to support film production by profit from television production. Cross-subsidies on a larger scale were seen in countries such as France and Indonesia where the television industry has become a major investor in or source of income to the film industry.

While it is difficult to say whether local and national television industries will single-handedly save national film industries from their demise, we can predict, with a rather comfortable level of confidence, that local and national cultural industries as a whole will not wither and die even if transnationals are reaching into the remotest corners of the world. According to Cantor (1994), mass culture is becoming extinct; today American products – the best in "universal programming" – may be available everywhere, but are not dominant anywhere.

Also worthy of notice from our observation of the local and national cultural industries, is the nature of the relationship between the local and the global. International trade statistics did provide us with some reasons for apprehension as American films and programs are taking a bigger share of the international market. However, statistics also showed that while the supply of foreign programs grew by large quantities as channel capacity multiplied, they were usually behind in viewing rates. Until the late 1990s major global media in many parts of the world were still struggling to get out of the red. This led one to suspect that the market dominance of global television, its globalizing function and purported impact on values and cultural identities had been overstated at this stage.

As global media kept researchers occupied, a number of cultural-lingual markets have emerged. In some of the formerly most peripheral third-world nations, such as Egypt and India, local, cultural industries have been transformed into regional exporters, challenging global, as well as national and local cultural industries in the same geographic area or ethnic community – a development which was not part of the globalization theories.

Indeed, when local and national cultural industries manage to prosper under competition from the transnationals and sometimes stay ahead in the rating game, when local industries eagerly globalize and the transnationals avidly localize, it is no longer clear whether treating them as opposing tendencies is still the best way to conceptualize their relationship. Television may be globalizing, as indicated by Barker (1997) and Giddens (1990); however, the same technology and capitalist pursuit of profits also push it to localize and regionalize. In fact if the major overseas markets for US audiovisual products were found in nations of a similar social cultural background and mainly sharing the same language (Waterman, 1988) , then could we call this a "global" market, or is it just a super-sized cultural market, like the others?

More detailed analyses of industry data are needed to answer the above questions, however, there is enough evidence to warrant another attempt to redefine the relationship among the local, regional and global cultural industries. In a discussion of globalization theories, Braman (1996: 22) suggested that globalization and localization processes can be conceptualized as a "mutually constitutive" relationship between parts and the whole. Perhaps the same may be said of global, regional, national, and local cultural industries. Rather than opponents in a zero-sum game, they may all be interacting parts of a global communications system. Changes in regulatory environments and technological advances bring new opportunities and new patterns of interaction which favor certain market players but discourage some others. As interacting parts of a system, they compete, yet not necessarily against one another; they strive to highlight their uniqueness, but also learn from one another.

Anthropological studies of cultural flow suggest that the process of transnationalization will lead to an increasingly "hybridized," rather than a "homogenized," world. As a result, people on the periphery will increasingly be subjected to imported meanings and forms, while the imported forms will be interpreted and recycled by local cultures, and the two scenarios are woven together, according to Mattelart (1994: 230).

Human history tells us that neither transnational cultural flow nor "hybridization" began with global media, just as modeling, mutual learning and imitating are not just practices of the audiovisual industries – they are part of human nature. In this sense, it is perhaps both inevitable and necessary for the global cultural industries to localize, and for the national and the local industries to globalize.

Is there, then, life after globalization for the local/national cultural industry? Yes; but what is a local or a national cultural industry? Or more precisely, has there been a genuine globalization of the cultural industries?

Notes

1 The authors would like to thank Ma Li-chun and Wang Ying-yu for their assistance in data collection.
2 Personal interview with Ming-jia Yao, assistant manager of Wei-lai Corporation, January 16, 1998.
3 Profit margins of terrestrial television networks were "notorious" because year-end bonuses for employees at the networks can be as much as five-sixths of their annual salary.
4 Personal interview with Chiu Fu-sheng, CEO of Era Video Enterprise, March 19, 1998.

References

"Advertising statistics." *Advertising Magazine* (1977). April: 52 (in Chinese).
Barker, C. (1997). *Global Television*. Oxford: Blackwell Publishers.
Braman, S. (1996). "Interpenetrated globalization: Scaling, power, and the public sphere." In S. Braman and A. Sreberny-Mohammadi (Eds), *Globalization, Communication and Transnational Civil Society*, 21–36. Cresskill, NJ: Hampton Press.
Canova-Lamarque, G., Perrot, M. and Lopez, B. (1995). "France: Identity crisis of regional television and expansion of local television." In M.de Moragas and C.Garitaonandía (Eds), *Decentralization in the Global Era*, 43–64. London: John Libbey.

Cantor, M. (1994). "The role of the audience in the production of culture: A personal research retrospective." In J. Ettema and D. Whitney (Eds), *Audiencemaking: How the Media Create the Audience*, 159–70. Thousand Oaks, CA: Sage.

Centre National de la Cinematographie (CNC). (1997). *Les Chiffres Cles du CNC*. Paris: CNC.

Collins, R. (1993). "The internationalization of the television program market: Media imperialism or international division of labor?" In E.M. Noam (Ed.), *The International Market in Film and Television Programs*, 125–45. Norwood, NJ: Ablex Publishing.

Dowmunt, T. (Ed.) (1993). *Channels of Resistance: Global Television and Local Empowerment*. London: BFI and Channel Four.

Du Gay, P. (Ed.) (1997). *Production of Culture / Culture of Production*. London: Sage.

European Audiovisual Observatory (1997). "Statistical yearbook: Film, television, video and new media in Europe" (1998 edn). Strasbourg: European Audiovisual Observatory.

Featherstone, M. (Ed.) (1990). *Global Culture: Nationalism, Globalization and Modernity*. London: Sage.

Feng, J. and Su, H. (1994). An analysis of European Commission GATT video industry policy and its impact on Taiwan. Unpublished research report (in Chinese).

Ferguson, M. (1992). "The mythology about globalization." *European Journal of Communication*, 7, 69–93.

Golding, P. and Harris, P. (Eds) (1997). *Beyond Cultural Imperialism: Globalization, Communication and the New International Order*. London: Sage.

Goonasekera, A. (1997). "Cultural markets in the age of globalization." *Intermedia Special Report*, December, 25(6).

Gross, S.L. (1995). *The International World of Electronic Media*. New York: McGraw-Hill.

Groves, D. and Espiritu, C. (1997). "Biz Dilemma Rx: $Infusion." *Variety*, 47, July 28–August 3.

Iwabuchi, K. (1997). "The sweet scent of Asian modernity: Japanese presence in the Asian audiovisual market." Paper presented at the 5th International Symposium on Film, Television and Video, on "Media globalization in Asia Pacific Region," May 20–22.

Lee, P.S.N. and Wang, G. (1995). "Satellite television in Asia." *Telecommunications Policy*, 190(2), 135–49.

Lu, F. Y. (1997). "Study of the Taiwan movie market: Using 1994 as an example." *Radio and Television*, February, 3(1), 167–90 (in Chinese).

Lull, J. (1995). *Media, Communication, Culture: A Global Approach*. Cambridge: Polity Press.

Mattelart, A. (1976). "Cultural imperialism in the multinational age." *Instant Research on Peace and Violence*, 6(4), 160–74.

Mattelart, A. (1994). *Mapping World Communication*. Minneapolis: University of Minnesota Press.

Minton-Beddoes, Z. (1997). "A world view." Online. Available: http://www. economist.com/editorial/freeforall/18-1-98/index_sb232.html (October to December).

Mohammadi, A. (Ed.) (1997). *International Communication and Globalization: A Critical Introduction*. London: Sage.

Moragas Spà, M. de and Garitaonandía, C. (Eds) (1995). *Decentralization in the Global Era*. London: John Libbey.

Morley, D. and Robins, K. (1995). *Spaces of Identity: Global Media, Electronic Landscapes and Cultural Boundaries*. London: Routledge.

Ohmann, R. (1996). *Making and Selling Culture*. Hanover: Wesleyan University Press.

Sepstrup, P. (1989). "Implications of current developments in west European broadcasting." *Media, Culture and Society*, 11(1), 29–54.

Sepstrup, P. (1990). *Transnationalization of Television in Western Europe*. London: John Libbey.

Sepstrup, P. and Goonasekera, A. (1994). *TV Transnationalization: Europe and Asia*. Paris: UNESCO.

Sinclair, J., Jacka, E. and Cunningham, S. (Eds) (1996). *New Patterns in Global Television: Peripheral Vision*. New York: Oxford University Press.

Smith, A.D. (1990). "Towards a global culture?" *Theory, Culture and Society*, 7, 171–91.

Sreberny-Mohammadi, A. (1996). "Globalization, communication and transnational civil society: Introduction." In S. Braman and A. Sreberny-Mohammadi (Eds), *Globalization, Communication and Transnational Civil Society*, 1–20. Cresskill, NJ: Hampton Press.

Street, J. (1997). "Across the universe: The limits of global popular culture." In A. Scott (Ed.), *The Limits of Globalization*, 75–89. London: Routledge.

Taylor, P.W. (1995). "Co-production and change: International television in the Americas." *Canadian Journal of Communication*, 20, 411–16.

Tomlinson, J. (1996). "Global experience as a consequence of modernity." In S. Braman and A. Sreberny-Mohammadi (Eds), *Globalization, Communication, and Transnational Civil Society*, 63–88. Cresskill, NJ: Hampton Press.

To, Y. and Lau, T. (1998). "Media trade or cultural invasion?" *Journalism Research*, 57, 77–89 (in Chinese).

US Department of Commerce (undated). *Globalization of the Mass Media*. NTIA Special Publication 93-290. Washington, DC: Author.

Varis, T. (1974). "Global traffic in television." *Journal of Communication*, 24(1), 102–9.

Varis, T. (1984). "International flow of television programs." *Journal of Communication*, 34(1), 143–52.

Wang, G. (1997). "Protecting local cultural industry: Regulatory myth in the global age." Paper presented at IAMCR conference in Oaxaca, Mexico, July.

Wasser, F. (1995). "Is Hollywood American? The trans-nationalization of the American film industry." *Critical Studies in Mass Communication*, 12, 423–37.

Waterman, D. (1988). "World television trade: The economic effects of privatisation and new technology." *Telecommunications Policy*, 12(2), 141–52.

This chapter has also used information from personal interviews and trade publications, including *Screen Digest* and *Variety*.

5

THE GLOBAL, THE LOCAL AND THE PUBLIC SPHERE

Colin Sparks

The title of this chapter could be mistaken for an amalgam of all that is fashionable in the study of the mass media. On the one hand, the pairing of "the global and the local" occurs everywhere in books and articles on communication. On the other, "the public sphere" is the subject of endless debates about democracy and the mass media. Almost the only thing missing in the title is the term "civil society."

There are two things to be said about this. The first is that, despite the fact that these terms are fashionable, they nevertheless point to some very important issues about the contemporary role of the mass media. The questions which this title address us to are therefore worth spending time upon and taking seriously. The second is that, perhaps as a condition of their being fashionable, they lack agreed and precise definitions. Very often, it seems as though they are terms that mean just what the particular author wishes them to mean. Consequently, if we are going to have a valuable discussion of these issues, we need start off by being clear as to what is here meant by the terms, and why they are important. It is very unlikely that the usage I adopt here will be the one that magically commands universal support, but at least if I spell it out, readers will know what exactly it is I am talking about.

Consequently, I begin this chapter with a brief account of what I mean by the term "public sphere," and why I think that this is a central category for discussions about the mass media. I then look at some of the problems involved in the global/ local pairing. Thirdly, I briefly recount the results of some recent work that I have done on the status of the global public sphere. I then look at the local public sphere. In conclusion, I draw out what I believe to be the general implications of my discussion.

My examples and evidence are disproportionately drawn from the UK, for obvious reasons. I have tried to broaden the discussion, however, by taking some account of other European countries and the USA. I believe that the conclusions that I reach are valid for the countries that I have looked at, but of course they could be inadequate in other circumstances. It may well be that, outside of this narrow and charmed circle of developed Western countries, the issue of the public sphere, and the ways in which it interacts with the global/local nexus, are quite different. I very much look forward to a discussion that will illuminate my occidental darkness and improve the scope of my findings.

The public sphere

Habermas's concept of the public sphere has been one of the most used, and most challenged, ideas in the field of media studies in the last decade. Many contemporary discussions of the relationship between the media and democracy have been conducted in terms of the public sphere. Despite numerous debates, however, the term remains deeply problematic. Part of the problem is that historical investigation has shown that what Habermas called the "bourgeois public sphere" of eighteenth-century England and France never existed, and what did in fact exist differed systematically from the kind of communicative space that the theory requires, indeed in important respects reality was directly contrary to the claims of theory (Curran, 1991; Schudson, 1992). It has further been argued, I believe convincingly, that Habermas's belief that the development of the modern commercial mass media and of public broadcasters led to a "refeudalization" of the public sphere in which democratic debate was replaced by displays of corporate power, was wrong in some of its central propositions (lc Mahieu, 1988; Scannell, 1989). These media in fact both extended the range of topics open to public debate and opened those debates to wider layers of the population, although it is also true that they acted to limit and constrain that debate, and access to it, in important ways. Finally, I think that few writers would claim that any of the existing media, in any country of the world, actually embody the formal criteria that Habermas specified were characteristic of the public sphere.

It is obviously tempting to ask: "Why, then, continue to employ this category?" My answer lies in the dual nature of the concept. While its empirical claims do not seem to be sustainable, its normative value remains considerable. The formal requirements for the constitution of a public sphere are, it can be argued, the essential conditions for the conduct of a democratic polity. While we may not expect to find them fully embodied in actual media systems, they remain an aspiration. That does not imply that they are wholly abstract and without practical utility. On the contrary, they provide a guide to media policy. It is the level of policy that provides the mediator between social scientific accounts of what is and philosophical accounts of what is desirable.

It is from this perspective that I wish to highlight three key attributes of Habermas's account of the public sphere. In the formulation which was first translated into English, Habermas gave as defining characteristics of the public sphere that "access is guaranteed to all citizens" and that they "confer in an unrestricted fashion" (Habermas, 1974: 14). He went on to say that, if there was a public sphere in contemporary society, this would necessarily be embedded in the mass media. We can use these as norms against which we can measure the performance of actually existing media systems. We can ask: to what extent are they open to all citizens? We can ask: to what extent is debate free and uncensored? We can ask: to what extent are citizens participants in, rather than spectators at, the debate? It seems likely that most media systems do not fully embody those desiridata. Certainly, the one I am most familiar with, that of the UK, falls a long way short on all three axes of measurement. Others, like the USA, do very much better on the axis of freedom and censorship, but perhaps worse on the other two axes. Some European examples, notably Sweden, seem to do much better on all axes; all though are still well short of the ideal. To the extent that we are concerned with policy formation, we can then use the results of such a study to help formulate proposals to improve the functioning of the media in these respects.

There are three other, more general, questions raised by the concept of the public sphere which should be mentioned at this point. The first is to note that the public sphere can be usefully contrasted with the notion of "public opinion," which is its major competitor for discussing the role of the media in contemporary democracy. The latter sits most comfortably with theories of elite democracy. It is concerned with measuring what the public think, and with understanding how that opinion comes to be formed, not to say manipulated. It produces relatively little space for discussions of the public as the initiators of, and participants in, the formation of their own views. This is a radically different focus from that of the public sphere, which is primarily concerned with the public as the active subject of discussions, and focuses discussion on the mechanisms in the mass media by which this is either encouraged or impeded: public opinion is what is formed as a result of discussion in the public sphere. The theory of the public sphere sits more comfortably with radical theories of democracy which value active and participatory citizens.

The second point to note is that it is an historical limit of the debate about the public sphere that its greatest reach has been that of the state system of modernity. This should hardly be surprising, in that the category, and the problems it proposes to address, are exactly those of the modern, capitalist, state. It shares this limitation with theories of democracy, which have, perforce, been concerned with how the citizens of particular states might exercise greater or lesser degrees of control over their own governments. Categories formed on this basis evidently need to be rethought to confront a situation, like that suggested by theories of globalization, in which the decisive locus of public affairs has shifted beyond the state to the world economy, world institutions, and a world polity. Accordingly, there are writers who have argued for the necessity of constructing a global public sphere to allow people to exercise some degree of control over these global political and economic forces that are determining more and more aspects of life (Garnham, 1992; Hjarvard, 1993).

The third point to note is that Habermas argued for the existence of two kinds of public spheres. The first is the familiar, political, public sphere concerned with rational discourse directed to reaching agreement about matters of public policy. The second is the literary public sphere, more concerned with matters of taste and general social beaviour, although, of course, having profound political implications. We are here concerned almost entirely with the first, political, public sphere, although at some points I touch upon the latter. This is largely for reasons of space, and it implies a serious limitation to this study, since it has often been argued that the issues of globalization and localization are most clearly articulated in the contemporary approximation to the literary public sphere (Negus, 1996).

The conclusions of this study should be read with that limitation in mind, although I believe that a fuller consideration of the question would in fact demonstrate that the same conclusions held for the literary public sphere as for the narrower political public sphere.

Finally, there are two terminological difficulties. The dual nature of the concept of the public sphere leads to potential confusion about which aspect we are discussing. On the one hand, in the normative sense, we are speaking of an ideal media system against which we are measuring actually-existing media. On the other hand, we are discussing those actually-existing media, which we expect to find do not embody many, or any, of the desirable characteristics of the norm. I am faced with the difficult choice of whether to try to coin a new term for one or the other, or to use the same term for both. I have come to the conclusion that it is best to follow the majority of authors and use just one term. I hope that it will be clear from the context when I am discussing defective real public spheres and when I am discussing ideal normative public spheres. I apologize in advance for any difficulties that might ensue. The second problem concerns the complex of terms around "nation" and "state." The normal English-language usage is "nation-state." This particularly commends itself to US writers, since it allows them to distinguish the USA from Alabama: the former is a "nation state," the latter simply a "state." To European sensitivities, that usage conceals too many problems. We are only too aware of nations without states (Scotland, Catalonia, etc.), states that contain more than one nation (the United Kingdom of Great Britain and Northern Ireland, the Spanish state, etc.), and states that do not contain within their borders the whole of the nation (the Republic of Ireland, Hungary, etc.). We are also only too well aware of the conflicts that can result from these disjunctures. I have here tried to use the term "state" to describe sovereign entities, which the US idiom would term "nation-states," although this has made for some ungainly constructions. I apologize in advance for any confusion that may ensue.

The global and the local

The terms global and local are often, although not invariably, conjoined in discussion, but the relative values of these terms differs widely from theorist to theorist, and there are very many theorists of globalization to choose from. Within this diversity, it is possible to identify three general classes of theorizing that assign different values to the local/global pair. We can consider each in turn, both with regard to their viewpoint on the general terms and their more precise implications for the mass media.

The first of these consists of those theories of globalization that see it as a generalization of existing, and usually Western, trends. The most obvious representative of this current is Giddens, who views globalization as the generalization of modernity. There is certainly a "local" in this account, but it is that characteristic feature of western modernity, the nation state, that is globalized. "Local," here, means "state:"

The nation state system has long participated in that reflexivity characteristic of modernity as a whole. The very existence of sovereignty should
be understood as something that is reflexively monitored. ...One aspect
of the dialectical nature of globalization is the "push and pull" between
tendencies towards centralization inherent in the reflexivity of the systems
of states on the one hand and the sovereignty of particular states on the
other.

(Giddens, 1991: 69)

If we attempt to operationalize this (very difficult with Giddens, and something
a grand social theorist like him never stoops to) in media terms, it seems to imply
the global diffusion of "modern," and therefore essentially state-based, mass media.
It might reasonably be taken as a view which corresponds closely to that phase of
thinking about resistance to media imperialism that spawned New World
Information and Communication Order (NWICO) as part of a defence of national
sovereignty.

The second group of theories are those that propose a uniform and homogenous process spreading throughout the world. Ritzer, for example, wrote of the
process of bureaucratic rationalization he termed "McDonaldization" that:

The spread of American and indigenous fast-food throughout much of
the world means that there is less and less diversity from one setting to
another. The human craving for new and diverse experiences is being
limited, if not progressively destroyed, by the national and international
spread of fast-food restaurants. The craving for diversity is being replaced
by the desire for uniformity and predictability.

(Ritzer, 1993: 138–9)

In this kind of theory, the process of globalization is one which destroys the
local, at whatever level it is manifested, and replaces it by a single, standard, and
usually US-inspired, society. Translated into media terms, this would suggest that
the development of global media means the progressive erosion of local media
and their incorporation into, or replacement by, their larger predators. Neither
the state, nor any more genuinely local formation, provides the basis for an
alternative to this process of homogenization. One specifically media-based articulation of this position is that offered recently by Herman and McChesney (1997),
in their analysis of the ways in which very large media companies, operating on an
international scale, tend to ensure the dominance of a US-inspired model of
advertising-financed media at the expense of a diversity of different national forms.

The third kind of theory proposes a state system under siege. It is attacked by
globalization "from above," with abstract forces, notably the world market, acting
at a level more general than that of the state, and imposing solutions upon the
state and its citizens. But it is also attacked "from below," with other forces relating

much more directly to the immediate experience of the population within a more limited scope. Raymond Williams put the issue clearly in an early formulation:

> It is now very apparent, in the development of modern industrial societies, that the nation state, in its classical European forms, is at once too large and too small for the range of real social purposes. It is too large, even in the old nation-states such as Britain, to develop full social identities in their real diversity…At the same time it is obvious that for many purposes…the existing nation-states are too small… (because of) the trading, monetary and military problems which now show this to be true, and which have so heavily encroached on the supposed "sovereignty" of the nation-states.
>
> (Williams, 1983: 197–8)

If we attempt to operationalize this view in terms of the mass media, it would seem to suggest that we would observe a simultaneous process of the erosion of the power and influence of the state-based media on the one hand, and a parallel strengthening of both the local and the global media. We would expect to find media organizations, and regulatory structures, migrating "up" to global forms or "down" to local forms. We would expect the audiences for state-oriented media to decline relative to those for local and for global media.

For the purposes of this chapter, I propose to bracket the first two of these theoretical positions. From our point of view here, the first contains little of theoretical interest. The second, while stimulating and intriguing, directs us away from a confrontation with the issues we are examining. Both of these positions invite us to consider only the process "from above." The third position provides a much more fruitful starting point, in that it proposes a dual movement that corresponds to the issues we are addressing, and it provides the basis for a research effort that might provide evidence that could illuminate the extent of its explanatory power. I therefore propose to concentrate my discussion on this account.

To say that it provides a useful starting point, however, is not to say that it provides a complete and coherent account of the issues at stake. It is possible to identify two major problems that need exploration. The first concerns what level is being specified when we use the term "local." The "global" might not be very well theorized, but there is a commo-sense usage that is adequate for most purposes: it refers to some level of social, economic, political and cultural organization that is more extensive than that provided by the states that divide the world. The local, on the other hand, can mean widely different things, and the media forms in question can be quite different. Some writers, indeed, have made a postmodern virtue out of this lack of definition: "I…have refrained from burdening (the local) with a definition that might have constricted analysis" (Drilik, 1996: 42).

We, unfortunately, are obliged to constrict our analysis to the public sphere, and so do need to undertake the burden of at least some definitional work. An obvious starting point is the fact that there is social space for a number of different levels below that of the state, and it is not clear exactly which of them is pertinent to the global/local discussion. There is a common distinction between what is often termed the "regional," meaning some geographically and, possibly, culturally defined unit of large extent, and the more properly "local" in the sense of the relatively small community of the town, district or urban neighborhood. In this chapter, I shall provisionally adopt that distinction, although it has two major shortcomings. In the first place, it ignores possible intermediate levels, for example the city, that are an important focus of social life, both in general and in terms of the mass media. In general, I shall assign things like cities to the regional level, for reasons that I hope will become obvious below. Secondly, it is clear that, within both the categories of region and locality, there are major differences in the kinds of phenomena under discussion. The Basque Country, Catalonia, or Wales, are all "regions," in the sense used here but they are qualitatively different kinds of social constructions than is the region of south-west England. Each of the former has the kind of characteristics that usually lead them to be considered nations, albeit "stateless nations." In particular, they all have distinctive languages, historical traditions and political trajectories that mark them off from the surrounding territories. In the latter case, a handful of reactionary eccentrics not withstanding, "Wessex" is an entirely literary entity. There is not, today at least, any distinctive language (although we don't quite manage to speak English properly) and the customs of the country are barely distinguishable from elsewhere in England. Such a distinction is even stronger when we consider those formations which are not historical and administrative locations, but rather are constructed as "fluid and relational space(s)" purely in terms of their position of relative advantage, or disadvantage, with regard to the operations of the global economy (Robins, 1991: 35). We may term those regions that are marked by the coincidence of strong cultural markers and a particular historical territory "old" regions, since they often pre-date the modern state system, which was frequently constructed in an attempt to eradicate precisely such differences. We may term the other forms "new" regions in that they exist either as administrative units of the modern state, perhaps because the state was successful in eradicating their marks of difference, or, more strongly, "in and through (their) relation to the global" (Robins, 1991: 35).

At the more immediate level, "local" community can mean different things in different situations. The sort of small market towns studied by Lunby (1992) are likely to have different internal social structures, for example in kinship and employment patterns, to a neighborhood in a vibrantly diverse city such as London or New York. We might reasonably hypothesize that in the smaller town, the general direction of social ties will be what we may term "integrative," with shared languages, uniform and largely endogamous kinship structures, relatively undifferentiated employment patterns, similar life-trajectories, and so on. In the metropolitan neighborhood, on the other hand, we might suppose that there would be many social ties that are "externalizing," with linguistic diversity, varied and dispersed kinship structures, highly differentiated employment patterns, radically different life-trajectories, and so on. We would also hypothesize that the media present in those communities would be different and, in the latter case, much more diverse and less bounded by the locality.

The second major problem concerns the fact that the common-sense use of the term is spatial in reference: "local" is linked etymologically and semantically with "locality." As Featherstone puts it:

> Usually when we think of locality we have in mind a relatively small place in which everyone can know everyone else, this is social life based on face to face relations. It is assumed that the intensity of the day-to-day contacts will generate a stock of common knowledge at hand which makes misunderstandings less frequent. It is the regularity and frequency of contacts with a group of significant others which are held to sustain a common culture.
>
> (Featherstone, 1996: 52)

This sense, at its extreme developed into a notion of territoriality, is clearly one of the ways in which both the regional and the immediately local can be understood. The local is a defined space that is distinguished by borders of some kind, although they need not be as policed and impermeable as are those of the state. We might call this an "old" sense of locality, since it is linked to patterns of life, and therefore embodies structures of feeling, that predate capitalism, let alone the twentieth century.

There is, however, a second important sense in which the local is used in contemporary discussion. One of the undeniable features of the contemporary world is the international movement of vast armies of peoples, creating what Appadurai (1990) called "ethnoscapes" across at least the major cities of the developed world. The perceptions of this reality has recently gained increased salience, particularly through the recent focus upon "identity." Stuart Hall articulated this sense of the local with a strident proclamation of its newness:

> The emergence of new subjects, new genders, new ethnicities, new regions, new communities, hitherto excluded from the major forms of cultural representation, unable to locate themselves except as decentered or sub-altern, have acquired through struggles, sometimes in very marginalized ways, the means to speak for themselves for the first time...Just as I tried to talk about homogenization and absorption, and then plurality and diversity as characteristic of the new forms of the dominant cultural post-modern, so in the same way one can see forms of local opposition and resistance going through exactly the same moment.
>
> (Hall, 1991: 34)

This is a quite different sense of local, which in Hall's words is unable to "locate" itself except in terms of power relations between it and dominant groups.

Particularly with regard to Hall's main theme, that of ethnic identity and diasporic self-consciousness, this conception of the local implies no particular sense of place. On the contrary, as the origins of the term diaspora remind us, it proposes an identity held and maintained independent of any, probably temporary, physical location. The attributes that Featherstone identified in the localized community are ones which are supposed to exist amongst these dispersed communities independent of their physical separation, and a similar structure of feeling can be discovered independent of geographical location. The social and cultural links between the members of these "dispersed localities" are, it is said, stronger than those between them and their immediate physical neighbors.

Similar, if much less remarked upon, movements of people have been active in the formation of the populations of Britain and France, among other countries, at least since the birth of capitalism. London has long had a population descended from French Hugenots fleeing religious persecution, press-ganged African sailors and escaped slaves, Irish peasants forced out by famine, Jewish workers driven from Eastern Europe by Tsarist pogroms, and very many other groups, all contributing alongside the proletarianized descendants of the peasants who had come to Britain from Germany, Denmark, Norway, Sweden and France in earlier waves of immigration. Nevertheless, despite the historical record, this version of the local represents itself as a new consciousness arising from new conditions.

When we consider these two sets of distinctions together, we can construct a matrix, as in Figure 5.1, which specifies different possible versions of the general term "the local." If it is true that the nation state is being attacked from both above and below, then it is reasonable to hypothesize that the media that are the most prominent markers of this from the point of view of the local are those which represent the two "new" dimensions of the local. The "older" forms, although perhaps very important, are far from being the distinctive products of a new phase of globalization. On the contrary, they are strong markers of the impossibility of the task that the modern state set itself of eradicating internal differences and producing a homogenous people inhabiting an homogenous administrative space.

Bringing together both the local and the global, it seems reasonable to say that, to the extent that there is a tendency towards globalization which is manifested in and through localization, the old media based on the state system are being eroded, while the global and local media are in the ascendant. The old, imperfect, state-based public spheres are being eroded and new, albeit possibly even more imperfect,

Old and local	New and local
Old and regional	New and regional

Figure 5.1 Types of locality

global and local public spheres are emerging, particularly around the new forms of the local. The propositions can be reformulated in terms of more or less testable hypotheses:

- the state-based public spheres are eroding as a consequence of globalization
- a global public sphere is emerging and growing relative to the state-based forms
- local public spheres are growing in strength relative to the state-based forms
- this growth is more marked for the new forms of locality than for the old
- the growth of the new local public sphere is articulated with, if not an embodiment of, the tendency towards a global public sphere.

We can therefore move on from the rather arid plateau of theoretical analysis to the lusher pastures of empirical investigation.

A global public sphere?

Most writers in this vein point to the emergence of satellite broadcasting, and global media corporations, as evidence for the fact that we are living in age in which the necessary media infrastructure for a global public sphere does already exist. If there is indeed a global public sphere coming into being, then we should be able to find concrete television and radio channels, or newspapers and magazines, that embody that sphere. Since I have already written extensively on this, it would be wrong to burden you with the details that are available elsewhere. I therefore present in this section a summary, in which all the evidence cited is to be found, except where specifically noted, in what I discovered when I first went out to look for the global public sphere (Sparks, 1998).

In brief, my conclusion was that there is at present no global public sphere, nor is there any sign of one emerging in the immediate future. In the first place, the belief that the communication satellite is in itself is a global, or even supra-national, medium is mistaken on two grounds. The first concerns the regulation and control of satellites. These occupy slots assigned by inter-governmental agreements, and are subject to the regulatory efforts of particular states. The reception of satellite signals, particularly when it is mediated through a Satellite Mater Antenna Television (SMATV) system, is again subject to state-based regulation. It is possible for states to force signals they don't like off particular satellites. The most notorious example is the People's Republic of China (PRC) deal with Murdoch over the objectionably critical BBC news service he carried on the northern beam of Star TV, but there others like the British government's struggle against pornographic broadcasters, in which state-based regulation (the provisions of the 1990 Broadcasting Act) proved adequate to prevent the offending material being broadcast.

The second reason why it is a mistake to think of satellites as necessarily global communication media has to do with content. There is a tendency to think that the free-to-air model, either state- or advertising-supported, will be the dominant one for future satellite broadcasting, as it has been in the past. There are very strong grounds for thinking that this is not likely to be the case in the future. Various kinds of subscription and pay-per-view systems are already in operation, and these have no necessary connection with the global. In order to view such a service, it is necessary to have a decoder, and the running of that very terrestrial piece of equipment is controlled by a subscription management system. In order to attract audiences, and thus to maximize their revenue, broadcasters are obliged to seek premium content, particular for these services. But rights holders are also keen to maximize their revenue, and therefore characteristically attempt to subdivide the rights to broadcast their material. One of the traditional ways in which markets are divided up is along "national" lines, and the design of a subscriber management system makes that model replicable in the case of the satellite. It is therefore in the interests of both the broadcasters and the rights holders to continue with the national organization of audiences in the future, subscription-oriented television economy. From this perspective, the cross-border potential of satellite broadcasting is the temporary and accidental product of the undeveloped state of the technology prevailing in the 1980s.

If we shift our attention from technology to social form, and ask what channels there are that might constitute the basis for a global public sphere, we arrive at the conclusion that there is very little evidence for its existence. The obvious candidate for the role of embodiment of the global public sphere is CNN, and this is regularly cited as having transformed viewing habits. There are strong arguments that would say that this is essentially a US, rather than a global, news channel, but let us leave those aside. If we ask how large the audience for this global channel is, both absolutely and relative to the existing state-based broadcasters, we come to the conclusion that it is so small as to be irrelevant from the point of view of constituting a genuine public sphere. Even in the USA, even in 1991, the year of the Gulf War and CNN's finest hour, the channel got an audience rating of 3.7 percent; in more normal years it hovers around 1 percent (Greenberg and Levy, 1997: 139). Outside the USA, the audiences are even smaller. In the UK, in the first quarter of 1998, the ITC reported a viewing share of 0.1 percent for CNN. Everywhere, the terrestrial broadcasters have experienced an erosion of their audiences at the hands of cable and satellite, but it has not been to any significant extent caused by the rise of a global news service taking the viewers for their national products as part of the growth of a global public sphere.

A similar tale can be told about the global newspapers, like the *Wall Street Journal* and the *Financial Times*. These exist, and they circulate globally, albeit in differently inflected editions, but the fact is that their readerships are tiny compared with the national press of the countries in which they operate, and in those cases like the USA and the UK where the audience has a choice, it prefers the more localized product. What is more, an examination of the audience for these newspapers reveals another striking factor about globalization. The people who read these papers are rich, even by the standards of rich nations: in the case of *The Wall Street Journal Europe*, they have an average annual income of US$196,000 per annum.

One further important point concerning these media is that they are over-whelmingly in English. While this is the most widely diffused of languages, it is, of course, very far from the mother tongue of the vast majority of the world's population. The ability to use this language to a very high level, or maybe Spanish as an alternative, is thus an extremely restrictive condition on access to whatever kinds of discussions take place in the global media.

These three factors lead me to the conclusion that there is no such thing as a global public sphere at the moment. There are certainly media that are concerned to address issues on a global scale, but their audiences are too small, too rich, and too English-speaking to be considered inclusive. Nor can I detect anything in the dynamics of these media that is likely to make them more accessible in the near future: to the extent that they are profitable operations, they are profitable precisely because they do address an elite, and have little incentive to extend their reach significantly. At the same time, there is little in either the new television or in international newspapers that suggests any serious erosion of the state-based public sphere. This sphere may well be eroding, but I can see no evidence that this is because substantial numbers of citizens are defecting to global forms that correspond more readily to their experience of interaction with social power. It may indeed be the case that more and more significant events in the lives of ordinary people are determined by events over which the state has little or no control, as the current crisis in Indonesia suggests, and which are at least initiated by global factors, but there is no sign that this is what is leading to a crisis for the state-based media. On the contrary, I agree with critics of the general "globalization of the media" thesis that the state remains a significant actor in this realm (Schiller, 1991; Ferguson, 1992). Indeed, I would go rather further: a study of the British case reveals that in important respects the state has, over the last two decades, been increasingly ready to intervene in the working of the mass media (Sparks, 1995). My conclusion is therefore that talk of the erosion of the state-based public sphere from above by forces of globalization is at least premature and, at the present, quite mistaken.

A local public sphere?

The case with the local public sphere is quite different. It is very easy indeed to find examples of the mass media that are either entirely local in their orientation, or at least have a strong local dimension. What is more, these tend to have a substantial concern with issues of public discussion, and to be relatively open to the views and voices of their audiences. These media have many shortcomings and limitations, and vary widely between themselves as to how seriously and extensively they address public issues, but, to a surprisingly large degree, they do sustain a (limited and imperfect) public sphere. But while there may not be much doubt about the existence of a local public sphere, the issue of how this is related to the more general question of the global and the local is much more complex.

To begin with the question of the articulation between global and local, and the extent to which they are interdependent, we can note that one striking feature

t these local media, and the local public spheres that they sustain, is that they
to be relatively independent of the global media operators, as described by
nan and McChesney (1997), for example. Murdoch, to take the paradigmatic
example of a global media operator, and one who is most certainly concerned to
intervene in public debate, does not appear much interested in local operations,
outside of his original patrimony in Australia. In the UK, his newspaper operations
are entirely national in scope, as is his satellite service. In the USA, while it is true
that Murdoch has owned "local" papers (e.g. *The New York Post*), he has never tried
to build a chain of US newspapers in the manner of Gannett or Knight-Ridder.
In television, it is a distinctive feature of what has happened to Fox since Murdoch
acquired it is that it has tried to become the fourth national TV network: Murdoch
has not concentrated simply on acquiring lucrative stations in particular localities.
He nowhere appears to have a strategy of finding local partners and working with
them. His alliances are with companies that operate at the state level. There is
little evidence, in most of his main theatres of operation, that Murdoch wants to
undermine the state from above and below. (Indeed, there is precious little evidence
that, despite his public speeches, he wants to undermine even very despotic states
from above. Provided he can do business with them, butchers are quite OK.) The
famous slogan, attributed to News Corporation as well as to many other companies,
of "Think Global. Act Local" seems to mean, in practice, "Think Global. Act
National." If the local is articulated with the global, it is in more complex and
subtle ways than through direct relationships between the two kinds of media.

Providing evidence relating to the hypotheses that the local public sphere is
growing relative to the state-based sphere, and that it is growing faster with regard
to the new forms of locality, requires a more extensive discussion. We can begin by
considering the printed newspaper press. In many countries the press began locally,
and continues up until today to be predominantly local. The USA is the most
obvious case, in which there are more than 1,500 daily newspapers, only two of
which, *The Wall Street Journal* and *USA Today*, are properly "national" newspapers
in the sense understood elsewhere. In this respect, the UK experience of a daily
press dominated by London-based, large-circulation, national newspapers is an
unusual and extreme example of the opposite situation. In most countries in Europe,
there is a substantial local newspaper press existing alongside a small number of
titles that have a wider remit.

The long existence of the local press suggests that it has little to do with any
relatively recent shift in the direction of a global/local nexus that is dislocating the
state system. The newspaper press in the UK, as much as the USA, was primarily
local in its nineteenth century origins (Lee, 1976). These origins, and the continued
existence, of the local press are the product, first, of technical limitations that, up
until recently made it difficult, expensive, or downright impossible to print the
same product at widely different locations, or physically to transport the product
of centralized printing to widely dispersed individuals in time to effect a sale. While
it is true that the technical advances that have permitted remote printing have
been essential to the advent of a genuinely global press, they have also, in the case

of the USA, been the main technical factor leading to the emergence of a national press and this is, economically at least, far more successful than the global pretenders: the continuing success and profitability of *The Wall Street Journal* proper as a US national paper is the condition for the attempt to construct a global paper. The second condition for the continuation of a local press has been the local nature of important aspects of the advertising market – for example, classifieds – which have meant that it has been possible to make money from small-circulation newspapers, especially when they enjoy a local monopoly. Neither of these conditions are recent, or original to some new phase of history in which the impact of the global/local nexus is undermining the state.

The press example also provides evidence with regard to two other issues. In the first place, the local press is predominantly the press of the old locality. That is to say, most of the titles are geographically defined in their circulation and economics, and to the extent that they constitute a public sphere they tend to be concerned with place-bound issues like City Hall, local crime, and so on. It is true that there are some titles which are representative of the new locality. In the UK, for example, *The Voice* is a weekly newspaper that articulates the concerns and issues of an audience predominantly Afro-Caribbean in ethnic origin. It is uncertain whether this represents a new phenomenon. In the case of the USA, there was in the early years this century a flourishing non-English press that articulated the concerns and issues of linguistically-defined ethnic groups. It counted more than two thousand titles when Robert E. Park undertook his pioneering study in the early 1920s. A similar process, albeit on a smaller scale, took place with regard to the Irish and, later, Jewish populations of Britain in the nineteenth century. It may well simply be my ignorance that prevents me adducing more British or other European examples from an earlier period.

It is not clear whether this group of newspapers are growing in numbers, circulation, or influence. Two things are clear, however. In the first place, the economic well-being of these publications depends relatively heavily on advertising by the local and national state machine. Secondly, even though these newspapers are very important indeed to their readers, they are very small scale compared to the "old" local press. Against a handful of such titles, there are more than 450 paid-for old weeklies produced in the UK.

That is not to say that the local press is in a state of rude health and posing an increasing challenge to the state-based media. The other points to bear in mind here are that the local press, defined in the old sense, is only local up to a point, and that it is a declining force in society. There has always been a tendency, for powerful economic reasons, for local newspapers to be grouped into ownership chains, and this process has accelerated in recent years, notably in the USA. The development of these chains, and their increasing informatization, implies a "nationalization" of policy, of managerial personnel, of business arrangements, and so on. Editorial material is another matter. The non-local material in the local press has long been predominantly dependent on press agency supply, for example through AP and UPI in the USA and the Press Association in the UK, and this suggests that they have a "global" dimension that stretches back to the last century. It may be that the growth of chain ownership means an increase in syndicated material, as economic logic would dictate, but I have no hard evidence on that. It is also true that the overall circulation of the newspaper press is declining in many advanced countries, notably the USA and the UK, although it is growing in countries like India. The local newspaper press is the greatest victim of this decline, showing much greater, and more protracted, losses than the national press.

We can therefore conclude from a study of the press that, while there is undoubtedly a form of the local public sphere, this is so long-established as not to be considered an aspect of globalization. The main form which this local newpaper press takes is the "old and local" one. There are some very important examples of a "new and local" press, but they are, in overall terms, marginal in number and in circulation. The whole sector, however, is decreasingly local in terms of ownership, and at least some aspects of operation, and it is declining, rather than growing, at a rate faster than is its state-oriented cousin.

The case of broadcasting provides additional insights into these problems. There are certainly numerous examples around the world of radio and television broadcasters whose audience is defined by areas or groupings much less inclusive than those of states, although, by its nature, television in particular, tends to construct the "local" much more broadly than does the press. With this medium, we are mostly concerned with the regional level that we discussed above. Once again, there is very strong evidence, at least from Europe, that news and current affairs are the strongest aspect of the local and regional broadcasters (see Moragas and Garitaonandía, 1995; Jankowski et al., 1992). We can therefore say that there is evidence that there is something of a local and regional public sphere in broadcasting, albeit subject to many limitations. What is more, in most of Europe, although not the USA, these local broadcasters are a relatively new development, produced by political and economic action during the last two decades (Hollander, 1992: 9). We seem to have here evidence for a process which might constitute the local dimension of a global/local nexus.

This plethora of local or regional broadcasters, however, conceals a very considerable paradox. As is very well-known, the economics of broadcasting, both in radio and in television, lead in the direction of networking. According to the logic of economics, there should be a very rapid process of consolidation into one or a few chains of broadcasters with the whole territory and population of the state at their disposal. That this has not been the case has primarily been due to regulation. The Federal Commincations Commission (FCC) in the USA has always had very strict rules as to the number of stations that any one company can own, and these have survived, albeit in weakened form, in the recent deregulatory Federal Communications Act. Elsewhere, there are similar attempts to prevent the erosion of local interests. In other words, the continued existence and health of the local in broadcasting has been predicated on action by the existing state machines. This action has been under constant threat from the forces of commerce, and where the regulatory regime has been relaxed, for example in the UK, there has been a sharp trend towards the consolidation of ownership and operation into fewer, more centralized hands (Porter and Combe, 1998). These same pressures appear to be operating with a similar force in other circumstances, for example Denmark (Jauert and Prehn, 1997).

The second point to note is that the most successful attempts to construct local and regional broadcasting seem to have been those that rely on the most strongly marked of the old regions. The greater the degree of regional difference, particularly in language, the easier it seems to be to construct a viable broadcaster. The trend towards the regionalization of broadcasting was very marked in the 1970s and 1980s, but there seems to have been a general retreat since then. One study of the regional dimension of broadcasting in Europe concluded that:

> It would appear, then, that the autonomous regional television stations (except for those in the German *Länder*, or those in multilingual countries) are really exceptional in Europe. Thus, the establishment of the six Spanish autonomous television networks since 1983 has been a landmark in the regionalization of European television…It is likely that only regional television which is based on actual regional communities (which could either be within the bounds of a nation or a tranfrontier region) with economic interests and particular cultures and traditions, will remain and will be able to compete with the growing number of TV channels in the future.
>
> (Garitaonandía, 1993: 290)

The decentralization of broadcasting into regions in the "new" sense of the administrative regions of the state does not seem to have corresponded to any strongly expressed need on the part of the mass audience. It is in the "old" kinds of regions that the development of a robust broadcasting system seems viable. As it happens, however, many of these old regions are also nations without states, which at least an identifiable body of opinion thinks should acquire states. In other words, it may be that the construction of these broadcasting systems is correlated not with an erosion of the state, but with a move to redefine and re-divide the existing state system into a new one that has greater legitimacy amongst the population.

A number of these new broadcasters, notably S4C in Wales and the Gaelic Broadcasting Trust in Scotland, are not economically viable on their own. They only exist because they are supported by the state. In the case of S4C, more than 95 percent of its income comes in the form of a subsidy direct from London, and in addition it receives free from the BBC more than 500 hours of Welsh-language programming per year. The production of news and current affairs, not to mention programs like the very popular soap-opera *Pobol I Cwm*, are possible because the high cost of sustaining broadcasting in a lesser-used language are borne, quite rightly since they should have equal cultural rights with other citizens, by the state of which speakers of that language are members (Sparks, 1996).

The problem of financing broadcasting is even more acute for local groups. It seems to be a problem that has haunted many of the efforts in Europe over the last decade, and undoubtedly lies behind much of the pressure to produce networks out of stations set up for specifically local purposes. If we examine the broadcasting of "new and local" groups, we can certainly find examples of radio broadcasting – London Greek Radio, for example – which are representations of some of these collectivities. Here the factors that permit a local broadcaster are similar to those that permit local broadcasting based on the old localities: available spectrum and the existence of an advertising market able to sustain a limited amount of production. Television, on the other hand, is much more problematic. The costs of producing genuinely local programming are so high that such broadcasters tend to be dependent upon state-based institutions. In some cases, for example in terms of British news and current affairs television that represents new localisms, this is mediated through the existing state-based broadcaster. In the case of Amsterdam, subsidy from the local state seems to have been crucial (Gooskens, 1992). In other cases, the relationship to the state structure does have more of a global dimension, since it is a broadcaster based in another state that provides programming. Zee TV in Britain is a good example of this. It began as a local channel, then with a different name, which produced some of its own programming. Eventually, the economic logic of its position has forced it into the situation of being exclusively a re-broadcaster of material originated by its parent Zee TV in India. In this sense, it is an example of globalization, but one which hardly fits most theorizations, since whatever public sphere is being facilitated is dominated by the discourse of a political situation in another state. This, surely, is reminiscent of an older form of "immigrant" culture, with an orientation on "home," rather than evidence of a genuinely hybrid and diasporic culture appropriate to an epoch of globalization.

Overall, then, the analysis of the local public sphere certainly suggests that there are examples (albeit imperfect and limited ones) of this category in the contemporary world. They do not appear to be obviously linked with global media companies. With regard to the newspaper press, the majority of these local forms have existed for a long time and relate primarily to the old forms of locality, based on physical proximity. There are some newspapers which represent new forms of locality, but these are very much the minority. The local public sphere, as articulated in the printed press, is eroding rather than growing, and aspects of its localism are declining in favor of state-wide organization. In the case of broadcasting, there are indeed local public spheres in radio, and to some extent in television. The strongest of these are in the old forms of regional organization. Those in the new regions seem to be stagnating if not declining. Even some of these successful old regional forms of television are dependent upon subsidy from the state. The forms of television appropriate to the new localities do exist, although they are few in number, and they are not generally economically self-sufficient. Subsidy from the state is an important condition for the viability of many of them. It seems reasonable to say that the local public sphere does indeed exist, but that there is little evidence that it is growing, disproportionately linked to new forms of localization, or articulated closely with the process of globalization.

Conclusions

None of the hypotheses regarding the global and the local that we suggested might be tested seem to be supported by the evidence we have reviewed here. On the contrary, the evidence directly contradicts them. We can conclude that formulations such as the following are, simply, wrong (as well as atrociously badly written):

> The nation-state, in effect, having been shaped into an "imagined community" of coherent modern identity through warfare, religion, blood, patriotic symbology, and language, is being undone by this fast imploding heteroglossic interface of the global with the local: what we would here diversely theorize as the *global/local* nexus. The dissolution and disinvention of *e pluribus unum* narratives can be seen happening in the United States from various angles and within multiple genres of discourse.
> (Wilson and Dissanayake, 1996: 3)

There is no sign that a global public sphere is coming in to being. There is little sign that the local public spheres are at all the product of a phase of globalization, and there is little evidence that there is an interface, heteroglossic or otherwise, between the two. Those public spheres that are produced by new localisms may well see as one of their aims the dissolution of grand narratives like the USA or the UK, but they very often turn out to be dependent upon these grand narratives to pay the bills.

If all that was at stake was an issue of theoretical clarity, we could stop there. The fashionable formulations are wrong. But there is more at stake than just having the right ideas. Theory is important, but so too is practical action. The issues which we have been discussing, and which most theorists of globalization tend to mis-recognize or exaggerate, are important practical questions. There is no doubt that the international money markets, and in their wake the International Monetary Fund (IMF), have an enormous importance to people's lives in Indonesia, Korea, Thailand, Russia and Brazil today, and perhaps elsewhere tomorrow. There is no doubt that the populations of many advanced countries are ethnically very diverse. There is no doubt that the democratic system in the USA, and to a lesser extent elsewhere, is experiencing some kind of a malaise, if not a fully-fledged crisis. These issues have implications for our understanding of the public sphere, whether global, state-based or local. Mis-recognizing the issues at stake as some kind of vaguely formulated process of globalization in fact disables us not only from understanding the real dynamics of the situation but also from developing any policies that could make it easier for people to exercise their democratic rights. I want, in closing, to develop three issues that seem to me possible extrapolations that one could draw from the analysis I have sketched here.

First, there are real forces, beyond the direct control of even the most powerful of states (i.e. the USA), that affect, directly or indirectly, the life experiences of all the world's population. It would be an extension of democracy, although not an antidote to the destructive effects of global capitalism, if these forces were placed under the same kinds of surveillance and control as are many states. To take an example, the IMF does not publish the details of its policies. The best that one can obtain are press releases and reports of speeches. What the IMF does matters, both to the people to whom it does things and to those whose money it risks when doing it. There can be no serious discussion of the role of the IMF without access to the information it is acting upon and the agreements that it is reaching. Simply assuming that a global public sphere is coming into being obscures the need for real pressure to bring the doings of the IMF into the public sphere, even to make its policies transparent, let alone to subject it to democratic control. To the extent that these globalising forces gain in strength and impact, so the need for an open and accessible global public sphere will become all the more urgent. Left to themselves, there is no chance that the existing fora for global debate will evolve towards inclusive public spheres. To produce a public sphere on a global basis will require a sustained and conscious effort.

Second, the state is not withering away as a result of a siege from above and below. It is true that the scope for activity of even the most powerful of states is circumscribed by global forces. It is true that neo-liberal policies have meant that many of the social-services functions of the state, and many of the industries it ran, are being privatized. What is left, however, is still the essential "special bodies of armed men with prisons etc. at their disposal," which show no signs of disappearing. At the same time, the state remains the most powerful of social actors, and many states are subject to some democratic controls. The function of the state-oriented public sphere remains crucial. It is today under threat, for example because of the fragmentation of broadcasting consequent on the end of channel scarcity. Defending and extending that public sphere remains a central democratic task.

Third, the "old" local and regional public spheres are in varying states of health, and some need assistance to survive. On the other hand, many of the "new" public spheres are in a very uncertain state, particular with respect to their ability to represent the lived contemporary experience of the diverse groups whose homes are in the great metropolises of the developed world. There are, for example, around 275 languages spoken in London and more than 190 first languages spoken in London schools. In inner London, more than 40 percent of children speak a language other than English at home. More than 30 percent of those who speak another language at home are not fluent in English. In my daughter's class of six year olds, there are half a dozen or so languages spoken at home. Admittedly, London is the most cosmopolitan city in the world, today more so, apparently, even than New York, but I think that the reality of complex and diverse ethnoscapes will be generally recognized, albeit in less extreme forms. It goes without saying, from the point of view that values a public sphere, that all of these children, when they become adults, and their parents as of today, have the same democratic right to enter into the public sphere as I do. The notion that an elite of confidently bilingual "community leaders" could fully represent these diverse populations does not fit easily into a theory of democratic involvement. What is more, the impact of new technologies of communication, the famous 500 channels that we hear so much about, means that it is technically possible to realize that right. But that, of course, is not what is happening. The 500 channels are going to be used to give us NVOD (Near Video On Demand) and sport. There are two obstacles to realising the desirable state of an inclusive local public sphere which could embrace all of these new groups. The first is regulatory: the imposition of the obligation to carry such material as a condition of a franchise. The second is economic: the provision of the same kind of subsidy that enables Welsh speakers to enjoy a developed public sphere for other language-defined groups like speakers of Bengali, Turkish, Cantonese, and so on. Whether either of these objectives could be realized or not is an open question: I am not in the short term optimistic. But the point is that, in order to realize either of them, it would be necessary that the existing state be forced to take action. Very far from replacing the state, the new localities need the state in order to represent themselves.

I hope that I have shown that "getting it right" with regard to the global, the local and the public sphere is more than just a matter of the correct formulations. How we understand these complex developments in the world, and in the public sphere, has a direct bearing on the kinds of policies that are appropriate to extend democratic debate and involvement.

References

Appadurai, A. (1990). "Disjuncture and difference in the global cultural economy." In M. Featherstone (Ed.), *Global Culture: Nationalism, Globalization, Modernity*, 295–310. London: Sage.

Curran, J. (1991). "Rethinking the media as a public sphere." In P. Dahlgren and C. Sparks (Eds), *Communication and Citizenship*, 38–42. London: Routledge.

Moragas Spà, M. de and Garitaonandía, C. (Eds) (1995). *Television in the Regions, Nationalities and Small Countries of Europe*. London: John Libbey.

Drilik, A. (1996). "The global in the local." In R. Wilson and W. Dissanayake (Eds), *Global/Local: Cultural Production and the Transnational Imaginary*, 21–45. London: Duke University Press.

Featherstone, M. (1996). "Localism, globalism, and cultural identity." In R. Wilson and W. Dissanayake (Eds), *Global/Local: Cultural Production and the Transnational Imaginary*, 46–77. London: Duke University Press.

Ferguson, M. (1992). "The mythology about globalization." *European Journal of Communication*, 7(1). 69–93.

Garitaonandía, C. (1993). "Regional television in Europe." *European Journal of Communication*, 8(4), 277–94.

Garnham, N. (1992). "The media and the public sphere." In C. Calhoun (Ed.), *Habermas and the Public Sphere*, 359–76. Cambridge, MA: MIT Press.

Giddens, A. (1991). *The Consequences of Modernity*. Stanford, CA: The Stanford University Press.

Gooskens, I. (1992). "Experimenting with minority television in Amsterdam." In N. Jankowski, O. Prehn and J. Stappers (Eds), *The People's Voice: Local Radio and Television in Europe*, 225–34. London: John Libbey.

Greenberg, B. and Levy, M. (1997). "Television in the changing communication environment: Audience and content trends in US television." *Studies in Broadcasting*, 33. 131–74.

Habermas, J. (1974). "The public sphere: An encyclopaedia article." *New German Critique*, 3(1), 14–21.

Hall, S. (1991). "The local and the global: Globalization and ethnicity." In A. King (Ed.), *Culture, Globalization and World-System*, 19–40. Basingstoke: Macmillan.

Herman, E. and McChesney, R. (1997). *The Global Media: The New Missionaries of the Global Capitalism*. London: Cassell.

Hjarvard, S. (1993). "Pan-European television news: Towards a European political public sphere?" In P. Drummond, R. Patterson and J. Willis (Eds), *National Identity and Europe*, 71–94, London: British Film Institute.

Hollander, E. (1992). "The emergence of small scale media." In N. Jankowski, O. Prehn and J. Stappers (Eds), *The People's Voice: Local Radio and Television in Europe*, 7–15. London: John Libbey.

Jankowski, N., Prehn, O. and Stappers, J. (Eds) (1992). *The People's Voice: Local Radio and Television in Europe*. London: John Libbey.

Jauert, P. and Prehn, O. (1997). "Local Television and Local News." *Communications*, 22, 31–56.

Lee, A. (1974). *The Origins of the Popular Press: 1855–1914*. London: Croom Helm.

Le Mahieu, D. (1988). *A Culture for Democracy*. Oxford: Clarendon Press.

Lunby, K. (1992). "Community television as a tool for local culture." In N. Jankowski, O. Prehn and J. Stappers (Eds), *The People's Voice: Local Radio and Television in Europe*, 27–41. London: John Libbey.

Negus, K. (1996). "Globalization and the music of the public spheres." In S. Braman and A. Sreberny-Mohammadi (Eds), *Globalization, Communication and Transnational Civil Society*, 179–96. Cresskill, NJ: Hampton Press.

Porter, V. and Combe, C. (1998). "The restructuring of UK independent television, 1993–1997." Paper presented to the conference "Media Beyond 2000," April 16–17. London.

Ritzer, G. (1993). *The McDonaldization of Society*. London: Pine Forge Press.

Robins, K. (1991). "Tradition and translation: National culture in its global context." In J. Corner and S. Harvey (Eds), *Enterprise and Heritage*, 1–44. London: Routledge.

Scannell, P. (1989). "Public service broadcasting and modern public life." *Media, Culture and Society*, 11(2), 135–66.

Schiller, H. (1991). "Not yet the post-imperialist era." *Critical Studies in Mass Communication*, 8(1), 13–28.

Schudson, M. (1992). "Was there ever a public sphere?" In C. Calhoun (Ed.), *Habermas and the Public Sphere*, 146. Cambridge, MA: The MIT Press.

Sparks, C. (1998). "Is there a global public sphere?" In D. Tussu (Ed.), *Electronic Empires*, 108–24. London: Arnold.

Sparks, C. (1996). "Television, culture and minority groups." In M. Ledo Andión (Ed.), *Comunicación na Periferia Atlántica*, 185–93. Santiago de Compostella: Universidade de Santiago de Compostella.

Sparks, C. (1995). "The survival of the state in British broadcasting." *Journal of Communication*, 45(4), 140–59.

Williams, R. (1983). *Towards 2000*. London: Penguin.

Wilson, R. and Dissanayake, W. (1996). "Introduction: tracking the global/local." In R. Wilson and W. Dissanayake (Eds), *Global/Local: Cultural Production and the Transnational Imaginary*, 1–18. London: Duke University Press.

6

THE AMBIGUITY OF THE "EMERGING" PUBLIC SPHERE AND THE THAI MEDIA INDUSTRY

Ubonrat Siriyuvasak

In this chapter I want to demonstrate the struggle between the capitalist and the bourgeois classes on the one hand and the working and the new middle classes on the other hand over the question of access and control of the mass media in Thailand. The rise of the new middle classes during the past decade is largely due to the high rate of economic growth. But as Preecha Piempongsanti (1993) and Nithi Aewsriwong (1993) argued, the Thai middle classes linked themselves economically and culturally with the capitalist class, nationally and internationally. Their income, their professional security and the way they manage information are all interconnected with the economy of the advanced industrialized countries in the West and in Asia, Japan in particular. In a sense, they are closely allied with the capitalist class of the global economy.

From this point of departure the chapter discusses how the new middle classes exercise their economic freedom *vis-à-vis* freedom of expression. The wealth generated by the economic growth in the late 1980s to the early 1990s has provided for the rapid commercialization and, to a lesser extent, the industrialization of the Thai media industry. The media sector, similar to other services and industrial economic sectors, depended directly and indirectly on Western media technologies, production paradigms and content. Hence, we see a booming consumerist society, not a democratic society.

The open space in the Thai social system since 1992, at first, appeared to be an open arena which would contribute to the empowerment of the masses and the expansion of a civil society (Ubonrat Siriyuvasak, 1994, 1996). But with the influence of the advertising industry over the media industry we are witnessing more corporate expressions than citizen expressions. It is not a public space or public sphere which opens the expressions of the rich and the poor alike, the Thais and the indigenous peoples, the urban and the rural people, nor does it include the voices of children and the disadvanged in the society. The question is, are the new

Thai middle classes building a new social space in the media of their own? Is the media industry also enjoying the economic freedom and leaving the question of democratic expression aside?

Economic growth and socio-political transition in the 1980s and 1990s

In the 1980s the economic growth rate and the wealth generated by such rapid growth seems to indicate that Thailand and her Association of South-East Asian Nations (ASEAN) neighbors have crossed over the threshold of the newly industrialized economy (Table 6.1). But the economic crises in these countries in the 1990s and the collapse in 1997 reveal the weaknesses of a society without either solid economic foundations or the social and political basis for an industrialized capitalist economy.

While the intense economic growth rate of Thailand between 1987 and 1991 grew at 9.5, 13.2, 12.2 and 10.0 percent it did not reflect a positive trend on the income distribution in Thai society. Neither does it signify any real change in the social and political power of the rural and disadvantaged people. On the contrary, they affected the structure of production and employment in the various economic sectors (Voravit Charoenlert, 1991).

Two significant economic indicators demonstrate how unequal development was taking place in Thailand during this period of economic growth. First, the income distribution between 1976 and 1986 showed that the top 20 percent received the largest and growing share of the total income which was 49.26 percent in 1976, 51.47 percent in 1981 and 55.63 percent in 1986. On the contrary, the bottom 20 percent of the population received less than 4.55 percent of the income distribution in 1986. The share dropped from 6.78 percent in 1976 – a 2.23 percent drop (Table 6.2). However, the middle classes (2nd, 3rd and 4th 20 percent) received a larger share between 1976 and 1981, from 41.74 percent to 44.12 percent, but

Table 6.1 Economic growth rate of the New Industrializing Countries (NICs) in Asia, 1990

Country	Population	Per capita		Economic growth rate (%GDP)	
	1990	in baht[a]	in US$	1965–80	1980–90
Hong Kong	5.8m	287,250	11,490	8.6	7.1
Singapore	3.0m	279,000	11,160	10.0	6.4
Taiwan	20.0m	147,596	5,904	8.9	7.3
Korea	42.8m	135,000	5,400	9.9	9.7
Malaysia	17.9m	58,000	2,320	7.4	5.2
Thailand	55.8m	35,500	1,420	7.3	7.6
Philippines	61.5m	18,250	730	5.7	0.9
Indonesia	178.2m	14,250	570	7.0	5.5

a   In 1990 the exchange rate of US$1 was equal to 25 baht

Source: Pasuk Pongpaichit (1993: 110)

Table 6.2 Thai income distribution, 1976–86

	1976	1981	1986
Top 20%	49.26	51.47	55.63
Second 20%	20.96	20.64	19.86
Third 20%	14.00	13.38	12.09
Fourth 20%	9.00	10.10	7.87
Bottom 20%	6.78	5.41	4.55
Total income	100.00	100.00	100.00

Source: TDRI in Voravit Charoenlert (1991: 36)

Table 6.3 Taiwan income distribution, 1964–86

	1964	1970	1975	1980	1986
Top 20%	41.1	38.7	37.9	36.8	38.2
Second 20%	22.0	22.5	22.3	22.8	22.6
Third 20%	16.6	17.1	17.3	17.7	17.4
Fourth 20%	12.6	13.3	13.6	13.9	13.8
Bottom 20%	7.7	8.4	8.9	8.8	8.3
Total income	100.0	100.0	100.0	100.0	100.0

Source: TDRI in Voravit Charoenlert (1991: 37)

fluctuated to 39.82 percent in 1986. They resumed a larger share of the income distribution in the 1990s since their work reside with the service sector and in the non-manual and managerial class of the industrial sector (Voravit Charoenlert, 1993: 134–5).

When compared with Taiwan the top 20 percent received 38.2 percent and the bottom received 8.3 percent of the income distribution in 1986. During the 1980s the gap between the rich and the poor has decreased compared with the 1960s (Table 6.3). If compared with Korea, the top 20 percent received 42.3 percent of the income distribution and the bottom 20 percent received 18.9 percent in 1984 (Table 6.4). Between Thailand, Taiwan and Korea the bottom 20 percent of the Thai population received the least share of wealth and is getting poorer as the economy grows larger.

The second indicator of unequal development is the contrast between the growth rate of the agriculture sector and the industrial and service sectors. The industrial and service sectors grew steadily in the 1960s to 1980s while the agriculture sector was on the decline (Table 6.5). Statistics showed that in 1960 the large majority of the people, or 84 percent, were employed in the agriculture sector while 4 percent were employed in the industrial sector and 12 percent in the service sector. In 1990 there was a sharp decrease in the agriculture sector. The employment ratio dropped from 84 percent to 67 percent – a 17 percent decrease. Employment grew by 8 percent in the industrial sector and by 9 percent in the service sector between 1960 and 1990. The GDP of the agriculture sector also dropped from 40 percent to 12 percent – a 28 percent decrease – while the industrial sector grew by

Table 6.4 Korean income distribution, 1965–84

	1965	*1970*	*1975*	*1980*	*1984*
Top 20%	41.8	42.6	45.3	45.4	42.3
Bottom 20%	19.3	19.6	16.8	16.1	18.9
Total income	100.0	100.0	100.0	100.0	100.0

Source: TDRI in Voravit Charoenlert (1991: 37)

Table 6.5 The growth rate, ratio of GDP and employment distribution by economic sectors, 1960 and 1990

	Growth rate			*% GDP*		*Employment distribution*	
	1960s (average)	*1989*	*1990–95*	*1960*	*1990*	*1960*	*1990*
Agriculture sector	5.5	4.1	3.5	40	12	84	67
Industrial sector	10.8	17.0	11.3	19	39	4	12
Service sector			7.5	41	48	12	21

Source: Voravit Charoenlert (1991: 38 for figures on growth rate); Pasuk Pongpaichit (1993: 111–12 for figures on GDP and employment distribution)

20 percent and the service sector grew by 7 percent during the same period. Taken together, the industrial sector and the service sector generated 87 percent of the GDP employing 33 percent of the total labor force. In 1990 the agriculture sector generated a mere 12 percent of the GDP, employing 67 percent of the total labor force. Hence, the gradual collapse of the rural or agricultural sector saw the rise of the industrial and the service sectors and the middle classes within these two sectors.

As Sungsidh Piriyarangsan and Pasuk Pongpaichit (1993) pointed out, the large labour force in the service sector provided for the making of the new middle classes whose works were being linked to external capitalist systems, the global economy and high technology. The "educated" segment of the new middle classes – the professionals, managers, technologists, skilled technicians, white-collar/office workers and non-manual workers, etc. – have grown at an exponential rate. Sungsidh and Pasuk believe that the new middle class wants not only economic liberalism but also political liberalism. And they see this growth as part of the democratization process. Their question is whether the new middle classes in the Thai society will contribute to building a new democratic system when they have gained their economic security.

There was a positive trend when the middle classes joined with the workers and other lower classes as the prime movers of the 1992 demonstration against the non-elected Prime Minister, Suchinda Kraprayoon. As an army general Suchinda was seen as the sign of political authoritarianism amidst the growing economic liberalism set out by the previous government. The demonstrators were seeking an openness in the political system and in the flow of information in order to continue the process of economic growth. Right after the May 1992 event, questions were asked if these newly politicized middle classes would advocate democracy and not only liberalism for their own classes (Sungsidh Piriyarangsan and Pasuk Pongpaichit, 1993; Anek Laothamathas, 1993).

I want to extract from the analyses of Preecha Piampongsanti and Nithi Aewsriwong of the Thai middle classes and their role in the democratization process before looking critically at the media. Preecha's work is a theoretical exposition of the role of the middle classes in Western industrialized economies. And the latter is a historical analysis of the role of the Thai middle classes. These would provide the necessary groundwork for my own argument on the relationship between the middle classes and the media.

Preecha Piampongsanti (1993) defined the new middle classes as social collectives made up of civil servants, corporate employees, intellectuals, office workers, business people, managers, executives and other white-collar workers and some small producers. The new middle classes are separated from the capitalist class but they are not the real producers or labor force. On the political dimension the new middle classes are in control of the working class who work on the production line. On the idealogical dimension the new middle classes monopolize the knowledge on production and the economy. The new middle classes are non-manual workers of all professions. They work with information and manage and control the production system. From their social formation their class consciousness is starkly different from the working-class consciousness. In short, the new middle classes are part of the capitalist class and they work to assist in the legitimization of the capitalist system in the political and ideological realm.

Preecha investigated the Marxian concept of class analysis and the Weberian social stratification categories within the German theoretical articulation of the new middle classes prior to the rise of Nazism. The traditional and mainstream Marxian analysis of Karl Kautsky argued that there was no middle class as such. There were only the capitalist class and the working class, while Eduard Bernstein held a reformist view of the middle classes. He expounded that in a modern capitalist society the classes between the capitalist class and the working class would expand rapidly and they do not belong to the working class. The new middle classes have their own economic, socio-political and cultural identities. They have their particular way of life and their own ideologies. They are the intermediary between the capitalist and the working class. But since they have formed their own identities and ideologies they would most probably not ally themselves with the working class politically.

Nithi Aewsriwong (1993) saw the importance of the historical role of the middle class in Thailand at this particular juncture. He searched Thai history to demonstrate the culture of the middle classes, of the young intellectuals, civil servants and journalists. His point is that the Thai middle classes have always looked up to the monarchy who initiated the socio-cultural role model for the Thai society. But ultimately, the role model was drawn from the West. This was due to the fact that the Thai monarchy often appropriated from Western culture since the early Rattanakosin period. What is interesting is that the Thai middle classes shared the ruling ideology which is firmly grounded on the concept of merit, patronage and power. Both the middle classes and the ruling class believed in benevolent dictatorship as an ideal state.

Taken together, Nithi Aewsriwong asserted that the Thai middle classes basically do not believe in democracy nor egalitarianism. In recent times, the new middle classes have linked themselves directly to the West via modern communications and information link-ups, education abroad and travel, etc. They are culturally more dependent on the capitalist and the middle classes' influences from the West. Individualism and consumerism are the key cultural values drawn from the West. Nithi argued that the middle classes are more concerned with their class interests. They are not committed to freedom, equality nor democracy.

Both Preecha Piampongsanti and Nithi Aewsriwong saw the central role of the new middle classes in the Thai society in moving the capitalist economy forward. But both were rather pessimistic on the "democratic role" of the new middle classes. For Nithi, if the present rising middle classes follow the path of history they would not side with democracy nor the majority of the peasantry in the rural areas and the working classes. This is because they are alienated from the peasants and their culture. The peasants are the real "other" for the Thai middle classes. For Preecha, he believed that the capitalist ideologies would permeate deeply into the consciousness of the new middle classes to the detriment of democracy. They would embrace individualism, which means competitiveness in business dealings. They would compete to seek power in their organizations and would focus on accumulation, be it of materials, income, profits, knowledge or resources. And finally, the new middle classes would seek economic freedom in the name of democracy. Embedded within these ideologies, it would not be far fetched to foresee the new middle classes allying themselves with the capitalist class, and becoming the new priests or ideological producers for the capitalist economy.

From the above analyses I would like to follow the line of argument on the role of the media and the middle classes in the present democratization process in Thai society. It is quite clear that the recent economic boom has brought about structural changes in the social formation of new classes. On the other hand, the media industry also mushroomed during the boom period. We have seen new media spaces in the entire range of the media industry – books, magazines, news-papers, television – both cable, satellite and over-the-air broadcasting, radio and music, films and videos, etc. Our question is to inquire if the mushrooming of the mass media signifies freedom of expressions and cultural formation for the new classes. And also to inquire further into the relationship between these expressions, the capitalist ideologies and democracy. The inquiries would be carried out by way of investigating the penetration of the global media and consumerism in Thai society on the one hand and the globalized form and content of the local (Thai) media *vis-à-vis* the present democratization process.

The extension of the global media market and the growth of consumerism

This section attempts to examine the relationship between the advertising industry and the media industry and their connection with the global media market and consumerism. In demonstrating the expansion of advertising on consumer products through the penetration of international advertising agencies we would be able to see how the global economy reaches out for new markets in this part of the world. We would, at the same time, be able to understand how these agencies sell their products along with consumerism. In addition, we would be able to show some examples on the close relationship between the advertising producers and the way they advertise the ideologies of the new middle classes.

Looking at the advertising industry during the economic boom period in the 1990s, advertising expenditure for television tripled. It grew from 6,502.1 million baht in 1990 to 20,771 million baht in 1996. This is also true of radio, newspapers and magazines (*The Advertising Book*, 1997–98). Between the 1980s and 1990s the advertising industry grew at a steady rate of 25 percent per annum. However, statistics show that seven out of the top ten advertising agencies in Thailand are international advertising agencies, two are Thai agencies and one is a joint verture company (Table 6.6). Together they have a 58 percent share of the total advertising revenue in the industry, or 22,124 million baht out of the 38,295 million baht revenue in 1996.

When we follow closely the kinds of products advertised in the media we find a mixture of consumer goods and luxurious/status products as the major categories of advertisers. The media are also included among the top ten advertising categories (Table 6.7).

If we examine the above categories in more detail we can see that the top ten advertisers share 16 percent of the total advertising expenditure in the industry (Table 6.8). Out of these, six are international corporations. They are the world (Western) major consumer product producers, namely, Lever Brothers, Procter & Gamble, Nestlé, Colgate and Palmolive and one Japanese automobile company, Toyota Motors. These global brand names are the market leaders which dominate the local market with their products. But furthermore, they produce the symbolic product of the "modern" images in their presentation of the characters wrapped in the new middle-class setting, lifestyle and languages in the ads. The modern city estate with green surroundings, big living rooms and kitchens, luxurious shopping malls, bars and pubs are the general backdrop of these advertisements. Consuming these modern products is, therefore, the key to a successful life and a happy family for an individual.

In products which deal with the sphere of work and production the advertisements show the images of modern office with hi-tech office and communication equipment. It is the ideology of efficiency, speed and reliability of the information technology at work.

Table 6.6 Top ten advertising agencies in Thailand, 1994–96 (unit: million baht)

Rank	Name	Revenue 1996	1995	1994
1	Lintas	4,553	3,820	3,500
2	Ogilvy & Mather	4,137	3,395	2,772
3	Spa Advertising[a]	2,000	1,540	1,000
4	Prakit & FCB[b]	1,900	2,000	1,500
5	J. Walter Thompson	1,850	1,520	1,512
6	Leo Burnett	1,824	1,600	1,400
7	Far East Advertising[a]	1,700	1,600	1,450
8	Dentsu, Young & Rubicam	1,500	1,300	1,200
9	McCann-Erickson	1,500	1,440	1,400
10	Dentsu (Thailand)	1,250	1,100	1,000
	Total of top 10 agencies	22,214	19,315	16,734
	Total advertising revenue[c]	38,295	34,024	30,608

a   Thai advertising agency.
b   Joint venture between Thai and international agencies.
c   Radio and outdoor advertising not included.

Source: The Advertising Book (1997–98: 53)

Table 6.7 Top ten advertising categories, 1996 (unit: million baht)

Rank	Product categories	Television	Papers	Magazines	Films	Billboards	Total
1	Real estate	332.56	2,362.20	237.64	–	2,529.87	5,462.27
2	Alcoholic drinks	1,830.80	284.15	124.82	4.78	48.74	2,293.29
3	Automobiles	759.52	840.46	135.76	–	56.54	1,792.28
4	Office equipment	407.88	1,017.20	62.45	1.57	94.98	1,584.08
5	The media	459.75	854.86	54.81	0.17	13.34	1,382.93
6	Cosmetics	1,091.42	39.46	227.62	1.30	2.08	1,361.88
7	Hair shampoo	1,181.67	4.95	19.71	0.43	3.25	1,210.01
8	Cooking oil	886.73	198.94	51.62		31.18	1,168.77
9	Social campaigns	816.20	202.05	9.74	–	0.20	1,028.19
10	Computers	117.18	633.84	249.08	0.01	23.15	1,023.26
	Total 10 categories	7,883.71	6,438.11	1,173.25	8.26	2,803.63	18,306.96
	Total 97 categories	22,962.48	11,433.05	3,876.09	24.08	3,695.71	41,991.41

Source: The Advertising Book (1997–98: 143)

A similar kind of concept is used with advertising cosmetics such as shampoo, body and skin-care products as well as detergents and other cleaning agents. Scientists presenting the product in the laboratory under the microscopic lens and with a chemical formula are a guarantee of the high quality of the scientifically proven product. These global advertisers are selling not only the goods but the new ideology of the power of information and knowledge, and professionalism in modern production. It is evident that these images are selective and represent the

Table 6.8 Top ten advertisers, 1996 (unit: million baht)

Rank	Name	Advertising expenditure
1	Lever Brothers (Thailand)	1,764.19
2	Procter & Gamble (Thailand)	754.43
3	Nestlé (Thailand)	612.57
4	Boonrod Brewery	527.51
5	Toyota Motors (Thailand)	478.66
6	Osothsapha (Teck Heng Yoo)	441.90
7	United Winery & Distillery	421.47
8	Colgate-Palmolive (Thailand)	410.95
9	T.C. Pharmaceutical Industrial	404.38
10	Land and House (Property)	350.72
	Total	6,166.78

Source: The Advertising Book (1997–98: 140)

life and work of the new middle classes whose works deal with the production of information and services in the service and industrial sectors of the economy.

Advertising is part of the media structure in a capitalist economy. Its first function is to sell the product by speeding up the flow of goods. Its second function is selling the ideology of capitalism (Garnham, 1979). But in addition, the advertising industry has direct impact and control on the media industry (Murdock and Janus, 1985). This is a more subtle relationship between the media and the global capitalist economy for which advertising is the key mediator. In the Thai milieu the media industry relies heavily on the advertising industry. While television and radio depend entirely on advertising revenue, newspapers and magazines receive 60–80 percent of their income from advertising. The content in these media is, therefore, circumscribed by the marketing strategy of advertisers. Popular programs on television prime time, for example, are confined to two or three genres. These are news, drama and game shows. For magazines, general magazines for women and men are the most popular ones supported by the advertising industry. The target viewers and readers are the new middle classes and lower middle classes. But we shall examine in more detail later on how the media industry under the influence of the advertising industry promotes consumerism and individualism in the mainstream media genre and content.

Let us now look at the Thai media industry and its connection with the ideology of the global economy through the direct sale and consumption of media products. Examples will be drawn from three major media – magazines, films and cable television – which saw a rapid rise of imported products since 1994. Our point of inquiry is that, although it is clear the Thai middle-class audiences are consuming more global media products, what kinds of symbolic construction of the capitalist ideology are they consuming?

Since 1994 several international magazines have launched Thai versions to attract the young and modern working men and women in the city. These are printed on luminova paper imported from Finland in order to keep the standard

Table 6.9 Examples of Thai version of international magazines, 1994–97

Name	Reader	Thai publisher	International publisher
Penthouse[a]	Men	May Media	General Media International (US)
Esquire[b]	Men	May Media	Hearst Magazine International (US)
Cosmopolitan[c]	Women	Pacific Group	Hearst Magazine International (US)
Cleo[c]	Women	Post Publishing	Hachette Filipacchi (French)
Elle[c]	Women	Post Publishing	Hachette Filipacchi (French)
Seventeen[a]	Women	Golf Digest	Golf Digest (US)

a Franchise *Penthouse* and *Seventeen* closed down in 1998.
b *Esquire*'s copyright fees is lifted for the time being.
c Joint venture.

Source: *Nation Sudsabda* (1998: 20–1)

and the look of the magazines. *Elle*, for example, declared that it would lead the fashion trend and lifestyle of Thai women. The publisher was certain that the Thai market was ready for such an international magazine and it would broaden the worldview of the Thai readers (*Puchadkarn Daily*, 1994, October 3). *Penthouse* and *Esquire* were also expected to be the leader magazines amongst the same group of men's magazines published locally. Penthouse folded in March 1998 due to the heavy copyright fees (400,000 baht/month, which was increased to 800,000 baht/month after the economic crisis in July 1997). However, since *Penthouse* has become one of the major popular soft porn magazine, May Media, the Thai publisher, put out *For Men* which is exactly the same as *Penthouse*, instead.

Most of these imported titles carry between 60 and 80 percent of the content from the original magazines, including advertisements. The attractive columns in these magazines are fashion, entertainment news, celebrity interviews, sex stories and columns, and most of all advertisements of international brand-name cosmetics, leather goods, clothing, watches and jewelry; there is also indirect advertising of CDs and films through the entertainment columns. The consumption of these products is to acquire the status symbols which form the identity of the new middle classes.

The second example is the expansion of Hollywood and Hong Kong film exhibition *vis-à-vis* the decline of the local film industry. For nearly two decades the Thai film industry has been able to produce over 100 films a year. It provided for the debut of new film directors and a variety of genres. One of the reasons was due to the high tax rate levied on imported films in 1976.[1] The tax rate was set at 30 baht/meter and the Motion Picture Export Association of America (MPEAA) boycotted the measure for five years before making a return in 1981 (*Puchadkarn Daily*, 1993, August 16). During the 1980s, the MPEAA and the American film studios came back to test the market while Thai politics during this period began to stabilize and the economy resumed its constant growth. The significant change, however, was in the 1990s when the Thai government negotiated with the US government for special export rights on agricultural products under Section 301 over the imported film tax. Hence, the film tax was lowered in 1993 (*Puchadkarn Daily*, 1993, August 26). Hollywood and Hong Kong films began to flow in by the hundreds as opposed to the number of Thai production which went down dramatically from 113 in 1990 to thrity-two in 1996 (Table 6.10).

The rapid decline of the Thai film industry has had at least three major effects. The first is on the diversity of the genre. If we look at the genres of Thai productions there are five major genres – real-life drama, comedy, action, ghost and pornography. Among these, ghost movies and pornography have disappeared. Comedy and real-life drama are the two major genres which survived with a small number of action movies. The second is on the size of film producer. Only the major production studios and big productions could weather the storm. These are Sahamongkol Film, Five Star, Nakorn Luang, Grammy and R.S. Film. The latter two are affiliated to the largest music corporations in the coutnry. Small producers of grade B movies whose films are popular in the countryside are completely wiped out in 1995. Hong Kong films and smaller productions from Hollywood take their place (Sutakorn Santithawat, 1997: 129). The third effect is on the revenue of the industry. During 1991–92 Hollywood films marketed in Thailand were worth around 100–120 million baht. Critics saw 1994 as the watershed year when Spielberg's *Jurassic Park* alone made over 74 million baht in Thailand and the major American studios together made 334 million baht.[2] On the contrary, the Thai film industry in 1997 made a total of 310.8 million baht (Thai Post, 1998, January 17: 8). The trend in 1998 showed an even rougher competition when *Titanic* already reaped 200 million baht from Thai viewers over its three-month exhibition. Its global revenue, in March, was recorded at US$ 10,000 or 40,000 million baht.

Our investigation, so far, shows three important changes in the film industry and the socio-economic context in the 1990s. First, the tax rate on imported film was lowered as an exchange for other export tax privileges. Second, the growth of the economy and the rise of the new middle classes and the elite and the upper classes who are seeking information and entertainment from within and from abroad in order to form their new class and cultural identities. These are the people who have the financial capability and consumption power who make up the significant part of the new media market. This is also true of the consumption of imported magazines exemplified above and the information and news media such as CNN, BBC, NHK, ABC, etc. Third, the large cinema theaters in Bangkok have been

Table 6.10 Number of Thai films and foreign films, 1990–97 (unit: million baht)

	1990	1991	1992	1993	1994	1995	1996	1997
Thai films	113	107	91	64	53	42	32	(17)
Foreign films[a]	n.a.	n.a.	293	242	n.a.	200	n.a.	n.a.

a The majority of foreign films come from Hollywood and Hong Kong and a small number come from Europe.

Source: Sutakorn Santithawat (1997) and *Thai Film 1993* (1993)

replaced by multiplex theaters in the new shopping centers and total replacement is expected by 2000. This means a large increase in the number of cinemas to ensure exhibition capacity in order to accommodate the deluge of foreign films.[3]

The change in the size of the cinema theaters came with the new sound technology of the multiplex cinema, the SRD, SDDS, DTS, THX systems. In 1993 there were 100 standard cinema theaters with seating of 1,500–2,000 in Bangkok. These were renovated into groups of three to five mini-multiplex theaters of 200–300 seats. In 1997 there were 250 cinema theaters in Bangkok. Outside of Bangkok there were 700–800 cinema theaters of standard and medium to small capacity seating. Among these, there were 270 standard and multiplex theaters (*Puchadkarn Daily*, 1993, August 26 and *The Advertising Book* 1997–98: 203). Over half of the cinemas in Bangkok show Hollywood films and the rest show Hong Kong and Thai films while the majority of the cinemas in the countryside show Hong Kong films and Thai films with Hollywood films taking a smaller share of the rural market.

The final example is on satellite and cable television. During the 1990s, satellite and cable/subscription television also came in vogue in Bangkok. In 1997 there were around 230,000 subscribers to IBC, Thai Sky and UTV cable television. These are the middle classes and upper classes who can afford the 400–890 baht/ month subscription fees plus 5,000–9,000 baht installation fees. These new media channels are the direct link-up with the global information and media centers and the global economy. There are news programs, focusing on economic and politics, and current affairs programs from the major international news services, sports, documentaries and most of all, Home Box Office which is one of the most popular channels on cable television (Ubonrat Siriyuvasak, 1996).

At present, the economic crisis in 1997–98 is having serious repercussions on the quality and quantity of the media industry. This means restructuring the industry one way or the other. Cable/subscription television, for instance, must downsize its organization or close down in order to survive. IBC and UTV already announced their merger at the end of 1997 (*Krungthep Thurakit*, 1997, October 14). This is due to the decreasing number of subscribers and the high cost of copyright fees on imported programs. In the process, IBC is inviting AIA Insurance to become its new major shareholder while CP, the holding company of UTV, is negotiating with Microsoft to invest in CP's Asia Multimedia for technology transfer and development in optic fiber and cable transmission (*Thai Post*, 1998, February 27 and March 28).

The examples of the imported magazines, films and cable programs discussed in this section indicate the kinds of information and entertainment consumption of the new middle classes in the 1990s. While they seek freedom of information and entertainment and the content which relates to their new economic contexts and aspirations they move closer to the global media and information center. It is clear that the media industry was prepared to mediate these marketable products for the rising Thai middle and upper classes. What happened shows a quick and growing liberalism in media consumption. This means greater consumption of the media products themselves and, at the same time, consuming the ideology promoted in the program content and columns and in the advertisement of these media products. Questions still remain whether these global media bring along political liberalism, equality and democracy in their content or whether they are essentially the instrument of global consumerism?

The localization of globalized media content and the middle-class worldview

In the areas where direct link-ups are not suitable in terms of languages, market, production technology and economy of scale the media industry devised the "localization" of content as a means of appropriation of the globalized media. We will investigate three important areas of the media which are related to the life and work of the new middle classes. These are: family and child care magazines, computer and information technology (IT) magazines and business handbooks. They form the core of information for modern living and professional development of the rising middle classes. It is interesting to find that the majority of information is appropriated from sources in the US and Europe, to a smaller extent. While all of these media introduce new information and technology to the readers they also portray the desirable worldview of the yuppie generation of material abundance, good education, happy family, and well-paid professions.

We take a look first at the mother and child-care magazines. There are six monthly magazines which are aimed at readers who are young working mothers. These magazines started off as handbooks for pregnant mothers. Most of the editors said that young mothers of today read more and want to get the right information for themselves and their family. They are providing information and knowledge for human resource development.

Mae Lae Dek (Mother & Child), the first magazine of the group, monopolized the market for nearly ten years during a period when the middle classes were still quite small. *Rak Luke* (Loving Children), the second magazine which started in 1983, struggled to survive for the first few years and then took off in 1987 coinciding with the growing number of the new middle classes. The rise of the new middle classes in the late 1980s and 1990s made it possible for the industry to expand this segment with four new publications. In 1995, Plan Publishing extended its new publication, *Duangjai Paw Mae* (Heart of Dad and Mum), to the mass readers in the provinces and rural areas. In 1996, *Life and Family* was launched for the upper middle classes in the city. The market value of this entire segment is estimated at 100 million baht/year.

The signification of the family and child-care magazines is on its break with local knowledge on child rearing and health care for the family, particularly mother and children. The symbol of modern child rearing and health care is the doctor. Child rearing and health care are combined into one whole system that relies mainly on modern medicine, doctors and the hospital. The worldview reinforced by these magazines is that modern families must be looked after professionally.

Table 6.11 Family and child-care magazines, 1996

Name	Year	Publisher	Readership focus
1 *Rak Luke* (Loving Children)	1983	Plan Publishing	Young, pregnant mother/child care and with pre-teen children; new outlook
2 *Duangjai Paw Mae* (Heart of Dad and Mum)	1995	Plan Publishing	Young, pregnant mother/child care and with pre-teen children accessible to mass, rural readers
3 *Life and Family*	1996	Plan Publishing	Family with teenage modern living children home and family
4 *Mae Lae Dek* (Mother & Child)	1977	Nung Jed Karn Pim	Young, pregnant mother/ additional with pre-teen children reading for mothers
5 *Bantuk Khun Mae* (Mother's Diary)	1993	Family Direct	Young, pregnant mother/child care with children <12 years
6 *Luke* (Children)	1992	Lunar International	Young, pregnant mother/child care with pre-teen children

Source: Puchadkarn Daily (1996, August 8: 10)

Knowledge on child care from the previous generations is not reliable and is no longer valued. Doctors and academics become expert columnists and consultants for the readers. But in raising children with modern knowledge there are certain formulae which must be followed and special health-care products to go along with. These are milk, nutritious drinks and food, disposable diapers, skin-care products, toys for children and health products for mothers, etc., most of which are imported goods. In addition, this new worldview is centered on the physical heath of the mother and child and the child's intelligence. The mother is designated as the main carer of the child. There is little emphasis on role sharing between father and mother in child rearing. And there is a lack of social dimension in this "new" concept of family and community and society. The worldview is firmly based on the individual family and its well (best) being.

Stepping out of the family into the modern office and we find computer and IT magazines providing the bulk of information and knowledge for the managers, professionals, technicians, and office staff. In the 1980s, information on IT and computers were popularized in new technology and IT sections in both Thai and English newspapers and IT magazines. According to the survey carried out by Karnjana Karnjanatawe there are three major categories of IT magazines (*Bangkok Post*, 1997, April 16). These are: the hardware-oriented IT magazines, the software-oriented IT magazines and the newly launched Internet magazines. The cover price of the magazines ranged from 40–180 baht. A large number of these magazines are market guides for computer buyers and game users. There is information on new hardware and software products, pricing as well as articles on step-by-step usage of various software and information on technology trends (Table 6.12). These magazines came out in the 1990s except for *Office Technology* which started in 1983. While they are meant to expand the IT market they are also transmitting the "hi-tech" worldview and experiences to students, young office workers, technicians, managers, professionals, etc. The consumption of these products is part of the new middle classes' professional advancement which would lead to both higher income and higher social status.

Another area which localizes the globalized media content is in translated books. The most popularized titles are on business management, office and technical know-how such as computer and information technology, and the global economy. The manager of Chulalongkorn University Book Center pointed out that during the last few years book consumption has increased tremendously in the areas of information technology, computer, business investment and the stock exchange, and the economy in general. This is due largely to the globalized economy, in which new information and communication technology played a key role linking Thai society with the world economic and political centers. It has become a necessity for Thai readers to keep abreast with the latest trends and developments (*Puchadkarn Daily*, 1994, September 8: 10). The editor of Praew, one of the leading publishing houses, gave an analysis on the trend in book publishing that novels and all forms of fiction have a much smaller market share when compared with books on business management and technical handbooks. The 30-years and older book buyers who make up the bulk of consumers are more interested in their professional development and in the trends in world affairs. Books on *Globalization* by Sondhi Limthongkul and *Globalization 2000* by Tienchai Wongchaisuwan are examples of bestseller titles in 1993–94 (*Puchadkarn Daily*, 1995, January 10: 10). Before the economic downturn in 1997, book publishing and book stores have mushroomed in Bangkok and in the provinces. Se-Ed Book which specializes in science and technology, for example, has been expanding rapidly in recent years while Brain Center of Manager Media Group planned to specialize in computer, business management and academic books but folded due to the present economic crisis. These are all aimed at the new middle classes who can afford to buy books on a regular basis and whose lives and work are connected with the global economy and the development in new technology one way or the other.

Our examples in this section and the previous section have attempted to demonstrate the kind of media environment surrounding the new middle classes. On the one hand, the Thai media industry connects itself with the global media industries, such as the advertising industry, the film industry and the publishing industry, in order to import the globalized media content for the Thai consumers. These media are primarily concerned with entertainment. On the other hand, it has appropriated other types of globalized media and reproduced them in a localized form for the consumption of the new middle classes. These are in the areas of child rearing and professional development, which are directly linked to the lives and works of the new middle classes.

Table 6.12 Thai IT magazines, 1997

Name	Price	Content and main focus
Hardware oriented		
Com Plus	40 bht	Hardware and software news and reviews for beginners and how-to articles.
Computer	40 bht	An academic journal of the Computer Association of Thailand. Focus on reports and analysis of computer technology.
Computer Review	70 bht	Hardware and software product review and information on new technology and products with *Home Computer Buyer's Guide.*
Microcomputer Magazine	60 bht	New trends in IT technology and how-to articles on software applications. For advanced readers.
Micro Computer User	50 bht	Special features on product review from particular disk manufacturers and in-depth stories on PC products.
Office Technology (started in 1983)	50 bht	IT news and trends, interviews, section on Apple Macintosh software and price index.
Communication Technology	50 bht	For technical reference on new technology magazines such as *EDI, Tele-medicine.*
PC Magazine (Thailand)	75 bht	Most articles are translated from the English edition of *PC Magazine.* Offers in-depth news and articles on PC technology.
Shopping Computer	65 bht	Popular guidebook on computer prices for users. News and articles on product testing.
Software oriented		
Business Computer	50 bht	Business usage of IT technology; cyber magazine banking, telephone banking, world outlook on technology trend, Mac software review.
Byte Thailand	60 bht	News and analysis on computer products in Thailand written by Thai and foreign authors. Features on Windows NT software and state-of-the-art hardware.
Computer Time	50 bht	Information on new software and how-to guide on software usage on work and enter tainment for beginners.
Computer Today	50 bht	Information on new software and how-to guide on software usage. Buyer's guide.
How.DTP	125 bht	For digital publishing professionals on Macintosh and Windows. Some software review.
IT.Soft	60 bht	News summary on latest IT technology and events in Thailand. Translated articles from *Information Week* and *Fortune Magazine.* Information on Internet and interesting websites.
Multimedia Guide (started in April 1997)	120 bht	For home users with free CD ROM. Information on games, software for kids, new products, websites, Windows.
Computer Gamer	180 bht	For computer game users with free CD ROM. Information on how to play the latest games from the US.
Windows Magazine	50 bht	Articles translated from English edition of *Window Magazine.* How-to articles on using Microsoft Office 97, PageMaker for beginners.
Internet magazines		
Internet/Intranet Magazine (started in 1996)	50 bht	Information on internet 'phone, network computer, Java language, interesting Websites.
Internet Today	40 bht	Internet guide book on Thai web pages, music, movie, travel and new technology.

Source: Karnjana Karnjanatawe, *Bangkok Post* (1997, April 16: 3)

But does the growing import of the globalized media and the quantitative consumption of these products signify the interiorization of the global ideology of capitalism and consumerism? Kasien Thechapira (1997) argued in his "Consuming Thainess" that the process of production and consumption (and reproduction) of mass culture have consequently deconstructed the self-identity of being Thai or Thainess and created the desire to be un-Thai. Hence, the media have unleashed our desire to become global consumers of the symbolic and identity commodities. In the twin process of the sublimation of un-Thainess and the sublimation of Thainess which he explicated from a selection of advertising campaigns and the official campaigns on the Thai Culture Years (1993–97) (government project to promote tourism), our cultural subjectivity, as consumers, has become fragmented and finally alienated from the very Thainess for which the state was desperate in promoting. Once the self-identity or the Thai cultural subjectivity has been purged by turning our consciousness inside out or the exteriorising of Thainess takes effect the interiorising of the global cultural subjectivity could readily penetrate into our consciousness. In "Consuming Thainess" Kasien has expressly analysed the process in which the Thai media turned the Thai consumers into global consumers. If we apply his analysis to the media consumption of the new middle classes we could argue, then, that a similar process is at work in turning the cultural subjectivity of the new middle classes into consumers of global media products and constructing a global cultural subjectivity along the process.

The "emerging" public sphere, civil society and citizenship

In this final section, I want to investigate the emerging media spaces I explored in "Limited competition without re-regulating the media" (1996) in parallel with the expansion of the globalized media space exemplified in the previous sections. In "Limited competition without re-regulating the media" I identified the structural changes of state monopoly in the broadcast media to one in which the large media corporations and the advertising industry are competing fiercely to break this monopoly. The important area is in the production of news and information, and current affairs programs on radio and television. Evidently, the economic boom and liberalization in recent years have put serious pressure on the state to liberalize the broadcast media economically and politically. There are at least five independent news agencies producing radio news as opposed to the state's Public Relations Department and the Mass Communication Organization of Thailand (MCOT). The rights to information and freedom of expression have been extended as a result despite the state effort to control the news content. It appears, then, that a "public sphere" is emerging and the audiences are addressed as citizens not mere consumers of products. But over a short span of time the media spaces created after the political confrontation between the deomocratic forces and the state on instituting a non-elected prime minister in 1992 have been on the decline. The expectation of a growing civil society based on the strength of community- based groups and democratic forces, especially the middle classes and the progressive media, expounded by several social critics and theorists such as Prawes Wasi (1995), Tirayut Bunmi (1997), Chuchai Supawong (1997) and Chai-anand Samutwanit (1997), has become more ambiguous.

Drawing from Anderson's *Imagined Communities* (1995), that the media, photographs and print, especially, played a key role in constructing nationalism and a nationalist consciousness in the former colonized nations of Southeast Asia, I would like to explicate its signification on the making of a new imagined community for the Thai people. In his revised edition of *Imagined Communities* Anderson traced back three institutions of power – census, map and museum – invented by European colonizers since the mid-nineteenth century. He showed how the census's abstract quantification/serialization of persons, the map's logoization of political space and the museum's "ecumenical" profane genealogization interlinked to form the colonial-state imagined dominion (for more detail see Chapter 10: 163–85). But for "un-colonized" Siam, Thongchai Winichakul's study on *Siam mapped* (1988) inquired into how the monarchy appropriated from the Europeans the technology of mapping and thus created her geographical domain during the reign of King Rama V. Although Siam was uncolonized by the Western powers her borders were colonially determined. Hence, the emergence of a new state-mind within a "traditional" structure of political power. The establishment of a special mapping school in 1882 and the compulsory subject of geography, *Phumisat Sayam* (Geography of Siam), at the junior secondary level in 1892 came after print-capitalism swept into Siam during the reign of King Rama IV (King Mongkut). Thongchai saw that the vectoral convergence of print-capitalism with the new conception of spatial reality presented by these maps changed the traditional visual images of *krung* (sacred capital) and *muang* (population centers), into a new invisible term: *prathet* (country of bounded territorial space). In Thongchai's words,

> a map anticipated spatial reality, not *vice versa*...a map was a model for, rather than a model of, what it purported to represent...The discourse of mapping was the paradigm which both administrative and military operations worked within and served.
>
> (Thongchai Winichakul, 1988: 310)

While maps mark out geographical borders, the census marked out racial, ethnic and religious borders among the local population or the ruled. The census, therefore, is the demographic triangulation which filled in politically the formal topography of the map.

Borrowing from Anderson's and Thongchai's metaphor of the "imagined communities" and the mechanical reproduction of powerful institutions of census, map and print-capitalism and language I would like to take a short cut from its colonial genealogy to the modern electronic/digital reproduction of present-day local, national and global media discourse. My assumption is that if the territorial borders of the old map are a model for the spatial reality of Siam for the rulers, the coverage areas marked out by the modern-day eletronic media (and satellite link-ups) offer a concretized and bird's-eye view of that spatial reality. Each station would have its logoized map determined by its coverage area. Some might overlap with the others. This media map is interconnected by the relay stations and local electronic networking enabling home television and radio receiving sets to hook up with the transmitting stations. The inter-linkages of programs from the national, regional and provincial studios enable the audiences/citizens to visualize and audioize the modern nation-state in split seconds. The imagined geographical space is being concretized through the extension of the mass electronic media.

Let us investigate further on how the media industry organizes its imagined communities in the new political, economic and cultural arrangements. If the census signified the political, ethnographical and religious groupings of the population, the market economy classification of media audiences into category A, B, C and D according to their household income, socio-economic status, sex and age represents the typologies of imagined communities within the media territorial space (*The Advertising Book 3*, 1989: 360). These categories exclude or marginalized ethnic groups and their religious affiliations from the main categorization. The Hill Tribes, the Muslims, for example, are usually collapsed into a low-income, rural audience category. The Indians, Sikhs, Khmers and Burmese are unaccountable for unless their income or socio-economic status puts them into one or the other of the income and socio-economic categories. Hence, the media map and audience categories, based primarily on economic classifications, sit uneasily with the reality these models purport to represent. They turn the political citizens of the official census into depoliticized market consumers.

If the broadcast coverage areas of both state and commercial radio and television could be taken as the electronic map or modern political/cultural map we would see the official political *vis-à-vis* the new political economic/capitalist space competing against each other. Within this new map there is a complex combination of media actors with different modes of interpellation constructing the cultural subjectivity of the Thai people. While the state national media broadcast news and information from the government and the centralized bureaucracy, the private national media (television and radio) address the audiences as citizens in their news and current affairs programs, and as consumers in their entertainment programs and in their advertisements. In essence, it was in the 1980s, when Channel 7, the most popular private television station, gained nationwide coverage, and in the 1990s, when private radio stations, linked up via satellite, were able to broadcast nation-wide, that the "imagined community" of the Thai nation-state in its modern form began to materialize. The Hill Tribe people or the indigenous people in the north and northeast and the Muslims in the south are able to watch and listen to the same nationwide programs and simultaneous national and regional news reports from both the state and private stations. Hence, the new electronic map represents the political geographical domain while juxtaposing it with the economic domain of the global market economy.

But if the new electronic map is in the process of making and shaping the "imagined communities" or the "imagined Thai state" it is, at the same time, breaking this very community at the same pace if not speedier. Our previous examples showed that the globalized media such as films, international news, imported magazines, translated/localized media content and most of all, advertising have been penetrating deeply into the national and mainstream media which meant that it is cracking into every grain of the new media map. Audiences at the center as much as those at the periphery are imagining the Thai nation-state and an un-Thai nation-state or a globalized state concurrently. They are being politicized as Thai citizens and depoliticized into global consumers at the same instant.

Two examples are given below to demonstrate the conflicting juxtaposition of the "citizens" during the political election period against the "consumers" of drama and advertising on prime-time television. This puts into sharp focus the notion of a fragmented subjectivity and the ambiguity of the public sphere created by a media industry closely connected to and dependent on the global economy. The election campaign is selected on the basis that it represents mass democratic movement and civic participation. And drama is chosen as the ultimate form of daily mass entertainment of the large majority of the people.

During the election periods in 1992 (March 22, 1992, September 13, 1992) and 1995 (July 2) Poll Watch, a concerned citizen organization, financed by government budget, was set up to monitor the election. One of the main mandates of Poll Watch was to promote citizens' rights and freedom and their responsibility and participation in the election. The campaign section of Poll Watch was responsible for campaigning for popular involvement in the election process or for participatory democracy. Poll Watch mass media programs included posters, banners, leaflets, audio cassettes, videos, television and radio interviews and television drama, civic education at the local level such as schools, factories, villagers and open democratic fora for dialogue between politicians and their constituencies. Callahan's study on *Poll Watch, elections and civil society* (1995) found that the media programs of Poll Watch had been able to organize a broad network of people's organizations, non-governmental organizations, educational institutions (universities and teachers' training colleges in all regions) and 60,000 volunteers to monitor the polls on the election day. During this short period of time, between four and six weeks, the civil society was extended and activated in the center and the periphery, inside the top social and political institutions and between the grassroots organizations, women's groups, district and village authorities and the media. They rallied to campaign for "good and uncorrupted MPs" and they questioned the candidates on local issues and to press for their inclusion in the Party platform. As Cohen and Arato (1992) pointed out:

> The political role of civil society in turn is not directly related to the control or conquest of power but to the generation of influence through the life of democratic associations and unconstrained discussion in the cultural public sphere.
>
> (Cohen and Arato, 1992: ix)

In *The media campaign during the 2 July 1995 election* (Ubonrat Siriyuvasak *et al.*, 1997) the study found that the mass media were extremely active in the election campaigns since 1992. On the one hand, the media coordinated with Poll Watch for information on election monitoring, civic education and the open democratic fora. On the other hand, the media produced new programs and columns to cover a range of issues on the competition tactics and strategies of political candidates and parties, vote-buying, political policies and past performances, etc. prior to polling day. On election day, the Public Relations Department re-organized its programs and devoted the entire day on Radio Thailand national service for news and analysis on the election. There were open telephone lines for regional reports, voters' comments and complaints as well as professional comments on the election. On television, most of the television stations set up their newsrooms to report on the election results. The programs ran from four o'clock to midnight or thereafter until the official results were announced. The active channels were Channel 9, 3, 11 and 7. These special programs were organized in conjunction with the print media, banks (using their nationwide computer network) and some large corporations. Channel 3, for instance, joined with *Matichon*, *Khao Sod* and *Prachachat Thurakit* papers, Pacific Intercommunication (radio news agency and documentary producer), U & I Corporation (one of Channel 3's affiliated companies) and the Bangkok Bank. And Channel 9 joined with the Nation Multimedia Group and Krung Thai Bank for its special election day programs.

During the election campaign and on the election day the electorate were constantly interpellated as citizens or politicized subjects by both the state media and commercial private media. There were some advertisement spots and music programs which supported voting – signifying democratic participation – and campaigning against vote-buying and corrupt politicians. On this kind of occasion, the usual corporate speech and discourse shifted its articulation in order to participate in the politically open space of the public sphere. It was also on this very occasion that the media map merged with the political map of the state. The Poll Watch local democratic fora, the Travelling Poll '95 of Channel 9 and the regional reports and phone-ins on election day, for instance, converged the political and media map with the visualization of a modern nation state. They placed the citizens into this "imagined public sphere" as the spatial reality of the "imagined communities."

Now let us turn to the prime-time drama on television (18.30–19.30 and 20.30–22.15) and their advertisers which are the most popular daily television fare. Among the five national television stations three out of five indicated that drama programs are their marketing strength.[4] The other stations, Channel 9 and 11, place their focus on news and current affairs and edu-tainment programs (*Krungthep Thurakit*, 1997, January 24: 2). Television is the medium which gets the largest share of the advertising expenditure. Between 1992 and 1996 television alone received 57 percent, 56 percent, 54 percent, 54 percent and 59 percent of the total advertising expenditure respectively compared with print – newspapers and magazines, radio and films (*The Advertising Book* 1997–98: 184). The most expensive advertising rate is the prime time drama slot followed by the evening news bulletin, game and talk shows, variety program and Chinese dramas (*The Advertising Book* 1997–98: 204–8).

Kanjana Kaewthep (1993) pointed out that there are two basic features central to Thai television drama. Firstly, they are meant to appeal to the female audiences so they choose to present love and romance and family sagas in which the stories are built around the family and their sexual relationship in the confine of the domestic sphere. In these kinds of drama the majority of the characters are not grounded in any occupational role. We could translate this in two different ways. Either the major characters belong to the elite class (the property class who live on rent and inheritance) or that the stories are so engrossed in the domestic and individual relationship that the world outside the family does not matter whatsoever. Secondly, they are the construction of the media industry which reinforces the representation of the unequal gender relations in the Thai society. Although the patriarchal relation is reflected in the drama the happy ending of the story usually closes off any alternative decoding or criticism on the unequal relationship.

In the mid-1980s to 1990s, the prime-time dramas developed two additional features. One was on the un-Thainess of the major characters and another one was on the "foreign setting" of the drama. This was when the twin process of sublimation of un-Thainess and sublimation of Thainess became intertwined at the same instance, as Kasien (1997) would have it. In 1985 the Miss Thailand pageantry awarded its nomination to Miss Pornthip Nakhirankanok, a Thai girl who grew up in California. She became Miss Universe and set the tradition of the globalized beauty in the Thai cultural spirit. Miss Pornthip is tall, pretty and intelligent. Most of all she speaks good English. Her Thai, on the contrary, is poor. But she proudly represents Thailand in the juxtaposition of Thainess and un-Thainess. This seems to provide Thai society with a sense of psychological security in competing successfully in the global arena.

Since then, a new tradition of an "imported Miss Thailand" for the pageantry was introduced. And it orchestrated this new cultural subjectivity and identity onto a whole range of personae in the entertainment world and the media industry. Actors and actresses, singers and fashion models, television hosts etc. now have a combination of Western appearances. They are tall with a light complexion, having a prominent nose and light-colored eyes and hair which reflect the desirable images of un-Thainess. In addition, the names and the pet names are all Westernized, such as Ann, Pete, Johny, Sam, Bird, Tata, etc. The exteriorization of un-Thainess is, thus, completed. Some of these celebrities are half-Thai who can speak perfect Thai. They have Scottish parents, some Italian and some American parents. But a large number of these actors/actresses and singers who grew up abroad and joined the entertainment industry in recent years could not speak nor write Thai. Some perform as key characters despite their inability to read the scripts nor speak properly.

A good majority of the prime-time drama during this period were set in foreign locations such as Switzerland, New York, New Zealand, Australia, Germany, France and England. The stories are mostly about the lives of middle- class teenage students studying abroad or family travelling for sight-seeing or fictionalized tales of foreign lands. They became one of the more popular genres despite heavy investment on production. The middle classes are well represented in prime-time drama with overwhelming support from advertisers. This means that most of these dramas are the kind of "cultural commodities" which are both profitable and ideologically desirable.

It is not surprising that the prime-time dramas, together with the advertising industry, work to reinforce the media and the middle classes' desire for un-Thainess and their fragmented cultural subjectivity (see detailed explication on advertising campaigns in Kasien's *Consuming Thainess*, 1997). They are happily being made into a new class of global consumers. When we contrast this daily fare with the periodical media campaign on election and democratic participation we find a deep imbalance. The irregularity of the open public sphere which produced the kind of politicized subjectivity needed for the interaction between economy and state in a civil society is thus, lacking. This was evident during the economic crisis in 1997–98. The media industry has been seriously affected and a large number of media practitioners are unemployed. Since their lives and works, and their mind-sets, depend on the wellbeing of the economy, similar to other groups of middle classes, they have become depoliticized, not politicized, by the whole economic crisis. In their effort to seek information to regain their economic status they have lost the sense of direction and their mission of watchdog and critical commentators for the civil society.

If we take a close look at the regular media fare of news and current affairs we find that the media report less on the plight of the economic crisis affecting the agricultural sector, the rural poor and the protest by the Forum of the Poor. They are more concerned on reporting the money market, export figures and the international economic fora which expect to bring in foreign currency to prop up the economic crisis. The media are not only less interested in the welfare of the majority of the people but they are openly biased against them. The reports, advertorial and advertised news on the recent controversial issue on energy consumption on the one hand, and the conservation of the environment and the people's way of life at Huay Kayeng on the other, Kanjanaburi is a case in point. The Petroleum Authority of Thailand (PTT), a powerful state enterprise, contracted the Burmese government on the Yadana gas pipeline project which runs from the Andaman sea to the western border of Thailand. It cut through 50 kilometers of national forests in Kanjanaburi province and a number of villages along the pipeline. Conservationists and villagers protested against the project and its environmental assessment report. But few of the media reported on both sides of the issues and there was little investigative reporting to inform the public. On the contrary, a large number of the print media reported and printed special features by PTT while radio and television ran short features and commercials supported by PTT (Tirayut Yuwanimi, 1998).

From the above explication I have demonstrated how two major contradicting forces are juxtaposed through the media representation during the election period and the representation in the daily fare of prime-time drama on television. Combining this with the previous examples on the expansion of the global media and the localization of the globalized media content by the Thai media industry (the majority are the new middle classes themselves) I hope to have shed some light on the inquiry into the ambiguity of the public sphere and the role the middle classes play in constructing a democracy for the Thai society.

Notes

1 This occurred at the time of the 1970s political crisis in which the student movement and the Left were suppressed by the military and the Rightist government. There was no freedom of expression and the media was strictly censored. It was interesting to see that all other forms of media expression were suppressed while the film industry received special treatment. This might be an open response to US sanctions on human rights in Thailand. And secondly, the privilege of the film industry on production did not cancel out the government measures on censorship of political and social commentary in the film.

2 There are two large agencies which import films from the major Hollywood studios: Major represents Disney, Twentieth Century Fox, Columbia/Tri Star and Warner, and UPI represents Paramount, Universal and MGM.

3 In order to draw the largest number of movie-goers for this growing influx of films, advertising and promotions are the key to business success. Some of the promotion strategies of the foreign film studios are: increasing the number of radio and television programs and the print media on film review, introducing special news sections on film and entertainment on television, and launching new programs such as the Movie Game on the most popular TV channel on prim-time (beginning April 1998). Hand bill is used to attract film buffs. And in March 1988, a pre-Oscar party for film critics and the media was held, for the first time, to predict the outcome of the Oscar winners.

4 ITV, the newly established station, does not have a nationwide coverage. Its main strength is in news and current affairs programs.

References

The Advertising Book 1997–98 (1997). Bangkok.

Anek Laothamathas (1993). "The business and Thai democracy." In Sungsidh Piriyarangsan and Pasuk Pongpaichit (Eds), *The Middle Class and Thai Democracy*. Political Economy Center, Faculty of Economics, Chulalongkorn University and Friedrich Ebert Stiftung.

Anderson, B. (1995). *Imagined Communities* (revised edn), London: Verso.

Callahan, W.A. (1995). *Poll Watch, Elections and Civil Society: A Comparative Study of Thailand and the Philippines*. Bangkok: Friedrich Naumann Stiftung.

Chai-anand Samutwanit (1997). "Interview." In Chuchai Supawong and Yuwadi Kadkarnklai (Eds), *Pracha Sangkom: Tasana Nak Kid nai Sangkom Thai* (*Civil Society: The Views of Thai Social Philosophers*), Bangkok: Matichon Press.

Chuchai Supawong (1997). "Naewkid Patanakarn lae Kor Picharana Kiewkab Pracha Sangkom Thai" (Concept, development and observations on the Thai civil society). In

Chuchai Supawong and Yuwadi Kadkarnklai (Eds), *Pracha Sangkom: Tasana Nak Kid nai Sangkom Thai (Civil Society: The Views of Thai Social Philosophers)*, Bangkok: Matichon Press.

Cohen, J.L. and Arato, A. (1992). *Civil Society and Political Theory*, Cambridge, MA: The MIT Press.

Garnham, M. (1979) "Contribution to a political economy of mass communication." *Media, Culture and Society*, 1(2), 123–46.

Kanjana Kaewthep (1993). *Maya Pinit: Karnmuang tang Pes kong Lakorn Thoratat (Critics of Illusion: Gender Politics in Television Drama)*, Bangkok: Gender Press.

Karnjana Karnjanatawe (1997) "Sifting through Thai IT magazines", *Bangkok Post*, Wednesday, April 16, 3.

Kasien Thechapira (1997). "Consuming Thainess" in Chaiwat Satha-anand (ed) *Imagining 2000: Paradigm Innovation on Thai Studies*. Bangkok: Thai Research Development Fund.

Krungthep Thurakit (1997). Friday, January 24, 2

Krungthep Thurakit (1997). "IBC and UTV merger materialized, economic pressure-down sizing." Tuesday, October 14, 1–4.

Krungthep Thurakit (1998). "IBC merged with UTV laid off 780 workers." Saturday, March 28, 1–4.

Murdock, G. and Janus, N. (1985). *Mass Communication and the Advetising Industry*. Reports and Papers on Mass Communication, No. 97. Paris: UNESCO

Nithi Aewsriwong (1993). "The cultural dimension of the Thai middle class." In Sungsidh Piriyarangsan and Pasuk Pongpaichit (Eds), *The Middle Class and Thai Democracy*. Political Economy Center, Faculty of Economics, Chulalongkorn University and Friedrich Ebert Stiftung.

Pasuk Pongpaichit (1993). "The middle class of Asia NICs and Thailand." In Sungsidh Piriyarangsan and Pasuk Pongpaichit (Eds), *The Middle Class and Thai Democracy*. Political Economy Center, Faculty of Economics, Chulalongkorn University and Friedrich Ebert Stiftung.

Puchadkarn Daily (1993). "Nang Jean Krong Muang Rab Lod Pasi Film Nang" (Chinese films dominated the city in the midst of lower film tax). Monday, August 16, 1–8.

Puchadkarn Daily (1994). "Mong Nae Nom Karn Boripoke Nangsue Pan Puchadkarn Soonnangsue Chula" (The trend on book consumption through the eyes of the manager of Chula Book Center). Thursday, September 8, 10.

Puchadkarn Daily (1994). "Post Jab Mue Elle Farangses Ok "Elle" Pasa Thai Por Yor Ni" (Post joined hand with French *Elle* to publish Thai "*Elle*" this November). Monday, October 3.

Puchadkarn Daily (1995). "Pocket Book: Kruangmue Tang Watanatham Ti Song Amnad" (Pocket Book: The powerful cultural instrument). Tuesday, January 10, 10.

Prawes Wasi (1995). *Yuthasart Tang Panya Hang Chat (National Intellectual Strategies)*. Bangkok: Thai Research Development Fund.

Preecha Piampongsanti (1993). "The middle class: concepts and theories." In Sungsidh Piriyarangsan and Pasuk Pongpaichit (Eds), *The Middle Class and Thai Democracy*. Political Economy Center, Faculty of Economics, Chulalongkorn University and Friedrich Ebert Stiftung.

Sutakorn Santithawat (1997) "*Nang Thai Nai Tosawat Lang: 2530–2539*" (Thai Film in the last decade 1987–96), *Sarakadi – Feature Magazine*, 13(150), August 1997, 129–32.

Thai Film 1993 (1993). Bankok, Film Critic Club, Thai Film Working Group.

Thai Post (1998). "Satanakarn Nang Thai Pi 2541" (The situation of Thai film in 1998). Saturday, January 17, 8.

Thai Post (1998). "IBC add new board member after merged with UTV, invite AIA to buy share." Friday, February 27, 8.

Thai Post (1998). "IBC merged with UTV laid off 780 workers." Saturday, March 28, 7–8.

Thongchai Winichakul (1988) *Siam Mapped: A History of the Geo-Body of Siam*. PhD Thesis, University of Sydney.

Tirayut Bunmi (1997). *Pradya Hang Karn Patirub Karnmuang* (*The Philosophy of Political Reform*). Bangkok: Walaya Press.

Tirayut Yuwanimi (1998). "Advertorial and media ethics: the case of the pipeline project." *Matichon Weekly*, March 24, 68–9.

Ubonrat Siriyuvasak (1994). "The development of a participatory democracy: raison d'etre for media reform in Thailand." *Southeast Asian Journal of Social Science*, 22(double issue) (Cultural Studies in the Asia Pacific), 101–14.

Ubonrat Siriyuvasak (1996). *Limited Competition Without Re-Regulating the Media: The Case of the Broadcasting Industry in Thailand*. Paper presented at the International Seminar on a Comparative Analysis of (Tele)Communications Policies in Cultural and Historical Perspectives on the Convergence Issue, Bruges, July 1996.

Ubonrat Siriyuvasak (1997). *Karn chai sue nai karn ronarong luektang tuapai wanti song Karakadakom 2540* (*The media campaign during the 2 July 1996 election*). Bangkok: Poll Watch.

Voravit Charoenlert (1991). "Introduction: The middle class and democracy in Thailand." In Sungsidh Piriyarangsan and Pasuk Pongpaichit (Eds), *The Middle Class and Thai Democracy*. Political Economy Center, Faculty of Economics, Chulalongkorn University and Friedrich Ebert Stiftung.

Voravit Charoenlert (1991). "Setakit Thai nai Rabob Setakit Loke" (The Thai economy in the global economy). In Pasuk Pongpaichit and Sungsidh Piriyarangsan (Eds), *Polawat Thai* (*Thai Dynamics: A Political Economy View*). Political Economy Center, Faculty of Economics, Chulalongkorn University and Friedrich Ebert Stiftung.

Voravit Charoenlert (1993). "The middle class and May 1992." In Voravit Charoenlert (Eds), *The Middle Class and Thai Democracy*. Political Economy Center, Faculty of Economics, Chulalongkorn University and Friedrich Ebert Stiftung.

7

CONSTITUTIONAL CHANGE, MEDIA, AND THE NATIONAL PUBLIC SPHERE

The case of Scotland

Philip Schlesinger

Introduction

This chapter considers the relationships between constitutional change, the news media, and the reshaping of political and communicative boundaries in the United Kingdom. We need to think again about these spaces because they are being transformed from above and from below. First, there is the ineluctable march of the European Union (EU) into the heartlands of British political life. And secondly, the UK has embarked on a process of devolving power to Scotland, Northern Ireland and Wales. In May 1999, the first elections took place for the new Scottish Parliament and Welsh Assembly. These are part of a wider process of constitutional reform that will bring about the restructuring of the upper chamber of the Westminster Parliament, the House of Lords, a directly elected Mayor for London, and eventually perhaps, some more representative form of government for the English regions. Although the EU provides the wider framework for this discussion, the devolution of powers to a new Scottish Parliament is my principal focus here since it has involved the most extensive concession of powers by the British state to any of its constituent parts – which may ultimately prove to be a key driving force for wider change.

Political communication and the nation-state

Political communication – the purposive communication by political actors about public affairs – conventionally takes the nation-state as its framework. In everyday political life it is still generally assumed that the United Kingdom is a bounded, sovereign polity, with its own national political agenda, communicated by its own national media. This dominant view of the relations between national political space and national communicative space is still supported by a well-established perspective in the theory of nationalism, which needs to be revised, and is beginning to be so.

Consider the line of work represented by, successively, Karl Deutsch (1966), Ernest Gellner (1983, 1997), Benedict Anderson (1983), and more recently Michael Billig (1995). All share a broad concern with how nations speak to themselves, how they mark themselves off, or flag themselves, as different from others. All theorize from within what Deutsch first labelled a "social communication" perspective whose axial premise is that nations are set apart from other collectivities because of the special nature of their internal communication. Consequently, it is held that a given cultural collectivity tends to build up and secure a separate national identity over time. While each theorist may differ as to the key explanatory factor, it is commonly argued that educational systems, the media, standardized languages or shared cultural practices and symbols are key elements in the historical process of national-culture building. Such national cultures and resultant identities are assumed to be both politically underpinned and continually developed by a state.

This underlying assumption has also been shared by the critical theorist Jürgen Habermas (1989) whose influential theory of communication initially took as its framework the nation addressed as a political community. Political communication within the nation need not necessarily take a democratic form. However, in Habermas's theory, and in the work of the many scholars who have tried to develop it further in recent years (cf. e.g. Keane, 1991; Mayhew, 1997), it is precisely how to ensure access to communicative power by citizens that has become a central concern.

Much current discussion has centered on the so-called "public sphere," a term promoted in academic discourse through the English translation of Habermas's work, and now in relatively wide use. This refers to the domain of debate that exists outside the state, but which is centered on the state's activities and engages all who are concerned with matters of public interest. This is the space of civil society, where political parties, voluntary associations and organized interests may intervene in the political process. The existence of such a domain – in which the media are also situated – is central to the freedom of expression commonly associated with democracy. Thus conceived, the public sphere presupposes a nation-state in relation to which civil society can think and organize politically.

The public sphere is therefore commonly seen as co-extensive with the political form of nation-statehood. This view has a bearing on the present-day functioning of political communication in the United Kingdom because in reality the dominant model of the nation-state as a unitary political community, as a stable locus in which we speak to ourselves about politics and public affairs, is breaking down.

Symptomatic is the persistent line of media commentary on the difficulties of defining "Britishness." An important, and highly visible, part of Tony Blair's New Labour government's politics has been the effort to "rebrand" the United Kingdom and give it a new identity. The discourse of modernized Britishness has been the happy hunting-ground of the think-tank intelligentsia (Leonard, 1997). Following New Labour's victory on May 1, 1997, a sequence of events and processes was annexed to the party's aim of effecting a cultural transformation. This included the political appropriation of the sentiments generated by the death of Diana, Princess of Wales (apparently, for some, a rediscovery of Britons' lost capacity for feeling), the vigorous selling of "cool Britannia" as an image of national revitalization, the enforced quasi-modernization of the monarchy, and the aspirations for an undefined grandeur embodied in the Millennium Dome at Greenwich. In keeping with this broad interest in the presentation of culture, the "creative industries" have been seen as at the cutting edge of reshaping both Britain's image and its workforce (DCMS, 1998; Smith, 1998). All of these have betokened attempts to grapple with a deep-seated problem of collective identity whose sources probably lie in Britain's post-imperial drift.

With devolution in Scotland and Wales, arguably "Britain" and "Britishness" have started to disaggregate. The attempts to characterize "Englishness" have gathered pace, generating both book-length disquisitions and increasingly obsessive commentary by columnists (e.g. Paxman, 1998). This is unquestionably a response to the reassertion by Britain's smaller nations of their distinctiveness through the new arenas of representative politics. Along with the reactive concern that this has provoked in the English heartland, it seems plain that "Englishness" will itself be a contested space, with resistance in the north to an exclusively metropolitan, southern, definition of the nation. So whether the first-term program of New Labour constitutional reform will result in a more united kingdom remains to be seen. As a modernizing program it is certainly intended to result in a new cohesion of the state, but conceivably it could provoke gradual disintegration.

The communicative challenge of "Europeanization"

We can less and less sensibly think of the UK as a sovereign political and communicative space because issues arise, and agendas appear, that derive from the broader political domain of the European Union, and these cannot simply be screened out. The compelling question of Britain's position on European Monetary Union (EMU) is the prime illustration of this. By opting to delay entry to the European single currency, the present British government first placed itself on the sidelines and then decided to recoup the situation by preparing the public for entry. On this decision hangs the future economic performance of the UK as well as the British state's wider political influence. A telling, if less fundamental, example has been the EU's key role in repeatedly deciding the terms of trade and outcomes of the bovine spongiform encephalopathy (BSE) crisis.

The British practice of politics has been steadily "Europeanized" as Westminster has ceased to be the sole arbiter of decision-making. Moreover, increasingly, the question of Britain's approach to European integration has the capacity to make and break political parties. After all, long-standing internal divisions over "Europe" had a decisive role in shattering the long Conservative hold over the country both before, and during, the General Election of 1997. They remained disruptive as that party approached the European parliamentary elections in June 1999.

The increasing centrality of European integration for the future of British politics deeply affects how we should think about the nation-state as a locus of political communication where journalism plays a key role alongside the promotional activities of a range of political actors including state agencies, parties, and pressure groups. As debates about major European policy issues routinely occur in the domestic heartlands of the polity, and are manifestly central to the agendas of British news media, the lines between "us" (the British) and "them" (the Continentals) are becoming increasingly blurred.

So while, routinely, the EU may be represented as external to the British political system, in reality it is increasingly internal to it. The often distance-taking political rhetoric and prevalently negative media coverage obscure this fact (cf. Anderson and Weymouth, 1999). However, these are surface reactions to a deeper movement. It is hard to see clearly the real, underlying, extent of the current change in politico-communicative boundaries precisely because how the highly complex relationship between the EU and the UK is handled both politically and in news coverage varies from moment to moment. Two brief illustrations from my research on contemporary political communication support this view.

In May 1996, for example, the volume of radio and television coverage of a number of European stories (notably reconsideration by the EU of the export ban on British beef) showed a marked increase over previous months. Moreover, the range of political figures given access to the airwaves significantly increased, with sources from several EU member states playing a major role in British debate. At the time, a matter of major UK national interest was being decided not at Westminster but in Brussels. Irrespective of the arguments, it was evident that the UK's broadcast forums of political argument and reporting had opened up to include the EU's spokespeople. In a marked shift, then, the EU's political space for a moment directly overlapped with the UK's, becoming an integral part of British communicative space.

Although such moments of relative openness occur, there may also be a countervailing tendency to closure, illustrated during the British General Election campaign of 1997. On April 21, Jacques Santer, then President of the European Commission, intervened with a swingeing attack on "Eurosceptics." General election campaigns are moments of national self-enclosure, when domestic concerns swell in importance and completely dominate political debate and media agendas. The polity could hardly be more self-absorbed at such times, so Santer's attack on the Eurosceptics, coupled with his uncompromising federalist agenda, played directly into the British political battlefield. Both the political class and the press were largely unanimous about putting Jacques back in his box, with some chauvinistic insults thrown in for good measure. For the Conservative Prime Minister, John Major, this was a chance to defend the British national interest and reassert his anti-federalism, whereas for the Labour aspirant, Tony Blair, it was a moment to blow the patriotic trumpet and reaffirm his gold-plated Britishness. On this occasion the EU, through the symbolic figure of the Commission's President, could easily be represented as alien and intrusive, even dictatorial, and

125

the speech as a gross interference in domestic politics – an affront to national sovereignty.

Such divergent instances suggest that both the political debate and media reporting of the EU in Britain may shift along a continuum of relative openness and closure to European perspectives and arguments. However, the introjection of European matters into British political and communicative space is undeniable and not as just another story, but rather as one integral to the secular melting-down of EU member states' boundaries. The EU has become a key locus for the evolution of a trans-border political community centered on its institutions and embodied in a politico-bureaucratic class and its surrounding networks, as well as elite media (Miller and Schlesinger, 2000; Schlesinger, 1999). European integration is beginning to have an unevenly distributed impact both on conceptions of citizenship and of collective belonging. After all, since the 1991 Treaty of Union (signed at Maastricht), the category of EU citizenship has existed alongside established national citizenship, and although its precise implications have been a matter of debate, it has introduced a new layer of complexity and of potential loyalty. This may, in time, produce another form of collective identity – "European-ness" – for the citizens of member states.

Political theory is beginning to catch up with the realities on the ground. Indicatively, in his more recent work, Jürgen Habermas (1994) has written of the European Union as itself constituting a complex public sphere, where the historic nation-states articulate with an emergent federal state – a viewpoint, incidentally, that neglects the place of stateless nations. If such a new European polity is indeed emerging, it is still embryonic. However, this rethinking of political space transforms the conventional role of political communication as a vehicle for addressing a nation-state-centered public and compels us to consider its relation to a putative supranational public. The corollary of the enlargement of the public sphere is that a European civil society must eventually emerge, the nucleus of which already exists in the policy communities clustered around the EU's executive and legislative institutions.

We might now, in retrospect, re-read almost two decades of tortured debates in the EU about the role of the media as variously helping to build a common culture, or an information society, or a democratic public, as reflecting the Union's developing impact on the communicative spaces still jealously guarded by the member states. This effect is likely to increase as European Monetary Union impels greater de facto federalization and as communication policy frameworks established in Brussels increasingly constrain member states (Schlesinger, 1997).

Scotland's quiet "democratic revolution"

If "Europeanization" is by stages redefining the space of political communication in Britain, so too is the current internal reshaping of the state due to the devolution of power to Scotland and Wales. Decentralization is a widespread feature of contemporary politics in most EU member states, and the UK is finally aligning itself with the European trend towards "subsidiarity," the doctrine that no political issue should be decided at a level higher than is absolutely necessary. The New Labour victory on May 1, 1997 placed home rule for the two countries firmly back on the British political agenda after almost two decades, initiating what constitutional reformers such as Anthony Barnett see as a "democratic revolution." Constitutional change is truly fundamental, as Barnett (1997: 149) notes, because it embodies "the set of relationships that proposes how a country is run," and therefore profoundly affects the institutional core of a society and how people live their everyday lives.

In Scotland, the government published its devolution White Paper, *Scotland's Parliament*, in July 1997 (The Scottish Office, 1997). This was rapidly followed by a two-question referendum on September 11, 1997 in which voters were asked to decide whether there should be a Scottish Parliament and whether this body should have the power to vary taxation. A telling majority of Scots voted for political autonomy. After the devastation of the Conservatives in the May election, there was little serious opposition from those in favor of the centralist status quo. The "Yes-Yes" campaign unprecedentedly brought together Scotland's two main devolutionist parties, Labour and the Liberal Democrats, with the pro-independence Scottish National Party (SNP). The referendum implicitly identified the Scots as a civic nation, as voting was open only to residents of Scotland, irrespective of their ethnic backgrounds or places of birth. Ethnic Scots outside the country had no voting rights. This was an important benchmark, though still little appreciated, for future political discourse about "the nation" in Scotland.

On a turnout of 60.4 percent, in response to the first question, 74.3 percent supported the creation of a Scottish Parliament, while, in response to the second, 63.5 percent agreed that the proposed legislature should have tax-varying powers. The 1997 vote was a milestone, as it turned around the result of the previous referendum of 1979. Support for a Scottish Parliament with wide powers, within the United Kingdom, finally addressed the "unfinished business" of constitutional reform, expressing "the settled will of the Scottish people," in the two resonant phrases of the late Labour Party leader and convinced devolutionist, John Smith. Any future choice will now be between remaining in the Union and outright independence.

The extensive pro-devolutionary shift during the Conservative years did not come out of the blue. The Tories had become steadily more beleaguered north of the Border. By the 1992 General Election, the Conservatives had been returned in only eleven of the seventy-two Scottish seats. The turning-point was 1997 as they lost all their Scottish seats. The disjuncture between increasingly unpopular Conservative rule from Westminster and the small Tory representation in Scotland had contributed to a widespread sense of disenfranchisement over the years. The various campaigns waged against devolution after 1992 by the Conservative Prime Minister John Major and his successive Scottish Secretaries, Ian Lang and Michael Forsyth, thus proved to be ineffective in saving the party from electoral collapse in 1997.

Much of the groundwork for the July 1997 White Paper and subsequent Scotland Bill was prepared through the patient work of the Scottish Constitutional Convention, which first met in March 1989. Little known outside Scotland, this was a crucial vehicle for key elements of Scottish civil society to devise a common approach to devolution. Contributing to the Convention's initial impetus was a resentment of the strident centralism of the long-ruling Conservative Prime Minister, Margaret Thatcher. This had led to the widespread sense that Scotland was not adequately represented by Westminster politics. The Convention brought together Scotland's dominant Labour Party and the Liberal Democrats, also including other minor parties and representatives of a wide range of interests such as the Scottish Trades Union Congress (STUC), the women's movement, local councils, and the churches. The core of its political project was the restoration of Home Rule to Scotland within the framework of the United Kingdom. Both the anti-devolution Conservatives and the independence-oriented SNP refused to join (Kellas, 1990; Wright, 1997).

To legitimize its opposition to the constitutional status quo, the Convention invoked the will of the Scottish nation. By seeing sovereignty as vested in "the people" rather than in the Crown-in-Parliament at Westminster, it drew a sharp distinction between Scottish and English constitutional thinking (MacCormick, 1998). The Convention also pointed to decentralizing developments in the European Union to bolster its intellectual case. As an expression of civil society, it could draw both on the legacy of the Scottish Enlightenment and find inspiration in civic movements intent on promoting political change and democratization in East-Central Europe. Crucially, the work of the Constitutional Convention was coupled with the largely supportive agenda-setting role amongst the "blethering classes" of the Scottish broadsheet press, which showed a consistent interest in its activities, as did Scottish broadcasters.

The Convention managed to maintain a remarkably broad political consensus over a period of eight years. It produced a series of key documents – notably *A Claim of Right for Scotland* (1989) and *Scotland's Parliament, Scotland's Right* (1995) – which set the stage in 1997 for the eventual White Paper, *Scotland's Parliament*, and the subsequent historic, and far-reaching, Scotland Bill (House of Commons, 1997).

Devolution, as laid out in the Scotland Act of November 1998, has given the Scottish Parliament legislative competencies in all major areas except those reserved to Westminster: principally, the constitution, UK financial matters, foreign policy, defence, social security and citizenship. Given our present concern with communication, it is crucial to note that powers over broadcasting have been reserved to Westminster. Major powers devolved to Scotland encompass key areas such as health, education, local government, economic development and transport, environment, agriculture, forestry and fishing, law and home affairs, sport and the arts. The Scottish Parliament has a tax-varying power of up to 3 percent of basic income tax.

The first general election under the Scotland Act was held on May 6, 1999. It provided for 129 Members of the Scottish Parliament (MSPs), seventy-three of whom were elected by the first-past-the-post system in existing Westminster constituencies, with an additional member voting system electing 56 members from party lists, seven from each of the eight European parliamentary constituencies. Labour won fifty-six seats, the SNP thirty-five, the Conservatives eighteen, and the Liberal Democrats seventeen. In addition, one Independent, one Scottish Socialist and one Green were elected. After some haggling, a Labour–Liberal Democrat coalition government was formed, headed by the veteran devolutionist, and first Secretary of State for Scotland in the Blair government, Donald Dewar.

Scotland's press and national identity

Since the Acts of Union of 1707 (when Scotland's last parliament was dissolved), the country has retained its separate legal and educational systems and church, all of which, with differing importance over time, have contributed to the shaping of a distinct national culture. Since 1886, the national institutional matrix has also had a territorial political and administrative dimension in the shape of the Scottish Office. The case for a parliament was latterly made in terms of the need to extend democratic control over this bureaucratic structure.

Scotland's media are a crucial element of the country's civil society. Their role in the development of the new Scottish political culture once the parliament is established will be substantial. They are part of the range of institutions that have been the substratum of Scottish distinctiveness within the UK. It is not surprising, therefore, that Scots have the option of a dual national identity, Scottish and/or British. The current evidence suggests that Scottishness is increasingly preferred over Britishness (McCrone, 1997).

The creation of a Scottish Parliament is a key test bed for sociological and political analyses concerned with the "stateless nation." It seems that the British multi-national state is likely to experience the strains of "asymmetrical government" if English regionalism does not take off following Scottish and Welsh devolution (Keating, 1997; McCrone, 1992; Paterson, 1994). Thus far, there have been some competitive regionalist stirrings in England's north-east and Yorkshire, but it remains to be seen whether this can translate itself into a sustained political campaign for representative institutions.

Unlike any other British region, for most Scots the "national media" are based not in London, but rather "located in Scotland, within a UK framework of ownership, control, finance and regulation. The semi-autonomous status of the Scottish media thus parallels that of other features of Scottish political and economic life." It has been argued that "in many respects the media in Scotland have their own distinctive characteristics and can be said to contribute, particularly in the case of the press, to Scotland's self-perception as a nation" (Meech and Kilborn, 1992: 258).

In fact, it is unclear to just what extent the self-conscious identification with Scotland of the Scottish-based press, radio and television promote a sense of distinctive Scottishness amongst the public. While some might argue that the media do significantly shape Scottish identity, others have speculated that the distinctiveness of the Scottish media has been shaped by the pre-existing national culture (McInnes, 1993). Whatever the precise causal relation, for present purposes we may assume that there is an intimate reciprocal connection between the media consumption patterns of the Scottish public and Scottish national and regional identities.

In the long run-up to the 1997 General Election, devolution was a topic of exceptionally intensive and extensive media interest north of the Border, especially so when systematically compared with coverage in the London-based press and broadcasting. Subsequently, this distinctive pattern of attention was sustained during the reporting of the devolution White Paper, the referendum and the publication of the Scotland Bill, and during Scotland's first General Election campaign, maintaining the south's communication deficit. It could be argued that a fracture line runs through the UK when it comes to public dissemination of the implications of Scottish devolution.

My concern here is with political communication strictly understood. I shall limit myself to giving a brief account of some of the most significant Scottish news media, underlining how they differ from the London-based UK media. Clearly, to explore other dimensions of the relationships between media and national identity one would cast the net much more widely in the media culture, to take in mainstream broadcast sport, music, comedy, drama, talk shows, phone-ins, magazines, advertising and cinema as well as Scottish Office-supported Gaelic television production.

Readership figures are a crude indicator of consumption preferences, and tell us nothing of the meanings attributed to what is read. However, they do indicate the strong hold that Scottish-produced and headquartered newspapers exercise in the country, when compared with most of those published south of the Border. Scotland has an old-established daily quality press in the shape of *The Herald* (Glasgow, founded 1783) and *The Scotsman* (Edinburgh, founded 1817). Jointly, these newspapers dominate the opinion-leading market in, respectively, west and east central Scotland, the belt where most of the population is concentrated. Between them, in 1996–97, these two titles reached more than 13 percent of readers, whereas the five London broadsheets together attracted some 8 percent.

The popular end of the daily newspaper market is also extremely distinctive. It is dominated by the *Daily Record* (founded 1895, and Britain's oldest popular daily newspaper). The country's leading daily tabloid, the *Record* has a readership of more than 1.8 million, or a reach of 44 percent of Scotland's adults, and is especially read in the west of the country. Its nearest rival is the *Scottish Sun*, with around a quarter of the readership. Against these front-runners, London titles such as the *Daily Mirror* or the *Daily Star* have very modest sales by the usual tabloid standards.

The middle market has recently been prone to penetration by Scottish editions of London newspapers, with both the *Scottish Daily Mail* and the *Scottish Daily Express* each building significant readerships of over a quarter of a million. However, their undeniably significant reach needs to be considered in relation to the continuing "city state" character of Scotland's press. Mid-market tabloid circulations are matched by those of Dundee's *Courier* and Aberdeen's *Press and Journal* (founded 1748).

Sunday newspaper sales are also markedly dominated by Scottish titles. *The Record*'s stable-mate, the *Sunday Mail*, reaches almost half the adult Scottish readership, with the *Sunday Post* pushing near to 40 percent. The only southern title to come close is the *News of the World*, with virtually a quarter of Scottish readers. The quality end of the market shows the *Sunday Times* to be a close rival to *Scotland on Sunday*, each reaching some 7 percent of readers. Unlike its southern broadsheet counterparts, however, the *Sunday Times* sold north of the Border is thoroughly Scottish in content and perspectives (NRS, 1996–97: np).

The Scottish press, therefore, penetrates everyday life, and while it is certainly true that some Scottified English titles have made major inroads of late, they have had to adapt themselves to the Scottish market in order to succeed. Pressures to focus even more on Scottish developments can only increase as the Edinburgh parliament assumes a major role in national life.

The media politics of the market-place

Prior to devolution, significant changes of ownership occurred in the two quality daily newspapers, which have a disproportionately significant role in setting the agenda of Scottish affairs. In one case, that of *The Herald*, this was part of the pre-devolutionary manoeuvrings of what was to become the Scottish Media Group (SMG) in May 1997, provoking concern about media concentration, the more so after SMG bought up Grampian Television. In the second case, that of *The Scotsman*, editorial changes had ramifications for the debate on devolution.

In July 1996, Caledonian Newspapers, owner of *The Herald* and the *Glasgow Evening Times*, accepted a bid from Scottish Television, the ITV central Scotland licensee. Scottish Television's then executive chairman, Gus Macdonald, unashamedly played the Scottish card in a pre election year, arguing that combining the businesses would avoid decision-making power being sucked down to London. Following expressions of public concern about the possibility of ownership concentration in the newspaper market, the Scottish Television-Caledonian merger was officially cleared by both the Independent Television Commission (ITC) in October 1996 (applying a public interest test) and the Department of Trade and Industry (following a report from the Office of Fair Trading).

Scottish Television's other growth point was in its home territory of television. It had long been supposed that the Glasgow-based company, broadcasting to the major Scottish central belt market, would bid for Grampian Television, headquartered in Aberdeen in Scotland's north-east. Once the provisions of the 1996 Broadcasting Act had come into effect, Grampian, which was showing improved pre-tax profits, became particularly vulnerable to takeover, as the Act allowed a single television company to reach up to 15 percent of the entire UK audience. The bid came in June 1997, the month following the British General

Election, and was accepted by the Grampian shareholders. The proposed merger brought 4.7 of the 5.1 million Scottish viewers within SMG's purview.

Concern was expressed in various quarters about a concentration of television ownership, about job losses, and the possible loss of a regional programming identity for Grampian viewers – a touchy issue since regional politics are likely to be rather significant in the Scottish parliament. The ITC mounted an inquiry on public interest grounds and found in SMG's favor, saying that it expected the regional provisions of the two companies' separate licences to be honored, a point subsequently re-emphasized by the ITC's chairman.

What was thrown into relief, and fuelled the continuing, if still sporadic, expressions of public concern, was the recognition that the rules designed to regulate concentration and audience share in the UK-wide market were simply not designed to take account of Scotland considered as a political entity, as opposed to its being regarded as a territory divided among three ITV regions. The politics of home rule are bound increasingly to underline the extent to which Scotland is a distinctive national market – that is, a political economy – in its own right.

Grampian's incorporation into SMG meant that the group now controlled some ninety percent of the Scottish television audience for the main terrestrial commercial television channel. Only those viewers served by Border Television remained outside SMG's reach. From a UK perspective, the Scottish-Grampian merger was small beer and merely part of a flurry of government-facilitated takeovers in the ITV sector that had led to three big players south of the Border. However, in a small country, a unique multi-media concentration both has a good deal of influence and considerable political visibility.

Presently, one question on the agenda is whether SMG will be able to retain its unique position in Scotland or rather become, in effect, a subsidiary of one of the bigger UK players. At this time of writing, while Scottish Television's majority ownership is in Scottish hands, the 18.6 percent of the company's shares owned by the London-based Mirror Group Newspapers (MGN) have been bid for by the Granada Group and referred to the Monopolies and Mergers Commission. The bid has aroused speculation that this may be the start of an eventual takeover process and that it might cause political conflict over whether or not SMG retains its "Scottishness."

SMG preemptively built up its strength during the last year of Tory rule. Recognizing that UK legislation dealt with Scotland as a market but not as a polity, it sought assurances that Labour, if elected, had no intention of changing this. Politicians of all stripes were willing to play the Scottish card in 1996. SMG's subsequent calculation – correct, as it turned out – was that UK regulation would stay in place and that the Edinburgh parliament would have no regulatory or legislative competence in the field of broadcasting. With 80 percent of its programs and 85 percent of its advertising coming through the ITV network, Scottish Television stresses its place in British broadcasting. Complaining that ITV was already overregulated, Bob Tomlinson, SMG's one-time head of public affairs, maintained that vesting any powers in Edinburgh would be "unwarranted, impractical and costly" and that the approach needed was "hands off, light touch, and let us get on with the job" (Speech to the Broadcasting in Scotland Post Devolution Conference, Stirling, November 29, 1997).

Despite this call for the status quo, it is difficult to believe that questions of cross-media ownership and concentration in Scotland will remain off the new parliamentary agenda. Pertinent questions were first raised by the Broadcasting for Scotland Campaign when Caledonian Newspapers was bought, reflecting concern about an eventual take-over of Scottish Television by the Mirror Group. Criticism has more recently been clearly articulated by the SNP, which, without impugning SMG's record, has argued that it would be generally prudent to have separate "anti-trust" laws for the media sector. SNP leaders have subsequently made it clear – both in public and privately to this author – that the issue of broadcasting regulation remains high on their agenda.

Change at *The Scotsman* has been of interest because of editorial rather than structural changes, at least for the present. In October 1996, Andrew Neil was appointed editor-in-chief of Scotsman Publications. The company, owned by Frederick and David Barclay's European Press Holdings, groups *The Scotsman*, *Scotland on Sunday*, and the *Edinburgh Evening News*.

Neil's appointment caused a stir among media commentators, given the long-standing commitment to devolution of *The Scotsman* and its Sunday stable-mate. His adamant opposition to independence and his dismissive views of what he sees as Scotland's "monotonic" left-of-center consensus goes back to his time at the *Sunday Times* which consistently attacked devolution in its Scottish edition (Smith, 1994). Neil's appointment, and consequent editorial changes, brought more astringent questioning to the practicalities of devolution, tempered by an acceptance that this would now indeed be the new political order. Neil summed up his mission thus in June 1997:

> I had laid down that our titles must be broadly in favour of the market economy, defenders of the union between Scotland and England and prepared to tackle head on the many outdated Scottish shibboleths and collectivist attitudes which still dominate politics north of the border. None of this conflicted with backing Blair ... [who] ... himself told me he hoped I might be able to stir things up ...
>
> (Neil, 1997: xvii–xviii)

In the run-up to the establishment of the parliament in Edinburgh, a new phase of struggle for primacy in the quality market began between *The Scotsman* and *The Herald*. This was linked to the ancient rivalry between Edinburgh and Glasgow, with fears in the west of Scotland that the country's biggest city would lose out to the capital's reinforced importance. At the start of the new parliamentary era, *The Herald* appears to have positioned itself editorially as the critically supportive voice of the new administration, whereas the *The Scotsman* has taken the role of principled detractor.

Broadcast journalism and regulation

At the same time as building an increasingly dominant position in Scotland's media landscape, Scottish Television also used its Scottishness to argue for more independence from the UK network, notably in news scheduling. This initiative, in Gus Macdonald's words to me, "detonated the debate," with Scotland's other big terrestrial television player, BBC Scotland, subsequently initiating a far-reaching review.

Macdonald argued for "country" membership of the ITV network – in effect, for a looser, affiliate status – in late 1996. The aim was to reduce Scottish's commitment to the network, paying only for the programs it wanted. In justification, Scottish Television claimed that it could choose to produce more programs with high production values, such as drama and entertainment, with benefits for local audiences. Relatedly, around this time, SMG spokesmen suggested that Scottish Television might opt out of network programming to cover the Edinburgh parliament and floated the idea that Scottish news delivered by the early evening flagship program, *Scotland Today*, might be combined with UK and international stories in a 60-minute program. Such a Scottish news program would have had a major impact on the broadcast media agenda north of the Border and would have challenged the London-based ITN's statutory role in supplying identical UK-wide news to all commercial television contractors. However, as devolution approached, these arguments were quietly shelved by the commercial station and instead became the mission of BBC Scotland.

As the date for devolution drew closer, BBC Scotland, and the corporation more generally, had to decide on the appropriate journalistic response to major constitutional change. Even if its management wished to, it could not easily effect a semi-detached relationship to London since, like its Welsh and Northern Irish counterparts, it has historically operated as a "national region" within a unitary corporation. Each "national region" has a special Broadcasting Council to act as a policy forum, and its own controller and senior management, with lines of responsibility to London.

Although it is the only pan-Scottish terrestrial news and current affairs broadcaster, the BBC's Scottish radio and television services differ. BBC Radio Scotland is a general national station – a rarity these days – and has no single direct competitor in Scotland, although it does compete with commercial local radio. The station has had a broad remit since being launched in 1978 in anticipation of a Scottish Assembly. Created with the expectation of constitutional change in mind, its journalistic role as the leading source of informed analysis and commentary in a devolved Scotland has been preordained. While Radio Scotland's news and current affairs coverage has its detractors, it is nonetheless wide-ranging, and puts a distinctive Scottish slant on the stories and issues covered. Radio Scotland's *Good Morning Scotland* operates as the equivalent of Radio 4's *Today* program. In ways analogous to the Scottish broadsheet press, Radio Scotland's morning news progam has a major agenda-setting role. Significantly, it attracts four times more Scottish listeners than its London-based counterpart.

BBC Television Scotland provides a distinct news service and some current affairs programs, as well as other programs such as drama, music, comedy and sport. However, by contrast with the comprehensive Scottish national radio service, it takes the bulk of its programming from the two BBC UK networks, opting-out with specific programs for Scottish viewers. It also supplies network programming, notably drama and comedy. While the Scottish ITV stations retain a regional remit, the "national regional" BBC Scotland takes the whole country as its territory in news and current affairs coverage, such as the early evening flagship news program, *Reporting Scotland*, and the current affairs program, *Frontline Scotland*.

The BBC's role under a devolved Parliament was summed up thus by the Controller, Scotland, John McCormick, in November 1997: "Our aim is to ensure that we provide an unrivalled journalistic service that matches the new pattern of governance of the UK" (the BBC and the Changing Broadcasting Environment, Town and Gown Lecture, University of Strathclyde, November 4, 1997). The centrality of journalism both accords with the corporation's public service mission and the BBC's global strategy of developing its presence as a news and information provider. In his lecture, McCormick made it clear that the corporation was going to retain its unitary structure. At the same time, BBC recognized that its activities would be properly scrutinized by the Scottish Parliament. But this was not seen as replacing the existing form of accountability through the governors to the Secretary of State for Culture, Media and Sport. The stance taken by commercial television has been identical. The chairman of the ITC, Sir Robin Biggam, has dismissed the prospect of separate Scottish broadcasting regulation, while conceding that national sensibilities would have to be addressed.

While Scottish Television initiated the debate on the journalism most suited to Scotland's new political landscape, it was BBC Scotland that eventually had to face the flak. In the autumn of 1998, there was intense pressure from BBC Scotland management, backed by its national advisory body, the Broadcasting Council for Scotland, for a Glasgow-produced television news program with an international and national remit, to be broadcast at 6 pm, the peak viewing time for news. This demand for a so-called "Scottish Six" became a cause célèbre north of the Border as it came up against the determined resistance of the BBC's director-general and a majority of the corporation's governors. The BBC's leadership was publicly concerned that the proposed change might be outrunning the proper pace of constitutional change; it was also privately worried that a distinctive Scottish news might contribute to the break-up of the United Kingdom (Schlesinger, 1998: 15).

The outcome, after much angry debate, was a revamped *Six O'Clock News*, first launched immediately after the Scottish and Welsh elections in May 1999. The program was set the task of better reflecting the new constitutional make-up of the UK through the closer integration with the London newsroom of the editorial and reporting priorities of the Belfast, Cardiff and Glasgow operations. At this time of writing, the *Six O'Clock News* is in its infancy, and it is too early to judge whether or not this will satisfy the various requirements of viewers in the devolved nations at the same time as pleasing the UK-wide audience. Nevertheless, its creation has reflected the BBC's effort to grapple with the mutating constitution, as has the corporation's staff guide, *The Changing UK*, issued in March 1999 by the Controller Editorial Policy, which has aimed to make staff sensitive to various national political, legal and cultural differences and how these might best be described.

The BBC has sought to hold the ring as a state-wide broadcaster. Like all the other networks, its position is ultimately defined by the reservation of broadcasting powers to Westminster under the Scotland Act. This has not been accepted by the SNP. The party considers that in order to protect the national culture both public-sector and commercial broadcasting should be under the legislative control of Edinburgh. This argument is likely to be revisited in future. Aside from the Liberal Democrats' general expressions of concern about media concentration and the maintenance of ITV's federalism, both Labour and the Conservatives seem content with the status quo.

The SNP's position as the official opposition will allow it to achieve some prominence for its views, although the composition of the Edinburgh parliament should ensure that no short-term challenge to the present broadcasting dispensation is likely to succeed. Extra-parliamentary debate may also be fuelled by producer interests and elements of the Scottish policy community. For instance, the Campaign for Broadcasting in Scotland has proposed that BBC Scotland control both the Scottish licensing fee and the scheduling of network services in Scotland, and that Channel 4 develop a distinct Scottish service on the lines of the Welsh S4C (Smith, 1997). Others have argued for the Scottish Parliament to have a say in the forthcoming renewal of the ITV franchises whereas the consumer lobby, Voice of the Listener and Viewer, provided platforms for major discussions of broadcasting and devolution in 1997 and 1998.

A developing political culture?

The new Scottish Parliament may well be something of a political laboratory. The use of the additional member system in parliamentary elections – modifying Westminster's first-past-the-post tradition – denied Labour an outright majority in the May 1999 elections. The Labour–Liberal Democrat "partnership" is an unprecedented departure in the post-war period, which has seen no previous formal coalition. In its working procedures, the new parliament has begun by breaking with Westminster's formality and aims to keep "family-friendly" hours. The parliament's gender-balance is quite remarkable, with forty-nine women out of 129 MSPs. Much touted as an innovation has been the important role attached to pre-legislative consultation in the parliamentary committees. These factors could all contribute to giving Scottish political culture a quite distinctive style and flavor.

It remains to be seen how the new Executive will interact with the media. When still Secretary of State for Scotland, Donald Dewar, now Scotland's First Minister, said of political reporting: "We are not likely to wish to recreate the lobby system" (speech at the Understanding Constitutional Change Conference, Edinburgh,

November 21, 1997). As arrangements are worked out with the new Edinburgh political press corps, can the high aspirations that lay behind the institution-building process translate themselves into an approach to government information distinct from that of Westminster?

The Scottish parliament has become a focus not just for the news media. For instance, British Telecom declared its interest in the restoration of trust in the political process, and underlined the role of information and communication technologies in promoting electoral involvement through training and education and remote working for MSPs. Of the mainstream media, Channel 4 made an adaptive gesture towards devolution by establishing a new "Nations and Regions" office in Glasgow, intended to be a new hub for the development of independent television production outside London.

A political market place has begun to develop, with a range of organizations jockeying for influence. Scotland has its home-grown think-tanks in the shape of the Scottish Council Foundation and the Centre for Scottish Public Policy, which were active in policy debate in the run-up to devolution and are now an established part of the scene. A group of professional lobbyists, bearing recent Westminster experience in mind, and intent on trying to establish a "sleaze-free" rule-book, have created the Association for Scottish Public Affairs (ASPA). Formally inaugurated in December 1998, this body has drawn up a voluntary code of conduct for the regulation of lobbyists" activities in relation to the Scottish Parliament. It remains to be seen whether ASPA will gain credibility with the new legislature and also how widely its writ will be accepted. A print journalists" body, the Scottish Political Press Association (SPPA), has been set up to represent the interests of political correspondents, and has shaped debate about reporters" accreditation to the Parliament. It, too, has drawn up a code of binding conduct for its members. Alongside these professionals of political communication, the Scottish Civic Forum was launched in March 1999, driven principally by the voluntary sector, and aiming to provide a complementary space to the Parliament, open to the whole range of Scottish civil society, for public debate and policy development.

A closing perspective

The boundaries of political communication in Britain are undergoing profound change. First, the European Union is redefining both British domestic politics and media agendas. And second, the devolution of powers to Scotland is producing a new national parliamentary center. As a result of the latter, the fault-lines running through British statehood will become much more apparent as "north of the Border" comes to signify wide-ranging democratic autonomy for the Scots.

It is an open question whether ultimately the new constitutional settlement will push the wider British polity in the direction of federalism, or instead ultimately lead to Scottish separation. The first Scottish parliamentary elections have in effect endorsed the continuance of the Union, while at the same time giving the SNP the role of official opposition. Whatever the eventual outcome, we are already facing a change of historic significance that will unleash a new political dynamic and reshape national identities both in Scotland and in the UK as a whole.

Within multi-national states such as the UK, it is plain that nationhood and statehood may pull in divergent directions, creating new fields of force. In the process of "stateless nation-building" (Keating, 1997) that is entering a decisive phase in Scotland today, the reconfiguration of politics has been intimately related to media and communication.

For instance, consistent media coverage in Scotland certainly played a major role in preparing the ground for the Referendum. The strong support for devolution showed that there was an informed public, precisely because of the airing given to the lengthy debate (both pro and con) amongst the political classes, key interest groups, and the intelligentsia. By contrast, the radical implications of devolution are not so well understood south of the Border, where media attention has been somewhat sporadic and rather superficial. There is at present a communication deficit which may have important consequences for relations between the parliaments at Westminster and at Holyrood and also for how the different parts of the UK react to major political change.

Arguably, therefore, "cross-border" communication via the news media will have an increasingly crucial role to play in the reporting and interpretation of devolution within the United Kingdom. The BBC, in the words of its director of National and Regional Broadcasting, Mark Thompson (1999: 5), has found itself with the difficult task of being "the only broadcaster committed to articulating the new politics and of sharing the different experiences of devolution with audiences across the UK." The corporation is having to reinvent its mission as broadcaster to a diversifying state – but one in which it continues to conceive of itself as the cultural cement. As Thompson puts it:

> We're not a unionist organization in the sense of favouring any one constitutional settlement over another, but we can and should be a clearing house not just for national differences, but the value and heritage that we hold in common. This is a public purpose of the BBC which will grow in importance as devolution develops.
>
> (Thompson, 1999: 5)

Of course, this recast role presumes the relatively untroubled development of the new order.

But there are likely to be tensions in the political dealings between Edinburgh and Westminster. A recurrent debate – that began just after the devolution referendum – has concerned the "Barnett formula" which determines per capita expenditure in the different parts of the UK: the present favoring of Scotland has led English MPs to question current arrangements. There can be little doubt that the country's financial settlement under devolution will be a major focus of political and media attention. Another issue is the repeatedly articulated concern about the role of Scottish MPs at Westminster when English and Welsh legislation is debated. Labour's present dominance at Westminster, and its predominance in Edinburgh, should ensure a short- to medium-term smoothing out of major difficulties. However, in due course future political developments both north and south of the Border could make the UK's new asymmetrical politics much more difficult to manage.

From a quite different angle, we might note how devolution has focused attention on Scotland's media regime. To date, discussion has touched on regulation, the concentration of ownership, regionalism, the organization of political reporting, and broadcasting economics and it is likely that these questions will be revisited.

However, so far as both broadcasting and the press are concerned, the parameters of policy change are located not at Westminster alone, but also increasingly in Brussels. The options available to Scotland's media will be influenced by a context in which global economic competition and technologically-driven change are decisive counters, as are supranational processes of political and economic integration.

Unavoidably, therefore, the Scottish media will also be increasingly affected by the rapid drive towards "convergence" in the fields of broadcasting, telecommunications, and interactive technologies. As new strategic alliances and mergers come thick and fast, these are transforming the entire media landscape in Britain, as elsewhere. There is also the wider European Union dimension to consider. The European Commission's Green Paper on Regulation (EC, 1997) raised far-reaching questions about whether current regulatory systems were blocking the growth of an "information society." These have still to be addressed. Furthermore, European policy-makers akso have to devise rules able to secure pluralism in a wide variety of media markets. Consequently, how Scotland's tranforming politico-communicative space is elaborated will depend not only on decisions taken in London but also on those made in Brussels.

Acknowledgement

The present chapter is a revised and updated version of "Scottish Devolution and the Media," 55–74 in Jean Seaton (ed.) *Politics and the Media: Harlots and Prerogatives at the Turn of the Millennium*, published by Oxford: Blackwell Publishers and first appeared in Political Quarterly (1998), © The Political Quarterly Publishing Co. Ltd. The author is grateful to the editor and publishers for permission to republish this version. The research was conducted as part of a project on "Political Communication and Democracy" with the support of the UK Economic and Social Research Council's "Media Culture and Media Economics" Program, (Reference No.: L126251022). The author thanks the Council for its support.

References

Anderson, B. (1983). *Imagined Communities: Reflections on the Origin and Spread of Nationalism*. London: Verso Editions.

Anderson, P.J. and Weymouth, A. (1999). *Insulting the Public? The British Press and the European Union*. London: Longman.
Barnett, A. (1997). *This Time: Our Constitutional Revolution*. London: Vintage.
Billig, M. (1995). *Banal Nationalism*. London: Sage.
DCMS (1998). *Creative Industries Mapping Document*. London: Department of Culture, Media and Sport.
Deutsch, K. (1966). *Nationalism and Social Communication: An Inquiry into the Foundations of Nationalism* (2nd edn). Cambridge: The MIT Press.
EC (1997). "Green Paper on the convergence of the telecommunications, media and information technology sectors, and the implications for regulation: towards an information society approach." European Commission, Com (97) 623, Brussels, 3 December .
Gellner, E. (1983). *Nations and Nationalism*. Oxford: Basil Blackwell.
Gellner, E.t (1997). *Nationalism*. London: Weidenfeld and Nicolson.
Habermas, J. (1989). *The Structural Transformation of the Public Sphere: An Inquiry into a Category of Bourgeois Society*. Cambridge: Polity Press.
Habermas, J. (1994). "Citizenship and national identity," 20–35. In B. van Steenbergen (Ed.), *The Condition of Citizenship*. London: Sage.
House of Commons (1997). Scotland Bill, Session 1997–98, online. Available at http//www.parliament,the-stationery-office.co.uk/pa/cm1999798/cmbills/104/19997104.htm (accessed 18 December).
Keane, J. (1991). *The Media and Democracy*. Cambridge: Polity Press.
Keating, M. (1997). "What's Wrong with Asymmetrical Government?" Paper presented to the ECPR Standing Group on Regionalism, conference on "Devolution," Newcastle-upon-Tyne, February.
Keating, M. (1997). "Stateless nation-building: Quebec, Catalonia and Scotland in the changing state system." *Nations and Nationalism*, 3(4), 689–717.
Kellas, J.G. (1990). "The constitutional options for Scotland," *Parliamentary Affairs*, 43(4), 426–34.
Leonard, M. (1997). *Britain TM*. London: Demos.
MacCormick, N. (1998). "The English constitution, the British state, and the Scottish anomaly." In *Scottish Affairs*, "Special issue: Understanding Constitutional Change," 129–45.
McCrone, D. (1992). *Understanding Scotland: The Sociology of a Stateless Nation*. London: Routledge.
McCrone, D. (1997). "Unmasking Britannia: The rise and fall of British national identity." *Nations and Nationalism*, 3(4), 579–96.
McInnes, J. (1993). "The broadcast media in Scotland." *Scottish Affairs*, 84–98.
Mayhew, L. (1997). *The New Public*. Cambridge: Cambridge University Press.
Meech, P. and Kilborn, R. (1992). "Media and identity in a stateless nation: The case of Scotland." *Media, Culture and Society*, 14(2), 245–59.
Miller, D. and Schlesinger, P. (2000). "The changing shape of public relations in the European Union." In R.L. Heath and G.M. Vasquez (Eds), *The Handbook of Public Relations*. London: Sage.
Neil, A. (1997). *Full Disclosure*. London: Pan Books.
NRS (1996–97) "Daily and Sunday newspapers in Scotland." National Readership Survey July 1996–June 1997.
Paterson, L. (1994). *The Autonomy of Modern Scotland*. Edinburgh: Edinburgh University Press.

Paxman, J. (1998). *The English: A Portrait of a People*. London: Michael Joseph.

Schlesinger, P. (1997). "From cultural defence to political culture: Media, politics and collective identity in the European Union." *Media, Culture and Society*, 19(3), 369–91.

Schlesinger, P. (1998). "Start spreading the news." *The Scotsman*, October 27, 15.

Schlesinger, P. (1999). "Changing spaces of political communication: The case of the European Union." *Political Communication*, 16(3), July–September.

Smith, C. (1998). *Creative Britain*. London: Faber and Faber

Smith, M. (1994). *Paper Lions: The Scottish Press and National Identity*. Edinburgh: Polygon.

Smith, N. (1997). "Broadcasting and a Scottish Parliament." *Scottish Affairs*, 19, 29–41.

The Scottish Office (1997). Scotland's Parliament, Cm 3658, Edinburgh: The Stationery Office.

Thompson, M. (1999). "This country of nations." *Media Guardian*, May 17, 5.

Wright, K. (1997). *The People Say Yes: The Making of Scotland's Parliament*. Glendaruel: Argyll Publishing.

8

TO GLOBALIZE, REGIONALIZE OR LOCALIZE US, THAT IS THE QUESTION

Japan's response to media globalization

Koichi Iwabuchi

This chapter explores the Japanese response to and involvement in media globalization. It identifies three processes by which Japanese cultural industries enter international markets – globalization, regionalization and localization. Globalization is evident in the popularity of animation and computer game software, the principal markets for which includes Western countries as well as Asian countires. And it is the Western reception that has made these recognized as global media products by Japanese media industries. If the circulation in the West is the requirement of the globalization of Japanese animation and computer game software, the boosting export of Japanese TV programs, particularly dramas, to Asian markets attests to the regionalization of Japanese popular culture. Although Japanese TV industries have been relatively passive in entering Asian markets, since the early 1990s the export of programs has been increasing with the active promotion by local cable and satellite TV industries in East and Southeast Asia. In those Asian markets, localization, which aims to tailor media products to local preferences, is also a key strategy of Japanese cultural industries. Japanese TV industries are trying to produce something new in conjunction with other Asian cultural industries through format trade and coproduction. Although different in terms of products, markets and strategies, I will suggest that all three patterns of Japanese involvement in transnationalizing processes of media culture – globalization, regionalization and localization – testify to an ever-increasing integration of global markets and transnational cooperation among world-wide media industries at various levels.

The return of Black Ship: opening the country

The development of communication technologies such as VCRs, cable TV and satellite TV, and the concurrent emergence of global media corporations in the late twentieth century, has brought about an unprecedented abundance of audiovisual space all over the globe. While the impact of media globalization has been discussed in relation to various locales, including Western countries, the high rate of economic growth and the emergence of a wealthy middle class in Asia has urged global media industries to enter the new market in the 1990s (e.g. Lee and Wang 1995; *Asiaweek* October 14, 1994). The pioneer was Star TV which started its operations in 1991. Fascinated with the size of the potential audience in the region, Western global players such as News Corp., CNN, BBC, MTV, ESPN, HBO and Disney followed Star TV's idea of pan-Asian mega-broadcasting. The emergence and proliferation of global media conglomerates prompted several Asian governments to react against the foreign (mostly American) invasion from the sky. For example, Malaysia, Singapore and China have advocated the protection of "Asian" values from decadent Western morals which are transmitted through the media. In those countries, the globalization of the media tends to be talked about in terms of the defending of a national cultural identity against Western cultural imperialism (concerning Asian governments' various responses to Star TV, see Chan, 1994).

The transnational flow of media has also had repercussions in Japanese broadcasting policy and media industries, but in a different way. As Japan is not only the second biggest TV market in the world but also the only self-sufficient market – where more than 95 percent of programs on Japanese TV are produced domestically – outside the United States, media globalization has not been talked about in the same way in Japan as in other Asian countries. It was Star TV that first had a significant impact on the amendment of Japanese policies of transnational broadcasting. When Star TV broadcasts first reached Japan in 1992, the Japanese government had a regulation of banning the distribution of the intercepted transnational broadcasts within Japanese territories for commercial purposes, although it did not prohibit people with their own satellite dishes for private purposes watching transnational broadcasts. Immediately after the Japanese government concluded in 1992 that the broadcasting of Star TV was not for deliberate commercial purposes but due to the spilling over of its airwaves across the Japanese territory, the government set about amending a transnational broadcast policy which had been based upon the self-contained domestic broadcast system and decided in April 1993 to deregulate the transnational satellite broadcasting service (Shimizu 1993)

Further impact on Japan by transnational satellite TV came from a global player, Rupert Murdoch. In June 1996, Murdoch announced his plan to launch JSkyB, stating that Japan was the last unexcavated gold mine in the world of satellite broadcasting. Just ten days later, his company, News Corp. – together with a Japanese computer software company, Softbank – bought about 20 percent of the shares of TV Asahi, one of the five key commercial TV stations in Japan. The threat posed by Murdoch to Japan was not that of transnational broadcasting, as with Star TV, but was rather the possibility of control of the Japanese media industry by foreign capital.[1] Responses from the Japanese media included some hysterical suggestions that Murdoch was trying to control a TV network in Japan, as he did with Fox in the United States, but the overall reaction was marked by a sober recognition that the time had come to restructure the highly domestic-oriented Japanese TV industry in the global satellite age. The then Prime Minister, Hashimoto Ryūtarō, commented that the current move towards liberalization of the Japanese industry made the influx of foreign capital inevitable and that the consequences of this depended on how the Japanese media industry responded to such challenges from overseas (*Nikkei Shinbun*, June 24, 1996). Behind this sober response lay a recognition that the Japanese media industry has inevitably been incorporated into the global media war. The two incidents made it clear that Japan could no longer enjoy a self-contained domestic market.

Japanese mass media have often compared the impact of transnational satellite broadcasting to the mid-nineteenth-century incident when the American Commodore Perry arrived with his fleet of Black Ships and forced Japan to open to the outside world after a two-century-long closed-door policy. Academics, media industries and journalists (e.g. Furuki and Higuchi 1996; Ryū 1996) frequently make the comparison, referring to *kurofune shūai* (the invasion of Black Ships), *kaikoku* (opening the country) and *sakoku* (closed country). The implication was that the Japanese TV market was once closed but is now under threat of being forced to open its doors to the world. The influx of foreign satellite TV such as Star TV and digital satellite services such as JSkyB brought about the proliferation of satellite TV channels in Japan, which inevitably increased the import of foreign TV programs to Japan. However, the influx of foreign media products does not seem to be posing a real threat to Japanese national identity. This is mainly because Japan has never closed its doors to foreign cultural goods such as TV programs, films and popular music since the Second World War. For example, it imports many films, particularly from the United States. In 1996, foreign films occupied 64 percent of total box office sales figures (*Yomiuri Shinbun*, August 31, 1997). As for the TV market, Japan is one of the few countries which has no quota on importing programs. Nevertheless, the Japanese TV market shifted from a high dependency on American programs in the 1960s to a high level of self-sufficiency in the 1970s. As early as 1980, Japan imported only 5 percent of total programs and this trend has continued (Kawatake and Hara 1994). The absence of a defensive discussion on the protection of national culture in Japan, in contrast with many other countries (e.g. France), is a testimony to the confidence held by the Japanese government as well as media industries that the influx of foreign programs into Japan would not have a great impact on the audience's preference for domestic programs (*Nikkei Entertainment*, April 28/May 5, 1993).

The global media industries' "opening the country" has thus dual implications for Japan: the expansion of Japanese media industries into global media markets and the influx of transnational media products and industries into the Japanese market. This time, unlike in the mid-nineteenth century, what is at stake seems less a foreign invasion of Japan than Japanese advance into global media markets and the enhancement of the competitiveness of Japanese TV software. The Star TV incident prompted the Japanese government and Japanese media industries to take the age of global communications seriously, but the main issue of deregulation was not about the reception of transnational broadcasts but about the dispatch of its broadcast to the world (Shimizu 1993). Similarly, the Murdoch shock urged the Japanese government and media industries to realize that in the age of global communications, Japanese cultural industries have to compete with various kinds of foreign software not only in the domestic market but also in international, particularly Asian, markets (e.g. Furuki and Higuchi 1996; Ryū 1996).

Japan goes global: animation and computer games

With the notable example of Sony, which is a global media giant, Japan is no doubt one of the main players in media globalization. However, it is often argued that Japanese cultural influence and presence in the world is secondary to its economic power. As Herman and McChesney (1998: 104) argue, "Japan is supplying capital and markets to the global media system, but little else." For example, a most conspicuous Japanese involvement with media globalization is the activity of Japanese trading companies such as Sumitomo and Itōchū, which invested in several American media giants (e.g. Sumitomo-TCI; Itōchū-Time Warner). What those Japanese companies are trying to do is to strengthen American cultural hegemony by investing in the production of Hollywood films and by facilitating the distribution of them all over the globe.

However, Japan is not only increasing its capital and market share in the audiovisual global markets but also its cultural presence on the global scene. It is animations and computer games that have attained a certain degree of popularity in the Western countries as well as in non-Western countries. Since Ōtomo Katuhiro's hugely popular animation film, *Akira* (1988), the quality and attraction of what is called "Japanimation" has been acknowledged by the American market. In November 1995, the animated film, *The Ghost in the Shell*, was shown simultaneously in Japan, America and Britain. Its video sales, according to *Billboard* (August 24, 1996), made it to No. 1 on the video chart in the United States. The export of Japanese animations and comics to the American market amounted to US $75 million in 1996 (*Sankei Shinbun*, December 14, 1998). Computer games are dominated by three Japanese manufacturers, Nintendo, Sega and Sony. The popularity of Japanese game software is exemplified by the fame of the Super Mario Brothers and Sonic. According to a survey, as a director of Nintendo pointed out, Mario was a better-known character among American children than Mickey Mouse (Akurosu Henshūshitsu, 1995: 41–2).

It is not just an accident that Japan has become a key player in the globalization of animation and computer games. These Japanese industries have always had overseas markets in mind. Since Tezuka Osamu's *Astro Boy* in the early 1960s,

Japanimation has long been consumed overseas. Japan routinely exports animation films. Animated films occupied 56 percent of TV exports from Japan in 1980–81 (Stronach, 1989) and 58 percent in 1992–93 (Kawatake and Hara, 1994). While other genres are mostly exported in the original Japanese language, only 1 percent of animated exports were in Japanese. This means that animation is routinely intended for export (Stronach, 1989: 144). The characters of computer games do not look Japanese because the producers and creators of game software are clearly conscious that the market is global (Akurosu Henshūshitsu, 1995). Mario, for example, does not invoke the image of Japan, because Mario, designed to be an "Italian" character, is not associated with the dominant image of Japan. Consumers and audiences of Japanese animation and game characters may know the Japanese origin of those commodities, but they have little "Japanese cultural odor" for the consumer (Iwabuchi, 1998a).

The popularity of Japanimation and computer games in the West in turn endorses the global appeal of those products in Japan itself. In the 1990s, Japanimation and computer games have attracted massive media attention in Japan, because they signify a new icon of Japanese global hegemony. There have been many articles in Japanese popular and academic magazines and daily newspapers which deal with the global popularity of animations and computer games. To just mention a few, "*Sekai wo seihasuru kokusan anime*" (Japan-made animation conquers the world) (*Hōsō Bunka*, October 1994); "*Nihon no manga ga sekai wo seifuku!?*" (Japanese Manga conquering the world!?) (*Elle Japon*, April 1996); "*Nihon Anime no sekai seifuku*" (Japanese animation conquers the world) (*Bart*, January 22, 1996); "*Manga ha sekai no kyōtsūgo*" (Manga becomes a world common language) (*Nihon Keizai Shinbun*, May 25, 1996). According to a conservative bi-weekly magazine, animations and computer games have become two of the few things that Japan can pride itself on (*Sapio*, June 11, 1997). All these articles boast of the global appeal of Japanese popular culture, but they actually deal with the popularity of Japanese animation and computer games principally in Western countries. In this sense, in Japan, the meaning of "global" is predominantly associated with the affluent Western market, especially the American market. As Hall (1991) argues, the West is positioned as the "dominant particular" in the global cultural flow. Making Japanese products "global" entirely depends upon their reception in Western markets.

Domestically, the most important factor in the 1990s which made Japan turn to the global popularity of animations and computer games was the recession in the Japanese economy. After the collapse of the so-called "bubble" economic expansion in the late 1980s, the Japanese economy has been suffering a long slump. This dark picture of the Japanese economic future makes the popularity of Japanimation overseas a positive contrast. Many saw a brighter future for Japan in its ability to produce universal digitalized software represented by Japanimation and computer games (e.g. *Dime*, February 7, 1991; *Nikkei Shinbun*, February 5, 1996; *Nikkei Trendy*, December 1998). For example, Sakaiya Taichi, who is an ex-bureaucrat of Ministry of International Trades and Industries and was appointed the director of Economic Planning Agency in 1998, argues that Japan should be proud of comics and animations as a global culture of Japanese origin. He sees the possibility of comics and animations breaking through the stratified Japanese social system by creating a new image of society in the age of the multimedia (*Nihon Keizai Shinbun*, February 25, 1996). Clearly, animations and comics are playing a significant role in the multimedia business. The characters of comics can be used in various other media such as computer games, movies, TV series, CD ROMs and toys. Kinder (1991) calls this multiple possibility of transmedia intertextuality a "supersystem of entertainment" which has come to be a dominant force in the global entertainment business. Japanese comics and animations would be the main features of a supersystem.

However, the euphoria concerning the dominant status of Japanese comics and animations in the supersystem is accompanied by a negative picture of its future. Precisely because they have become universally consumed, they are destined to be copied, studied and indigenized outside Japan. What is happening here is an "Americanization of Japanimation." In this respect, Japanese animations are often compared in the Japanese media to the *Ukiyoe*, premodern Japanese color prints of people's everyday life, whose beauty and values were appreciated as Japanesque by the West and had a significant impact on Western artists. It is often suggested that animation faces the same dilemma as *Ukiyoe*, many of which were taken out from Japan and exhibited in Western art galleries since the mid-nineteenth century; that the West (America) again deprives Japan of animations while Japan fails to recognize their (commercial) value (e.g. *Dime*, October 6, 1994; *Bart*, January 22, 1996; *Nikkei Trendy*, October 1996). Thus, Hollywood is trying to develop a new global genre by making use of Japanese animations. American film producers and directors are recruiting Japanese animators to develop American animations and computer graphics (*Aera*, July 29, 1996; *Nikkei Shinbun*, January 5, 1997; June 9, 1997). American production companies with the help of Japanese animators began producing Japanimation in the United States (Ōhata, 1996; *Nikkei Trendy*, October 1996). Also the South Korean government has decided to support the promotion of the local animation industry for the future development of the national economy. A Korean conglomerate has entered the animation business by investing into domestic as well as Japanese animation industries (*Nikkei Shinbun* 3 September 1996; *Aera*, 29 July 1996).

In contrast, although the potential of the animation industry for the Japanese economy has been recognized, it has not yet led to the encouragement of and investment in the industry in Japan (Takemura, 1996: 72–105). The Japanese government is a target of criticism for its failure to promote Japan's most lucrative cultural software industry in the digitalized world (e.g. *Dime*, June 2, 1997). Oshii Mamoru, the director of *The Ghost in the Shell*, lamented the lack of support for the development of the animation industry in Japan, and predicted the decay of the industry in the near future (*Nikkei Entertainment*, May 1997). Responding to criticism, the Agency for Cultural Affairs belatedly decided to support multimedia software contents in 1997 and held a Media Art Festival in Tokyo in February 1998. Its purpose was to encourage the domestic production of animation, comics, computer graphics and computer game software. The Agency for Cultural Affairs also decided to set about exterminating the piracy of Japanese software in Asia (*Asahi Shinbun*, 22 January 1998). Animations and digitalized software have become an officially recognized Japanese culture.

However, it should be stressed here that it is Western (American) money and the global distribution power that have made Japanese animation a global popular culture. For example, it was the investment and the distribution channels of a British and American company, Manga Entertainment – established in 1991 under the conglomerate of Polygram, then a major recording company – that made *The Ghost in the Shell* a hit in Western countries. Similarly, in 1996, Disney decided to distribute Miyazaki Hayao's animated films globally. With the help of the global prestige of Disney, Miyazaki's latest animation, *Mononokehime*, became a phenomenal hit in Japan in 1997. Its box office revenue went beyond the until then record figure of *E.T.* for the first time in Japan and exceeded 10 billion yen (*Nikkei Shinbun*, November 29, 1997). The production cost was 2.3 billion yen and more than 2 billion yen was spent on publicity in Japan (*Nikkei Shinbun*, June 9, 1997). The exceptional box-office hit of *Mononokehime* was realized thanks to a business tie-up with Disney. As the producer of the film acknowledged, the fact that Miyazaki's animations are highly appreciated by the global animation giant, Disney, worked well as the publicity for giving the film an international prominence (*Nikkei Entertainment*, January 1998: 42). The director of *The Ghost in the Shell*, who is now producing a new animation film, plainly stated that he takes Western markets into consideration (*Nikkei Shinbun*, January 16, 1998). The budget for the film was 2.3 billion yen. The director of *Akira*, which attracted the attention of Western audiences to Japanese animation in the late 1980s, is also producing a new film with a budget of 1.6 billion yen. As is the case with Hollywood, Japanese animation is now becoming a big, though risky, business by taking global distribution into consideration at the production stage. These cases clearly suggest that Japanese animation's inroad into the global market is closely related to the ever-growing global integration of markets and the media industries. The Japanese animation industry is able to become a global player only by exploiting the power of Western media insustries.

Japan goes to Asia: export of TV programs to cultural neighbors

Secondly, what has also become conspicuous in the 1990s is the export of Japanese TV programs to booming Asian markets. While what Japan can export to Western countries is still limited to animations and computer games, much broader selections of Japanese TV programs and popular music are increasing their presence in East and Southeast Asian markets. The popularity of Japanese TV programs in other parts of Asia suggests that media globalization also activates the intra-regional flow of cultural commodities (Straubhaar, 1991; Sinclair *et al.*, 1996). Although the textual appeal of Japanese TV programs to Asian audiences is a significant factor in the prevalence of Japanese TV programs in Asian markets (Iwabuchi, forthcoming), I argue, the promotion by "local" industries is a significant factor which facilitated the diffusion of Japanese TV programs in Asian markets. And it is this local initiative that have given Japanese TV industries more confidence in the exportability of Japanese TV programs.

Although the possible impact of the recent financial crisis in Asia on the media markets is yet to be seen, Asian markets have become the hottest battlefield for global media corporations in the 1990s. About three billion people live in a region which achieved high economic growth and where the states are increasingly privatizing the media and communication industries. The huge potential of the Asian market is likely to attract entrepreneurs from all over the world. Since the emergence of Star TV, as mentioned earlier, there have been discussions about the Japanese role in the booming Asian markets, but Japanese media industries have not been as keen as Western and other Asian counterparts in exporting their products to the booming Asian audiovisual market. Until 1993, Japan has not had any intention of expanding its satellite broadcasting services outside the country. The reluctance of the Japanese media industries to export their products partly reflects the historical obstacle of Japanese imperialism as well as the existence of a profitable and wealthy domestic market. After its defeat in the Second World War, the Japanese government has tried not to face its imperialist past in Asia. With the help of the American Cold War policy which utilized Japan as a model capitalist country to counter communism in Asia, Japan suppressed its past by camouflaging itself with an image of a weak victim of the war defeated by the United States and successfully eschewed confronting its colonial history. The suppression of a Japanese cultural visibility is a desirable strategy for enabling the Japanese economy to expand to Asia. Kawatake (1995), for example, found that many Japanese companies wanted to remove apparent "Japaneseness" from their advertising material in Asian markets. It was thought that a Japanese appearance in Asia should be avoided as much as possible in order to pursue further profits.

When the Japanese government amended its policy on transnational satellite broadcasting in 1994, NHK quickly announced the launch of a satellite service to Europe, but still hesitated to broadcast to Asia (*Nikkei Shinbun*, July 14, 1994; *Asahi Shinbun*, September 7, 1994). The main reason was fear of being accused of cultural imperialism. It was an Asia Broadcasting Unity (ABU) meeting which was held in Kyoto in November 1994 that dispersed the anxiety regarding criticism of cultural imperialism. What the Japanese media industries realized during the meeting was a sudden shift in other Asian countries' policies from protection to promotion of local industries to counter Western "cultural invasion" (see Wang, 1996). This change finally convinced NHK to launch its service in Asia as well, but a Japanese scholar still lamented that what the ABU meeting told us was that Japan had fallen far behind Asian countries as well as the West in terms of the development of transnational broadcasting (*Nikkei Shinbun*, November 26, 1994). Many industry people and journalists pointed out the belatedness of the Japanese TV industries to enter the Asian markets, arguing that Asian markets have already been dominated by American and local industries and that there is no space for the Japanese TV industries (e.g. Shima, 1994; Asai, 1997; *Nikkei Shinbun*, November 26, 1994).

There are two economic and structural reasons why Japanese TV industries are not very active about the promotion of the export of Japanese TV programs to Asia. The first is the difficulty in making profits in Asian markets. American industries quickly entered Asian markets, because this was just an extension of their existing global businesses. Including Star TV, almost all the satellite and cable channel suppliers cannot make profits in Asia, but the deficiency is compensated for by profits in the affluent Western market. However, Japan, without entering the Western markets, would not be able to make profits in Asia until the price of TV programs becomes as high as the Western counterparts. According to a survey by the Ministry of Posts and Telecommunication, the total hours of program imports in 1992 was 6,800 hours, worth 481.2 billion yen. As for exports, the figures are 16,471 hours, valued at 2.1 billion yen (Nakazora, 1994). As for the unit price of programs per hour, import is 7 million yen but export is just 127 thousand yen, almost fifty-five times. The average budget of a one-hour drama production in Japan is about 30–40 million yen, but the same drama can be sold for only 200,000– 400,000 yen in Asia.

The second reason is copyright and royalties. In Japan, the production of TV programs has been for the domestic market and there have been no incentives to develop copyright contracts for second and third broadcasts. Since the early 1990s, as Japanese TV programs were increasingly exported to Asia, Japanese TV stations have come to realize that copyright issues are an obstacle to selling their programs overseas. To sell a drama overseas, for example, Japanese TV stations have to get permission from the cast and music composer of each series. Therefore it takes at least six months to clarify all the copyright issues for the second broadcast. Some talent management offices demand fees, which are more expensive than the TV stations can afford. For this reason, Fuji TV for example cannot sell even one-third of the twelve drama series it produces annually.

In the 1990s, according to my interviews with the Japanese TV industries, the wholesale figures of programs in Asian markets has become three times higher than before, but it still occupies much less than one percent of the total sales figures of a TV station.[2] Given the low price of the programs, the cost of copying and packaging, and the extremely small proportion in the total profits of the station, it is no surprise that Japanese TV stations have not been active in exporting their programs to Asian markets

In addition to these economic and structural obstacles, Japanese cultural industries have tended to be pessimistic about the competitiveness of Japanese TV programs and popular music in Asian markets. It was speculated in Japan that Japanese TV programs other than animation would not attract Asian audiences due to Japanese cultural and language uniqueness (*Nikkei Shinbun*, November 26, 1994). The pessimistic view has also something to do with the prediction held by Japanese cultural industries of the quick development of local industries in East and Southeast Asia. In 1994, Dentsu, the biggest advertising agency in Japan, organized a committee to promote the export of Japanese audiovisual products and submitted a report to the Ministry of International Trade and Industry. The report clearly saw the good possibility of Japanese products being further accepted into Asian markets and suggested the necessity of developing more export-oriented production systems, including market research and language dubbing, to expand export. However, many members of the committee also pointed out the likelihood of Japanese cultural products soon being superseded by local ones. This view corresponds with my own research. In November 1994, I interviewed more than twenty cultural producers in Japan concerning the popularity of Japanese products in Asia. Interestingly, almost every producer thought that the popularity of Japanese products in Asian markets, if any, would be transient and the markets would be sooner or later dominated by local products. I will return to this point later.

Despite the pessimism about the competitiveness of Japanese software and the relatively passive attitude of the Japanese TV industries in entering Asian markets, the export of Japanese TV programs has been increasing in the 1990s. The total export hours of TV programs increased from 2,200 in 1971 to 4,585 in 1980 to 19,546 in 1992 (Kawatake, 1994). The proliferation of media space in Asia has dramatically increased the demand for Japanese programs. However, it is important to note here that the promotion of Japanese TV programs was facilitated mainly by local industries rather than by active promotion by Japanese media industries. Star TV has from the beginning constantly broadcast Japanese TV programs, particularly dramas, in prime time. A manager of the Star TV Chinese Channel told me that Japanese programs are indispensable for Star TV's strategy of localization in Asia.[3]

The local promotion of Japanese TV programs is best exemplified in Taiwan, where there are five cable channels which broadcast Japanese programs exclusively. Apart from NHK Asia, which simultaneously broadcasts most programs from Japan by satellite, four other channels – Video Land Japanese, Gold Sun, Po-shin Japanese and JET (Japan Entertainment Network) – buy whole programs from Japanese commercial television stations. These channels broadcast exclusively Japanese programs twenty-four hours a day (repeating the basic programming of six to ten hours a day). In addition, other cable and free-to-air channels also regularly broadcast Japanese programs. The number of Japanese TV programs exported to Taiwan has drastically increased since 1994. In 1992 the total amount exported from Japan to Taiwan was about 600 hours (Kawatake and Hara, 1994). There are no exact figures available for Japanese program export to Taiwan after 1993. However, in 1996, one Japanese commercial TV station, TBS, alone exported 1,000 hours of programs to Taiwan

The popularity of Japanese TV programs in Asia has given Japanese media industries more confidence in exporting their programs to Asian markets. In 1997, Sumitomo Trading Co. Ltd launched the first Japanese pay-TV channel, JET (Japan Entertainment Television) with TBS, a commercial TV station whose profits from selling programs overseas are the highest in Japan. JET plans to supply seven

Asian countries (Taiwan, Hong Kong, Thailand, Singapore, Malaysia, Indonesia and Philippines) with one channel exclusively devoted to Japanese dramas, variety shows and cartoons by satellite up-link from Singapore. Taiwan is the most important market and the company started operation there in January, several months before other markets. JET dubs Japanese into three languages – English, Mandarin and Thai – but, significantly, only the Taiwan version is subtitled to meet Taiwanese viewers' taste. Since JET covers eight different markets, the advertisements are not about particular commodities but about general images of companies and products like Star TV. Taiwan JET inserts local advertisements. In 1997, the expected audience number reached was 3.5 million in Taiwan (JET), 350,000 in Hong Kong (Warf Cable), 50,000 in Thailand (UTB) and 120,000 in the Philippines (Sun Cable). JET will also start operation in Malaysia (Mea Sat) and Singapore (Cablevision) soon. It is estimated that JET has reached an audience of more than four million in Asia.

A manager of Dentsu, who expressed a pessimistic view of the long-term popularity of Japanese TV programs in Asian markets in an interview with me in 1994, changed his view when I met him again in January 1997: "What has been made clear is that Japanese TV programs have gained a certain universal appeal. The next step is to produce programs whwhich target international, particularly Asian markets."

Endorsing this shift, Japanese TV industries are increasingly becoming seriously engaged in setting up a principle of royalties for the second and third use of programs as well as in controlling piracy. In September 1998, Japanese TV industry for the first time made a raid on Sino Center in Hong Kong which is (in)famous for pirated VCDs (Video CDs) of Japanese animations and TV dramas with the help of the Hong Kong Customs (*South China Morning Post,* September 11, 1998). What has become clear to the Japanese media industries is that Japanese TV programs have huge market potentials in Asian markets, thanks to the promotion of other Asian media industries.

Localization as hybridization

Apart from government regulation policies, one of the difficulties which transnational cultural industries have faced in entering Asian markets is the diversity of culture, religion, language and race in the region. Combined with such culturally diversity, audience preference for "local" TV programs (Straubhaar, 1991) has proven to be a significant obstacle in exporting TV programs for Japanese as well as Western media industries, as some countries such as Hong Kong and India have long-established and powerful cultural industries whose products have won the hearts of their people. As expressed in the cover story of *Asian Business* (October 1996): "The battle for a share of Asia's huge television audience is in full swing, with international broadcasters pouring in vast amounts of cash. But it's the players who provide local programming content that look likely to succeed." It is precisely these issues that Star TV is struggling with. By overestimating the omnipotence of

American cultural products, Star TV mistook the centralization of distribution for centralization of transmission and neglected the existence of multiple "locals." The lesson Star TV has learned is that exporting English-language programs produced in Hollywood is no longer enough. As Rupert Murdoch said, "We've committed ourselves to learning the nuance of the region's diverse cultures" (*Asian Business Review,* May 1994). Rather than pursuing the old-fashioned "communication as transmission view" of broadcasting pan-Asian programs in one language, the strategy of Star TV is changing to one of localizing programs by finding local partners which assure them of local programs. (*Far Eastern Economic Review,* January 27, 1994). Coupled with highly political reasons, Star TV replaced BBC World News and the American MTV with more Chinese-sensitive drama and music programs (*The Australian,* May 11, 1994). MTV Asia also struck back with much more localized programming.

Similarly, Japanese media industries acknowledged the significance of producing local products and have tried to penetrate the booming Asian markets through a localization strategy in the 1990s, but differently from Western and other Asian local industries. Clearly indicated in the above-mentioned report of the Dentsu-organized committee, Japanese cultural industries were not as keen to export Japanese products as to be somehow involved in the production of "local" products in various Asian markets as a long-term strategy. Japanese cultural industries had a conviction that "foreign popular culture such as TV programs and popular music will be soon superseded by domestically produced ones, as local cultural industries develop their production capacity by absorbing foreign influence," as the organizer of the committee told me in an interview. I argued elsewhere (Iwabuchi, 1998b) that Japan prides itself on most successfully hybridizing and indigenizing Western cultures. With this confidence in their experience of negotiating Western (American) popular culture, the Japanese cultural industries are trying to fuse things global (American) and local in Asian markets. As the director of Epic Sony told me in an interview:

> Japaneseness of Japanese popular cultural production can be found in its capacity for cultural mixing which makes the original source irrelevant. I think we are good at appropriating best parts from American popular music and reconstructing our own music. ...In the same vein, if we produce something stunning, trendy and newly stylish in local languages by local singers, I am sure that it can sell in Asian markets. The basic model [of the stunning style] is American popular culture.

While Japanese cultural industries have been somewhat unsure about the exportability of distinctively Japanese products, they are confident that other Asian countries will follow the same path as Japan in terms of a rapid indigenization of foreign (American) popular culture. If the ascent of Japanese TV programs in Asian markets is based upon the "localization" strategies of local cable and satellite channels, the localization strategy that Japanese cultural industries have tried to deploy in Asian markets is thus the export of Japan's know-how for producing "local" popular culture through the indigenization of American cultural influence (Iwabuchi, 1998a).

While the Japanese recording companies and talent agencies have actively held auditions in various Asian countries to find local pop stars in the 1990s (see Iwabuchi, 1995), the Japanese TV industry has also begun to promote "concept trade" (*Asahi Shinbun*, September 10, 1993). This means that Japan sells program concepts rather than the programs themselves to other countries, and thus includes the sale of video materials which hardly contain any Japanese "odour." Although it is a common business of TV industry in many parts of the world, the concept trade or format sales has been actively promoted by Dentsu since early 1990s. Like Hong Kong's TVB, Dentsu sells the program concepts of chat shows and game shows which have been well-accepted in Japan, together with the video material, the supervision of production and Japanese sponsors to Asian TV stations (*Far Eastern Economic Review*, June 16, 1994). All local TV stations have to do is to provide local celebrities and audiences, and to learn the know-how of TV production from Japanese producers. For example, NTV, a commercial TV station in Japan, sold the format and visual material of the quiz show, *Show-by Show-by*, to Spain, Italy, Thailand and Hong Kong. The original of *America's Funniest Video Show* can also be found in TBS's variety show. The merit of concept trade for Japanese TV industry is that it can be sold to affluent Western markets. It is also advantageous in that if American production houses sell *Funniest Video Show*, for example, to another TV station, a Japanese TV station still receives another royalty.

Another move is coproduction. Fuji television is now jointly producing a TV program with Singapore, Malaysia, Indonesia, and South Korea (Taiwan joined in 1994 after the Taiwanese government abolished its policy of banning the broadcasting of Japanese-language programs, but left the program due to its predominantly Southeast Asian flavor). The title of the program is *Asia Bagus!*, which means "Asia is terrific!" in Malay/Indonesian. Each week, four amateur singers from five countries compete with one another. The grand champion is assured of making his/her/their debut as a professional act. The program has two presenters, a Japanese woman and a Malay-Singaporean man. Both presenters speak English and in addition each speaks, respectively, Japanese and Malay/Indonesian. And a Korean translator occasionally appears.

This program has been broadcast in each country since April 1992; in Singapore, on TCS 5, in Malaysia, on TV3 (NTV9 from 1997), and in Indonesia, on TVRI (TVRI quit the program in 1995 because the Indonesian Government does not like to broadcast Mandarin, but in 1996, a private TV station, RTCI, joined the program). While it is scheduled at midnight in Japan, most of the other countries broadcast *Asia Bagus!* in prime time – TCS 5 and TV3, for example, broadcast it at 7.30 pm on Sunday night which is a most significant time for TV programming – and it has been popular in terms of ratings (*Yomiuri Shinbun*, October 27, 1994; *Mainichi Shinbun*, December 8, 1994). Although *Asia Bagus!* is directed and produced mainly by Japanese staff, the program is produced in close cooperation with the local TV industries and filmed in Singapore, in order to make the program "Asian." In my field research in Singapore, most studio audiences replied to my questionnaire that they did not think it was a program produced by Japan and that the attractiveness of the program has much to do with its "Asian" flavor which cannot be reduced to a single country.

In 1997, NTV, another popular commercial TV station in Japan, also started coproducing an information program, *Chō Ajiaryū* (Super Asians), with Hong Kong (TVB), Taiwan (CTV), South Korea (SBS), Thailand (ITV) and Singapore (TCS8). NTV started a variety show which dealt with Asia-related topics in 1996 with the production cooperation of CTV, TCS8 and ITV, but developed the idea of coproduction further. What is interesting is that all the TV stations do not broadcast the same program. SBS, ITV and TCS8 used some of the film coverage as a component of an information program. Only CTV broadcasts the same program with subtitles as NTV. Each week, there is a main topic, such as fashion or karaoke, and each station covers the topic locally. Actually this difference itself has become a main topic of the program.

It should be remembered that both *Asia Bagus!* and *Chō Ajiaryū* are programed at midnight in Japan; 2.30 am and 1.15 am respectively. This means that the programs are not for Japanese consumption but for other Asian markets. It is also important to note that NTV and Fuji TV do not make a profit by producing the programs. Neither sell the programs nor the concepts. The main reason for coproduction is to establish a corporational tie and to experiment with coproduction. NTV's main purpose is to promote what they call "syndication," with NTV selling the commercial time for Japanese sponsors in several Asian countries by coproducing a program.

One production house, Amuse, actively promotes coproduction of films in East Asia. Amuse coproduced with Shanghai TV a drama series (twenty-five episodes of a one-hour program), *Shanghai People in Tokyo*, in 1995. The drama is about the lives of overseas students from Shanghai in Tokyo. It is another version of *Beijing People in New York*, which became phenomenally popular in China in 1992. The director and the protagonist are both Chinese, but Amuse provided the production budget of 400 million yen (*Nikkei Shinbun*, January 12, 1996). The program was finally broadcast in China in 1995 and 1996 and got high ratings (*Asahi Shinbun*, evening edition, February 24, 1996). It was also broadcast in Japan in 1997, but it was scheduled at midnight and never attracted a wide audience. Amuse also sold commercial time to various sponsors including South Korean and Chinese companies, but allegedly could not cover the production costs. The main purpose was, like NTV and Fuji TV, to establish a relationship with Chinese TV industries and to learn the system of Chinese production and the know-how of selling programs and commercial times in China. Amuse is also very active in coproducing films with Hong Kong production houses. Since 1994, it has coproduced several films such as *Nankin no Kirisuto, Hong Kong Daiyasōkai, Kitchen*. In 1997 Amuse finally established a joint production house, Golden Amuse, with Goldenharvest Entertainment in Hong Kong to produce a string of love stories (*Nikkei Shinbun*, December 11, 1997).

Japanese strategies of localization in Asia reflects a widely observed tendency that the global distribution of the same commodities and media texts does not bring about cultural homogenization but generates a new cultural diversity, through the process of hybridization/creolization or localization/indigenization (e.g. Appadurai, 1996; Hannerz, 1996). In contrast to a globalization-as-homogenization thesis, a hybridization thesis is concerned more with the site of local negotiation with the global. It elucidates how foreign goods and texts are creatively cross-fertilized, indigenized and differently translated according to local contexts. As seen in the Japanese strategies of format trade and coproduction, Japanese media industries, together with local cultural producers, are attempting to produce something new in modern, urbanized Asian nations. In other words, I suggest that it is the process of local indigenization rather than the product *per se* that the Japanese media industries attempt to exploit in conjunction with other Asian media industries through localization strategies.

Global-regional-local: an interconnected triangle

John Tomlinson (1997) points out three reasons why we should reframe the issues posed by the "cultural imperialism" thesis with the globalization theory perspective. They are the question of the impact and the ubiquity of Western cultural products in the world; the dialectic nexus between global and local in terms of ongoing cultural hybridization; and the de-centring process of Western cultural domination. The ascent of Japanese media industries in the process of media globalization seems to be a testimony to the three – the increasing flow of Japanese TV programs in other Asian markets refutes the unambiguous power of Western cultural products in the world; the localization strategies of Japanese cultural industries is grounded in the global-local dynamics; and finally the global circulation of Japanese animations and the involvement of Japanese corporations in global media conglomerates shows the diffusion of cultural power. The activities of Japanese media industries at three levels – global, regional, local – suggest the complex and de-centring processes of cultural globalization, but it also shows that such processes themselves are coming to be at the mercy of the strategies and activities of trans-national media industries.

The analysis of the involvement of Japanese cultural industries in global, regional and local markets testifies to the increasing integration and cooperation among world-wide cultural industries. As Pieterse argues: "What globalization means in structural terms, then, is the *increase in the available modes of organization*: transnational, international, macro-regional, national, micro-regional, municipal, local (1995: 50, emphasis original).

At each level of the market, Japanese cultural industries and Japanese media products cannot operate effectively without partners. Morley and Robins point out three patterns of activities for global media corporations: producing cultural products; distributing products; and owning hardware which delivers products (1995: 13). Global media corporations try to combine at least two of the above three, particularly production and distribution. American media industries have no doubt unambiguous global hegemony with the latter two. As the recent buy-out of Hollywood studios – for example, Fox by Rupert Murdoch and Columbia by Sony – shows, the fundamental factor for the success of global media corporations in global media markets is securing good products. The serious shortcoming of the Japanese TV industries which have mature production capabilities and techniques is the lack of international distribution channels. As we saw in this chapter, it is American and other Asian media industries that act as distributors of Japanese programs.

Although the products and strategies corresponding to each of the three levels differ, the same player often runs through these levels. Japanese animations cannot be distributed globally without the support of American media giants. The latter, for their part, need Japanese animations to advance out to every corner of the globe. This is not just to exploit a new genre and product for the global market, but also to enter Asian markets where Japanese comics and animations have been most consumed. It is said that the ultimate purpose of Disney's distribution of Miyazaki's animations is to acquire the know-how of Miyazaki's production technique and "Asian" flavor (*Aera*, August 4, 1997). It is also speculated that the real intention of Murdoch's entry into the Japanese market is to secure attractive programs for the Asian market (Ryū, 1996; Inoue, 1996).

Even intra-regional coproduction in Asia cannot escape the shadow of the global corporations. In concept trade, for example, *Oshin*, a globally popular Japanese melodrama series, is now being re-made in Indonesia through the Australian production house, Beckers Group, which exports TV programs globally. A most powerful music producer, Tetsuya Komuro, is now trying to debut several Chinese, Hong Kong and Taiwanese pop singers in the American market. This movement from local (Asia) to global (the West) is forged by his joint venture with News Corp., TK NEWS. TK NEWS has produced a star search TV program, *TK Magic*, for the Taiwan market alone and established a new record label, rojam com, from Sony Music Entertainment, for the American market.

Conceiving the global as an aggregation of multiple locals, which are mostly equated with national markets, transnational corporations desparately attempt to maximize the number of local markets that they penetrate. As the merger and the cooperation of transnational corporations of different countries of origin intensifies, various markets are increasingly united and interrelated. The development of communication technologies also contributes to the simultaneous spread of information and images of a new product around the world. The speed and the quantity of transnational distribution of cultural commodities has been rapidly accelerating. The recent instantaneous spread, and the quick dying down of the popularity, of Spice Girls and Tamagocchi in the world testifies to this trend. The proliferation of media space and the recognition of the significance of producing "local" products encourages media industries to appreciate the many kinds of media products, including those of non-Western countries, for various levels of markets. This clearly articulates the gradual de-centralization of Western cultural hegemony. However, the rise of non-Western transnational media corporations in the global arena has not so much countered long-standing West-centric power relations as coopted it by joining the alliance. De-centralization of Western cultural hegemony is accompanied by the re-centralization of the still West-dominated cooperative transnational media system, which interpenetrates the global, regional and local markets.

Notes

1 It soon became clear, however, that Murdoch's intention was not to control a free-to-air TV station in Japan when he suddenly decided in March 1997 to sell the shares of TV Asahi to its parent company, Asahi Shinbun. Murdoch had concluded that the acquisition of shares in a particular Japanese TV station deterred other stations from cooperating with JSkyB and thus would do more harm than good in securing good Japanese programs. Murdoch's decision was to the point. Two months after Murdoch's selling of TV Asahi shares, the most popular TV station, Fuji TV, and Sony, which owns Columbia, decided to join JSkyB

2 For example, the business earning of Nippon Television Network in the 1997 financial year was 283 billion yen. However, according to my interview with the station, the international sales earning was less than 1 billion yen.

3 It should be noted that this strategy was deployed by Star TV from 1992, well before Murdoch's takeover and the beginning of his localizing strategy.

References

Akurosu Henshūshitu. (1995). *Sekai Shōhin no Tsukurikata: Nihon Media ga Sekai wo Sēshita Hi. (The making of world products: The day when Japanese media conquer the world)*. Tokyo: Parco Shuppan.

Appadurai, A. (1996). *Modernity at Large: Cultural Dimensions of Globalization*. Minneapolis: University of Minnesota Press.

Asai, M. (1997). "Ajia Ēsei Hōsōshijō ni Deokureta Nihon" (Japan's belated entry into Asian satellite markets). *Shinbun Kenkyū*, 551, 67–70.

Chan, J.M. (1994). "National responses and accessibility to Star TV in Asia." *Journal of Communication*, 44(3), 112–31.

Furuki, M and Higuchi, M. (1996). "Ēsei Kurofune no Shūrai de Nemutteirarenakunatta Terebikyoku" (Satellite Black Ships have awakened Japanese TV stations). *Hōsōbunka*, July, 56–71.

Hall, S. (1991). "The local and the global: Globalization and ethnicity." In A. King. (Ed.). *Culture, Globalization, and the World-System*, 19–39. London: Macmillan.

Hannerz, U. (1996). *Transnational Connections: Culture, People, Places*. London: Routledge.

Herman, E. and McChesney, R. (1998). *The Global Media: The New Missionaries of Global Capitalism*. London: Cassell.

Inoue, H. (1996). "Ēsei Jidai no Ajia to Nihon no Hōsō" (Satellite broadcasting in Asia and Japan). *Minpō*, October, 4–7.

Iwabuchi, K. (1995). "Return to Asia? Japan in the global audiovisual market." *Media Internatinal Australia*, 77 August, 94–106.

Iwabuchi, K. (1998a). "Marketing 'Japan': Japanese cultural presence under a global gaze." *Japanese Studies*, 18(2), 165–80.

Iwabuchi, K. (1998b) "Pure impurity: Japan's genius for hybridism." *Communal/Plural: Journal of Transnational and Crosscultural Studies*, 6(1), 71–85.

Iwabuchi, K. (forthcoming). "Becoming culturally proximate: A/scent of Japanese idol dramas in Taiwan." In B. Moeran. (Ed.), *Asian Media Worlds*. London: Curzon.

Kawatake, K. (1994). "Nihon wo chūshin to suru terebijouhou furō no genjō to mondaiten" (The current issues on the flow of information through television: A Japaese perspective). *Jōhōtsūshin Gakkaishi*, 12(1), 54–63.

Kawatake, K. (1995). "Ajia Kyōtsū no Terebibunka Kōchiku ni mukete" (Toward the construction of the common TV culture of Asia). *Kōkoku*, 310, May–June, 20–4.

Kawatake, K. and Hara, Y. (1994). "Nihon wo Chuushin to suru Terebi Bangumi no Ryutsu Jyokyo" (The Intenational flow of TV programs from and into Japan). *Hoso Kenkyu to Chousa*, November, 2–17.

Kinder, M. (1991). *Playing with Power in Movies, Television and Video Games*. Berkeley: University of California Press.

Lee, P.S.N. and Wang, G. (1995). "Satellite TV in Asia: Forming a new ecology." *Telecommunications Policy*, 19(2), 135–49.

Morley, D. and Robins, K. (1995). *Spaces of Identities: Global Media, Electronic Landscapes and Cultural Boundaries*. London: Routledge.

Nakazora, M. (1994). "Hōsōbangumi Sofuto no Kokusai Ryūtsū Jōkyō" (The current situation of international flow of TV programs). *Jōhōtsūshin Gakkaishishi*, 12(8), 48–53.

Ōhata, K. (1996). "Animerika he no Shoutai" (An invitation to the world of American animations). *Yuriika*, August, 88–94.

Pieterse, J.N. (1995). "Globalization as hybridization." In M. Fetherstone, S. Lash and R. Robertson (Eds), *Global Modernities*, 45–68. London: Sage.

Ryū, M. (1996). "Hōsōkai Kiro ni Tatsu" (Japanese media industries stand on the crossroads). *Hōsōhihyō*, September, 28–33.

Shima, K. (1994). "Mohaya Ajia ha Teokureda" (It's too late to enter the Asian media markets). *Hōsōhihyō*, 300, July, 28–33.

Shimizu, S. (1993). "The implication of transborder television for national cultures and broadcasting: A Japanese perspective." *Media Asia*, 20(4), 187–93.

Sinclair, J., Jacka, E. and Cunningham, S. (1996). *New Patterns in Global Television; Peripheral Vision*. Oxford: Oxford University Press.

Straubhaar, J. (1991). "Beyond media imperialism: Asymmetrical interdependence and cultural proximity." *Critical Studies in Mass Communication*, 8(1), 39–59.

Stronach, B. (1989). "Japanese television." In R. Powers and H. Kato (Eds), *Handbook of Japanese Popular Culture*, 127–65. Westport: Greenwood Press.

Takemura, M. (1996). *Dejitaru Japanesuku* (Digital Japanesque). Tokyo: NTT Shuppan.

Tomlinson, J. (1997). "Cultural globalization and cultural imperialism." In A. Mohammadi (Ed.), *International Communication and Globalization: A Critical Introduction*, 170–90. London: Sage.

Wang, G. (1996). "Beyond media globalization: A look at cultural integrity from a policy perspective." Paper presented to the seminar on (Tele)communications Policies in Western Europe and South-East Asia, Bruges, Belgium. August 29–September 1.

9

EXPORT OF CULTURE OR COPRODUCTION OF CULTURE?

Vignettes from the creative process at a global advertising affiliate, Beijing

Jian Wang

The world's leading corporations have become "stateless," and advertising agencies have also followed their footsteps to business frontiers around the world. As Armand Mattelart (1991: ix) has put it, "[t]he question of advertising has long ceased to be a national question..."

In 1960, only 17 percent of the ten largest US ad agencies' total worldwide billings were generated from overseas markets; but by 1989 their overseas billings had risen to 54 percent (Kim, 1995: 209). The overseas share in the worldwide income of the top 500 US-based advertising agencies grew from less than 25 percent (US$2.15 billion) in 1986 to more than 40 percent (US$7.15 billion) in 1995 (*Advertising Age*, April 1995: s15). The advertising agency Young & Rubicam, for instance, has established a global network of more than 300 offices, spanning from Africa and Asia to Europe and the Americas. Grey Advertising, founded in New York City in 1917 and still headquartered there, now operates in over fifty countries.

The entry strategy of Western multinational advertising agencies in various parts of the world has taken three basic forms (Kaynak, 1989: 178–9). In an "associate" arrangement, the parent company is loosely or tightly connected to a local advertising agency but has no official equity. For an "affiliate," the parent company has substantial but not 100-percent control of the overseas agency. A "brand agency" is a local office or subsidiary of the parent company. Almost all of the major multinational advertising agencies are now present in the world's largest potential consumer market: China. Since the Chinese government still does not allow wholly foreign-owned advertising businesses inside the country, many multinational advertising agencies have adopted the strategy of establishing an affiliate by forming a joint venture with a local Chinese agency while retaining majority equity share and management control in the new entity.

In the early 1980s, when China had just reopened its market to outside investment, the global advertising industry viewed the Chinese market with "guarded optimism" (Seligman, 1984: 17). But such a cautious approach has since given way to expressed confidence in the bright prospects of the Chinese consumer market. There were, for instance, only four sino-foreign joint-venture advertising agencies in 1990, and by 1997 the number of international advertising agencies in China had reached about 250 (*Modern Advertising*, 1, 1997: 15). Among the top ten advertising agencies in China in 1995, four were joint-venture agencies (Saatchi & Saatchi, Ogilvy & Mather, Densu and McCann & Erickson) (*China Advertising Yearbook*, 1996: 33), and in that same year, multinational advertising grew much faster than the domestic advertising sector (172.2 percent versus 51.7 percent) (*International Advertising*, September 1997: 14).

Along with the Western/American entertainment establishment, multinational advertising has also been in the spotlight of the media imperialism debate. It has in fact been criticized as a venture of Western media imperialism. Herbert Schiller (1972) called the internationalization of advertising an act of "Madison Avenue imperialism," and Michael Anderson (1984) simply termed it "advertising imperialism." Research on the experience of multinational advertising agencies in the third world, such as South and Southeast Asia (e.g. Anderson, 1984; Frith and Frith, 1989, 1990; Kim and Frith, 1993; Sengupta and Frith, 1997) and Latin America (e.g. Mattelart, 1979; Fejes, 1980; Janus 1980, 1981a, 1981b), has centered on the transformative impact of multinational advertising in the local cultural milieu.

The media/advertising imperialism research has primarily focused on aspects of structure and content of the communication process. How messages of Western media and, in this case, advertising messages are actually created for the consumption of the third world has not received much research attention, but it certainly deserves to be more closely examined.

In this chapter, I will first present the advertising imperialism debate with its major arguments and counter-arguments. I will then use examples from the creative process at a global advertising affiliate in Beijing to illustrate the characteristics of advertising production in a cross-cultural/national context. Finally, I will suggest the emerging concept of cultural glocalization as a viable analytical tool for the study of contemporary production and circulation of advertising and culture.

Advertising imperialism

As represented by its proponents such as Herbert Schiller (1969, 1976, 1991), the media imperialism thesis holds that, as cultural agents, the Western media industry and its dissemination in the third world constitutes an act of cultural assault and domination. As a corollary, the expansion of Western advertising, emblematic of Western consumerism, is symptomatic of media imperialism.

Michael Anderson (1984) provided a detailed account of the multinational advertising industry in Southeast Asia. His theoretical framework, largely based on Johan Galtung's structure of imperialism, viewed advertising as an important dimension of the international power structure, and emphasized the uneven flow of advertising between the Center and the Periphery countries. He (Anderson, 1984: 49) defined advertising imperialism as "the way in which advertising exchange between nations is structured internationally with the effect that some nations may dominate other nations and create a disharmony of interest between them." He argued:

> It is one way in which advertising-rich Center nations penetrate into, and maintain a hold over, weaker Periphery nations whose indigenous communications resources are less sophisticated...The concept implies great, as well as unequal, power over advertising in and between nations. It also implies that the development goals of Center and Periphery nations are incompatible, even though these societies are closely coupled.
>
> (Anderson, 1984: 49)

Anderson's data, collected in 1977–78 in Malaysia, Singapore and Indonesia (and China), appeared to support his main thesis. In his concluding remarks, he wrote,

> This analysis of the "Madison Avenue connection" and the structure of advertising in four Asian nations has suggested that the TNAAs (transnational advertising agencies) have power over value-forming institutions within each of these societies except China, where the evidence is not in yet, and that the overall picture of advertising remains characteristic of colonialism, with ex-colonies at a disadvantage.
>
> (Anderson, 1984: 336)

Overall, the advertising imperialism discourse encompasses mainly three dimensions of cultural impact produced by multinational advertising in the third world (see also Kim and Frith, 1993): the export of Western advertising and its professionalism; the transnationalization of consumer culture; and the commercialization of local mass media.

First, studies on multinational advertising in Southeast Asia (e.g. Anderson, 1984; Frith and Frith, 1989) have argued that multinational advertising in the third world has introduced and implanted Western advertising norms and professional values in the developing countries. For Anderson (1984), ownership patterns, market domination, and staff composition are clear indications of economic and cultural control by multinational agencies in the advertising industry in these countries. Similarly, the Frith and Frith (1989) study suggested that the dominance of multinational advertising in Southeast Asia is tantamount to "cultural invasion." The cultural invasion in their study has two manifestations. One is that the producers of advertising in multinational agencies are Western expatriates and local staff socialized into Western advertising professionalism. "As a result," they concluded, "advertising messages are encoded in alienated pockets and decoded in host cultures that exhibit quite different values and mores" (Frith and Frith, 1989: 180). The other aspect of the cultural invasion is manifested in the divergence in symbolic representations between foreign and local ads. In their semiotic analysis of ads, Frith and Frith found that cultural values expressed in foreign ads were incompatible with local traditions. They used pairs of words and phrases (e.g. "we" or group feeling versus individualism; intuitive problem-solving vs. logical problem-solving) to compare and contrast between Eastern and Western cultural values as represented in ads.

The second cultural impact of multinational advertising in the third world is the transnationalization of consumer culture. The MacBride Report (1980) held that commercial advertising tends to "promote attitudes and life-styles which extol acquisition and consumption at the expense of other values." As Cees J. Hamelink (1983: 16) argued, foreign advertising in developing countries cultivates an identification with the culture of the more affluent classes in developed countries. The promotion of socially and economically low-priority goods also impedes the desirable path of development. Furthermore, multinational advertising is prone to "inform very little but persuade very strongly" (Hamelink, 1983: 13). To pursue the "world consumer," according to Noreene Janus's (1981a) research on foreign advertising in Latin America, international ad agencies cooperate with multinational manufacturers and launch marketing campaigns to introduce new products and teach new consumption habits. Multinational ad agencies therefore help to foster a standardized global consumer culture.

Third, when multinational ad agencies establish their dominance in the advertising industry in a third-world country, their influence also extends to the operation of the local mass media. In Latin America, for instance, it was not a coincidence that the growth of mass media (especially broadcast media) was accompanied by that of transnational advertising (e.g. Janus, 1980). Both private and government-owned media (especially television) in Latin America became increasingly dependent on (multinational) advertising as a source of income (Fejes, 1980).

Aside from these three recurring themes and emphases in the study of cultural impact of multinational advertising in the third world, Armand Mattelart (1979) pointed out that multinational advertising's influence could even seep into the political process of the local government as shown in the case of Chile. Noreene Janus (1980) also called attention to the economic effects of multinational advertising in the third world in terms of market competition and entry of new products.

To sum up, as Michael Anderson (1984: 66) argued:

> In effect, the TNAAs do far more than provide mere advertising services. They also on a daily basis – mostly during a person's leisure time – transmit consumerism and other values, communicate information, influence behavior both of individuals and of institutions, and affect development policies and plans. In a word, they exercise *power*.

Criticisms of advertising imperialism

Suffice it to say, the conceptualization of advertising imperialism is identical to that of the broader media imperialism research. The critique of advertising imperialism, as a result, also falls along the same line as that of general media/ cultural imperialism. To the critics, the underlying assumptions of advertising imperialism research are that ownership means control of advertising practice and content and that advertising content is appreciated uniformly by audience. The imperialism perspective seems also to assume that there is a pure local/ indigenous culture that is not only antithetical to Western values and norms but invariably vulnerable to Western cultural "contamination" and domination as well.

Charles F. Frazer (1990) presented some of the arguments to challenge the claims of the advertising imperialism thesis. Among his arguments, Frazer questioned the existence of the "great power" that is ascribed to Western advertising in the third world and the assumption that advertising effects are "unique and separable from those of other social forces" in the process of social and cultural change (Frazer, 1990: 78). When discussing whether advertising creates a consumer society, Frazer cited studies which showed that advertising only "changes the composition of consumption, not the level of consumption," and that advertising is the result (rather than the cause) of rise in income and consumption (Frazer, 1990: 79–80). He also challenged the assertion of the vulnerability of local cultures and the alleged culturally destructive nature of advertising.

In sum, Frazer found that there is a lack of compelling evidence to support the advertising imperialism thesis. He concluded:

> The foregoing discussion is not intended to suggest that TNCs (trans-national corporations) and TNAAs (transnational advertising agencies) ought to operate with global impunity, nor is it intended to suggest that whatever consequences occur as the result of their activities are inconsequential. I have tried to suggest that many of the charges connected with the view of US communications technologies, organization and content as cultural imperialism (...) are based on evidence which is, at best, limited. Indeed, the charges themselves are quite grave, which gives good reason for attending to them carefully. However, it seems that the role of TNCs and TNAAs in a host country are matters of national policy, not merely corporate preference.
>
> (Frazer, 1990: 87)

The question of media production

In an earlier study (Wang, 1997), I have pointed out some of the limitations in the conceptualization of the media imperialism thesis. Here, I would like to highlight one aspect of the cultural transaction which is often neglected in international media studies, namely, the condition of media production under the new global context.

For Western countries, media export used to be secondary to domestic audience. The media products that found their way to the third world had originally been made for the consumption of the domestic audience in the West. Since these media products were created without the international audience in mind, the reality embodied in them tended to reflect the expectations of the Western audience.

But nowadays, like in other product and service industries, domestic audience is no longer the first or only concern for Western media companies for they depend more and more on the international market for profits. Therefore media products (e.g. films, TV series, advertisements) are increasingly manufactured and marketed for an international/global audience (also see Robertson, 1995: 38). Examples include the promotion of Michael Jackson's album "HIStory" as a global album (*New York Times*, November 25, 1996: C7) and the international success of the Hollywood blockbuster *Titanic*. Another case in point is Coca-Cola's red paper pinwheel TV spot in 1997, which was filmed entirely in China and aired in several global markets (*Advertising Age*, February 10, 1997: 18). The phenomenon of "product life cycle" has thus become increasingly obsolete and irrelevant in the contemporary cultural and media flow.

The changing makeup of the market leads to adaptive changes in media organizations and their content production. Media organizations have grown *international* rather than *transnational*.

> An organization is international if the control is explicitly shared among representatives of two or more nationalities. An organization is transnational if, even though the control is within a single nation, it carries on operations in the territories of two or more nation states.
>
> (Bell, 1978: 210–11)

"Transnational" suggests that corporations are nationally based and extend their business to other countries; whereas "multinational" (or "international") more so signifies international allocation of resources and production, and most importantly, international management and ownership (Modelski ,1979: 2). To some scholars (e.g. Miyoshi, 1996: 86), "transnational" means that business organizations transcend national borders and defy political ideologies. Despite the semantic differences, we do see that researchers are pointing at the same phenomenon, that is the production and circulation of some products and services becoming globally rather than nationally/locally oriented and coordinated.

Media messages created by an *international* organization are likely to be different from those created by a *transnational* organization because the former is an international team of message producers and thus is more likely to understand audience needs from the *inside*, whereas the latter is foreign-based and can only view audience needs from the *outside*. Therefore we can argue that as a result of the structural changes in the global media economy, "export of meaning," the basis of media imperialism, is giving way to a collective mode of cultural production. It is, of course, presumptuous for us to suggest that the joint efforts of the foreign and the local in the production process always take place on an equal level. What seems to be interesting and important, then, is to explore and explain how the different roles are *negotiated* in the contemporary production and circulation of media culture.

Vignettes from the creative front

In this section, I will present several ethnographic fragments of the creative process at a global advertising affiliate in Beijing to illustrate the collaborative nature of advertising production.[1] The Agency is a joint venture between one of the world's largest ad agencies and a Chinese advertising agency. It was established in Beijing in the early 1990s. The foreign partner has majority stockholding and management control in the joint venture. The Agency mostly handles multinational business accounts in the Chinese market.

Like any standard advertising companies, the three key departments involved in the making of adverts at the Agency are account service, media and creative. The process normally begins with the account service receiving instructions from a client on product marketing goals and plans. In consultation with the client, the account staff generate a brief, which details marketing objectives, target audience, market information, etc. The brief is then shared with the media and creative departments. According to the marketing objectives outlined in the brief, the media and creative staff begin their work by interpreting the objectives and then considering campaign strategies.

The media department articulates its own objectives in terms of how to reach target consumers via selected advertising media. The media staff make recommendations about the types of media and the amount of media time or space deemed appropriate for the proposed advertising campaign. In the meantime, the creative staff have their own brainstorming sessions. Their task is to make recommendations about creative executions – headlines, body copy, or a storyboard for a television commercial. In this study, I will only focus on one aspect of the production process – the creative department.

At the time of the study, the director of the Agency's creative department was an expatriate from Hong Kong. The Asia-Pacific regional office in Hong Kong also periodically dispatches art directors to Beijing on special projects. At the time there were three expatriate art directors working at the Agency. Besides, there were three graphic artists, one copywriter and one production executive, all of whom were local employees.

The expatriate art directors work closely with local employees. Taking into account the huge size of the country and the cultural differences among regions within China, the Agency often needs to design different versions of the same advert to cater to the various regional markets in the country. It is therefore imperative for the expatriates to communicate with the locals in order to arrive at the appropriate language and image for a specific region.

"Gift giving" or "giving gift"

One of the responsibilities of the copywriter at the Agency is to make sure that the expressions in the headlines and body copies of the adverts are acceptable and understandable in mainland China. Although mainland Chinese and overseas Chinese share the same Chinese language, some grammatical and syntactic differences are often obvious. Therefore, when advertising copies or storyboards arrive from the Agency's Asia-Pacific office in Hong Kong, the copywriter edits them mercilessly to ensure the correct sentence structure and diction.

For example, two Chinese characters – "*zeng*" and "*song*" – make up the Chinese phrase "gift giving." In Hong Kong, it is customarily expressed as "*song zeng*." But in mainland China, the phrase is "*zeng song*." Even though local Chinese can still understand the meaning of the phrase in the reverted word order, they will find the expression odd and unauthentic.

"Sedan, hatchback, wagon,..."

The local copywriter runs out of her vocabulary when she writes for automobile advertising. What is a sedan? A hatchback? A wagon? She turns to her thick English-Chinese dictionary. But the dictionary only translates "sedan" as "a car." The translation of "wagon" is lengthy with detailed descriptions. Nor does the dictionary have a straightforward translation for "hatchback."

Automobiles for private consumption are a rather new phenomenon in China. Most people do not drive. The Chinese terms for the various types of cars and other auto gadgets (e.g. "sunroof") have not yet made their way into everyday language. The copywriter only understands the differences among the various types of automobiles but does not know the right terms in Chinese for "sedan," "hatchback," or "wagon."

"Beer at wedding banquet?"

One of the expatriate art directors is pondering over a TV spot for a joint-venture beer producer. "In north China," he asks the local staff, "what do people usually drink at a wedding banquet?" "Beer at a wedding banquet" appears to be his idea. He continues to ask, "What do people in this part of the country normally say when they invite others to come for a beer?" and "How do they say it?" A local staff suggests to him several possible ways of saying "come and have a beer" in the north China cultural context.

Although not totally culturally incorrect, the local staff thinks the association between beer and wedding banquet is less than appropriate. Chinese do drink beer at wedding banquets, but they find beer more of a refreshment drink consumed in summer rather than a drink at a wedding banquet.

Production and adaptation

With growing cooperative efforts in advertising production, it is virtually impossible to assert that the production of a commercial at the Agency is genuinely local or foreign. Local production companies in China are often hired to produce TV commercials even though they are not equipped with the most advanced technologies and facilities. But it is still cheaper to produce a TV spot in China than having it done overseas. Some of these companies contract art directors from Hong Kong and Taiwan to improve their creative concepts. For the Agency, some of its TV commercials are shot locally, and their post-production is finished in Hong Kong where top-line facilities are available.

In TV spots, local production companies are more experienced than overseas production teams in shooting outdoor scenes (e.g. natural landscape in China). But for domestic scenes, such as spots inside a house or apartment, overseas production seems more desirable. The local production companies have limited direct experience with modern homes and their ambiance. Such a lack affects the quality in their interpreting and shooting of advertising concepts that make use of homes as a lifestyle symbol.

The difference in adaptation of foreign advertising at the Agency is often that of degree rather than kind. The advertising production always involves some aspects of coproduction between the local and foreign partners. Some adverts for foreign and joint-venture brand-name products are mostly done overseas with only little local adaptation while others are conceived and produced primarily inside the country.

In general, the client's global marketing strategy often influences the degree of global-local involvement. A centralized approach requires less local adaptation while a decentralized brand/product management demands significant local adaptation. Research has also shown that high-tech, high-touch and high- fashion products are easier to market globally than other product categories (Moriarty and Duncan, 1991: 324).

Cultural brokers

International advertising agencies, such as the Agency, stand between the global manufacturer and the Chinese consumer and make advertisements of global products for local consumption. They therefore play the role of a cultural broker in the advertising transaction between the global and the local.

The expatriates at the Agency advise and supervise the production of advertising. They tend to understand better and are able to interpret effectively the needs of their international clients. Their knowledge of the local market and culture is, however, limited. The local staff supply necessary cultural information in advertising planning and production. In order for any advertising to have resonance with the Chinese consumer, the Agency has to be sensitive to local cultural traditions and localize messages whenever necessary. In short, the expatriates and the locals at the Agency are mutually complementary in creating "an effective juncture" (Geertz, 1960: 229) between the global product and the local consumer.

From a historical standpoint, foreign advertising's reliance on local knowledge and expertise to reach the Chinese market is nothing new or unusual. One of the big foreign advertisers in China in the early part of the twentieth century was the British-American Tobacco Company (BAT).

> To design appealing advertisements, BAT quickly learned to rely on Chinese who had a knowledge of Chinese traditions, an awareness of local customs, and a sensitivity to the popular imagination – cultural sensibility which Americans and other Westerners on the staff simply did not possess.
>
> (Cochran, 1980: 36)

BAT first hired Westerners to design adverts. Their use of German fairy tales, for instance, and advertising slogans that hardly made any sense to local Chinese was unsuccessful. BAT then decided to have Chinese artists design its adverts. Chinese artists often drew from the wellspring of Chinese folklore and popular culture, and BAT's advertising was thus adapted to the Chinese setting (Cochran, 1980).

Cultural hybridities: globalization and localization

The media imperialism discourse has demonstrated the critical vigilance in the face of growing cultural flow in the increasingly complex, variegated media world. However, students of international communication have also raised questions about the adequacy of the imperialism framework as an effective analytical and explanatory tool. The imperialism thesis tacitly assumes the power and control of media production of foreign media companies on the one hand and the vulnerability and uniformity of media reception of local customers and audience on the other.

For both academic scholars and social commentators, media imperialism is generally interpreted as a process of cultural homogenization. Yet, as it is indicated in the vignettes from the creative process at the Agency, the dynamics in cultural/media production (and flow) would find this outlook incomplete. What has been overlooked is the dimension of heterogenization in cultural contact. As Jan Nederveen Pieterse (1995: 53) pointed out,

> This is not to say that the notion of global cultural synchronization (Schiller, 1989; Hamelink, 1983) is irrelevant, on the contrary; but it is fundamentally incomplete. It overlooks the countercurrent. The impact non-Western cultures have been making on the West. It plays down the ambivalence of the globalizing momentum and ignores the role of the local reception of Western culture; for example, the indigenization of Western elements. It also fails to see the influence non-Western cultures

have been exercizing on one another. It leaves no room for cross-over culture – as in the development of "third cultures," such as world music. It overrates the homogeneity of Western culture and overlooks the fact that many of the standards exported by the West and its cultural industries themselves turn out to be of culturally mixed character if we examine their cultural lineages.

Contemporary cultural change and formation is characterized by the inter-locking duality of globalization and localization. The notion of globalization in both the academic and popular press tends to refer to "social process in which constraints of geography on social and cultural arrangements recede and in which people become increasingly aware that they are receding" (Waters, 1995: 3). This suggests the development of cultural convergence but slights the heterogenizing force of local cultures (e.g. an example of this tendency is George Ritzer's [1996] McDonaldization thesis).

The concept of glocalization (a composite word of "globalization" and "localization") (see Robertson, 1995), however, takes into account both the global in the local and the local in the global. It is a dialectic process between universalism and particularism, and homogenization and heterogenization (see e.g. Appadurai, 1990; Friedman, 1990). As Jan Nederveen Pieterse (1995) contended, such a process involves "interculturalism" rather than either "universalism" or "multiculturalism." Pieterse (1995: 63) argued that viewing globalization "in terms of homogenization, or of modernization/Westernization," was empirically narrow and historically flat.

Hence, the process of glocalization is that of hybridization. Hybridities refer to a continuum of adaptation between the global and the local. Under different conditions, there are various combinations of the global and the local. We are not naive to suggest that elements of the global and the local, for instance, always carry the same weight in the cultural hybrid. The process of hybridization is complex and sometimes ambiguous.

In future studies of cultural/advertising globalization and localization, we need to address the following issues of hybridities and, more importantly, provide compelling evidence to bolster our theoretical stand:

First, what are the content and context of the hybridities of culture? In the study of international/intercultural advertising, it is necessary to identify the global and local elements in not only the ads but also the advertising production and circulation process. While we define what constitutes the global and the local, it is also important that we contextualize our understanding by examining the shifting levels and order of the local, regional, national, and global identities.

Second, what is the personal and social impact of such hybridities? In inter-national/intercultural advertising research, we need to discuss the significance and impact of a certain hybridity at both the personal and societal level. Do the hybrid-ities in, for instance, advertising production and consumption broaden or narrow the personal and social imagining of both audience/consumers and advertising practitioners?

Third, as social forms change over time and space, we need to address the process of formation, maintenance and transformation of the cultural hybridities. We need to examine how certain cultural hybridities, as represented in the field of advertising production and circulation, are modified or replaced by other hybridities, what the driving forces are behind the changing process, and what the direction of change is.

In summary, as we move from the cultural export model to the cultural coproduction framework, the concept of cultural glocalization becomes a more effective tool in helping us make sense of contemporary cultural phenomena. In this chapter, I used ethnographic vignettes from a global advertising affiliate in Beijing to demonstrate that multinational advertising (or transnational advertising) is not a simple matter of export of culture. At least, from the field of production at the Agency, we see that the global and local roles are both involved and negotiated during the process.

Note

1 I conducted fieldwork at this agency (we will call it the Agency for the convenience of discussion) as a participant observer for a period of one month in spring 1996. I gathered information about the Agency's structure and process of advertising production and circulation.

References

Anderson, M. (1984). *Madison Avenue in Asia: Politics and Transnational Advertising*. London: Associated University Press.

Appadurai, A. (1990). "Disjuncture and difference in the global cultural economy." *Theory, Culture and Society*, 7, 295–310.

Bell, D. (1978). *The Cultural Contradiction of Capitalism*. New York: Basic Books.

China Advertising Yearbook 1996. (Zhong guo guang gao nian jian) Beijing: Xinhua Press (in Chinese).

Cochran, S. (1980). *Big Business in China: Sino-Foreign Rivalry in the Cigarette Industry, 1890–1930*. Cambridge: Harvard University Press.

Fejes, F. (1980). "The growth of multinational advertising agencies in Latin America." *Journal of Communication*, 30(3), 36–49.

Frazer, C.F. (1990). "Issues and evidence in international advertising." *Current Issues and Research in Advertising* 12(1), 75–90.

Friedman, J. (1990). "Being in the world: Globalization and localization." *Theory, Culture and Society*, 7, 311–28.

Frith, K. and Frith, M. (1989). "Advertising as cultural invasion." *Media Asia*, 16(4), 179–84, 214.

Frith, K. and Frith, M. (1990). "Western advertising and eastern culture: The confrontation in Southeast Asia." *Current Issues and Research in Advertising*, 12(1), 63–73.

Geertz, C. (1960). "The Javanese kijaji: The changing role of a cultural broker." *Comparative Studies in Society and History*, 2(2), 228–49.

Hamelink, C.J. (1983). *Cultural Autonomy in Global Communication: Planning National Information Policy*. New York: Longman.

International Commission for the Study of Communication Problems. (1980). *Many Voices, One World: Towards a New More Just and More Efficient World Information and Communication Order (The MacBride Report)*. UNESCO.

Janus N.Z. (1980). "The making of the global consumer: Transnational advertising and the mass media in Latin America." PhD dissertation, Stanford University.

Janus N.Z. (1981a). "Advertising and the mass media: Transnational link between production and consumption." *Media, Culture & Society*, 3, 13–23.

Janus N.Z. (1981b). "Advertising and the mass media in the era of the global corporation." In Emile G. McAnany, J. Schritman and N.Z. Janus (Eds), *Communication and Social Structure: Critical Studies in Mass Media Research*, 287–316. New York: Praegers.

Kaynak, E. (1989). *The Management of International Advertising: A Handbook and Guide for Professionals*. New York: Quorum Books.

Kim, K.K. (1995). "Spreading the net: The consolidation process of large transnational advertising agencies in the 1980s and the early 1990s." *International Journal of Advertising*, 14, 195–217.

Kim, K.K. and Frith, K.T. (1993). "An analysis of the growth of transnational advertising in five Asian countries: 1970–1990." *Media Asia*, 20(1), 45–53, 56.

Mattelart, A. (1979). *Multinational Corporations and the Control of Culture: The Ideological Apparatus of Imperialism*. New Jersey: Humanities Press.

Mattelart, A. (1991). *Advertising International: The Privatization of Public Sphere*. London: Routledge.

Miyoshi, M. (1996). "Borderless world? From Colonialism to transnationalism and the decline of the nation-state." In R. Wilson and W. Dissanayake (Eds), *Global/Local: Cultural Production and the Transnational Imaginary*, 78–106. Durham: Duke University Press.

Modelski, G. (Ed.) (1979). *Transnational Corporation and World Order: Readings in International Political Economy*. San Francisco, CA: W.H. Freeman and Company.

Moriarty, S.E. and Duncan, T.R. (1991). "Global advertising: Issues and practice." *Current Issues and Research in Advertising*, 13(2), 313–41.

Pieterse, J.N. (1995). "Globalization as hybridization." In M Featherstone, S Lash and R Robertson (Eds), *Global Modernities*, 45–68. Thousand Oaks, CA: Sage.

Ritzer, G. (1996). "The McDonaldization thesis: Is expansion inevitable?" *International Sociology*, 11(3), 291–308.

Robertson, R. (1995). "Glocalization: Time-space and homogeneity-heterogeneity." In M. Featherstone, S. Lash and R. Robertson (Eds), *Global Modernities*, 25–44. Thousand Oaks, CA: Sage.

Schiller, H.I. (1969). *Mass Communication and American Empire*. Augustus M. Kelley Publishers.

Schiller, H.I. (1972). "Madison Avenue imperialism." In R.L. Merritt (Ed.), *Communication in International Politics*, 318–38. Illinois: University of Illinois Press.

Schiller, H.I. (1976). *Communication and Cultural Domination*. New York: International Arts and Sciences Press.

Schiller, H.I. (1991). "Not yet the post-imperialist era." *Critical Studies in Mass Communication*, 8, 13–28.

Seligman, S.D. (1984). "China's fledgling advertising industry: The start of something big?" *The China Business Review*, January/February, 12–17.

Sengupta, S. and Frith, K.T. (1997). "Multinational corporation advertising and cultural imperialism: A content analysis of Indian television commercials." *Asian Journal of Communication*, 7(1), 1–18.

Wang, J. (1997). "Global media and cultural change." *Media Asia*, 24(1), 15–22.

Waters, M. (1995). *Key Ideas: Globalization*. London: Routledge.

10

CULTURAL IDENTITY IN AN ERA OF GLOBALIZATION

The structure and content of Taiwanese soap operas

Yean Tsai

The predicted "global village" is closer than ever to realization following the improvement of the modern political environment and prosperity of advanced technologies. Theoretical discussions in recent media studies have therefore paid special concerns to ethnicity and cultural identity in the context of recent developments toward globalization and localization of culture (Gillespie, 1995). While researchers report that information and cultural products move mainly in a unidirectional way from Western societies to less developed nations (Straubhaar, 1994; Varis, 1991; Nordenstreng and Varis, 1974), the general public's tastes still show a different orientation. Exchange models, for example, are easily obtainable; famous Brazilian *telenovela* as well as Indian movies and the music television program *Made in India* are all accepted in countries like the United States and China, or in Europe. A further example is the Spanish popular music *Macarena*, which has thrived in markets around the world (Yeh, 1998; Hinchberger, 1997; Paxman, 1996).

As communication studies become increasingly interested in the many facets of globalization, it is recognizable that an integration of cultural, economic and political works has formed a quick way to understand cultural industries in an era of global communication. An understanding of individual cultural production in each different society also helps to provide a full view of the subject of globalization. As Straubhaar (1994) indicates that past research has greatly neglected the reporting of media content as part of cultural industries in third-world countries, there is indeed little documentation, if any, which has addressed the subject of Taiwan's TV soap operas. This study, therefore, aims to fill this gap by examining the content and structure of soap operas in Taiwan in order to provide internationally comparable categories (Barker, 1997: 84–95).

In essence, the focus of this paper is on one of the most popular new Taiwanese soap genres that has also been greatly accepted in the overseas Chinese markets in Southeast Asia, Australia, and North and South America this decade, the *hsiang-tu-chu* (or the rural soap). *Hsiang-tu-chu*, a soap genre which has been broadcast mainly in prime-time hours with highest ratings in recent years, forms a type of drama depicting Taiwan's local customs and practices. As distinguished from other soap genres, the lines of which are delivered in Mandarin, *hsiang-tu-chu* is presented mostly in Ho-lo tone, a dialect used in Taiwan and the southern Fukien province in Southeast China, and therefore is considered to hold the proximal feeling among its target audience.

The plots of *hsiang-tu-chu* are mixtures of love affairs, revenge and family conflicts, and characters act mostly against a stage background of southern Chinese buildings and are dressed in wardrobes popular either in modern Chinese or in folk styles in the past century.

Another notable fact, which also differentiates *hsiang-tu-chu* from other important genres like romance (*chung-yao-chu*) and history (*li-shih-chu*) soaps (see Tsai, 1997, for in-depth explanation), is the delineation of characters. A sorrowful unfortunate woman, for instance, is often placed with her sinister mother-in-law, and an evil male character marries a concubine, an act which shatters the family's peace. The plot, which is finalized by the restoration of justice to pacify the family conflict between good and evil roles, seems to be common to Brazilian *telenovelas* (Tufte, 1995; Barker, 1997).

In general, *hsiang-tu-chu*, representing a new soap genre reflecting the regional audience's search for cultural identity, flourished after Taiwan started various cultural and economic contacts with China in the last decade. It also became popular among the Taiwanese communities in Southeast Asia, Australia, and the Americas because its contents can sooth the emigrants' nostalgic feelings.

This paper purports to explore the *hsiang-tu-chu*'s content and structure, which are exclusively local, in order to add to our understanding of a communication and cultural issue under the influence of a global flow of information in a postmodern age.

TV soaps and cultural identity

Past studies of globalization have placed more emphasis on the economic and political rather than the cultural aspects, and related research has traditionally stressed issues of world economics, worldwide enterprises or new technologies. Little attention, if any, has been paid to media content; it is therefore difficult to gain a full spectrum of knowledge about the flow of images and ideas on a global scale.

In a sense, cultural patterns, customs and living standards, behavioral models, and value systems in a society are all basic elements of the creative foundations of dramatic dialogues and actions. Soaps, being one of the most complex social products, often aim at telling human stories in society. Cultural identity, which is intrinsically adopted in the story plot, reflects the relationship among the social classes in that society as a way to attract the audience's attention and thus elevate the reception rate.

As Scholes and Kellogg (1975: 14) indicate, fictional narrative, as in the TV soaps which delineate either beauty or goodness in one's mind and in the society, includes two main components: the romantic and the didactic. And it's true that all types of the Taiwanese soaps retain romance and moral instruction (Tsai, 1997), perhaps because the soap writers always intend to "influence" the audience with either joy or instruction. If the audience is indeed attracted by the soap plot, then it is possible to say that some kind of "conversation" has been successfully created through the soap plot, in which the same language is exchanged between the writer and audience.

A popular soap communicates the audience's own beliefs and shares the audience's dreams and hopes. With modern communication systems at work, it has become possible to change interaction among different cultures. As cable television systems bring in a large number of soaps from Japan, Hong Kong, the United States and China, the audience in Taiwan shares the least elements with American soaps. It is the sense of reality or identity that sustains the interest of the public (Koichi, 1998); such examples can be easily obtained, judging from the popularity of the Japanese *ou-hsiang-chu*, soaps with young Japanese idols, in Taiwan. Young Taiwanese adults identify with the struggles of the fictional characters as well as the romantic engagements in such Japanese soaps because the stories are convincing to the audience.

Other cases of such soap/audience relationships are the Taiwan-made *li-shih-chu* (historic soap) entitled *Pao Ching-Tien*, which has been popular in Thailand, and the Chinese-made *li-shih-chu* extensively welcomed in Taiwan. Basically, *li-shih-chu* presents a dramatic story that may spread across several generations throughout Chinese history and literature. As the political environment in Thailand is similar to that of Taiwan, for example, a "*ching-tien*," an upright official representing justice, or a judge or high-ranking politician with integrity, satisfies the expectations of a majority of the audience.

Further, some of the most successful *li-shih-chu* (historic soaps) made in mainland China are adapted from Chinese classics or history. Famous stories in previous dynasties or in great novels, such as *The Monkey King*, *The Three Kingdoms*, *All Men Are Brothers*,[1] are now being dramatized for prime-time TV audiences. On the other hand, Taiwan's *li-shih-chu* have concentrated on famous historical characters such as Liu Hsiu,[2] Pao Cheng,[3] Liu Bo-wen,[4] and Emperor Chieng Lung[5] (Tsai, 1996), all well-known historical figures with great achievements in the Han, Sung, Ming, and Ching Dynasties, respectively.

Other than the *li-shih-chu* (historic soaps), the most important TV soap genre which has made a major hit in Taiwan in the recent decade is *hsiang-tu-chu*, a drama depicting Taiwan's local history and regional customs. In order to attract an even greater audience, the TV company combines the *li-shih-chu* with a *hsiang-tu-chu* flavor. For instance, stories of Shih Kung, an honest official and a fair judge in the Ching Dynasty classic literature, is represented by using both Mandarin and Ho-lo dialect. The soap *Legends of Shih Kung* was a top-rated prime-time soap in previous seasons. The leading actor who played Shih Kung is well-known for his previous roles in *hsiang-tu-chu*. In a sense, *hsiang-tu-chu* in Taiwan may be said to be comparable to Western movies to Americans, *li-shih-chu* to the Chinese, or *novelas* to the Brazilians.

Researchers have argued that the electronic media play a restructuring role of social life in which traditional links between culture and community have been disrupted and the sense of locality destroyed. According to Harvey (1989) and Thompson (1992), the acceleration of communication has radically affected the transmission of social values, meanings, and identities. In the postmodern era, social identities are increasingly marked by "fragmentation, multiplicity, plurality and indeterminacy" (Gillespie, 1995: 12). Gillespie further asserts, basically from a bottom-up point of view, that "the popular search for 'roots' and the resurgence of concern with ethnic identity are signs of the decay of group identity rather than of its regeneration" (1995: 16).

The behavior and belief systems in soaps, then, come from a collective memory in history which reveals people's expectations in real life. As a domestic or social leisure appliance, television serves as reinforcement to certain identities and ideologies (Tsai, 1998). The remaining question to be explored here is what is the reality, in terms of cultural products and identity, that the *hsiang-tu-chu* proposes to the audience in the postmodern era?

In answering such an inquiry of how the television soap drama is linked with cultural identity, an assumption about identity needs to be clarified. First of all, gender, race, class, region, as well as ethnicity all contribute to the difference of identity (Gillespie, 1995), and, more importantly, identity can be reinvented and reinterpreted in each new generation. It was hypothesized by researchers that due to the powerful assimilation process produced by the international cultural enterprises, differences across national boundaries and racial gaps may be narrowed (Yeh, 1998: 43). A further theory even asserts that the tastes, desires and attitudes of third-world people are not likely to remain the same and will parallel those of Westerners under the long-term influence of TV soap operas. Similar analog hypotheses about globalization hint that when something works in one area, it is supposed to work in other. However, the question remains to be answered with regard to whether and how Taiwan soaps react to a tide of globalization.

Taking an example from the music industry, one important effect of globalization has been to start a hybrid fashion of music. As a new population in favor of pop music arises in recent years, people enjoy a tone hardly distinctive from American rock, jazz, or heavy metal. It is at the same time that throughout the world "the globalization process, as represented by the international music industry, is being countered by the production of unique music by local musicians" (Robinson, Buck and Cuthbert, 1991: 227).

On the other hand, there are also reports which indicate that popular songs aiming at a global market have been de-territorized. The theme of a song, it is found, is always love, and the production of the music video incorporate individualism without senses of social, historical or cultural heritages (Lee, 1998). In the end, as Lee argued against Robinson, Buck and Cuthbert, a balanced ecosystem in regional music is destroyed; the music products become monotonous, and the polysemy of world culture is then dispossessed.

Such a contrast in observing the world music industry reveals the fact that the impact of globalization or regionalization is still a debatable issue. It is believed that dialogues among nations and cultures remain necessary since the diversity of individual races, cultures, religions, habits and lifestyles cannot be easily overlooked. The lesson can also be learned from the example of selling Marlboro cigarettes in England and in Malaysia, where the favorable image of the American cowboy does not add to the gross sales at all.

People in the advertising industry now suggest that globalization may be better off taken as an idea, or a goal to expand the potential market to the whole world, since it is essential "to think globally and to act locally" (Cheng and Chou, 1991: 63). This tendency to turn away from the earlier optimism about globalization may hint at an anxiety about global homogenization.

Following the same trend, both Taiwan and China TV producers now target soaps for the local audience but later still market them to overseas Chinese. In the meantime, a lot of money is budgeted in order to develop high-quality television soaps, mainly *li-shih-chu* (historic genre) that are suitable for the world market.

As a variation of *li-shih-chu*, the *hsiang-tu-chu* (rural soap) also enjoys the surge of the tide. *Li-shih-chu* are dramas that depict stories relating to different people of successive generations throughout Chinese history, while *hsiang-tu-chu* are episodes regarding common Taiwanese in the past. *Li-shih-chu* exhibit important morals which associate modern Chinese with the spirit of the ancient classics, while *hsiang-tu-chu* are important programs which channel current Taiwanese culture with memories of Taiwan rural life. Finally, the central theme of many *li-shih-chu* always involves male authorities in ancient times, but *hsiang-tu-chu* often detail conflicts and power structures between females, particularly in-laws.

Hall (1992) specifies three possible consequences of globalization for cultural identities, including erosion, strengthening and the emergence of new identities or new ethnicities. Hall uses the term "global-postmodern" to refer to the perceived breakdown of all the established cultural identities, the fragmentation of cultural codes, or the pluralization of styles (1992: 17). He points out that one of the major debates in question comes from the assertion that inside the culture people can protect a familiar sense of value and a sound and safe environment against the encroachment of foreign ideology.

Cubitt (1991), on the other hand, argues that television presents itself as an absolute presence (here and now) and personal medium. One thing for sale these days is a mixture of feminist power, fantasy, and desire. With the development of high technology and the free flow of information, do soap operas in Taiwan reflect a fragmented culture as expected by scholars waiting for the arrival of a so-called global village and a global postmodern ideology? What are some reactions as revealed through media content in an age of global communication?

This paper aims to deal with these questions by utilizing a content analysis method proposed by Burke (1989), as well as a structural analysis proposed by Propp (1994).

Method

This research asks, what are the content and the structure of a specific Taiwan cultural product, the *hsiang-tu-chu*, in the age of global communication? Compared to other soap genres, the *hsiang-tu-chu* is probably the most locally favored type of TV program representing exclusive senses of Taiwan in transition. This style of soap portrays stories of love relations and family struggles with a historic background falling between the eighteenth century to the modern period. Eras such as the Japanese Occupation (1895–1945), Sino-Japanese War (1937–45) and Taiwan Retrocession (1945) are used to thread the plots of romance and affection among family members.

In a time period from April 1995 to March 1997, three Taiwanese TV networks produced twenty-six *hsiang-tu-chu* of varied lengths, including fourteen being broadcast at prime time between 8 and 9 pm, and five broadcast either at 6 pm or 6.30 pm, Monday through Friday, each for half an hour. The remaining six were broadcast at 12.30 pm or 1.00 pm, also half an hour a day, during the weekdays. Still one more was broadcast at 10 pm on weekdays.

This research purposely selected and reviewed fourteen titles with content mostly matching the definition of *hsiang-tu-chu* as previously described; all were broadcast at 8 pm to 9 pm on weekdays. A total of 665 episodes constitute the target genre from which 177 (26.6 percent) hours were sampled systematically for analysis. Each sample was then examined by two coders together and a mutually agreed result was transcribed into dramatic acts as prescribed by Burke in his Dramatism Theory (Cragan and Shields, 1995; Burke, 1989).

A dramatic act was defined in this research as a complete action in which agent, agency, scene and purpose were recognizable and the related event observable in one episode. An example would be that the female lead Meilin (agent) went to her brother's chamber at noon (scene), trying to buy an estate through deceit (act). Meilin's sweet-talk (agency) concealed her greed to monopolize the family wealth (purpose), and her motive was obviously overlooked by her brother.

Sometimes an act stretched over more than one scene. As the agent, act, and/ or agency changed, the dramatic act was coded as a separate one. The following section reports the collected data on how dramatic acts, including agent, scene, agency and purpose, were portrayed in the *hsiang-tu-chu*.

Before moving on, another important step needs to be mentioned. In order to understand the role structure in such a specific genre, a similar pattern in Western tales proposed by Propp (1994) was used for comparison. In his famous work,

Morphology of the folktale, Propp suggested that all folktales were structured by the relationships among different roles. That means, each role in a folktale or a story has its specific function, whose action contributes to the completion of the whole story. The seven major role functions that Propp identified include the actions of the Hero, the Villain, the Princess and her Father, the Donor, the Helper, the Dispatcher, and the False Hero.

As Owen (1993: 221) also indicates, characters in narratives are not merely individuals; in fact, they together form an embodiment of a "type," or a social category defined by the expression of a particular constellation of social norms and attitudes. In examining the dramatic acts in Taiwanese rural soaps, data on the function of a role, or an agent as reflected through relationships with others, are collected in order to report the structure of these soap episodes.

Content and structure of the soaps

The content

An investigation of 171 samples of the *hsiang-tu-chu* identified 453 dramatic acts[6] in thirteen different soaps. It was found that, first, the genre is in fact related to family stories about people in Taiwan during and after a historical period covering the Japanese Occupation and Taiwan Retrocession (1895–1945). Some important historical events, such as the Sino-Japanese War (1937–45) as a part of World War II, could only be "heard" from the lines.

Second, this study also found that the acts in *hsiang-tu-chu* were mostly about family members in interaction. Love affairs between couples appeared in 108 acts or 23.8 percent of the total acts under study,[7] and affection among family members (103 acts, 22.7 percent) was a theme that could be most commonly seen among all surveyed soaps. Violent interactions such as physical fights or smashing as well as conspiracies were each seen in sixty-nine acts (15.2 percent respectively).

Friendship (sixty-two acts, or 13.7 percent), truth revelation (forty-one acts, 9.1 percent), as well as rescuing (thirty-seven acts, 8.2 percent) were among the main dramatic acts counteracting misunderstanding (fifty-four acts, 11.9 percent), sickness (fifty acts, 11.0 percent) and threats (forty-three acts, 6.7 percent). Interestingly, a light or humorous mood was absent from the surveyed acts; instead, they were full of sorrow, anger, and grief.

Ironically, these soap stories always ended with pleasure and fulfillment. It was found that *hsiang-tu-chu*, similar to *li-shih-chu* or American soaps, used dramatic acts to contrast good and evil. An action of a Hero, for example, was always associated with romance and good deeds like helping others. After inquiring truth, rescuing the weak, and supplication for blessings, the Hero is successful and returns home. An action of a Villain, on the contrary, provokes fights, threats, deceit, blackmail, rape and, of course, murder.

Although the *hsiang-tu-chu* is literally a type of drama illustrating Taiwan's rural and rustic past, its stories frequently covered the people living in urban areas.

180

Excluding the four episodes which failed to specify any exact locales, stories were always related to events happening in Taipei (the metropolitan capital). Other locations were mentioned in different soaps without repetition, including cities like Tainan, Tamshui, Hsinchu and Hwalian; rural countries were rarely part of the plots from which stories originated.

From the 453 acts collected, 302 scenes[8] (66.7 percent) were acted in the home environment, such as a living room, bedroom, kitchen or dining room. Other interior scenes, including restaurants, police stations, temples, churches, jails, factories, hotels, hospitals, brothels, tea houses, pawn shops, and many different stores, totaled up to 149 scenes (or 32.9 percent). Exterior scenes comprised only 14 percent or seventy-five in number, including gardens, streets, waterfronts, woods, markets, villages, mountain roads, riversides, etc.

There was a total of ninety-two agents, or major roles, identified from the 453 acts; male characters accounted for forty-four and females for forty-eight. Twelve of the characters were mainlanders; except for two whose origins were unclear, all the rest were Taiwanese (84.8 percent). The range of age of these characters grew with the plots from youngsters to grandparents.

As past research has found that one unique and important characteristic in *hsiang-tu-chu* is its clearly represented profession of the characters (Tsai, 1997), a total of eleven soaps (84.6 percent) described the occupation of each major role. Of the sventy-nine major agents analyzed, it was found that almost all agents had jobs, mostly as small business owners or venders of varied types. Some changed their jobs as the plots developed, from poor boy to lawyer, from worker to factory owner, or even from whore to president of a company.

Evidently Taiwan's TV *hsiang-tu-chu* goes along with the soaps in other societies by utilizing popular narratives to project a neverending dream in which the loser wins, the poor get rich, and the discontented are fulfilled. A failure in love or career was often introduced in the middle to dramatize the plot and a glorious success is included toward the end in order to cheer up the audience.

Another general impression of *hsiang-tu-chu* has been its attempt to promote a positive image of modern Taiwanese women following the flourishing of world feminism. Although the titles often suggest that the soaps are about females and their life stories, the content shows otherwise. Very much like the *li-shih-chu*, which portrays romance, justice and the overthrow of the evil by the good, in *hsiang-tu-chu* male dominance and a power of tradition remain the major ideologies. Male agents always occupy a higher stratum in the family, while older father or father-in-law types often practice their images as authoritative and rich roles. Young male Heroes are full of reasonable and romantic ideas and they are the agents who practice honesty and bravery.

Older or higher-stratum female agents, however, are often represented as ignorant, selfish and superstitious, while younger female agents are either romantic, tender and kind, or, on the contrary, energetic, aggressive, and scheming.

The structure

As previous studies have found (Tsai, 1997), the structure of Taiwan's soap operas did support Propp's theory (1994) on plot as it actually consisted of various actions of the characters. In this study, the actions of the Hero, the Princess and her Father, the Villain, and the Helper were identified as the most common role functions in the *hsiang-tu-chu*; actions of the Dispatcher and the False Hero were the least significant, while the action of the Donor was totally absent.[9]

In a sense, some story elements found in the *hsiang-tu-chu* go parallel with those presented in the structure of Russian tales identified by Propp (1994). In the initial situation, for instance, the *hsiang-tu-chu* provides a temporal-spatial composition of family members as Propp similarly listed in his discussion of story structures. And Hero, Princess, and Villain are introduced to the audience at this stage, also following Propp's proposition.

Even so, differences between the *hsiang-tu-chu* and the Russian structure are observable. First of all, the dramatic acts in the *hsiang-tu-chu* most frequently reveal deceitful tricks that separate good from evil. No massive injustice nor any large-scale violence is seen in the plot. Second, no plot contains the absence of a family member or violations of any interdictions as the Russian tales usually do.

Besides these, the function of the Villain is an important structure in the *hsiang-tu-chu*. When Villains suffer from financial needs or emotional disturbances, they threaten, harm, or steal from and kidnap their family members who are closely related by blood or matrimony. Sometimes evil deeds come out of strong emotions, such as jealousy, anger, or dislike. Since the *hsiang-tu-chu* mainly involves descriptions of affection and hatred among family members and relatives, Villains often represent forces in opposition to the Hero's goals, and do not even come close to take the life of any Hero, at least intentionally.

On the other hand, the action of the Dispatcher is not an obvious plot structure in the *hsiang-tu-chu*. Perhaps misfortunes in the soaps are often associated with the Hero himself but not with his fellow beings. Usually it is the Hero himself, or herself, who figures out that some actions must be taken to prevent further destruction. A Dispatcher is therefore not an integral part of the plot structure.

Propp has further proposed that a story is often structured in succession by mediation, consent to counteraction, and departure. Mediation is a connective incident which places the Hero into action. Consent to counteraction leads the confrontation between Hero and Villain. Departure means the dispatch of the Hero from home to conquer the Villain or other obstacles (Propp, 1994: 150–1).

During this phase the *hsiang-tu-chu* does represent varied conflicts, tests and requests for Heroes and Villains in order to place both characters in dramatic action. However, all these actions happen at home. In fact, the *hsiang-tu-chu* starts its complication stage, in which forces of Heroes and Villains compete, mostly in a home environment. Also in this stage, functions of different roles, such as Princess and Helper, as well as the reactions of Heroes, start to be revealed. The process of the drama is prolonged by many struggles of the Heroes until there is a final victory over the Villains. Propp predicts that the ending in a folktale comes with the triumph of the Hero and his wedding; the structure of *hsiang-tu-chu* supports this prediction.

As the object of the search is obtained and misfortune prevented, *hsiang-tu-chu* comes to a conclusion with one culturally related resolution while the Villains are pardoned. Although this resolution departs from Propp's proposal of the Villain's function, it is still the final arrangement of the soap. This departure occurs because in this specific genre all Villains are in fact family members. When brothers and sisters reject their sins and return to virtue, their regret arouse the pity of the injured. Under the influences of authoritative parents and intimate brotherhood, the victims choose to forgive rather than to punish those sinners. When the separated reunites, bitterness transforms into contentment, happiness replaces sorrow, and happily a harmonious family relationship is regained.

A case of cultural integration

After a review of soaps that have gained so much popularity in Taiwan and among those emigrants in Chinatowns around the world, it seems an issue of cultural productions can be further explored.

In essence, this research has demonstrated that the content and structure of Taiwan's TV soaps follow to a large degree those theoretical propositions presented by Propp's. This may prove that some themes and structural elements in these stories are universally juxtaposed across cultures. In fact, there are not only similarities between Taiwanese soaps and Russian folktales, but also a close correspondence between the Western plot and Chinese soaps in romantic themes. As Scholes and Kellogg (1975) relate,

> A young couple fall in love, are prevented from consummating their love by various catastrophes which place them in grave danger while separated from one another, but they emerge chaste and unscathed, to marry at the end of the narrative.
>
> Principal characters in a typical romance are definitely human beings, but extraordinarily attractive ones, and usually virtuous and honorable despite extraordinary pressures.
>
> In the romance chastity becomes the most significant of all the virtues. As a rule in these tales, strict poetic justice prevails, and the truly virtuous characters are indestructible though always threatened with destruction.
>
> (Scholes and Kellogg, 1975: 68–9)

According to Scholes and Kellogg, romance is depicted more as an ideal world that playwrights everywhere search for, in which poetic justice prevails against wrongdoing. As soaps are one of the most complex cultural and social products, such identical patterns in stories around the world may confirm that a desire for romantic experience as well as justice and harmonious relationships among family members are only human. It is also perhaps appropriate to state that many cultural products (like soap contents) have a lot in common and thus make global attractions possible.

On the other hand, familiar ethics and traditional values are highly cherished in the soaps. The return to family love and a traditional value of forgiving, as shown in Taiwan's TV soaps, is a significant final plot arrangement in terms of structure. We may infer, therefore, that the influences of traditional practices in cultural and traditional customs are quite different from those of the American as represented in the soaps.

While some functions of roles and story elements expressed in Propp's theory are identified in Taiwan's soaps, Propp's other roles, i.e. the actions of the Donor and False Hero, cannot be observed at all.

In addition, Villains in the *hsiang-tu-chu* are addressed as a negative function but are always pardoned in the soap, which is in contrast with the American soaps where a Villain often stands for a conflicting power to that of the Hero and thus needs to pay for his vicious deeds. To employ such a negative role in the plot structure, *hsiang-tu-chu* intentionally invites strong emotion from the audience. Tears are shed due to the pitiful situations in which a weak character, usually a young and innocent female, feels in turmoil in a confrontation with other family members.

Another difference results from the Villain's role function; while in the American soap Villains who commit harmful deeds can rarely escape from punishment either by law or by other practices (Tsai, 1997), in the *hsiang-tu-chu* there is hardly a way to punish a cruel mother-in-law or an unfaithful husband.

One more cultural uniqueness in terms of story content in the *hsiang-tu-chu* is that almost all of the roles in the TV soaps have jobs. Being either business owners or landowners, they often move up the social ladder from being despised to respected, or from poor to rich. This kind of plot arrangement reflects an old Chinese motto which says that misfortune always changes into luck, thus the soap ends with hope and fulfillment. Similarly, repentance or reform somehow turns a vice into benevolence in the soap's final episodes.

It is true that in recent years popular culture has integrated different varieties of feminism and American ideologies (Tsai, 1996), but it is also notable that there are still cases in Taiwan, China, Malaysia, India, Brazil, Spain and England where social and regional identities remain popular in their television programs. It is possible that past literature has broadly underestimated the strength of local culture against the international cultural industry. It is also perhaps true that globalization should be considered as a concept subject to local needs and to each individual cultural and social environment. That is, behavior patterns and living attitudes of local consumers must be considered before globalization is to be achieved.

If the above assertions are meaningful, then it is about time to take seriously Mercer's suggestion (1990: 43) that "Identity only becomes an issue when it is in crisis, when something assured to be fixed, coherent and stable is displaced by the experience of doubt and uncertainty." We may then assume that although cultural elements change all the time following globalization, identity sometimes remains, only in different formats.

It is clear from this short essay that more empirical evidence is necessary concerning how the media shape identity if we want to traverse the maze of cultural products. Although Gillespie (1995) argues that the advancement of modern technology has compressed spatial and temporal differences and made cultural changes unavoidable, the current cases in Chinese soaps seem to tell a different story. The *hsiang-tu-chu* and *li-shih-chu* both show a clear pattern where local customs and practices react strongly to support unique flavors and traditions in specific regions.

Television as a discipline of cultural studies in Taiwan has grown in recent years, but academic descriptions of TV soaps are still absent in general; future research should continue to explore the related issues on this subject. Straubhaar (1994) suggests that other important themes in the area of global communication deserving more attention include the process of media flow, industrial structure, and the role of the government and cultural policy in, say, the change of technology. Regrettably, no connection of important social issues has been made to the content of TV soaps in either Taiwan or other developing nations. More research in this area is necessary before we can finally obtain a better understanding of the value of cultural products in an age of global communication.

Notes

1 The translation of Chinese classics varies. Other known titles of the same novel include *The Very Land of China / The Magic Monkey / Si-Yu-Ki; The Story of the Three Kingdoms / Romance of the Three Kingdoms;* and *Adventure of Chinese Giant / Water Margin.*

2 The emperor who revived the Han Dynasty (206 BC–219 AD).

3 A magistrate in the Sung Courts (960–1279 AD), and later a famous fictional figure in classic literature.

4 A prophet and a prime minister who helped Emperor Chu Yuanchang to found the Ming Dynasty.

5 A famous emperor of the Ching Dynasty.

6 This is the actual number of acts being analyzed for this research. One soap was cancelled by the TV station and therefore dropped from this research. The research also dropped all acts that were initiated by minor characters, and therefore analyzed only the acts which were initiated by ninety-two major characters in the soap operas.

7 Sometimes multiple themes, such as love, physical clashes and sickness are observable in one act. The percentage therefore totals more than 100 percent.

8 Some acts are completed in more than one scene.

9 The action of the Donor, a common function in *li-shih-chu* such as gods, fairies, old monks and kung fu masters was used to provide some sorts of magical power to the Hero. The most famous soap opera *Legends of Pao Chin-Tien* portrays the fair judge in the Sung Dynasty as a symbol of wisdom, righteousness and justice. As Pao travels and investigates crimes, he has two important magical agents, his sword granted by the emperor (Donor) and his "magical third eye" gifted by the heavens (Donor). In addition to inspecting evil in broad daylight, Pao's "third eye," represented by a crescent moon on his forehead, enables him to communicate with the deceased at night. After murderers, outlaws and corrupt officials were convicted by Pao's "three eye," the sward given by the Emperor allows Pao to behead even the most powerful villains.

References

Barker, C. (1997). *Global Television – An Introduction*. Oxford: Blackwell.

Burke, K. (1989). *On Symbols and Society*. J.R. Gusfield (Ed.). Chicago: University of Chicago.

Cheng, D.H. and Chou, Y.Y. (1991). "Introduction to the globalization of advertisement" (Trans.).*Advertising Magazine* (in Chinese), 10, 62–5.

Cubitt, S. (1991). *Timeshift – On Video Culture*. London: Routledge.

Cragan, J.F. and Shields, D.C. (1995). *Symbolic Theories in Applied Communication Research-Bormann, Burke, and Fisher*. Cresskill, NJ: Hampton.

Cunningham, S. and Jacka, E. (1996). "Australian television in world markets." In J. Sinclair, E. Jacka and S. Cunningham (Eds), *New Patterns in Global Television – Peripheral Vision*. New York: Oxford University Press.

Gillespie, M. (1995). *Television, Ethnicity and Cultural Change*. London: Routledge.

Hall, S. (1992). "The question of cultural identity." In S. Hall, D. Held and T. McGrew (Eds), *Modernity and Its Futures*. Cambridge: Polity Press.

Harvey, D. (1989). *The Condition of Postmodernity*. Oxford: Blackwell.

Hinchberger, B. (1997). "Actress has international spirit." *Variety*, October 20–26, 46–8.

Koichi, I. (1998). "Japanese culture in Taiwan." *Contemporary*, 125, 14–39.

Lee, T.D. (1998). "A political-economic analysis of cross-national media and Chinese music" (in Chinese). *Contemporary*, 125, 54–71.

Mercer, K. (1990). "Welcome to the jungle." In J. Rutherford (Ed.). *Identity: Community, Culture, Difference.*. London: Lawrence and Wishart.

Nordenstreng, K. and Varis, T. (1974). "Television traffic – a one-way street?" A Survey and Analysis of the International Flow of Television Program Material. UNESCO, No. 70.

Owen, A.S. (1993). "Oppositional voices in *China Beach*: Narrative configurations of gender and war." In D.K. Mumby (Ed.), *Narrative and Social Control: Critical Perspectives*. Newbury Park: Sage.

Paxman, A. (1996). "*Telenovela* delirium". *Variety*, October 7–13, 61–5.

Propp, V. (1994). *Morphology of the Folktale*. Austin: University of Texas.

Robinson, D.C., Buck, E.B. and Cuthbert, M. (1991). *Music at the Margin – Popular Music and Global Cultural Diversity*. Newbury Park: Sage.

Scholes, A. and Kellogg, R. (1975). *The Nature of Narrative*. New York: Oxford University Press.

Straubhaar, J. (1994). "Asymmetrical interdependence and cultural proximity: A critical review on the international flow of television programs." *Communication Culture*, 3, 165–85.

Straubhaar, J.D. and Viscasillas, G. M. (1991). "Class, genre, and the regionalization of television programming in the Dominican Republic." *Journal of Communication*, 41(1), 53–69.

Thompson, K. (1992). "Social pluralism and post-modernity." In S. Hall, D. Held and T. McGrew (Eds.), *Modernity and Its Futures*. Cambridge: Polity.

Tsai, Y. (1996). *An Analysis of the Value Systems and Social Ideologies in the Historic Television Drama* (in Chinese). Taipei: Television-Culture Research Committee.

Tsai, Y. (1997). "Television drama genres and structural formulas" (in Chinese). *Communication Research Monographs*, 1. Taipei: National Chengchi University.

Tsai, Y. (1998). "A legend of silence – Morality of historic television drama." *Mass Communication Research*, 56, 85–103.

Tufte, T. (1995). "How do *telenovelas* serve to articulate hybrid cultures in contemporary Brazil?" *The Nordicom Review of Nordic Research on Media and Communication*, 2, 29–36.

Yeh, S.M. (1998). "Overturning images of cross-national television (in Chinese). *Contemporary*, 125, 40–54.

Varis, T. (1991). "Trends in international television flow." In C. Schneider and B. Wallis (Eds.), *Global Television*. New York: Wedge.

11

TELEVISION AND GLOBAL CULTURE

Assessing the role of television in globalization

Paul S. N. Lee

The flow and consumption of global television

Much has been said about the flow of global television in the world market (Ang, 1985; Antola and Rogers, 1984; Elasmar and Hunter, 1997; Goonasekera and Lee, 1998; Katz, Blumler and Gurevitch, 1974; Katz, Gurevitch and Haas, 1973; Katz and Liebes, 1985; Nordenstreng and Varis, 1974; Sreberny-Mohammadi, 1996; Schiller, 1976, 1991; Schement and Rogers, 1984; Straubhaar, 1991; Straubhaar and Viscasillas, 1991; Varis, 1985). The general findings of nearly all empirical studies point to the fact that the viewing of global television has little impact on viewers, not to say changing their deeply entrenched values. It was found that global television was mostly shown in fringe hours in the non-English-speaking world and viewers usually preferred local to foreign programs.

Straubhaar (1991) considered that cultural proximity was a major factor contributing to the flow of global television. He pointed out that there was a preference first for national material, and when that cannot be filled, the audience would look next to regional productions, which were relatively more culturally proximate than were those from outside the region. The US television products are more likely to be imported and consumed in countries with British cultural heritages. In Latin America, products from regional centers such as Mexico and Argentina are more likely to be imported and consumed.

Lee (1998) has suggested a three-tiered model for television consumption in non-English speaking countries where local productions are weak. The first tier of programs consumed by local audience are local programs. The second tier consists of culturally proximate programs with popular genres like those in the first tier. The third tier comprises programs with less cultural proximity, and the genres are usually information-related, international sports or productions with high technical skills such as science programs and animation. Anglo-American productions have

188

a competitive edge in the third tier as they have larger economy of scale and support of a long production history and high-tech productions. Occasionally, some popular genres of global television such as serial drama would also be consumed in the third tier. Audience will select programs in the order of first, second and third tier.

Lee (1998) suggests that cultural absorption explains the flow of global television better than media-cultural imperialism. He defines cultural absorption as "a process whereby a country chooses to import global television on its own terms with a view to meeting local cultural needs" (1988: 282). Under the three-tiered model of television consumption, the influence of global television on local audiences is not as great as that perceived in the thesis of media-cultural imperialism.

In a study on five Asian countries by Hagiwara and his colleagues (1999), it was found that the majority of audiences did not consider the negative values portrayed in global television, such as greed, pre-marital sex, and individualism, had significant impact on local cultures or their own way of living. On the other hand, they considered that global television could enrich their knowledge and help them understand other cultures.

Ferguson (1992) also noted that Canada, a close neighbor of the US which is the dominant exporter of global television, imported 90 percent of its Anglophone TV drama. Yet, considerable evidence showed that Canada continued to maintain a value system and way of life distinctive from the US (1992: 81).

When people consume global television, they have different motivations – to get information unavailable at home, to get better entertainment, or to catch up with topics related to some popular foreign programs, movies or celebrities. On the whole, when local productions have better appeal, people prefer local to foreign. When local productions cannot meet their needs, and foreign productions have better quality and appeal, people will reverse their preference.

Local appeal versus expert-rated quality

The "quality" of cultural products is hard to define because the perception of it varies with cultures. In general, the quality of a television program can be assessed through three aspects, namely, the technical attractiveness of audio-visual images, appeal of story plots and performance of artists. Nevertheless, a good mix of these aspects need not assure audience viewing. There were cases when industry experts or critics rated a film or a program as high-quality, but the film or program failed disastrously. Consumers care about programs' "appeal" more than expert-rated "quality."

In the discussion of "quality" in cultural products, a distinction should be made between "appeal" and "quality." It is true that good quality is likely to go with good appeal, but it need not be always the case. The common mass may not like high-quality products as defined by industry experts or an elite class. When common masses talk about quality, they refer more to the "appeal" than "quality" of the cultural product. The evaluation of public television is a case in point. In audience surveys, respondents usually rate public television high in quality, but seldom watch it. On the other hand, they may rate a commercial program average in quality, yet they watch it frequently. Therefore, when the general mass talk about program quality, they are referring to program "appeal" rather than the expert-rated "quality."

Program appeal refers to "the ability of a program to put together elements that satisfy the informational, entertainment and cultural needs of the audience, and to induce consumption." Consumption of cultural products involves cultural tastes which change with time, generations, and cultures. As a result of the "changing" nature of cultural tastes, global television must adjust its appeal to the changing tastes of different cultures at different times. An increase in investment alone is no guarantee for a cultural product's "appeal," although it is likely to raise its "quality." A good quality product without appeal will fail in the global market. For example, Batman failed badly in Hong Kong although it was a class A production. Only products with appeal can succeed – big investment helps but it is not a panacea.

Quality plus local appeal is a successful formula for global television. Programs like *Ironside, Mission Impossible, Dynasty, Baywatch, The X-files*, etc. have possessed both quality and appeal in many places of the world. However, there were also many cases in which the program had quality but little local appeal, such as *M.A.S.H, Hill Street Blues, Three's Company, Cheers*, etc., and failed in non-Western markets. American sit-coms usually failed overseas because their plots were more culture-bound. Audiences with different cultures cannot enjoy the gags and punch lines.

The importance of local appeal to the reception of global television in local markets can be illustrated also by the experience of Star TV in Asia. Since its inception in 1991, Star TV has relayed mostly Western programs, with only one Chinese channel (Phoenix) in its north beam and one Hindi channel (Zee TV) in its south. Despite that fact that most Hong Kong people use the dialect of Cantonese rather than Mandarin, which is the language broadcast on Phoenix channel, this Chinese channel has become the most popular among all Star channels receivable in Hong Kong (Survey Research Hong Kong, 1996: 8). The Phoenix channel broadcasts programs originated from Taiwan, China, Hong Kong, Japan and South Korea – all sharing Confucian cultural heritages (Lee and Wang, 1995). Similarly, Zee TV which uses Hindi programming has become the most popular Star channel in India, surpassing the rating of Star Plus, Prime Sports and Channel V (Joshi, 1998: 22). Cultural proximity and local contents prescribe the relative success of Phoenix among the Chinese communities in Asia, and Zee TV in India, compared with other global channels or programs without local appeal or contents.

Studies on the elements that make global television "appealing" to local audiences are needed to increase our understanding of the flow and consumption of global television in the world market.

Global television and global culture

The fear of a homogenous global culture is ungrounded. The formation of a culture in a particular setting requires ongoing interactions among people in that setting.

Watching television and interacting with others on the basis of it is one among many activities in our society. The dominance of television viewing in leisure time has shown signs of decline in recent times. When television fails to appeal to them, people have many alternatives such as watching videos, playing video games, reading, or surfing on the Internet. Television has become a commonplace activity which people can ignore if it cannot serve the purpose people want.

The situation today is unlike the 1960s and 1970s when television was still a relatively new gadget for most people around the world. Although watching television remains a relatively important activity, taking up most of the leisure in most parts of the world, its glamour has been lost in time. The proliferation of television channels in the 1990s due to technological changes further reduces people's interests in television. Too many channels provide too much of the same things on screen. People might have never given serious attention to the fanfares of television; they give even less today. To attribute a powerful role to television in creating a global culture in the twenty-first century is to ignore the fragmentation and inattentiveness of audiences in the 1990s.

Global television will not be able to homogenize various cultures into a single one because it can neither dominate people's viewing in the host countries, nor have the impact to do so even if people consume it.

Homogenizing various cultures

To homogenize various cultures around the world, global television has to successfully complete all the following steps. First, it needs to have access to various host countries. Second, it must be shown during prime time so as to reach the largest possible audiences. Third, it needs to be consumed. Fourth, it must replace the audiences' existing values that are different from those carried in global television. Finally, the values carried by global television must be comprehensive so that they can cover and replace every important aspect of the host country's culture.

As long as global television has limited local appeal, it will not get much access to host countries and their prime–time slots, even if the governments of the host countries do not restrict its flow. Without local appeal, global television will be consumed minimally and have only little replacement effects in cultural values. At present, most global television has limited local appeal because it is mainly produced for home audiences and at best takes care of the "taste of the global market" by using some broad and superficial themes.

It is doubtful whether a common taste and a single global market exists, given the diversity of cultures in the world. What "global market" refers to is usually a few countries to which the cultural products are exported. Overseas market is a more accurate depiction for these host countries.

Globalization and the fear of homogenization

In the analysis above, homogenization of cultures by global television is very unlikely. The fear of homogenization of cultures itself, however, deserves more attention. The concern about the sameness of cultures at the end of this century is related to the phenomenon of globalization. One can see McDonald's, Coca-Cola and Disney almost everywhere. All cities in the world have similar skylines, road signs, constructions, shopping malls, chain stores, brands and products. The death of Diana and the Clinton-Lewinsky scandal were seen in every corner of the world through local media, CNN or the Internet. The economic meltdown in Asia threatened the US economy and consequently the European economy. International hedge funds created global financial turmoil by the turn of this century. Never before have people been bound so closely by the economic force. Globalization refers to "the rapidly developing process of complex intercon-nections between societies, cultures, institutions and individuals world-wide" (Tomlinson, 1997: 170). It involves a compression of time and space, shrinking distances through a dramatic reduction in time taken – either physically or represen-tationally – to cross them, so making the world seem smaller and in a certain sense bring human beings "closer" to one another. It is also a process which stretches social relations, removing the relationships which govern our daily lives form local contexts to global ones (Harvey, 1989; Tomlinson, 1997).

In the discussion about globalization, two dimensions are apparent – the state and the market. Giddens (1990) notes that the literature on globalization revolves around international relations and the theory of world systems. The former focuses on the interactions among nations and the development of interdependence in regional and international organizations. The state is an essential actor. The latter focuses on the economic relations resulting from the division of labor in the world market. Wallerstein's (1979, 1991) theories of core, semi-periphery and periphery are most influential. The conceptualization of a capitalistic world economy stresses the influence of capitalism in integrating the globe into a world market.

Internationalization

From the international relations perspective, globalization involves increasing inter-actions among the states. The formation of regional and international organizations, adoption of standard rules and behaviors, international collaboration in health, crimes and drugs, and collective actions against terrorism are part and parcel of globalization. Since the basic unit of interaction in this perspective is the nation-state, we can call it an "internationalization" process. Many nations today share similar political and social institutions, such as judiciary systems, political elections, universities, commercial broadcasting and the United Nations. Viewed from this perspective, a global system is in place. The emergence of the European Union is a recent example of internationalization.

However, this "internationalization" process – mingling different national systems into one – barely touches the cultural system of the nations involved. Most often, this process involves institution building and political compromises. Seldom does it deal with the social and cultural differences among the nations. Quite often, the nations would want to avoid highlighting their socio-cultural differences so as to strike a deal for all. An example is the US government's 1997 Framework for

Electronic Commerce. It calls for governance by "consistent principles across state, national and international borders that leads to predictable results regardless of the jurisdiction in which a particular buyer or seller resides" (Kobrin, 1998). It aims at a reconciliation of national law of various countries, rather than harmonizing the differences in basic beliefs and values. In the process of internationalization, the fear of homogenization of cultures is moot because the interactions rarely aim at bringing other sides to accept one's value system. The fear for cultural homogeneity is more a result of holding a conception of globalization in economic terms.

Marketization

From the world systems perspective, capitalism is inherently globalizing. Based on the growth data in the third world after the Second World War, Warren (1980) found that the underdeveloped countries were changing into capitalistic societies. According to Marxist analysis, capitalism will commodify all human activities and capitalize all backward sectors. Capital will flow to where profits can be made. Consumerism is the most important value carried by capitalism. The process of turning the world into a single market through multinational corporations can also be termed "marketization."

This process has turned many facets of human life alike. Factories, division of labor and assembly lines are standard features of production. Mass advertising and consumption of uniform products have become a "natural" part of life. Standardization of automobiles, living amenities, computer hardware and software, sports facilities, etc., reinforces the image of "sameness" in the world. In global television and advertising, the values of consumerism and individualism are explicitly shown and promoted. Since the United States is the most advanced capitalist state, it has become the central force to sell capitalism to the world and set standards for the formation of a single market. The deregulatory force was set in by the US to break down national barriers for capital flow and world marketization.

The fear of global television's role in homogenizing cultures is generated under this version of globalization. Under the conception of marketization, the US is seen as a center extending its particular culture or society to the rest of the world. Since the US is a major exporter of global television, which contains explicit cultural values, global television is naturally conceived to be the vehicle for globalizing and homogenizing world cultures.

This conception of globalization, however, overestimates the impact of capitalism on local cultures. It conceives that capitalist culture is one and the same. It also considers that capitalist culture can replace local cultures in all realms. Williams (1961) had a straightforward definition of culture – the day-to-day expression of shared human experiences. The commodification of human relations and consumption ethics of capitalism cannot substitute every realm of culture, or every major aspect of people's day-to-day social practices. A culture does not only deal with survival and material well-being, but also self-actualization and spiritual enrichment.

Capitalist values at best touch part of the spiritual realm of people's life. Global television can hardly sell values deep and entrenching enough to replace the central values of a culture, namely, the value concerning one's relationship with self, others, family, nation, life and nature. It is doubtful if global television contains commodification values all the time, and if it can persuade people to commodify very aspect of their everyday practices. Moreover, even if we assume that the audiences have adopted the values portrayed in global television, there are still many local forces in play, acting on and reacting against the "pick-up" values. Television has been assigned too great a role in cultural formation.

Inter-acculturation

The emergence of a global culture can result from a process of inter-acculturation in which different cultures interact on a day-to-day basis, with mutual influences, adaptation and absorption. Inter-acculturation is a process by which different cultures learn to adapt the values of one another's cultures and assimilate them into their own.

The distinction between inter-acculturation and internationalization can be seen from the identity of the medieval nobility who perceived themselves as European rather than national. These elites might have been linked to territories, and their titles were grounded in place, but they were not territorial in the modern sense (Kobrin, 1998). They considered themselves sharing common qualities and values across territorial boundaries.

Environmentalism is perhaps the best example of inter-acculturation in modern times. In the 1970s, only a few scientific and civic bodies in the industrial countries were alerted to the issues of pollution. In the 1990s, despite resistance from some governments, it would look bad for them not to pay at least lip service to environmental protection. It would also look bad for individuals to ignore environmental issues at all. The green value has been taken up by various cultures as part of their values through adaptation and absorption.

A global culture would be one having all its central values universally adopted by human beings. There have been some universal values adopted by mankind for a long time, such as "not to kill" and "not to steal." But these values apply more at home than outside, and need punitive measures to uphold their being practiced.

Today, apart from environmentalism, some values are getting the universal status as a result of inter-acculturation. They are liberty, equality and democracy. Although these values are not accepted by all states, most people in the world consider them desirable. The inter-acculturation process is conducted on a basis of voluntary exchanges among cultures, with mutual influences and respect. It is a spontaneous process without coercion imposed by any culture. Although dominance of some cultures in the process is inevitable, the outcome is not a simple transplant of the dominant cultures' values to the less influential ones.

Featherstone (1990) has pointed out that globalization should not be misunderstood as homogenization. He notes:

It is not sufficient to regard the intensification of the flows of commodities, money, images, information and technology as globalizing the
postmodern by exporting its cultural forms and complexity problematic
from Western centers to the rest of world…[T]here is an important spatial
and relational dimension to modernity which is lost when we conceive it
as coming out of one particular time and place with all others condemned
to follow the same route.

(Featherstone, 1995: 5-6).

[margin note: Globalisat more to do with the materiality of a society]
[margin note: Homogenisation more to do with the intrinsics]

Under this conception of globalization, the formation of a global culture will
involve a complex interaction of globalizing and localizing tendencies; a synthesis
of particularistic and universalistic values (Robertson, 1992; Scott, 1997). As
Hannerz (1990: 237) remarks, globalization is characterized by "the organization
of diversity rather than by a replication of uniformity." Global television can only
play a role of middleman in this process by relating cultural values of the West to
various cultures. The fear of a standardized global culture being imposed by global
television is not warranted if one shares the view of inter-acculturation in
globalization. If a global culture arises from a melding of diverse particularities of
different cultures, rather than a transplant of one single form, there is nothing to
be feared. All cultures today have experienced the same process for a long time.

[margin note: ↓ G.C. Sample of is just grouping of artificial sets together but not create a uniform.]
[handwritten across text: Basically .T.V does not have the power to form interacculturation]

Contest among market, state and culture

On the basis of Polanyi's analysis of the globalizing tendencies of market societies,
Scott (1997) points out the contest between the market and state in the process of
globalization. He observes that the recent trend of deregulation is not a *response* to
competition, but a means of extending it into areas which were previously protected,
or partially protected, from commodification. He notes, "the globalizing logic of
capital is always and already engaged in a struggle to escape political regulation,
while politics is constantly fighting to keep economic activity under its control"
(1997: 15).

In the discussion on the contest between state and market, the state is taken as
the guardian of local culture while the market is an intruder on it. This conception
tends to treat culture as a non-problematic and give it a subservient role on either
side in the contest. With closer examination, however, we can see that the state is
neither a protector necessarily welcome by people, nor the market an intruder
necessarily abhorred. People of the host country, for example, may be fond of
global television while the state imposes strict censorship on it. It will end up with
"illegal" watching of global television by satellite dishes or private cable setups.
People in China today receive Star TV despite the ban on private dishes. Taiwanese
people received Japanese programs by their own dishes and illegal cable long before
the ban was lifted in the 1990s. The two examples show that people may not agree
to the state's protection for them in cultural matters.

[margin note: State names culture. Market is a attempt to capitalise on it]

The conception of state-market contest also assumes that if the marketization force is not regulated, local culture will crumble. Evidence has shown that this need not be the case. In the five Asian countries studied (Hagiwara *et al.*, 1999), Japan, Hong Kong and the Philippines were found to impose no restriction on the import of global television, but one cannot see any sign that these three cultures are being replaced by a single foreign one, or losing their cultural particularities.

What is suggested here is that instead of conceptualizing globalization in terms of a state-market contest, the process should be viewed as a contest among state, market, and culture. Culture is subservient neither to the state, nor to the market. It is an active player in the process. If the state and local market cannot satisfy the cultural needs of people, people will look for substitutes from abroad. The state will fail to suppress people's unmet cultural needs. On the other hand, the market cannot dictate people's consumption and subsequent actions. Local cultures, especially those in non-English-speaking countries, are resilient and active interactants in the process of acculturation. Quite often foreign cultural products, including global television, have to adapt to local cultures in order to be accepted and consumed. In the process of globalization, local culture is an active player, perhaps the most important player, to arbitrate between the state and the market in their contest for dominance over people.

Conclusion

Global television has been assigned too important a role in the process of globalization and the formation of a global culture. From the above analysis, globalization can be conceived in three different ways – a process of internationalization with the state as the essential actor, a process of marketization with capitalism as the central force, and a process of inter-acculturation with the interactions among various cultures as the focal point for attention.

The fear for homogenization of various cultures by a single form is grounded only if one holds the conception of marketization in globalization. Even with this perspective, global television's role has been over-stressed because the values portrayed are usually superficial and limited. The contents and values of global television will also be modified to suit the local contexts if they are to be consumed and absorbed. The formation of a global culture can only result from the process of inter-acculturation which is a process conducted on a basis of voluntary exchanges among cultures, with mutual influences and respects. Without this process of inter-acculturation, the emergence of a global culture is not likely.

References

Ang, I. (1985). *Watching "Dallas": Soap Opera and the Melodramatic Imagination.* London: Methuen.

Antola, L. and Rogers, E. (1984). "Television flow in Latin America." *Communication Research*, 11, 183-202.

Elasmar, M. and Hunter, J. (1996). "The Impact of Foreign TV on a Domestic Audience: A Meta-Analysis." In B. Burleson (Ed.) *Communication Yearbook*, 20, 46–69. Thousand Oaks, CA: Sage.

Featherstone, M. (Ed.) (1990). *Global Culture: Nationalism, Globalization and Modernity.* London: Sage.

Featherstone, M. (1995). *Undoing Culture: Globalization, Postmodernism and Identity.* London: Sage.

Ferguson, M. (1992). "The mythology about globalization." *European Journal of Communications*, 7(1) 69–94.

Giddens, A. (1990). *The Consequences of Modernity.* Cambridge: Polity Press.

Goonasekera, A. and Lee, P. (Eds) (1998). *Television without borders: Asia speaks out.* Singapore: Asian Media Information and Communication Center.

Hagiwara, S., Joshi, S., Karthigesu, R., Kenny, J., Lee, P. and Pernia, E. (1999). "The reception of global television in Asia: An assessment of its impact on local culture." *Asian Journal of Communication*, 9(1).

Hannerz, U. (1990). "Cosmopolitan and locals in world culture." In M. Featherstone (Ed.), *Global Culture: Nationalism, Globalization and Modernity.* London: Sage.

Harvey, D. (1989). *The Condition of Post-Modernity.* Oxford: Blackwell.

Joshi, S. (1998). Transborer Television in India. In A. Goonasekera and P. Lee (Eds), *Television Without Borders: Asia Speaks Out*, 3–37. Singapore: Asian Media Information and Communication Center.

Katz, E., Gurevitch, M. and Haas, H. (1973). "On the use of mass media for important things." *American Sociological Review*, 138, 164–81.

Katz, E., Gurevitch, M. and Haas, H. (1974). "Utilization of mass communication by the individual." In J. Blumler and E. Katz (Eds), *The Uses of Mass Communication: Current Perspectives on Gratification Research*, 19–23. Beverley Hills, CA: Sage.

Katz, E. and Liebes, T. (1985). "Mutual aid in the decoding of Dallas: Preliminary notes from a cross-cultural study." In P. Drummond and R. Paterson (Eds), *Television in Transition: Papers from the First International Television Studies conference.* London, British Film Institute.

Kobrin, S. (1998). "Back to the future: neomedievalism and the postmodern digital world economy." *Journal of International Affairs*, 51(2), 361–86.

Lee, P. (1998). "Toward a theory of transborder television." In A. Goonasekera and P. Lee (Eds), *Television Without Borders: Asia Speaks Out*, 274–86. Singapore: Asian Media Information and Communication Center.

Nordenstreng, K. and Varis, T. (1974). *Television Traffic: One Way Street.* Paris: Unesco.

Schement, J. and Rogers, E. (1984). "Media flows in Latin America." *Communication Research*, 11(2), 305–20.

Schiller, H. (1976). *Communications and Cultural Domination*, New York: M.E. Sharpe.

Schiller, H. (1991). "Not yet the post-imperialist era." *Cultural Studies in Mass Communication*, 8, 13–28.

Scott, A. (Ed.) (1997). *The Limits of Globalization: Cases and Arguments.* London: Routledge.

Sreberny-Mohammadi, A. (1996). "Global and the local in international communications." In J. Curran and M. Gurevitch (Eds), *Mass Media and Society*, 177–203. London: Arnold.

Straubhaar, J. (1991). "Beyond media imperialism: Assymetrical interdependence and cultural proximity." *Critical Studies in Mass Communication*, 8(1), 39–59.

Straubhaar, J. and Viscasillas, G. (1991). "Class genre, and the regionalization of television programming in the Dominican Republic." *Journal of Communication*, 41(1), 53–69.

Survey Research Hong Kong (1996). *Satellite Television Broadcasting Survey 1995, Main Report*. Hong Kong: SRH.

Tomlinson, J. (1997). "Cultural Globalization and Cultural Imperialism." In A. Mohammadi (Ed.), *International Communication and Globalization: A Critical Introduction*, 170–90. London: Sage.

Varis, T. (1985). *International Flow of Television Programs*. Paris: Unesco.

Wallerstein, I. (1979). *The Capitalist World Economy*. Cambridge: Cambridge University Press.

Wallerstein, I. (1991). *Geopolitics and Geoculture: Essays on the Changing World-System*. Cambridge: Cambridge University Press.

Warren, B. (1980). *Imperialism: Pioneer of Capitalism*. London: NLB.

Williams, R. (1961). *Culture and Society*. Harmondsworth: Penguin.

12

CULTURE, LANGUAGE AND SOCIAL CLASS IN THE GLOBALIZATION OF TELEVISION

Joseph D. Straubhaar

There are many ways of looking at culture and the globalization of television. Ultimately we are looking here at culture as the individual and collective synthesis of identity. In this sense, this chapter argues that the identities of television viewers around the world are becoming more multilayered with elements that are very local, regional (subnational but larger than the very local), and national. The newest layers of identity are supranational – based on cultural-linguistic "regions" held together by language and cultural specifics, such as dress, style, ethnic types, religion, and values – and global. This chapter argues, however, based on an analysis of indepth interviews in Brazil, that the proportion of people whose identity is deeply globalized is actually quite small, that the traditional layers of identity at the local, regional and national levels are still the strongest for the large majority of people.

In a more practical and immediate sense, this chapter will use cultural capital as a concept to sum up a series of identifiable factors that people tend to use when deciding what they want to watch on television. While a number of studies have focused on the role of language in defining television markets (Wildman and Siwek, 1988), this chapter will try to define and demonstrate a number of the cultural factors which also define television markets, by defining what audiences' cultural identities and cultural capital leads them to prefer. Those are specific things like humor, gender images, dress, style, lifestyle, knowledge about other lifestyles, ethnic types, religion, and values. Cultural groups defined by their differences on these kinds of factors often overlap greatly with language groups. This study will elaborate the aspects of cultural capital that are most relevant to audience choices about global, cultural-linguistic regional and national television, as well as their ability to make sense of what they watch from such different sources.

Cultural capital, identity and language tend to favor an audience desire for cultural proximity, which leads audiences to prefer local and national productions over those which are globalized and/or American. However, cultural proximity is itself limited by social class stratification. Groups united by language and/or culture

199

seem to be increasingly fragmented by both economic and cultural capital in the senses defined by Bourdieu (1984). Economic capital (Bourdieu, 1984) gives some people in the economic elite of many countries access to television channels, particularly those delivered by satellite or cable, that the vast majority or the population cannot afford. Even more subtly, in most countries, only elites or upper middle classes have the education, employment experiences, travel opportunities, and family backgrounds that give them the cultural capital (Bourdieu, 1984) required to understand and enjoy programs in other languages. In fact, this chapter will argue that this also extends beyond language to culture, that the cultural capital required for wanting to watch many kinds of imported programs also tends to be concentrated in middle and upper classes. Thus, while cultural capital is separable from economic capital, the former is bounded and constrained by the latter, the economic aspects of social class.

Nevertheless, this chapter argues that aside from such relatively globalized elites and middle classes, there is an audience tendency in the majority of most television markets defined by cultural groups toward seeking cultural proximity or similarity in television, preferring the localization of television programs and channels. That is to say, most people prefer to watch television programs and satellite or cable TV channels which feature their own language or one close to it, familiar dress and style, topical and locally relevant humor, familiar stars and actors, familiar ethnic types, familiar values, and addressing relevant regional, national or local issues. For example, a certain idea for historical soap opera about a famous Chinese judge, Judge Bao, has been produced in several different Chinese language markets. While Taiwanese audiences did watch and enjoy a Hong Kong production, Taiwanese producers interviewed by the author indicated that a local production was more popular. The Taiwan production pacing was slower (which the audience apparently preferred), the Mandarin idiom more localized, and the national television stars were more familiar.

Overall, this study further defines and operationalizes, in indepth interviews in Brazil, the concept of cultural proximity. The general dimensions that tend to extend across social classes will be looked at in terms of cultural affinities, common values, perceived similarities and perceived relevance. The dimensions of the audience that divide social classes and limit cultural proximity will be looked at in terms of cultural capital, building on the manner in which Bourdieu used the concept to examine social class distinctions in taste within a culture, like France (1984).

Global TV flows: from dependency to rediscovering the audience

During the 1960s and 1970s, many studies pointed out to a one-way flow of television, news and music from a few first-world countries to the rest of the world (Nordenstreng and Varis, 1974; Boyd-Barrett, 1980). Several theoretical explanations were developed, notably cultural dependency Hamelink, 1983), dependent development (Evans, 1979) and media imperialism (Lee, 1980).

Both the empirical findings of a one-way flow and the theoretical explanations for it began to be challenged. While the US still makes a great deal of money exporting television programming, studies in Latin America (Antola and Rogers, 1984) and Asia (Waterman and Rogers, 1994) observed that national production was increasing in many countries, particularly in prime time. A twenty-nation study by Straubhaar, *et al.* (1992) confirmed that almost all but the smallest nations, such as the English speaking Caribbean, and those which share English as a native language with the US, such as Canada, seemed to be reducing US imports, producing more national programs, and importing more programs from within cultural-linguistic regions, such as Latin America, or Chinese-speaking Asia. Increasingly, while poor countries still import much of their programming, it no longer primarily comes in a one-way flow from the US For example, the Dominican Republic is now more likely to import many genres, such as comedies, variety shows, and news from Mexico, a dominant producer for the Latin American cultural-linguistic market, than from the US (Straubhaar, 1991). Mozambique imports about as much entertainment from Brazil, a dominant producer for Portuguese-speaking countries, as from the US, furthermore the Brazilian material is much more likely to be in prime time.

This constitutes a much more complex flow. Television programming now flows horizontally from one developing country to another quite frequently. Some programs even flow back to the US and Europe. Brazilian television now tends to dominate the prime-time programming of its former colonial power, Portugal (Marques de Melo, 1988, 1992). Mexico long dominated the television and radio programming of the Hispanic audience in the US, although more programming is increasingly created by US Latinos for the unique interests of that population itself. The flow of television is still asymmetric but there is now an interpenetration of cultures, both by migration and by media, which flows largely from developed North to the developing South but increasingly flows from South to South as well.

For some years in the 1960s and 1970s, many scholars thought that imported programming frequently was more entertaining or more desirable to the audience, anticipating "Wall-to-wall *Dallas*" (Collins, 1986). It does seem that there is still a powerful appeal of exotic, non-local programming, particularly in some genres like action-adventure films and programs. Violence still travels very well (Herman and McChesney, 1997). And, more positively, as Parameswaran points out, sometimes women or other particular groups can find certain imported genres to be more emancipating or supportive of their particular needs than much locally-produced material.

However, as more time elapses and television systems develop further, it begins to seem that relevance to local culture may give many kinds of local or national programming an advantage. In a study of television in Brazil, Kottak observes,

> Common to all mass culture successes, no matter what the country, the first requirement is that they fit the existing culture. They must be *preadapted* to their culture by virtue of cultural appropriateness. If a product is to be

a mass culture success, it must be immediately acceptable, understandable, familiar, and conducive to mass participation.

(Kottak, 1990: 43. Emphases in the original.)

Hoskins and Mirus (1988) have created a useful concept for examining the attraction of national programming to national audiences, the cultural discount.

> A particular program rooted in one culture, and thus attractive in that environment, will have a diminished appeal elsewhere as viewers find it difficult to identify with the style, values, beliefs, institutions and behavioral patterns of the material in questions. Included in the cultural discount are reductions in appreciation due to dubbing or subtitling...As a result of the diminished appeal, fewer viewers will watch a foreign program than a domestic program of the same type and quality, and hence the value to the broadcasters, equal to the advertising revenue induced if the broadcaster is financed from this source, will be less... the cultural discount explains why trade is predominantly in entertainment, primarily drama, programming, where the size of this discount is minimized. Informative programming is much more culture specific and hence, particularly for news and public affairs programming, subject to such a large discount that little trade takes place...

(Hoskins and Mirus, 1988: 500–1)

Using the idea of cultural proximity, this study tries to explain why television production is growing within Latin America and other regions of the world at both the national and cultural-linguistic regional levels. The argument, building on Pool (1977), is that all other things being equal, audiences will tend to prefer that programming which is closest or most proximate to their own culture: national programming if it can be supported by the local economy. A similar desire for the most relevant or similar programs also seems to lead many national audiences to prefer cultural-linguistic regional programming in genres that small countries cannot afford to produce for themselves. The US continues to have an advantage primarily in genres that even large third- world countries cannot afford to produce, such as high-budget feature films, cartoons, and action-adventure series.

Cultural proximity is based to large degree in language. Regional television and music markets are developing for Spanish, Chinese, Arabic and other multi-country language groups. However, besides language, there are other levels of similarity or proximity, based in cultural elements, per se: dress, ethnic types, gestures, body language, definitions of humor, ideas about story pacing, music traditions, religious elements, etc. Indian movies are popular in the Arab world for such similarities, Brazilian telenovelas (evening serials or soaps) dubbed into Spanish are more popular than *Dallas* or *Dynasty* because of such similarities (Straubhaar, 1991). Iwabuchi (1997) shows that Taiwanese young people see Japanese television and music as culturally proximate, sharing a sense of "Asian modernity," despite the language difference between Japanese and Chinese.

Continuing limits of asymmetrical interdependence

Many would-be producers of television programming are constrained by economic realities. The continuing results of conditions of dependency, such as low income resources, lack of industrial infrastructure, lack of support by weak governments, inappropriate models for production, and lack of trained personnel, keep a number of poorer countries from developing much local or national production, even if their audiences might prefer more national programs. This is particularly true for the smallest and poorest of nations, such as the English-speaking Caribbean (Brown, 1987).

However, many countries, like the Dominican Republic or Mozambique, which have extremely limited industrialization do produce significant cultural goods, particularly music, but also television. Rather than classic, almost complete dependency, most countries find themselves in a complex, asymmetrical interdependence. This is particularly true in cultural industries. First, because cultural industries are less capital intensive than others. Second, because the "raw materials" of cultural production are found almost everywhere, in local music, political talk, humor, and dramatic situations. Third, relatedly, because most people seem to like local productions better in most genres, particularly in music and television. So these factors do impel production, both at the national level in the most affortable genres, such as talk shows, news, live music, and live variety, and in the larger producers for cultural-linguistic regions, in more expensive genres such as soap opera, situation comedies, dramas, and action-adventure (Straubhaar, et al., 1992).

Cultural proximity modified by class

Dependency theorists argued that elites and middle classes would tend to be internationalized in their tastes, attentions, and loyalties (Chilcote, 1984; Dos Santos, 1973; Salinas and Paldan, 1979). This chapter will examine what has been happening with elite audiences, particularly as they come to have access to the new cable and satellite television services, which offer a new set of global and regional channels. As a working proposition, in line with dependency theory, these elites do in fact seem to be more internationalized in their television use than do lower middle classes, working classes and the poor.

There is another assumption hidden in theorizations by Dos Santos and Cardoso, that elite notions, tastes and interests would be passed down in a hegemonic process to the masses of the audience. One problem with this is the assumed passivity of the developing nation's mass audiences. Both behavioral science researchers, such as the uses and gratifications school (Blumler and Katz, 1974), and cultural studies researchers, such as Morley (1980), have consistently rejected the view of the audience as a passive entity. Fejes (1981) and Ang (1996), in reassessing the legacy

203

of critical theory, including international dependency theory, remark that political-economy based theories did often lose sight of the audience and its actual behavior. However, as Ang (1996) notes, it is also too easy to speak glibly of an active audience without considering the political economic context. Patterns of commercial television, for example, do limit audience options to the commercially successful formulas, even when locally-produced, and do tend to present a strong set of messages driving consumer behavior.

Class and television technology access

Primarily, this chapter is concerned with how language, culture and cultural capital tend to affect what audiences do with television once they have access to it. However, it is very important to continue to recognize that billions of people are limited in their access to television, particularly the newer television technologies, because they cannot afford access to them.

In 1978, the MacBride report noted that much of the world's population did not have access to many of the dominant communications technologies, including television (McBride Commission, 1980). Since that time, access to broadcast television has rapidly accelerated in many of the world's larger developing countries. In Brazil and Mexico, almost 90 percent of all the population have access, greatly increased since the 1970s. China has increased access to television even faster, from only three million television sets in 1979 to 230 million sets in 200 million TV households by 1992 (Karp, April 21, 1994). This is largely because a television set has emerged as the number one consumer purchase for much of the world's population, including much of the world's poor. However, in the poorest African countries, such as Mozambique, broadcasters estimate are that under one quarter of the population has access to television (from interviews by author with several Southern Africa broadcasters).

The economic capital aspect of social class is the most exclusive with the newest television technologies. Monthly fees for cable television tend to be in the US$20–30 range even in developing countries. When median monthly incomes are often still between US$100 and US$200 for much of the population in countries like Brazil, then access to cable or pay television is simply blocked by lack of economic capital, so that less than 5 percent of the audience has cable or satellite television as of 1997, whereas almost 75 percent of homes in increasingly middle-class Taiwan had cable. In most developing countries, cable television is a middle-class or even upper-middle-class technology which excludes most of the population. To date, direct broadcast satellite technologies (DBS) tend to be even more expensive, including the initial cost of the satellite dish.

When economic class/capital gives access to new television technologies, that permits privileged audiences a far more globalized form of media consumption. The new television technologies nearly always emphasize global, usually American, content, at least at first. The supply of films on videocassette in most countries is still dominated by Hollywood productions, although that may be changing in Asia,

Age and gender are other important demographic characteristics in this study. Many observers have noted that younger people tend to be more involved in global or at least transnational cultural patterns than older people. A number of studies have shown that young people tend to have more globalized music tastes, for instance (Robinson, Buck and Cuthbert, 1991), although young people are also divided by class, education, etc. in the same patterns discussed above (Straubhaar and Viscasillas, 1991). Young people in Brazil are very divided by class in terms of their preferences, as we shall see below.

Class and age seem to be directly related to general preferences for global, regional, national or local culture. Gender seems tied to cultural use patterns that are less general, more specific to genre. Gender is a powerful factor in patterns of interest, use and interpretation of a number of television genres. For example, there is evidence from India and from Greece that women find certain kinds of imported genres to be liberating in the sense that they offer messages that seem to show roles for women beyond those indicated by the local culture. Women in India may read romance novels (Parameswaran, 1997) or women in Greece may watch imported television and find such messages, that draw their interest further toward the imported genres (Zaharopoulos, 1997), and leads them to incorporate some of these messages in their own culture. There is some evidence from at least Brazil and the Dominican Republic that men do tend to prefer some major global cultural genres, such as action films or television series, more than women (Straubhaar, 1991a).

Gender does tend to work in noticeable patterns with national and regional genres as well. Women watch certain kinds of programming more, such as soap operas in the United States, while men tend to watch more sports in most countries. Men and women will also read the messages of national and regional productions differently. In Brazil, both women and men watch *telenovelas*, for example, but several studies have noted that women tend to pick up more messages about alternative women's roles and tend to interpret them in a more emancipating manner.

Brazilian case study

To examine cultural capital formation and its relation to television choices, the author has been conducting a series of in-depth interviews over a ten year period, 1989–98, in Brazil. Almost 120 baseline interviews were conducted in São Paulo in 1989–90 by the author and students working with him. They were structured but in-depth interviews on media habits and social class identity across a stratified sample based on age, class and gender profiles from the 1988 Brazilian census update (PENAD). Subsequent in-depth interviews were conducted in São Paulo, with working-class, lower-middle-class, middl-class, upper-middle-class, and upper-class people. Interviews were also conducted in Salvador and Ilheus, Bahia, with the same kinds of classes, plus urban and rural poor. These last two cities also provided an opportunity to focus on Afro-Brazilians, compared to those in São Paulo, who are disproportionately more likely to be of European origin.

There is some disagreement among Brazilian audience and market researchers about definition of social classes, particularly about the size of the elite and upper-middle class, who are the most avidly sought consumers. This study uses definitions based on Brazilian market research, particularly the ABIPEME social classification system,[1] that focuses on education and major acquisitions, like cars and appliances, that demonstrate purchasing power. This study also focuses on characteristics, like travel, occupation, family background and connections, type and qualitiy of formal education, and language education; and on media access, like Internet, satellite/cable television, print media, that relate to theoretical constructs about globalization that are important to the study.

By ABIPEME definitions, commonly used as a shorhand for class status even in Brazilian media, the elite – Class A – are roughly 3–5 percent of Brazilian society. The upper middle – Class B – is roughly the next 8–10 percent. The middle class – Class C – are about 15–20 percent. The working class – Class D – are about 25–35 percent, and the poor – Class E – are 30–50 percent, depending on the region of the country and fluctuating levels of poverty and employment. This study uses this rough five-category system and tends to confirm its proportions, but adds a number of factors about media access.

In this study, the elite respondents are defined as those who have at least $3,000 a month in income, have all major consumer appliances and a nice car. Although some of the older elite are self-made and uneducated, the younger members almost all have university education. In terms most relevant to globalization of media and culture, they have access to international travel, to learning foreign languages, to satellite and cable television, to computers and the Internet, and to all print media, often including foreign-language media. The most distinguishing thing about them, from these interviews, is that they have direct, unmediated personal access to global culture via travel, work, education and other direct experiences. They also tended to aspire to a lifestyle defined in global terms by both media and direct experience, like travel to Florida. This is the group that is potentially truly globalized, although many of the elite do not use their potential global access and have primarily national mediated and personal cultural and informational experience.

The upper middle class tends to have most of the same characteristics, but lacks some of the economic capital that would provide access to the highest level technology, like the Internet; to international travel; and to the kind of private primary and secondary schooling that permits the elite to get into the best universities, including education abroad. Upper-middle-class people do not have the same access to global interpersonal connections so their access to global information and culture tends to be mediated via the mass media and Brazilian schooling. This group does tend to aspire to achieve more direct global experience by travel, education, etc. They also aspire at least somewhat to a lifestyle defined in part by global media images received at home via television and movies, and are more likely to pursue global media content within Brazil on radio, television, and film.

208

The middle class in Brazil is largely defined in national terms. The working definition that emerged from the interviews was that middle class meant a car, a telephone, a respectable dwelling (defined in fairly local terms), a few major appliances, like a refrigerator, and good prospects for at least a high-school education, with hopes of university. Middle-class people were nationally rather than globally-focused in media consumption. Their material aspirations seem to be formed primarily by the dominant national media, such as television advertising, lifestyle images from *telenovelas*, variety shows, and, to lesser degree, by international music and foreign movies that are shown after 10.00 pm on television, although many middle-class people don't typically stay up for those. Their experience of the global is almost entirely filtered through Brazilian media, although some middle-class people are willing to spend scarce resources for international media, like pay-TV. Within Brazilian media, they are more likely to have access to print media, which carry more global content, as well as television and radio.

The lower middle class and working class are defined in terms of having decent housing (as defined locally), a fairly steady income and employment, and usually some education. They aspire to the national middle-class lifestyle, largely as defined by *telenovelas*, especially a better house, a car, a telephone, more appliances, and maybe a vacation. Their global images are formed almost exclusively by television and music, since print media are mostly priced out of their reach. They often do not realize that brands they aspire to are global – things are framed almost exclusively within a national context for them.

The poor earn little, often under US$100 a month, or less than the minimum wage. They can afford little consumption, although most who have a fixed dwelling also have a television. Most have a dirt floor, few have refrigerators or stoves. They aspire to the necessities of life, defined in local terms in style of food, clothing, etc. Few have anything beyond four years of primary education. Media access is either radio, which almost all have, or television: around 50 percent or so of rural dewllers have a TV, compared to 80 percent or more of the urban poor. Their media consumption tends to be local, provincial/regional or national. They express little interest in foreign or global content.

Culture and media commonalities across class boundaries

Despite the striking differences in class and in media access across classes, a striking amount of national cultural capital is common across classes in Brazil. This common cultural capital is almost all based in either basic schooling or broadcast media, particularly television. More specifically, an enormous amount of this common culture comes from *telenovelas*, popular music, carnival, and sports, particularly soccer. This replicates findings from Kottak's (1990) mammouth study in the mid-1980s of television and culture in Brazil in six coordinated but geographically dispersed ethnographic field studies. Kottak found that there was a mass, democratizing common knowledge across social classes at his sites, represented in telenovelas, soccer and carnival. The latter two are both directly experienced but also commonly experienced in terms of national television. He notes the existence of common "codes... well within the spectator's intellectual, verbal and pyschological repertoire" (Kottak, 1990: 43).

A base in terms of popularly held notions about Brazilian history and identity does seem to come from primary schooling, but most common culture seems to rely on broadcast media experience, rather than direct experience. Direct experience in Brazil is often still very localized, particularly for the working class and poor, in terms of local climate, local ethnic tradition, local cooking, local music and local groups and their leadership.

The existence of this broad common national cultural capital base in Brazil is relatively new. Brazilian cultural has traditionally been very regionalized. Even the national popularity of soccer and carnival has grown slowly in the twentieth Century impelled first by radio and then television, along with the slow growth in penetration of primary education. The achievement of the current degree of common national cultural capital and identity represents a substantial achivement of one of the main development goals set first by developmentalist regimes in the late 1950s and most specifically by the military regimes (1964–85). The military specifically saw the achievement of a consumer culture and a common national identity via national television as one of their main national security goals (Mattos, 1982; 1990). To achieve this, they poured a great deal of money into television, particularly one main commercial network, TV Globo (Straubhaar, 1984). Kottak noted that by 1985 TV Globo had indeed achieved this position as a primary source of cultural capital. "The cultural reason that Globo is such a powerful force in contemporary Brazil is its appeal across regions, classes and other social boundaries... Because Globo offers quality programming, its appeal even extends to upper class people" (Kottak, 1990: 44).

This common cultural capital is very largely national. The programs that almost everyone watches on television are *telenovelas*, some sports (soccer, basketball and volleyball), music shows, and one or two variety shows. The music that almost everyone is familiar with from the radio tends to be mostly from several national genres, with a limited amount of foreign rock and pop, mostly a few international songs that are included on *telenovela* soundtracks. There are some common consumer aspirations, focused on a few things that almost everyone consumes, such as clothes, sandals, beer, and soft drinks. Most of these, except Coca-Cola, are national brands, since the broad common level of consumption and aspiration throughout Brazil seldom even reaches the range of the kinds of products that most global manufacturers wish to manufacture. Other than Coca-Cola, most global firms don't try to make the kinds of things that poor people can afford. Even Levis remain out of most people's grasp. The average poor Brazilian wears rubber thong sandals, a T-shirt, and shorts. They like Coke but don't get to drink it that often; they are more likely to drink juice or local alcohol.

On the other hand, media exposure has produced some degree of globalization in almost all Brazilians. Very few have no global layer at all to their identity or cultural capital. At the simplest level, people are aware that there is an outside world, an America, a Japan, although "foreignness" is relative. More than one northeastern Brazilian that I have talked to thought Japan was down by São Paulo someplace and didn't realize that people speak languages other than Portuguese, since everything on television is in Portuguese and the dubbing isn't always obvious to people. Almost all people are aware of a few international figures (Kennedy, Hitler, Princess Diana – depending on the generation of the interviewee), a few brands (like Coke), a few stars, movies and music groups (although many people recognize Beatles' tunes without knowing who they were).

But these globalized symbols are also mostly localized in the minds of most people as they become part of the broad common Brazilian cultural capital. For example, for critics, Coke remains the apogee of globalization. It probably is, but it has been successfully de-Americanized in the process. Its meaning for local people has been woven into the fabric of their culture. Coke represents a new, global kind of consumption, but its meaning has also been hybridized. Many people do not think of it as American. One student of the author interviewed a São Paulo man in 1994 who worked at a Coca-Cola bottling plant, but did not realize that it was an "American" product. He argued vehemently that it was Brazilian. This is probably a mark of success for Coke's global marketing which localizes it in Brazil by putting Brazilian national soccer shirts on polar bears holding Coke bottles and soccer balls. The polar bears are themselves a global symbol of cold that has been hybridized into tropical Brazil, where a selling point for both beer and soft drinks is that they are sold very cold (*bem geladinha*). Global symbols like these are interpreted in a local context and, through hybridization (Canclini, 1995), eventually become part of the local context.

This minimum globalization that almost all Brazilians have is almost entirely a result of media exposure, particularly radio, television and movies on television. Interviews by both the author and students working with the author show that few Brazilians outside the upper middle and upper classes have any direct, unmediated contact with foreigners or with "global" culture. In contrast, interviews in the Dominican Republic in 1987–88 showed that almost everyone knew someone who has been in the US to work or live, so Dominicans participate much more in the diasporic or migrant approach to globalization, emphasized by scholars like Bhabha (1994). In contrast, due to its geographic distance to the US and its more self-contained economy, the vast majority of Brazilians participate only in mediated and very limited globalization, acquiring very little global cultural capital.

Cultural capital in Brazil

Cultural capital of poor Brazilians

Many rural and extremely poor urban Brazilians are only beginning to acquire cultural capital via media and schooling. Many are still relying very heavily on traditional oral cultures that tend to be very localized, so many poor Brazilians are only somewhat inserted into the national cultural context. As noted above, however, even most poor Brazilians are coming into increasing contact with radio and television. While radio is still often a localizing force in terms of music, news and particularly talk, television is very much a nationalizing force in the lives of poor people. Poor people have relatively little global cultural influence, however.

The vast majority of what little global influence reaches poor people does so through television. In rural areas, access to television varies with electrification, proximity to or coverage by broadcast television signals, access to satellite dishes, and economical capital, or income. The very poorest 10 percent or so are not geographically stable, migrating to look for land or work. Increasingly, those who are stable on land or have a permanent urban dwelling have access to television. Recent migrants to urbanized areas acquire television very quickly before almost anything else. Rural dwellers are working hard to acquire television. For example, in the Cajueiro land reform community settled about ten years ago near Una and Ilheus, Bahia, less than a third of the fifty-five settled families had television, although people could watch a solar powered set in the settlement school sometimes.

Rural dwellers are increasingly likely to share in the minimum common Brazilian national and global cultural capital described above. Writing of the mid-1980s, Kottak noted that "rural Brazilians' knowledge of the contemporary world ... is certainly greater now than it was before television. By the mid-1980s, as a direct result of exposure to television, villagers had become much more world wise" (1990: 134). Kottak and others, along with this study, observed that almost all of what rural and poor people in Brazil learn from television and radio is nationally-focused. People in this study and in Kottak's spoke of national soccer, characters and themes on *telenovelas*, awareness of a few national political issues, and a general sense of what Brazilians have in common. Kottak (1990) noted that one of the primary impacts of television in Brazil has been to make previously isolated people feel comfortable with other Brazilians and with being Brazilian. Kottak gave the example of one very shy rural woman who remained very isolated even within her new village until her family got television. With television, and more regular social opportunities, she gradually became more outgoing and socially integrated (1990: 133–4).

The results of both Kottak's study and the present one show that television tends to add a number of national factors to the cultural capital of rural Brazilians. They become aware of Brazilian city life, as portrayed in the *telenovelas*, but the actual motivation to migrate to the city has much more to do with interpersonal contacts with migrants, particularly among their own families. They become aware of new ideas about race and gender roles, which tend to change locally held definitions and stereotypes. Kottak considered this process a powerful and largely positive liberalization of attitudes (1990). They become aware of national holidays, foods, sports and music, which gradually begin to supplement traditional local activities and consumption. They do also tend to receive a very minimal global awareness as described above.

Interestingly enough, while relatively little global influence reaches rural Brazilians via television, other aspects of globalization can sometimes reach them more directly, if still in relatively small numbers. Rural dwellers do interact with aspects of the global economy in terms of who they work for, where they sell their crops, and what they aspire to buy. Because of global non-governmental organization (NGO) concerns over issues like land reform, forest preservation, and sustainable agriculture, rural dwellers have an increasing likelihood of direct contact with other Brazilians who are working for or with global NGOs. For example, rural organizations in Brazil, such as the Movimento dos Sem Terra (Movement of the Landless), have formed to obtain or defend land for landless or recently settled small farmers. The Cajueiro land reform settlement of formerly landless farmers is affiliated with that national organization and several local ones. Discussions in 1994, 1996 and 1998 with several Cajueiro community members showed that their knowledge and cultural capital was largely traditional, but they had been very much affected by several kinds of direct contact with both the landless movement and ecologically-oriented Brazilian NGOs funded by Conservation International and the World Wildlife Fund. They had learned how to organize cooperative work groups and had begun to build cooperative facilities to improve their access to fertilizers, crop processing, basic education, and medical aid. They had also become aware of the ideas of sustainable agriculture to preserve the rather fragile soils of their land and of preservation of some of the tropical forest that remained on the land they had seized to settle.

The urban poor tend to have more contact with media, but theirs is often limited to watching television with neighbors or in public places. Like rural people, those without permanent dwellings are least drawn into media contact with either the national or the global. Interviews in 1989 and in 1994 with homeless people in São Paulo showed that most of their cultural capital was based on interpersonal contacts within an oral culture context. Most are migrants to the city from rural areas and small towns. Much of their cultural capital is an adaptation of rural traditions to the city, but as they get drawn into urban social life and media use, their cultural capital becomes a hybrid of rural tradition and national urban culture. For example, the traditional music that rural migrants brought with them from the northeast of Brazil to the major cities of the southeast, like São Paulo, has been transformed into various hybrids that add electronic instruments, urban images and themes, industrial production and marketing, to rural tunes, stories and images. According to interviews, this kind of hybrid is welcomed by the migrants because it helps them adjust to life in the city while preserving a memory of the (oral) culture they grew up with.

Luiz Roberto Alves has studied the efforts of migrants to São Paulo's industrial suburbs to maintain the memory of their original rural cultures. In a 1992 interview with the author, he observed that migrants tend to use hybrid media that maintain rural elements, but even more importantly, the migrants form interpretive communities of interpersonal communication which help them interpret national mass media in ways that help them create hybrid identities that bridge the urban and rural, the new national televized culture and the old oral, local culture.

Interviews from 1989 to 1998 in São Paulo reflect that poor and working- class people tend to make television viewing choices that are somewhat different from the national majority. They do tend to watch the dominant popular culture in TV Globo's *telenovelas*, but frequently they turn away from TV Globo to watch other channels which target programs more directly at this very substantial number of urban poor, working poor, working-class and lower- middle-class people. Two networks target variety and talk shows at the rural and urban working class and poor. SBT (Sistema Brasileira de Televisão, owned by longtime salesman and variety show host Silvio Santos) aims its variety shows, game shows, talk shows, *telenovelas*, and music specifically at this segement of the population (Mira, 1990), as a strategy of segmented competition with TV Globo, which tends to dominate the general mass audience. More recently, the Record Network has re-targeted the same kind of working-class and poor audience with sensationalist talk/interview programs modeled on Jerry Springer, etc. in the US These kinds of programs are often denounced by Brazilian critics as tasteless, coarse, even grotesque, but as Muniz Sodre (1972) noted in early work on variety shows, such shows do revive and incorporate both the styles and content of traditional Brazil oral culture and rural folkmore. Further, as current critics like Esther Hamburger of the *Folha de São Paulo* do often note, these shows raise issues of genuine concern to the urban poor and working class, airing grievances about roads, health conditions, medical care and crime, as well as revealing sensational sexual scandals and provoking fistfights among participants. Hamburger (April 12, 1998) noted that one of the most sensationalist shows, *Ratinho*, (Little Mouse) on TV Record, actually beat TV Globo in the ratings one evening when Globo showed an imported series, *E.R.*, instead of a *telenovela* in late prime time. She observed that while *E.R.* was a very high quality import, *Ratinho* was arguably much more relevant to people's lives and much more within their areas of interest and awareness.

Interviews with urban poor reflect a cultural capital that is in transition from the kind of local and traditional rural cultural capital described above to the national televised common cultural capital described earlier. Their cultural capital tends to focus on increasing awareness of urban issues, of city and national leaders, of urban transport and working conditions, of working-class consumer aspirations (particularly in food, clothes, and basic household products), of national ethnic and religious images, of new urban gender roles, of less traditional sexual behavior and imagery, and a slightly greater knowledge of global culture than they had before coming to the city. While much of this comes from national television, interviews show that the urban poor rely mostly on oral communication with the people and groups they know for essential cultural capital for adjusting to city life.

Working class cultural capital

Not unlike the urban poor, from which they mostly come, working-class people in Brazil have cultural capital that is mostly focused on the local and the regional, to lesser degree on the national, and fairly little on the international or global. Interviews in São Paulo and Salvador, Bahia for this study show that the interpersonal sources of working class cultural capital are focused and based on the extended family, the neighborhood, groups of friends of the same age and gender, the workplace and union, and, most of all, the immediate nuclear family and the home. Jacks (1995) talks about the importance of the home and of daily life as the crux of people's reception and understanding of television in Brazil. While this was true of most of those interviewed for this study, it seemed particularly key for working class people who are working hard to establish and maintain a stable residence and home environment, aware of the danger of slipping back into the urban poor and maybe even into homelessness. Interviews from 1989 to 1992 evidenced a particularly strong sense of anxiety about this. The church, either Catholic or Protestant, is important for some, but not all, as an additional source of cultural capital.

Media sources, particularly radio and television, are very importat for most working-class people as a primary source of cultural capital. Among those interviewed, almost all global and cultural-linguistic "regional" cultural capital comes to working-class or poor people via media, or to a lesser degree, formal schooling. Working-class schooling is often limited, however, to four to six years of primary school, which limits schooling's role in cultural capital formation. However, working-class parents and youth with a certain amount of stability in the city tend to start focusing more on the school as a source of educational capital for upward mobility.

Working-class people, based on a locally or nationally-oriented store of cultural capital, tend to make media choices that reinforce what is familiar or culturally proximate to them. Working-class people are much more likely to listen to radio stations that play only national or local music genres, such as samba, forró (northeastern dance music), Axé (samba plus reggae), or Musica Popular Brasileiro (MPB – Brazilian pop music), whereas upper-middle- or upper-class interviewees were more likely to listen to stations that played either US/European pop music or a mixture of imported and Brazilian music.

Working-class print media exposure is much more limited and much more largely national than is the print media usage of the upper middle and upper class. Working-class people mostly read magazines and newspapers, rather than books, a trend noted across Latin America by Martin Barbero (1988). The books read by working-class interviewees tended to be either national popular literature or popular US/European genre novels in translation.

Working-class Brazilians travel between cities by bus while the upper-middle-class and upper-class tend to go by airplane. It is revealing therefore to compare what is in a large bookstore or newsstand in a São Paulo bus station with what is in an equivalent shop in the São Paulo airport. The bus station shop has more magazines, comics and cheaply printed chapbooks and pamphlets than books, although the book section is of a respectable size. Aside from the comics, many of which are Disney, Marvel and DC translations, and the translated novels, almost everything else is national in origins. At the airport, the same national newspapers, magazines, and books are available, as are the translated comics and novels. The selection in the latter two is different for a more affluent audience, with more expensive book editions and more HQ or "high quality" comics translations. What is most noticeable is much more foreign literature in translation and a significant number of foreign-language books, magazines, and newspapers aimed at both international travelers and Brazilians with elite cultural capital such as sufficient foreign-language skills to read comfortably for pleasure in another language.

Middle class cultural capital

Working-class Brazilians aspire to be middle class, at least lower middle class. That typically means a nicer dwelling, a car, more appliances, a telephone, and more and better education, aiming at completed secondary or maybe even university education. To the interviewees, it also implies a less blue-collar occupation, different neighborhoods, paying for private schools, and adherence to what is seen as a more conventional set of values and mores.

An image of what it is to be middle class seems to one of the main items of cultural capital that interviewees acquire from watching television, particularly the *telenovelas*. Although census statistics tend to indicated that mobility from working class or lower to the middle class is fairly low in real life in Brazil, this is very much the stuff of which telenovela plots are made, according to reviewers like Artur da Tavola (1984). Reviewing an ostensibly Americanized *telenovela* with discos, called *Dancin' Days*, in the late 1970s, da Tavola observed that it, like most novelas, was really about how to become middle class. The defining moment for him came not in the disco scenes, but when one of the characters asked his wife if she would like a refrigerator and she burst into tears of joy (cited in Straubhaar, 1981). Interviewees agree. They think *telenovelas* mostly focus on romance, getting ahead in life (upward mobility), and the urban middle class. Aside from consumer items, like refrigerators, the Brazilian cultural capital understanding or perception of "middle class" seems to focus on education, family stability, a better and varied diet, greater leisure options, better housing, and a sense of security, according to interviewees, both in the middle class and beneath it.

The cultural capital of those actually in the middle class still largely comes from television. Middle-class television choices are somewhat different, tending to disdain the working-class-oriented variety shows of SBT and focusing much more on the *telenovela*-oriented contents of TV Globo. Middle-class cultural capital is much more heavily supplemented beyond television, however, by education, print media use, personal contacts, and organizations like churches, clubs and networks of friends from school. Several newspaper critics and this study's interviewees note that one of the key differences between the working class and middle class is that the latter has more non-mediated options for information, entertainment and leisure ("TV – o pobre lazer dos paulistanos," 1977).

Middle-class Brazilians are somewhat more globalized than are the working-class in the kinds of media choices they make. Middle-class interviewees are much more likely to stay up after 10.00 pm so they can watch the American movies that are typically shown then on several channels. That both expresses cultural capital already acquired through schooling and media, and it also reinforces a more globalized cultural capital. Movies in the cinema houses have become very expensive, so even middle-class people go to them fairly infrequently. But between late movies on television and rented movies on video, feature films seem to be an important source of American and global cultural capital for a fair number of middle-class Brazilians, whereas American or other imported movies do not seem particularly important to working-class or poor Brazilians, who are much more likely to prefer the national programs broadcast on television. However, even middle-class or upper-middle-class Brazilians usually prefer prime-time *telenovelas* to watching movies on video, even when they have the VCR sometimes gathering dust on a shelf. While some middle-class Brazilians do have satellite dishes and/or cable connections, those interviewed for this study were more likely to be using them to get a good-quality signal for TV Globo than to buy pay-TV packages that would deliver dozens of extra channels in English.

Upper-middle and upper-class cultural capital

A greater degree of globalization, both in media choices and in direct personal experience, is perhaps the main thing that divided upper-middle-class and upper-class interviewees from those in the middle class and working class. The upper class are characterized by a number of globalized attributes: language skills, particuarly in English; higher education, with either study abroad or aspirations to do so; international travel, particularly to the US and Europe; occupations that lend themselves to contact with people in the US and Europe, or increasingly, Asia; interest in US and European lifestyles; knowledge of those lifestyles; identification with European standards of beauty, including ethnicity; detailed knowledge of both high culture and popular culture in the US and Europe. Upper-class Brazilians are often divided in whether their global cultural capital is linked to Europe or to the US, particularly for those who have been at least partially educated abroad, and who have learned English versus another of the European languages.

The upper-middle-class interviewees tend to aspire to all of this direct experience with the global. Their actual experience with global culture is likely to be more heavily mediated, however. Most upper-middle-class Brazilians have eventually made a trip to Miami and/or Disneyworld, but they have otherwise traveled far less that the elite. Upper-middle-class global cultural capital tends to be more focused on the US and less on Europe, perhaps because physical access to the US is cheaper, study of English as a foreign language is more prevalent, and because US culture is much more widely available in mediated forms. Upper-middle-class interviewees seemed to be the most likely to watch American movies on video or to make use of the movie channels on pay-TV packages for satellite dishes or cable TV.

Language skill is one sharp dividing between the upper class or elite, and the upper middle and upper classes. Comments by interviewees indicate that real skill in English, sufficient to watch and enjoy CNN, for example, is largely limited to the upper class. Middle class people find language a major barrier to access to globalized information. So do many in the upper-middle class, but many of them have set a serious goal to acquire better English as a tool to bridge the gap into elite-level media access to more global sources. English and access to information through it are seen by many in the upper middle class as a crucial tool to be acquired. However, for most of them it also remains a crucial barrier that ultimately tends to reinforce their use of national media, particularly the *telenovelas*, music shows, variety shows, etc. that are part of the broad national cultural capital.

Brazilian MTV provides an interesting case of globalization aimed at the upper, upper middle and some of the middle class in Brazil. MTV Brazil is a joint venture between MTV and the large publisher Editora Abril. It plays 70–80 percent US and European rock and pop music videos and only targets the upper 20–30 percent of the population, in terms of class status and buying power, according to interviews in 1994 and 1998 with MTV Brazil research and marketing staff members. They do that because their advertisers target the more affluent and the more globalized among Brazilian youth in terms of consumer preferences. They also target this group because it has the most interest in the US and European music that MTV has to offer. The target is reached. A 1997 MARPLAN study of eight major urban markets in Brazil shows that 22 percent of MTV's audience tends to be in class A (upper class), 44 percent in class B (upper middle class), 28 percent in class C (middle class), 6 percent in class D (working class) and none in class D (the poor) (*Perfil da Penetração MTV*, 1997).

These middle-, upper-middle and upper-class youths have the cultural capital base that leads them away from a strictly national cultural capital and in a more globalized direction. They have a more elite education, which often includes serious study of English. They are more likely to have traveled abroad, or know people there. They are more likely to be aware of American and European brands, due in part to MTV's own role in their cultural capital. They are more likely to be aware of American stars, lifestyles, and images, again partially due to MTV, as well as movies at both cinema and video. However, even these more upper-class youths still usually like Brazilian music, particularly that which incorporates rock, like Brazilian urban rock; reggae, like Axé; rap, funk and other global elements. Some Brazilian music is part of the broad cultural capital shared across class lines that was discussed earlier.

Conclusion

Language, cultural capital and social class do seem to be significant moderators of television flows between countries. While the original cultural imperialism paradigm did not seem to anticipate this, it does seem that language, culture and class can both facilitate and provide barriers against internationalizing and globalizing flows of television.

Media imperialism and dependency theorists did anticipate the internationalization of the bourgeoisie (Chilcote, 1984; Dos Santos, 1973). This study finds that both economic capital and cultural capital do encourage the elite and upper middle classes of Brazil to watch more imported programming, particularly US television programs and feature films.

Economic capital gives access to basic television in poor regions, like Africa, where broadcast television also tends to depend more on imported US and European programs, because they cost less (Read, 1976; Tunstall, 1977). Even when countries in regions like Latin America begin to produce much or even most of their own programming, economic capital still gives privileged classes a continued greater access to foreign programming, first through VCRs and now, increasingly, through cable and satellite TV. This was strongly demonstrated in the interviews in Brazil, where the top 5–10 percent of the population have much more globalized media access.

Cultural capital reinforces the use of this access to imported media and TV programming by giving elites and upper middle classes the ability to understand and enjoy programming imported from outside their cultural-linguistic region. This kind of cultural capital is clearest with language ability, which has been emphasized in economic studies (Hoskins and Mirus, 1988; Wildman and Siwek, 1988), but also includes education, travel abroad, familiarity with the ways of life of other countries, education abroad, work with international companies, and the kind of family life which is produced by and reinforces these kinds of advantages. This study found that non-mediated cultural capital from direct contact with global culture was decisive in making Brazilian elites far more globalized than the rest of the Brazilian population.

What media imperialism did not anticipate was the growth of national and regional (cultural-linguistic) television producers, protected and encouraged within national and cultural-linguistic television markets, it seems, by elements of cultural capital which seem to provide natural barriers against interest in many types of imported programming, when national or regional alternatives are available. These are causes of what Hoskins and Mirus (1988) call the "cultural discount" that many audiences apply against imported programming. These aspects of cultural capital seem to include lack of language ability, which is particularly important in the early phases of television technologies and in less developed markets where dubbing is not yet extensively used. In many African countries, such as Namibia and Mozambique, most imported programs are not dubbed. When VCRs first hit many markets, imported films were not yet dubbed or even subtitled – particularly when they were pirated copies (Boyd, Straubhaar and Lent, 1989). In the initial introductions of cable and satellite television, as in the Dominican Republic in the 1980s, when signals where taken straight from US distribution satellites, or as in the early-to-mid 1990s in Brazil, where local pay-TV services often carried undubbed US and European channels, language capital was also still crucial for watching the new undubbed channels.

Language is not the only significant aspect of cultural capital which favors national and cultural-linguistic market producers. The interviews cited above have shown the importance of national references in humor, national or regional/local ethnic types, national or regional/local historical references, local or national political references, unfamiliarity with ways of life outside the nation or cultural-linguistic region, preference for known national or regional stars, and familiar scenery and locales. Another, which is touched on in the Brazilian study, is familiarity with national and regional genres, which even if they have US or European roots, have taken on a life and trajectory of their own within the nation or region. The Latin-American version of the soap opera, the *telenovela* provides two cases in point. The *telenovela* form was created in Cuba by Colgate-Palmolive (Straubhaar, 1982) but has been heavily adapted and developed over almost five decades in Latin America. There is now a *telenovelas* genre archetype that any Latin-American will recognize, but which would seem decidedly odd to an American fan of soap operas. Within that genre development broadly shared by the Latin-American region, however, Brazilian and Mexican *telenovelas* have taken decidedly different turnings. Both countries are large enough to produce their own programming and import little from other Latin-American countries. In-depth interviews of viewers by the author in Santo Domingo in 1988 showed that they were aware of and consistent in their views of the Brazilian and Mexican variations: Brazilian *telenovelas* were seen as more socially and politically topical, more historical, and sexier; Mexican *telenovelas* were seen as more romantic, more traditional and lighter. In these Brazilian interviews, there is a distinct preference for the national form of the *telenovela*. Some of the people interviewed were aware of the Argentine and Mexican *telenovelas*, but none preferred them to national production. Since national production can fill prime time on several stations now, there is little motivation to watch imports.

To some degree, these attractions of national or culturally and linguistically similar forms of television programming can be summed up in the concept of cultural proximity. Audiences do seem to prefer that culture which is closest to their accumulated tastes, corresponding to their cultural capital. For the broad audience, consisting of lower middle, working and poor classes, that tends to translate into a preference for national production. Outside of large countries like Brazil, where national production does not fill prime time, that translates into a strong secondary preference for productions from within the cultural-linguistic market. However, both economic capital access to new technologies and cultural capital familiarity with cosmopolitan, developed world cultures seem to be leading elites and upper middle classes away from national and cultural-linguistic market television genres and productions. That was reflected in Brazil. While even elites still listen to Brazilian music and watch quite a bit of Brazilian television, they are strongly drawn to more globalized sources of culture and information.

One might speculate that as more national economies become globalized and as economic growth in many countries leads to a growth in middle classes, that their acquisition of greater economic and cultural capital will tend to lead to a steadily larger proportion of many nations' populations toward viewing more US and European programming. In-depth interviews by the authors in both Brazil and the Dominican Republic, however, suggest that this effect will tend to be only partial, however. In both those countries, groups across the cultural capital spectrum all watch national television productions. What seems more likely, from what was suggested in the in-depth interviews, was that those with increased economic and cultural capital begin to have more multi-layered identities. In Brazil, for example, elites still seem to identify heavily with Brazilian culture and like what they perceive as the best of Brazilian mass culture, including television and even *telenovelas*. They do, however, come to have other layers of taste for things and cultural products from US and European cultures.

Within a seeming globalization, there seems more of a potential for uneven, multilayered cultural productions, flow or sales, and consumption, a type of asymmetrical interdependence among various producing and importing television markets. On the production, sale and flow side, there is an asymmetrical interdependence in which Brazil imports more culture from the US than it sells to the US, but may compete quite successfully with US cultural exports to other countries in Latin America, other Portuguese-speaking countries, or even the world market for historical soap opera, in which, incidentally, Brazil has successfully sold programs to over 100 countries (Marques de Melo, 1988, 1992). On the consumption side, there is a sort of uneven balance between the draw of cultural proximity among most of the audience and the draw toward other global offerings available to those members of middle and upper classes with cultural and economic capital.

Note

1 In Brazil, the weight of cultural capital in determining one's social class standing seems to be clear in the index adopted by the Association of Audience and Market Survey Agencies (ABA/ABIPEME). These weighted point criteria balance the education of the head of the family with the possession of several key icons of acquisitive power to classify social classes in five hierarchical groups, from A to E. Illustratively, having a college degree is worth more points than completing only the elementary school or owning any home appliance.

References

Ang, I. (1996). *Living Room Wars: Rethinking Media Audiences for a Post-Modern World.* New York: Routledge.

Blumler, J. and Katz, E. (1974). *Sage Annual Review of Communication Research,* 3. Beverly Hills, CA: Sage.

Bourdieu, P. (1984). *Distinction: A social critique of the judgement of taste.* Cambridge: Harvard University Press.

Boyd, D.A., Straubhaar, J.D. and Lent, J. (1989). *The Videocassette Recorder in the Third Torld*. New York: Longman.

Boyd-Barrett, O. (1980). *The International News Agencies*. Beverly Hills: Sage.

Brown, A. (1987). *TV Programming Trends in the Anglophone Caribbean: the 1980s*. Caribbean. Occasional Paper No. 2. Institute of Mass Communication, University of the West Indies, Kingston, Jamaica

Canclini, N.G. (1988). "Culture and power: the state of research." *Media, Culture and Society*, 10.

Canclini, N.G. (1995). *Hybrid Cultures: Strategies for Entering and Leaving Modernity.* Minneapolis: University of Minnesota Press.

Chen, S.-L. (1987). "The flow of television rograms from United States to Latin America: A comparative study of two weeks television schedules in 1973 and 1983." Unpublished Master's thesis, Michigan State University.

Chilcote, R.H. (1984). *Theories of Development and Underdevelopment*. Boulder, CO: Westview Press.

Collins, R. (1986). "Wall-to-wall Dallas? The US–UK trade in television." *Screen*, May–June, 66–77.

Collins, R. (1990). *Television: Policy and Culture*. London: Unwyn Hyman.

International Commission for the Study of Communication Problems (McBride Commission) (1980). *One World, Many Voices*. New York: Unipub/UNESCO.

Da Tavola, A. (1984). *Comunicacao e Mito*. Rio de Janeiro.

Dos Santos, T. (1973). "The crisis of development theory and problems of departure in Latin America." In H. Bernstein (Ed.), *Underdevelopment and Development: The Third World Today.* Baltimore: Penguin.

Duarte, L. (1997). "Social class as a mediator for patterns of viewership of international programs." In East Lansing, Michigan: Michigan State University, unpublished paper.

Evans, P. (1979). *Dependent Development: The Alliance of Multinational, State and Local Capital in Brazil*. Princeton: Princeton University Press.

Featherstone, M. and Lash, S. (1995). "An Introduction." In M. Featherstone, S. Lash, and R. Robertson (Eds), *Global Modernities*. Thousand Oaks, CA: Sage.

Fejes, F. (1981). "Media imperialism: An assessment." *Media, Culture and Society*, 3(3), 281–9.

Ferguson, M. (1992). "The mythology about globalization." *European Journal of Communication*, 7, 69–93.

Getino, O. (1990). *Impacto del Video en el Espacio Audiovisual Latinamericano*. Lima, Peru: Instituto para América Latina.

Guback, T. and Varis, T. (1986). *Transnational Communication and Cultural Industries. Reports and Papers on Mass Communication*. Paris: UNESCO.

Hall, Stewart. (1982). "Encoding/Decoding." In S. Hall, D. Hobson, A. Lowe and P. Willis (Eds), *Culture, Media and Language*. London: Hutchinson.

Hamelink, C.J. (1983). *Cultural Autonomy in Global Communications*. New York: Longman.

Herman E. and McChesney, R. (1997). *The Global Media: The New Missionaries of Global Capitalism*. Washington, DC: Cassell.

Hoskins, C. and Mirus, R. (1988). "Reasons for the US dominance of the international trade in television programs." *Media, Culture and Society*, 499–515.

Huntington, S. (1996). "The West unique: not universal." *Foreign Affairs*.

Iwabuchi, K. (1997). "The sweet smell of Asian modernity: the Japanese presence in the Asian audiovisual market." Presented at the Fifth International Symposium on Film,

Television and Video, Taipei, Fu Jen University.

Jacks, N. (1995). "Pesquisa de recepção e cultura regional." In M. Wilton (Ed.), *Sujeito, o Lado Oculto do Receptor*, 151–68. São Paulo: Editora Brasiliense.

Kahl, S. (1995). "The cross-cultural effects of US programming on young cable and non-cable television viewers in Brazil." Unpublished MA thesis, Department of Telecommunication, Michigan State University.

Lee, C.C. (1980). *Media Imperialism Reconsidered*. Beverly Hills, CA: Sage.

McAnany (1984). The Logic of Cultural Industries in Latin America: The Television Industry in Brazil. In V. Mosco and J. Wasco (Eds), *Critical Communications Review*, 185–208. Norwood, NJ: Ablex.

McChesney, R. (1997). "Political economy and globalization." Association for Education in Journalism and Mass Communication. Chicago.

Marques de Melo, J. (1988). *As Telenovelas da Globo: Produção e Exportação*. São Paulo: Summus.

Marques de Melo, J. (1992). "Brazil's role as a television exporter within the Latin American regional Market." Paper at International Communication Association, Miami.

Martín-Barbero, J.M. (1988). "Communication from culture: the crisis of the national and emergence of the popular." *Media, Culture and Society*, 10.

Mattelart, A. (1991). *Advertising International: The Privatization of Public Space*. New York: Routledge.

Mattelart, A. and Schmuckler, H. (1985). *Communication and Information Technologies: Freedom of Choice for Latin America?* (Bruxton, D., Trans.). Norwood, NJ: Ablex.

Mira, M.-C. (1990). "Modernização e Gosto Popular – Uma História do Sistema Brasileiro de Televisão." Master's thesis, Catholic University of São Paulo (PUC).

Morley, D. (1980). *The Nationwide Audience: Structure and Decoding*. London: British Film Institute.

Morley, D. (1992). *Television, Audiences and Cultural Spaces*. New York: Routledge.

Nordentreng, K. and Varis, T. (1974). *Television Traffic: A One-Way Street. Reports and Papers on Mass Communication*. Paris: UNESCO.

Oliveira, O.S. (1989). "Media and Dependency: a view from Latin America." *Media Development*, (1), 10–13.

Page, J.A. (1995). *The Brazilians*. Reading, MA: Addison-Wesley.

Parameswaran, R. (1997). *Western Romance Fiction as Urban "English Popular Culture" in Post-colonial India*. Chicago Association for Education in Journalism and Mass Communication.

Pool, Ithiel de Sola. (1977). "The changing flow of television." *Journal of Communications*. Spring, 139–49.

Read, W.H. (1976). *America's Mass Media Merchants*. Baltimore, MA: Johns Hopkins University Press.

Robinson, D., Buck, E. and M. Cuthbert. (1991). *Music at the Margins: Popular Music and Global Cultural Diversity*. Newbury Park, CA: Sage.

Rodrigues, A. "Creating an audience and remapping a nation: Brief history of US Spanish language broadcasting, 1930–1980." *Quarterly Review of Film and Video*.

Rodrigues, A. (1994). "Latino panethnicity and panamericanism: The imagined audience of the Noticiero Univsion." Paper at International Communication Association, Albuquerque, NM.

Salinas, R. and Paldan, L. (1979). "Culture in the process of dependent development: Theoretical perspectives." In K. Nordenstreng and H.I. Schiller (Eds), *National Sovereignty and International Communiations*. Norwood, NJ: Ablex Publishing.

Simpson, A. (1992). *Xuxa*. Philadelphia: Temple University Press.

Sinclair, J. (1994). "Televisa-ization and Globo." Paper at Latin American Studies Association.

Straubhaar, J. (1982). "The development of the *telenovela* as the paramount form of popular culture in Brazil." *Studies in Latin American Popular Culture*, 138–50.

Straubhaar, J. (1990). Effects of Cable TV in the Dominican Republic. In Surlin and Soderlund, eds. *Mass Media and the Caribbean, Caribbean Studies, Vol. 6*. New York: Gordon and Breach, pp. 273-286.

Straubhaar, J. (1991). "Beyond media imperialism: Assymetrical interdependence and cultural proximity." *Critical Studies in Mass Communication*, 8.

Straubhaar, J. and Viscasillas, G. (1991). "Class, genre and the regionalization of the television market in Latin America." *Journal of Communication*, 41(1), 53–69.

Straubhaar, J., Campbell, C., Youn, S.-M., Champagnie, K., Elasmar, M. and L. Castellon. (1992). "The emergence of a Latin American market for television programs." International Communication Association, Miami.

Tomlinson, J. (1991). *Cultural Imperialism*. Baltimore, MD: Johns Hopkins Press.

Tracey, M. (1988). "Popular culture and the economics of global television." *InterMedia*.

Tunstall, J. (1977). *The Media are American*. New York: Columbia University Press.

Veii, V.S. (1988). "Foreign television entertainment programs viewing and cultural imperialism: A case study of US television entertainment programs viewing in Windhoek, Namibia." Unpublished PhD dissertation, Michigan State University, Department of Sociology.

Varis, T. and Nordenstreng, K. (1974). *One-Way Street*. Paris: UNESCO..

Von Garnier, C. (1986). *Katutura Revisited 1986*. Windhoek, Namibia: Angelus Printing.

Wallerstein, I. (1990). "Culture as the ideological battelground of the modern world system." *Theory and Culture*, 7, 31–56.

Waterman, D. and Rogers, E. (1994). "The economics of television program production and trade in Far East Asia." *Journal of Communication*. 44(3), 89–111.

Wildman, S. and Siwek, S. (1988). *International Trade in Films and Television Programs*. Cambridge, MA: Ballinger.

Wilkinson, K. (1995). "Where culture, language and communication converge: The Latin-American cultural linguistic market." Unpublished PhD dissertation, University of Texas-Austin.

Zaharopoulos, D. (1997). *US Television and American Cultural Stereotypes in Greece*. Las Vegas: Broadcast Education Association.

13

THE CHOICE BETWEEN LOCAL AND FOREIGN

Taiwan youths' television viewing behavior

Herng Su and Sheue-Yun Chen

The influence of television programs – especially that of imported, foreign programs – on audiences has long been a major concern for communication researchers. Although recent research has found audiences to be rather autonomous in their selection of programs and local in tastes, the question of foreign program consumption is left open as younger viewers have been found to be more oriented toward imported programs in general. If the finding is an indicator of what will come, there would be grounds for concern given the dramatic growth of satellite television and foreign program supply in recent years.

Taiwan, an island nation which used to have a controlled media environment, suddenly found it no longer possible to keep its borders clear of undesired cultural products. As a result of democratization, the television market was deregulated in 1992, and a tremendous amount of foreign TV programs were brought in from the United States and Japan. In the four years between 1993 and 1997, almost twenty satellite channels appeared, ten of which were American, seven Japanese, one from Singapore and one, CCTV, from mainland China. Taiwan's TV environment suddenly moved into an era where it was part of the global capital economic system and local stations no longer had an unchallenged position.

The trans-cultural imagination and cultural experience created by American, Japanese and other overseas channels has become a main theme in the current transformation of Taiwan's TV culture. What then, does this mean to audiences? Have local programs been able to maintain their attraction, or are they disappearing from the viewing agenda as more choices are made available?

This study concentrates on a single audience group, young viewers, for they were not only found to be avid consumers of foreign programs, but they also tended to be more susceptible to influences.

The discussion in this chapter pays special attention, but is not limited, to the theories of cultural capital and cultural proximity, for they provide an analytical framework that is especially pertinent to the study of viewing behavior *vis-à-vis* foreign programs. It is believed that an understanding of the extent to which foreign programs dominate youths' viewing agenda, the factors that may contribute to the formulation of such an agenda, and the significance of this exposure would be the first step to answering the question on the implications of cultural product flow in this age of global communication.

In this research, "foreign programs" refers to programs that come from overseas, including programs that are transmitted to Taiwan from overseas and also programs which originate overseas but are bought or re-packaged by local TV stations or channels, and which are broadcast on satellite channels or TV stations.

Re-contextualizing the globalization thesis

There are many reasons why Taiwan viewers – or viewers in any country – should watch foreign programs. Past research has found that educated and upper-middle-class Taiwanese watch more foreign programs produced in the US and Japan, a pattern which is similar to that in third-world nations (Wang and Tseung, 1988: 217, 271; Pan and Wang, 1989: 62; Tsang and Wang, 1990). There is, however, insufficient evidence to tell us what contributed to this viewing behavior.

In 1970, Schiller (1971), with his view of US cultural imperialism, severely criticized the one-way flow of US TV programs to other countries. He also accused the US of using its market power to forcibly sell media products to developing countries with the effect of creating a kind of branch media culture.

The analysis of media imperialism was not only reductionist; it was seriously lacking in discussion of the meaning of audiovisual culture and media reception. While some scholars believed that the social impact of foreign programs included the ideas, values, knowledge, behavior modes or even lifestyles of their audiences (Beltran, 1978: 184), research showed that the effect was either limited or uncertain.

Elasmar and Hunter (1992), in a meta-analysis involving thirty-six pieces of transnational broadcasting research from twenty-four countries, found that transnational broadcasting only had a limited impact on viewers. There was no clear relationship at all between exposure to foreign programs and viewers' knowledge, ideas, attitudes, values or behavior, still less a causal relationship. They also pointed out that past research lacked a theoretical perspective, and that in the future emphasis should be put on cultural theories, and the impact of language and religion, history on viewers should be considered.

Since the 1980s broadcasting industries have been deregulated in many countries. Thanks to advances in technology, the international flow of programs was increasingly common and this was one of the most striking phenomena of the 1990s. The cultural impact that might have accompanied this trend brought further discussion. However, in this wave of research, assessments of the cultural impact of the international flow of programs mostly focused on changes in the structure of the global media industry and on whether the transnational flow of programs was building a global media culture (Varis, 1974, 1984; Sepstrup, 1990; Wallis and Baran, 1990; Negus, 1993).The cultural impact of transnational media still needed to be clarified.

Globalization theories discussed the process and driving forces of change while recognizing the difficulty of observing the effects of transnationalism – especially when the effects involved widespread reception of and adjustment to foreign culture. The dominance of Western media products has led some to claim that media globalization equals "cultural imperialism." However, some significant counter-trends should be noted when we assess the impact of global media.

Not only were ownership and production concentrated in wealthier nations, but consumption, too, was skewed heavily toward the wealthier segment of the world's population – those with the necessary material resources to fully participate in the global media culture. In addition, differences or affinities of language and culture between partners to any exchange could either discourage or encourage flow (McQuail, 1994: 113).

Sepstrup (1990) warned against drawing conclusions about cultural effects from different characters of the product transmitted and consumed. According to Septstrup, each of the steps – from the export of international media content to the actual consequences for the receiving culture – whether or not it is actually received – were all different and there was a long road from the first to the third step.

By the end of the twentieth century, globalization concepts alone could no longer explain complex social phenomena, and the discussion of global and local as a symbiotic development was found more acceptable. The putting forward of concepts that were often analyzed together, e.g., global and local, global and tribal, national and social, and commonality and difference, reflected this trend. Robertson (1995: 30) and Pieterse (1995: 40) both suggested that on the road towards the global village, globalization and localization were intersecting phenomena. The process of globalization accompanied that of localization, but localization was a force against globalization. Thompson (1995) and Robertson (1995) also believed that global-local culture issues were becoming increasingly important.

Although the cultural imperialism model suggested that media products emanating from the West, especially the US, powerfully shaped the cultures of other nations, we could not assume that audiences interpret foreign media products in a single way, especially when the characteristics of the television industry are taken into consideration.

Several scholars have considered television to be more internationalized and "mass," and that broadcasters can easily make different program packages for the segmented audiences. Schlesinger (1991: 51) explained that TV that mixes international, local and regional levels does not necessary harm local culture and even in some respects will "support" local culture. In other words TV programs often cover local, regional, and international aspects and viewers move between different levels to find what pleases them. Therefore, TV program schedules and genres need to cover various levels. Because TV provides mixed images that combine international, local and regional programs, viewers will form dual acceptance or multi-acceptance.

But the viewer's power to make the meanings that suit his or her social experience is not unlimited because different audiovisual products are made to attract different audiences. For instance, action adventure films, like The A-Team, cater to a largely male audience, while soap operas, like Dallas and Dynasty, are directed at female audiences (Fiske, 1987). In Brazil, the American prime-time soap opera Dallas never caught on; Brazilians preferred their *telenovelas* (soap operas) (Croteau and Hoynes, 1997: 308–9). The example showed that there were limits to the appeal of certain cultural products, including foreign programs. The regionally or locally produced programs, finely attuned to the local culture, tended to be very popular.

To communication researchers, the rise of program flow within regions has opened up a new level of analysis – the question of linguistic/cultural regional markets and cultural proximity. Although globalization seemed to involve domination by programs from a few countries and cultural unification (Mattelart and Schmuckler, 1985; Schiller, 1991), the rise of local and regional production centers did contribute to program trading on the market.

Social class, cultural proximity and viewers' reception of foreign programs

In the early days of television, programs were made according to the principle of the common denominator, and this principle was upheld through the 1970s. In 1974, however, Ganz (1974: 157) discovered that the TV environment had changed and proposed the idea that people with different tastes watched different types of programs, e.g. women liked romantic comedies, men liked action drama and sports.

By the 1990s, viewers were categorized into more distinct groups. For example the biggest soap opera viewer group is 18 to 49-year-old women, and they are not the same type of women. Because of changes in society, soap operas need to attract women of different marital status and also occupation (Cantor, 1994: 163).

The new development in the world television market shows that the understanding of changes in program flow requires a better conceptualization of the audience and its divisions. Some researchers found popular or, more broadly, class-divided interests to have been reflected in various television genres, which, to be enjoyed, require different levels of cultural capital (Martín-Barbero, 1988; Canclini, 1988; Straubhaar and Viscasillas, 1991).

Using Bourdieu's (1984) theory that aesthetic distinctions were not innocent relative to class, Straubhaar pointed out that viewers had different levels of taste and that it seemed that class could be used as an indicator of cultural preferences and taste, and that cultural capital and economic capital could help to further identify social class.

According to Straubhaar and Viscasillas (1991), there were two aspects to social classes: one was economic – what Bourdieu called economic capital, which could be measured by income, buying power and possessions. The second was cultural capital, which was commonly gained from family, education, occupation and travel opportunities. As the two were often related, only viewers belonging to certain social classes would have the cultural and economic capital to enable them to access international programs, or programs from neighboring countries. Straubhaar and Viscasillas (1991) found that in the Dominican Republic, middle- and low-income people and blue-collar workers had a taste for local programs and programs from neighboring countries, whereas those from the upper social classes preferred foreign programs, especially programs from the US.

Bourdieu stressed the importance of educational establishments and believed that cultural capital was different to economic capital in one respect: the latter could be acquired instantly while the former needed long-term "investment."

According to the above theories, the commonality of culture and language meant that local viewers would "inevitably" like local programs. Other things being equal, local programs, e.g. news, morning talk shows and variety shows, should be more attractive to local audiences because they can reflect local cultural needs (Straubhaar, 1997). In this sense, local programs should have greater intrinsic appeal to local audiences and advantages which imports lack.

The theory of cultural capital explained why audiences preferred local products, but it failed to explain why audiences frequently watched a combination of international, regional and local programs.

In discussing the Latin American TV market, Straubhaar and Viscasillas (1991) suggested a hypothesis which divided viewing preferences into three levels: the first level consisted of purely local products; if there were not enough local products, people were likely to select the second-level preference – products with a degree of cultural proximity; third-level preference involved the selection of foreign products. Studies have found that, generally speaking, the closer the program origin was to the culture the audience attached to, the more popular the program would be with the audience (Zha, 1995: 27). To develop first-level preference, therefore, localization or customization would become the primary means.

Straubhaar and Viscasillas (1991) also pointed to the need to look at program viewing from a cultural relevance, or proximity, point of view. Generally speaking, they suggested, the closer the program is to the culture the audience attaches to, the more popular it should be. A good example is that American programs are most popular in, and also culturally proximate to, the English-speaking countries. The recent development of regional TV and music markets for Spanish, Chinese, and Arabic products, and the popularity of Indian films, Japanese cartoons and Hong Kong action films on the Asian market could all be explained by culture or language, based in cultural proximity (Straubhaar, 1997). In essence, language and cultural proximity have turned the TV market into a quite different one from the global market for consumer goods (Straubhaar, 1997).

Program genre and content

In the 1950s, the US began to export programs overseas, and by the 1970s it had achieved superiority on the market. Although other centers of production and distribution have emerged in recent years, the reasons for their success and that of the American programs were not the same.

According to the commercial model, the popularity of American programs on the international market did not represent an admiration of audiences for American culture, but that their quality was good (Waterman and Rogers, 1994). Program quality, a factor which is usually gauged by a shifting array of characteristics including novelty, popular genre, brand-name association, and authenticity are also considered critically important in drawing an audience.

Others also believed in non-economic factors for the popularity of American programs. According to Noam and Millonzi (1993), the reason for Hollywood's success was economy of concentration, not economy of scale – although the two are related. They suggested that to sell on the international market, program content should be universally understandable.

Genre is another useful factor to explain what people watch (Straubhaar and Viscasillas, 1991: 67). The term "genre," a French word for type, is constructed by the entertainment industries and audiences to categorize audiovisual products. In certain ways, the structural analysis of audiovisual products, such as television programs, has taken to episodic series and serials. However, a more sophisticated conception of genre is made to distinguish television programs, e.g. sitcoms, crime shows and soap operas.

Mattelart (1991) stressed the importance of program genre, and pointed out that after adjustment some program genres could easily flow around the world. For example American soap operas were popular in Cuba in the 1950s and in Mexico in the 1970s and 1980s. But the soap operas that have been popular in recent years in Latin America illustrated how local and regional producers learned to adjust themselves to get closer to the viewers and create new program genres.

Many Asian countries have been showing Western programs for years. In Taiwan, for example, feature films, cartoons, soap operas, action-adventure series, and variety shows are the most prominent foreign programs in broadcast schedules throughout Taiwan. This has helped to lay down the viewer base for Western programs. Foreign program genres such as action and thriller series, romances and comedies have achieved significant ratings on Star TV, and Western action series, animation, sitcoms and children's programs are usually high on Asian buyers' shopping lists. As of today, American romantic dramas, cartoons, and action series were still popular on the third world market, however, in Asia a schedule initially dominated by, or devoted exclusively to, US-made programs has gradually been replaced by Japanese programs.

In Taiwan, the middle classes have shown great interest in regional entertainment programs in local dialects (Zha, 1995: 31) and even Japanese drama, in contrast to Western programs which have often been categorized as their third-level preference. According to Iwabuchi (1997), Japanese drama has in recent years been diversified in terms of story lines, setting and topics which made it a new genre for Taiwan audiences. He also pointed out other reasons for Japanese drama to become attractive to Taiwan viewers, including the comfortable distance between Taiwan and Japan due to the narrowing economic gap and increasing information flow between the two countries.

In addition to program genre, Straubhaar and Viscasillas (1991: 67–8) proposed that viewers' general opinion of countries seemed related to their preference of programs from those countries. But in their study, the relation was significant only when viewers' home country was concerned.

Another reason for viewers' preference of foreign programs may be the dreams and lifestyles depicted in these programs. Some have argued that US programming can serve as an international promotional vehicle for the American way of life by focusing on the material abundance and consumer opportunities available in the United States (Croteau and Hoynes, 1997: 191). If this is the case, there should be a positive association between viewing frequency and the impression of the program-producing country, another dimension which is worthy of exploration.

In Taiwan lifting the ban on satellite television has produced a real expansion in the media available to viewers. Although local TV stations are aware of the threat from overseas programs, they have not come up with a response. Taiwan is unable to produce special genres (such as films, cartoons) to compete with Holly-wood films, Japanese cartoons and drama (Ishii et al., 1996). With the increase in channels, cable TV operators are more worried about programming sources than offering program genres that are missing from local production.

The audiovisual space which continued to combine local and international imagination, therefore, has formed a postmodern TV cultural scenario in Taiwan. But this does not mean American or Japanese popular culture has become mainstream. The resurrection of old ethnic, cultural and social questions in the postmodern world reprises familiar questions about the impact of imported media products, languages, values, and lifestyles on all of the above.

Youth and foreign programs

Studies (Findahl, 1989; Iwabuchi, 1997; Sen, 1992; Straubhaar and Viscasillas, 1991; Zha, 1995) have shown that youths were the most avid viewers of foreign programs. Some transnational programs were widely popular with youngsters in different countries. MTV, which featured rock and pop music, started off in 1981; it has attracted audiences mostly from amongst the young (Sherman and Etling, 1991: 373–5). Straubhaar and Viscasillas (1991) also discovered that the average young viewers in the Dominican Republican had a strong US and foreign-program orientation and a special liking for foreign movies.

The foreign programs shown in Taiwan were mostly from the US and Japan. After Star TV began showing a Japanese drama in May 1992, the three terrestrial stations began showing Japanese programs in 1994. The target audiences were young viewers. American programs included films from Hollywood, serials, talk shows, variety shows, news and cartoons, while most Japanese programs were cartoons, drama series and variety shows.

The showing times for cartoons were exclusively chosen to fit the schedules of the young. All three terrestrial television stations, for example, showed cartoons – mostly Japanese – from 4.00 pm to 6.00 pm, while some cable channels also ran them during the day. Magic Cartoon Channel, a cartoon channel, usually ran Japanese cartoons in cycles. These cartoons were mainly new, popular ones. According to Japan's *PUFF* cartoon magazine, the most popular cartoon in Japan was shown in Taiwan on Star TV Chinese Channel and the number fourth, sixth, seventh, eighth and nineth-placed cartoons were also shown in Taiwan, targeting middle and primary school students (*China Times*, April 13, 1998: 24).

Most American programs were not shown during prime time in the evening. Cable networks normally ran serials at 8.00 pm but the terrestrial stations would show serials after 10.00 pm. Movies were mainly provided by US channels like HBO. Overall, American programs were scheduled at less popular viewing times than Japanese programs in Taiwan, an arrangement which may reflect viewers' program preferences.

Despite the external factors, the audience's motivation to watch TV at all is directly connected with audience preference of particular TV programs. According to uses and gratifications theory, viewers watch TV in order to gain gratification of their needs. At this point, the audience's selection of TV programs is perceived as a goal-directed purposive behavior (Rubin, 1994). What the reasons are behind young viewers' choice of television programs, therefore, becomes highly important in view of the current theoretical debate.

Young viewers: a mixed viewing agenda

To have a clear picture of what, and how many, foreign programs young viewers in Taiwan choose to watch and why, a telephone survey was conducted. As a youth culture often refers to the subculture of 13 to 19-year-olds (Amit-Talai, 1995), this research surveyed 12 to 19-year-olds in the Taipei metropolitan area. The sample was taken by the systematic random sampling method. Altogether 1,096 respondents were interviewed with a refusal rate of 21.62 percent. In the end there were 602 valid respondents of which 329 were men, or 54.7 percent, and 273 were women, or 45.3 percent.

In the telephone survey respondents were asked for their opinions on the quality of programs from the US, Japan, and Taiwan and their overall impression of these places. Questions were asked regarding the viewers' cultural and economic capital, e.g., their educational level and average family monthly income. Because family factors were likely to influence the kind of programs young viewers watched, the survey also solicited information on their parents.

The survey found that respondents had a "hybrid" viewing pattern. As we can see from Table 13.2, we found that the most popular programs were live local variety shows, but Japanese cartoons took second place. Next to these two in popularity were films, including Hong Kong films, and news which provided local information and culture, serving as major channels for the promotion and expression of local culture.

Of the foreign programs, Japanese cartoons were most popular; 42.7 percent of the respondents watched Japanese programs regularly while only 2.3 percent

Table 13.1 Respondents' demographic variables

Gender	Number	Percentage	
Male	329	54.7	
Female	273	45.3	
Age			
12	67	11.1	
13	81	13.5	
14	93	15.4	
15	87	14.5	
16	93	15.4	
17	73	12.1	
18	53	8.8	
19	55	9.1	
Education			
Primary	349	58.0	
High school	253	42.0	
Total	602	100.0	

Table 13.2 Respondents' "frequently" watched genres[a] (n=602)

	Number	Percentage	
National			
Live variety show	367	61.0	
Taiwanese, HK films	151	25.1	
Local news	141	23.4	
Chinese dramatic series	111	18.4	
Sports	90	15.0	
Game shows	76	12.6	
Entertainment news	35	5.8	
Crime shows	23	3.8	
Taiwanese dramatic series	7	1.2	
Ghost shows	7	1.2	
Children's programs		2.3	
Other	9	1.3	
Japanese programs			
Cartoons	271	42.7	
Idol dramas	22	3.7	
Regional			
Hong Kong or Singapore dramas	36	6.0	
Mainland Chinese dramas	7	1.2	
US or international			
US films	144	23.9	
MTV	96	15.9	
Feature films	33	5.5	
NBA programs	22	3.7	
Documentaries	15	2.5	
Cartoons	14	2.3	

Note

a   Multiple choice up to three.

Table 13.3 "Frequently" watched programs from key regions and countries

Program source	n	Percentage
Taiwan	331	56.2
Japan	122	20.7
US	92	15.6
Hong Kong	38	6.5
Mainland China		3.5
Korea		1.2
Singapore		1.2
Other	1.2	
Total	589	100.0

watched US cartoons. US films, with a rating of 23.9 percent, were also much less popular than Japanese cartoons.

Why did young viewers have a marked affinity for local variety shows? Local material in these programs made them more attractive than imported programs. In the case of live local variety shows, solo comedies, local popular music and verbal humor in the programs formed a good base for appealing to a broad general audience. These formats are also interesting to young viewers. As for Japanese cartoons, the story line and characters are major attractions to the young audience. Since the costs of their production are largely recovered in Japan, producers were able to sell at whatever price the host market can afford – often much below the local costs of producing competing programming.

Local films (including Hong Kong films) and American films had an audience of a similar size. Respondents also watched other foreign programs like HK and Singaporean drama, and MTV. In terms of program origin, they displayed a hybrid pattern; 56 percent of the programs watched were local with the rest foreign, including Japanese, US and Hong Kong in rank order.

What is worthy of attention from the above finding is that the genres of popular foreign programs, e.g. Japanese cartoons and American films, were not produced in Taiwan. When local programs could not satisfy their needs with the genres they preferred, they turned to Japanese and American products.

As seen in Table 13.4, of the channels regularly watched by the young, the top three were local terrestrial stations, the fourth was HBO and the sixth MTV. The latter two were foreign, both entertainment channels.

From the list of the top 10 popular programs (Table 13.5), it was clear that respondents' viewing pattern were heavily entertainment-oriented with a multitude of genres. Of the top ten, four were foreign with two from the US and two from Japan. At the top of the list was a live variety show, the second, national news. Both of these were produced in Taiwan with a strong local flavor. At the third place there was a tie among three foreign programs – a Japanese cartoon, HBO, and NBA sports.

Table 13.4 Top ten "frequently" watched channels

Channel	n	Percentage	Target market
CTS	255	42.6	Taiwan
TTV	197	32.9	Taiwan
CTV	186	31.1	Taiwan
HBO	130	21.7	International
TVBS	83	13.9	Taiwan
MTV	73	12.2	Chinese region
Star TV	66	11.0	Taiwan
Chun-du Cartoon	63	10.5	Taiwan
TVBSG	61	10.2	Taiwan
Scholar Chinese Films	54	9.0	Taiwan

Table 13.5 Top ten "frequently" watched programs

Program	n	Percentage	Genre	Source
Super Sunday	112	29.8	Variety show	Taiwan
HBO movies	22	5.9	Films	US
Detective Ke-nan	22	5.9	Cartoon	Japan
NBA Sports	22	5.9	Sports	US
Judge Shi	19	5.1	Costume drama	Taiwan
Dragon and Tiger variety show	17	4.5	Variety show	Taiwan
Red and White variety show	14	3.7	Variety show	Taiwan
Tau's entertainment news	12	3.2	News	Taiwan
Dream game (Japanese cartoon)	10	2.7	Cartoon	Japan

Cultural and economic capital and frequently watched programs

This study found that age differences led to different TV menus. Respondents of the 16- to 19-year-old group watched less Japanese cartoons but more US films, local TV news, MTV and sport. The 12- to 15-year-olds mainly watched local variety shows and Japanese cartoons. It seems that while early teens in the sample liked to watch cartoons, late teens preferred dramas played by "real people."

Young people at this stage also began to show gender differences in their viewing behavior, as described in Fiske's notion of "Gendered Television." Girls preferred to watch variety shows and TV news, while boys liked local films, Hong Kong films and sports. However, there were no significant differences in watching Japanese cartoons, HK drama, Singapore drama and Japanese drama by gender. The results from age and education figures were similar: late teens watched TV news and US serials, while the younger respondents often watched cartoons (see Table 13.6).

As Table 13.6 indicates, respondents from lower-income families (under NT$50,000 per month) watched many more Japanese cartoons than those from

Table 13.6 "Frequently" watched genres from key regions and countries by gender, education and age

Program source and genre	Gender		Education		Age	
	Male (n=329)	Female (n=273)	Primary (n=349)	High (n=240)	12–15 (n=328)	16–19 (n=274)
Variety show	25.2	37.4	27.2	29.6	24.7	27.7
News	7.6	10.3	5.2	10.8	4.9	10.6
Mandarin or Hong Kong films	3.1	7.0	11.7	7.9	11.9	8.4
Sports	13.1	0.4	5.7	10.0	5.5	9.5
Mandarin dramatic series	3.3	4.8	4.9	2.9	5.2	2.6
Taiwanese dialect dramatic series	0.6	0.0	0.3	0.4	0.3	0.4
Hong Kong or Singapore dramatic series	1.5	1.5	1.1	1.7	0.9	2.2
Mainland Chinese dramatic series	0.6	0.4	0.6	0.4	0.6	0.4
Japanese cartoons	18.8	18.7	25.8	8.3	26.8	9.1
Japanese idol dramas	0.0	1.1	0.0	1.3	0.0	1.1
US feature films	11.9	8.4	8.3	12.9	8.5	12.4
MTV	3.6	8.4	4.0	8.8	3.4	8.8
Others	0.6	1.1	0.0	0.4	0.0	0.4
Chi-Square Test	p<0.01		not significant		not significant	

higher-income families (over NT$90,000); there was a 9-percent gap between the two. Those from high-income families watched slightly less drama, but more MTV and TV news. "Father's education" also seemed to make a difference. Respondents with highly educated fathers showed a preference for US serials and films. However, the popularity of Japanese cartoons among this group was similar to respondents whose fathers only had primary-school education. Those respondents whose fathers had high-school education showed less preference for cartoons, but preferred variety shows and MTV.

One possible reason for the 12- to 15-year-olds to prefer Japanese cartoons could be their content which provides many sub-genres like robots, cyberpunk, science fiction, animals, fantasy worlds, sports, romance, or police stories. There is usually a strong, but not overtly intrusive, moral element to the story structure. Programs are generally aimed at appealing to either boys or girls. Stories for girls normally contain as much action and adventure as those for boys, while those for boys often have strong, positive female characters as well as the expected young heroes (McCarthy, 1993: 40). The odorlessness of Japanese cartoons that mix school and home-life stories, retelling of classic tales, fairy stories and action/adventures, things that make up most children's programming, may be the main reasons for its attraction.

Table 13.7 "Frequently" watched genres from key regions and countries by income and father's education

	Income			Father's education		
Genre	Less than 50,000 (n=101)	50,000 to 90,000 (n=144)	90,000 and + (n=89)	Primary school (n=169)	High school (n=158)	University or above (n=204)
News	7.9	9.0	11.2	7.1	3.8	11.8
Sports	5.0	7.6	9.0	7.1	7.6	8.8
Japanese cartoons	20.8	17.4	11.2	18.9	12.7	19.1
MTV	3.6	8.4	12.4	5.9	7.6	5.9
Variety shows	32.7	30.6	31.5	27.2	31.6	21.6
Mandarin dramatic series	8.9	7.6	6.7	4.1	3.8	3.4
Taiwanese dialect dramatic series	0.6	0.0	0.0	1.2	0.0	0.0
Hong Kong or Singapore dramatic series	1.5	1.5	0.0	1.2	0.0	2.0
Mainland Chinese dramatic series	0.6	0.4	0.0	1.2	0.0	0.5
Japanese idol dramas	0.0	1.1	0.0	0.6	0.6	0.5
US feature films	11.9	7.6	10.1	5.9	12.1	13.8
Chinese or Hong Kong movies	11.9	13.9	6.7	11.8	10.8	5.4
Other	1.0	0.7	1.1	0.0	0.0	0.5
Chi Square Test	$p < 0.01$			not significant		

If program origin were the only factor taken into consideration, female, as versus male, respondents and those attending high schools would have a greater percentage watching local programs (Table 13.8). Males showed a preference for US programs, but there was not much gender difference for viewing Japanese programs. The data also showed educational influence. High-school students often watched local programs, while middle-school students liked Japanese programs. This preference was probably associated with age and program genre, as indicated earlier in our discussion. Respondents attending high school watched more local and US programs than those attending middle school. The popularity of Japanese cartoons declined with older age groups.

Because the young viewers were still in the process of receiving education so that their cultural capital cannot really be reflected, this item asked the level but mainly took father's educational level as an indicator. For economic capital, the monthly family income was asked but because some were not familiar with this figure, of the 627 respondents only 327 answered this question (52.1 percent).

Table 13.9 shows that cultural capital does seem to make a difference as a greater percentage of the respondents with highly educated father reported frequently watching foreign, and also regional programs. In other words, the higher the educational level of the father the more likely that they would be frequent

Table 13.8 "Frequently" watched program sources from key regions and countries by gender, education and age

Program source	Gender		Education		Age	
	Male (n=160)	*Female* (n=171)	*Primary* (n=343)	*High* (n=233)	*12–15* (n=322)	*16–19* (n=267)
Taiwan	49.8	63.8	53.4	60.9	50.9	62.5
Hong Kong	7.8	4.9	6.1	6.4	6.2	6.7
Japan	21.5	19.8	25.4	13.7	26.7	13.5
Korea	0.3	0.0	0.0	0.4	0.0	0.4
Singapore	0.3	0.0	0.0	0.4	0.0	0.4
US	19.6	10.8	14.6	17.2	15.5	15.7
Mainland China	0.6	0.4	0.6	0.4	0.6	0.4
Other	0.0	0.4	0.0	0.4	0.0	0.4
Chi Square Test	not significant		not significant		not significant	

Table 13.9 "Frequently" watched program sources from key regions and countries by income and father's education

Source	Income			Father's education		
	Less than 50,000 (n=100)	*50,000 to 90,000* (n=140)	*90,000 and +* (n=87)	*Primary school* (n=104)	*High school* (n=96)	*University or above* (n=98)
Taiwan	56.0	56.4	58.6	62.7	63.2	48.8
Hong Kong	6.0	8.6	8.0	6.6	5.3	6.0
Japan	25.0	20.0	13.8	20.5	14.5	21.4
Korea	0.0	0.0	0.0	0.0	0.0	0.5
Singapore	0.0	0.7	0.0	0.0	0.0	0.5
US	3.0	12.9	18.4	9.0	17.1	21.9
Mainland China	0.0	1.4	1.1	1.2	0.0	0.5
Other	0.0	0.0	0.0	0.0	0.0	0.5
Chi Square Test	not significant			not significant		

viewers of US and regional programs, and less likely frequent viewers of local programs.

But a closer look at the data shows that the differences related mainly to US programs. For example only 9 percent of the respondents whose fathers had primary education reported watching US programs frequently; however, the percentage grew to 17.1 percent with respondents whose fathers had high- school education, and 21.9 percent with those whose fathers were highly educated. Of the respondents whose fathers had received higher education, the percentage of frequent US and Japanese program viewers were almost the same: 21 percent.

It is worthy of notice that the level of fathers' education did not seem to make a difference in the percentage of respondents reporting frequently watching Japanese programs. The similarity may be attributed to the proximity of Japanese culture to Taiwan viewers; it could also mean that Japanese programs have

Table 13.10 Countries' program quality and countries' overall image

Program quality	Excellent	Good	Not good	Not good at all	Don't know	No answer
Taiwanese programs	3.8	75.4	16.1	2.5	2.0	0.2
Japanese programs	13.5	55.3	12.8	3.2	9.0	6.3
US programs	23.4	50.2	5.1	1.2	11.8	8.3
Overall image						
Taiwan	13.5	63.4	18.5	4.2	0.5	
Japan	18.6	62.0	12.0	4.7	2.8	
US	21.6	64.0	8.8	2.5	3.2	

successfully transcended cultural differences to become "neutral" products which are capable of attracting foreign viewers with, or without, cultural capital – a development which deserves further study.

In contrast to what was found with regard to cultural capital, no significant differences in viewing foreign versus local programs were found among respondents from high-, middle-, and low-income families. Regardless of the monthly family income over half of respondents from all three income groups were frequent viewers of local, as opposed to 30 percent foreign, programs, showing little support for the economic capital theory.

Impression of place of origin and assessment of program quality

Table 13.10 shows that respondents had a higher opinion of the US and Japan than of Taiwan, with the US topping the list. Correlation analyses found a significant association between what respondents thought of program quality and their impression of its place of origin. The strongest association was found with their impression of Taiwan and perceived quality of its programs, weakest with the US. The result was different from what Straubhaar and Viscasillas (1991) found in the Dominican Republic.

Conclusions and implications

The rapid expansion of the domestic market in Taiwan is a relatively recent phenomenon. Since 1990, cable TV has broadcast an increasing number of foreign programs, and youths have seemed more inclined to prefer and watch foreign programs. Although mainstream viewing is still Taiwanese, Japanese and US programs have an important place, especially Japanese cartoons. The direction of change is clear, and the following points are worthy of notice.

The first key issue regarding the impact of foreign programs on young viewers discussed here has been the complex interrelationship between "globalization" and "localization" of satellite channels and local TV. After deregulation of telecommunications policy, young viewers in Taiwan began to have access to a greater variety of foreign programs, and a new viewing agenda emerged. This study showed that local programs remained the main course of respondents' TV menus, with foreign programs subsidiary. Part of the reason is that the foreign program genres which the young viewers prefer, including Japanese cartoons and US films, are not made in Taiwan.

Japan's leading position in the popularity of foreign programs is worthy of notice. Japanese cartoon production is now a well-developed industry with products sold on the international market, often in concert with US-based companies. Although Japanese media products may display a somewhat different national image as part of the sales pitch, the story line and characters in Japanese programs are culturally neutral.

Secondly, the most likely explanation for the popularity of foreign programs is that time slots suitable for young viewers were dominated by foreign programs. For foreign programs to be seen there must be media accessibility. The heavy pressure of examinations on students – especially high school students – in Taiwan severely limited the time they could afford to watch television. As parents usually allow children to relax a while after school, late afternoon hours – usually time before dinner – would be their time for television entertainment. It was perhaps no accident that the showing times of Japanese cartoons were designed to be in tune with young viewers' habits, a factor which explains, at least in part, the heavy consumption (over 40 percent of the respondents reported frequently watching) of Japanese programs. Likewise the 20 percent of regular viewers of US films could be attributed to the availability of movie channels, e.g. HBO, offered over cable networks at the right hours.

If a global culture can be seen as pre-eminently a "constructed" culture (Smith, 1990: 177), we can see the barriers to transnational broadcasting disappearing; transnational programs are carrying more attributes of a conventional commodity. Besides satellite broadcasters, local TV services are also scheduling foreign programs to meet the needs of local youths in order to attain high ratings. In this sense, young viewers' preferences will certainly have special implications for international broadcasters and will exert a significant influence on the future of Japanese programming in Taiwan.

Research found that young viewers liked cartoons and films. Serials and NBA were among the most popular programs. In this study, we found that genre is indeed an important factor to explain what people watch. Live variety shows were the most frequently watched local programs. Most foreign programs watched by the audiences were of special genres, such as cartoons, professional sports, and films, genres that local audiences had to depend on imports for because it is almost impossible for local industry to generate large enough budgets to produce such high-quality programs. Program genre, however, did not seem to be sufficient to explain the hybridity of viewing patterns; cultural proximity also needs to be considered.

While terrestrial television bombarded audiences with Japanese cartoons in late afternoon hours, US cartoons were also available on the Disney and Cartoon

Network satellite channels. But youths in Taiwan seldom watched these programs; Japanese cartoons remained the most frequently watched for both junior and senior high-school students. The success of Japanese cartoons may be attributed to the young age of the major characters and the context of the stories. In contrast to the animal world depicted in American cartoons, the narration of school and home life made up the main theme of Japanese cartoon stories, something which youths can identify with. It is, therefore, both cultural and generational proximity that have brought young Taiwanese audiences to Japanese programs. This finding shows that imports from the first world will likely be reduced if local or regional cultural industries are capable of producing the genre of programs that are currently missing.

Consequently whether or not an increase in the supply of foreign programs results in increased viewing depends on program genre and content proximity – including, but not limited to, cultural proximity. This phenomenon does not necessarily represent the acceptance of US or Japanese culture.

The different preferences of foreign programs among different age groups also indicate that viewing patterns may change according to age, as a result of changes in lifestyle, tastes, or the development of the cognitive and affective abilities of the young viewers. This was the case with gender, too. More girls than boys liked to watch local programs while boys watched more Japanese, US, and Hong Kong programs, probably because the program genres (sports, action programs) are more attractive to boys.

In addition, in young viewers the influence of cultural capital was more significant than that of economic capital. The educational level of the father seemed to be an important factor – respondents with highly educated fathers had a much higher acceptance level of foreign programs than those whose fathers were poorly educated, a finding which was in agreement with what was found in previous research. In brief this study shows that the viewing of foreign programs is not just related to demographic factors; also present are social and cultural factors such as age, gender, cultural capital and program genre.

Therefore in Taiwan's case, Straubhaar's three levels of preference have to be taken into consideration with a number of other factors. First, youths looked to entertainment programs for relaxation after school and before homework. Within the entertainment category, local products might be preferred, but foreign programs would be chosen if they were of a genre that was missing in the local supply.

Second, statistics show that young viewers have different preferences for programs from different countries at different ages; the interest in viewing transnational programs increased when the program genres became more compatible with the lifestyle and subculture of the audience. This can not be called media imperialism. We need to find out why Japanese and US programs are attractive to youths and look into the reason for their growth.

Most interesting is the fact that choice among foreign programs was influenced by the combined effect of program genres and cultural proximity. Japanese programs have been increasing in supply and becoming more popular than US

241

programs in Taiwan recently. These audiovisual products offer a greater variety of sub-genres, and more importantly perhaps, are culturally more proximate in that they depict the life of characters with whom young viewers could identify. These features may facilitate the eventual building of a regional, or geographical-cultural, popular domain in Taiwan.

Last but not least, the abundant supply and scheduling of foreign programs also contributed to their popularity among the young. The gap in investment contributed to the differences in the variety of genres between local and foreign products. As it is almost impossible for local production to match Japan and Hollywood in terms of economy of scale, foreign programs will likely remain a major supplement to local programs.

From the development of the Taiwan TV environment it is evident that culture is dynamic and changing. While the Taiwan TV industry is subject to global, regional and local influences, it is also important to note that the viewing behavior of youths in Taiwan is neither purely regionally, nor internationally, oriented, despite their significant intake of foreign programs.

This study stayed away from the issue of the cultural influence of foreign programs. But if the hybrid viewing pattern is of any indication, the influence will be mixed, at best.

References

Amit-Talai, V. (1995). "Conclusion: The 'multi' cultural of youth." In V. Amit-Talai and H. Wulff (Eds), *Youth cultures: A cross-cultural perspective*, 223–33. London: Routledge.

Beltran, L.R.S. (1978). "Communication and cultural domination: USA-Latin American case." *Media Asia*, 5, 183–92.

Bourdieu, P. (1984). *Distinction: A social critique of the judgement of taste*. Cambridge, MA: Harvard University Press.

Canclini, N.G. (1988). "Culture and power: The state of research." *Media, Culture and Society*, 10(4), October, 467–99.

Cantor, M.G. (1994). "The role of the audience in the production of culture: A personal research retrospective." In J.S. Ettema and D.C. Whitney (1994) (Eds), *Audiencemaking: How the Media Create the Audience*. London: Sage.

Croteau, D. and Hoynes, W. (1997). *Media/Society: Industries, Images, and Audiences*. Thousand Oaks, CA: Pine Forge Press.

Elasmar, M.G. and Hunter, J.E. (1992). "The impact of foreign TV on a domestic audience: A meta-analysis." *Communication Yearbook*, 20: 47–69.

Findahl, O. (1989). "Language in the age of satellite television." *European Journal of Communication*, vol. 4, 133–59.

Fiske, J. (1987). *Television Culture*. London: Routledge.

Fiske, J. (1995). "Gendered television: Femininity." In G. Dinces and J.M. Humez (Eds), *Gender, race, and class in media*, 340–7. Thousand Oaks, CA: Sage.

Ganz, H.J. (1974). *Popular Culture and High Culture*. New York: Basic Books.

Ishii, K., Watanabe S. and Su Herng (1996). *Japanese TV Programs Viewed by Taiwanese People*. Housou, Institute of Policy and Planning Sciences: Discussion paper series (in Japanese).

Iwabuchi, K. (1997). "The sweet scent of Asian modernity: Japanese Presence in the Asian Audiovisual Market." Paper presented at the International Symposium, Media Globalization in Asia-Pacific Region, Taipei, Taiwan, May 20–22, 1997.

Martín-Barbero, J. (1988). "Communication from culture: The crisis of the national and the emergence of the popular." *Media, Culture and Society*, 10(4), October, 447–66.

Mattelart, A. (1991). *Advertising International: The Privatization of Public Space.* New York: Routledge.

Mattelart, A. and Schmuckler, H. (1985). *Communication and Information Technologies: Freedom of Choice for Latin American?* (Bruxton, D., Trans.). Norwood, NJ: Ablex.

McCarthy, H. (1993). *Anime! A Beginner's Guide for Japanese Animation.* London: Titanbooks.

McQuail, D. (1994). *Mass Communication Theory: An Introduction*, 3rd edn. London: Sage.

Negus, K. (1993). *Producing Pop.* London: Edward Arnold.

Noam, E.M. and Millonzi, J.C. (Ed.) (1993). *The International Market in Film and TV Program.* Norwood, NJ: Ablex.

Pan, C. and Wang, H. (1989). *The Relationship Between Music Television and Leisure Culture.* Taipei: Culture Foundation Commission.

Pieterse, J.N. (1995). "Globalization as hybridization." In M. Featherstone, S. Lash and R. Robertson (Eds), *Global Modernities*, 45–68. London: Sage.

Robertson, R. (1995). "Glocalization: Time-space and homogeneity-heterogeneity." in M. Featherstone *et al.* (Eds), *Global Modernities*, 23–44. London: Sage.

Rubin, A.M. (1994). "Media uses and effects: A uses-and-gratifications perspective." In Jennings, Bryant and D. Zillmann (Eds), *Media Effects: Advances in Theory and Research.* Hillsdale, NJ: Lawrence Erlbaum Associates.

Schiller, H.I. (1971). *Mass Communication and American Empire.* Boston: Beacon Press.

Schiller, H.I. (1991). "Not yet the Post-Imperialist era." *Critical Studies in Mass Communication.*

Schlesinger, P. (1991). "Media, the political order and national identity." *Media, Culture and Society*, 13(3), 297–308.

Sen, A. (1992). "The import of American pop culture in the third world." *Media Asia*, 20(4), 208–17.

Sepstrup, P. (1990). *The Transnationalization of TV in West Europe.* London: John Libbey.

Sherman, B.L. and Etling, L.W. (1991). "Perceiving and processing music television." In Bryant, Jennings and D. Zillmann (Eds), *Responding to the Screen: Reception and Reaction Processes*, Chap. 16: 373–88. Hillsdale, NJ: Lawrence Erlbaum.

Smith, A. (1990). "Towards a global culture?" In M. Featherstone (Ed.), *Global Culture: Nationalism, Globalization and Modernity.* London: Sage.

Straubhaar, J. (1997). "Global or regional? Cultural and language markers for television." A paper presented at the 5th International Symposium on Film, Television and Video. Media Globalization in Asia-Pacific Region, May 20–22, 1997, Taipei, Taiwan.

Straubhaar, J. and Viscasillas, G.M. (1991). "Class, genre, and the regionalization of television programming in the Dominican Republic." *Journal of Communication*, 41(1), Winter, 53–69.

Thompson, J.B. (1995). *The Media and Modernity.* Cambridge, Polity.

Tsang, K. and Wang, G. (1990). "Indigenising foreign culture: the case of Taiwan." *Mass Communication Research*, 43, 117–33.

Varis, T. (1974). *Television Traffic: a One-Way Street.* Paris: UNESCO.

Varis, T. (1984). "The internationalization flow of television programs." *Journal of Communication*, 34(1) 143–52.

Wallis, R. and Baran, S. (1990). *The World of Broadcasting News*. London: Routledge.

Wang, G. and Tseung, W. (1988). *The Second Generation Media*. Taipei: Tung Hwa.

Waterman, D. and Rogers, E.M. (1994). "The economics of television program production and trade in Far East Asia." *Journal of Communication*, 44(3), Summer, 89–111.

Zha, H.Y. (1995). "Transnational television programming: media globalization in East Asia. With an emphasis on the People's Republic of China." Thesis for MS, University of North Texas.

14

THE PRODUCTION AND CONSUMPTION OF NATIONAL AND LOCAL CULTURAL PRODUCTS IN THE AGE OF GLOBAL COMMUNICATION

Gérard Pogorel

The decade-long debate over monopoly in telecommunications is now coming to an end, with pro-competitive policies having gained the upper hand. A further step in this direction has been taken by the February 1997 agreement by the World Trade Organization (WTO) on a set of liberalization principles to be implemented in domestic telecom regulation (WTO, 1997). Three issues, however, prevent a full shift to the market paradigm in the world of telecommunications (WTO, 1994; 1998). First comes the legacy of telecom monopolies, which confront us to a transition period toward normalcy, whose length still has to be determined. Second, although the natural monopoly argument is no longer prevalent, telecom peculiarities and technicalities leave us with a range of issues to be dealt in with at policy, industry, and firm level. Those issues are, *inter alia*, interconnection modes and prices, the provision of universal service, implementing actual competition, and its expected outcomes in terms of enhanced innovation and decreasing costs of services. Lastly, the issue of satellite communication has been raised during the negotiation. It has been considered, however, that satellites were still mostly dealing with television broadcasting, that telecommunications were the focus of the negotiation, and subsequently media-related issues have eventually been kept aside in the agreement. Under these circumstances, and given the looming occurrence of "convergence," the WTO agreement might appear in the future more like the end of an era than the beginning of a new one.

We would like here to concentrate on an issue, which is common to the worlds of telecommunications, the media, and computers, i.e., the issue of market *dominance*. Although it is commonplace in anti-trust theory and policy, is specifically critical in this context, as we have to address the issue in all its industrial, social and cultural dimensions.

Dominance is an apparently touchy concept, as the word itself is kind of taboo among the former telecom monopolies, who now proudly advocate their full conversion to competitive doctrines and practices, and tend to deny the use of the word, for fear maybe of confronting its reality. In software, we are presently witnessing a titanic struggle, with the questioning of the effects of dominance in operating software and Internet browsers. As for the media, and specifically the movie and TV broadcasting industries, sensitiveness to dominance is present in most countries, even if a whole spectrum of answers can be observed in various regions of the world.

If we look for instance at telecommunications, the opinion has been widely held that the regulator(s), whoever they are, should devote special attention to the behavior of former monopolies, to prevent uncompetitive practices. Speakers for the historical telcos are symmetrically advocating that any overshooting in this respect should be avoided. In the media, a parallel process is taking place, although it is not clear whether the present situation could last. The present paper will survey *dominance* concepts, as inherited from the anti-trust tradition, and articulate it to the localization-globalization debate. It will confront them with the specificity and practicalities of communications at large, and with the new issues arising from the overlapping of telecommunications and media activities (convergence). It will survey the present experience, and tentatively address issues to arise in the predictable international structures and environment (Pogorel, 1994).

Market dominance in communications

It is clear that the usage of the term "market dominance" in anti-trust debates and circles, as opposed to straightforward monopolies, cartels and the like, denotes a change in paradigm and reality. In a "world of monopolies," monopolies are no longer the primary concern. More tricky issues have emerged, generic, relating to the prevalent oligopolistic industrial structures, or specific, relating to communications peculiarities.

The monitoring of market dominance in communications takes place against a background which has been subject to a recent shift on global markets. Increasing attention is being paid to the competitive dynamics observable in networks, media and software activities. The Federal Trade Commission and the Department of Justice in the USA has devoted considerable attention to possible consequences deriving from the vertical integration of the various components and layers of computer and network equipment and software. The market supply structure of microprocessors, operating systems, application software, and Internet browsers are being placed under close scrutiny. Briefly stated, the emphasis on horizontal integration, which accounted for most of anti-trust policy in the past, in Europe as well, is now complemented with increasing concern concerning the advantages accruing to vertically integrated firms versus those which are not. Similarly, if price caps are commonly in use to curb excessively high tariffs, along the lines of traditional anti-trust policy, preventing barriers to entry in the form of predatory pricing and price squeezes build up to an always more complex set of "postmodern" anti-trust thought based on medium- to long-term strategic considerations.

Asymmetric regulation, whether it should be acted and for how long, is also part of this line of thought, especially in the telecom context.

Aims and tools of communications regulation

Equity and "fairness" considerations loom high among the concerns of the telecom community, if we still can call it this. Arguments based on fairness considerations are likely to strongly interfere with the issue of dominance. Opposed opinions can be heard from incumbents and insurgents on telecom markets. Incumbents deem it fair to ask for due consideration to be given to the historical costs of their investments. The economic and managerial perspective is quite clear on the only value to be considered for investments: it should be based on the present (i.e. replacement). If an incumbent is clogged with higher book values for its investments, some write-offs should occur. Whether the burden of this operation should be borne by the company, or by any other means, is a policy issue too delicate, unfortunately, to have been actually addressed.

Conversely, insurgents are vocal in demanding initial offsetting advantages for the historical integration and subsequent market power of the incumbent. This should of course only be considered as part of the transition phase toward a competitive environment. A strong caveat should be made for possible overshooting in that respect. It has to be kept in mind that the competitive means should not unwittingly allow anti-trust authorities to give undue emphasis to the protection of competitors rather than to competition.

Various aims appear to be pursued in the name of fairness:

- allowing the incumbent operator to recoup its historical costs
- accounting for the special provisions imposed on it by the legislator (in the case of France: universal service, lifelong employment for the staff, setting up a pension fund from scratch)
- providing cost-based (i.e. in this case today's costs, as determined by present technological alternatives) interconnection tariffs to new entrants.

Those aims appear to be largely conflicting. If the tariffs, interconnection costs, and rules for entry and regulation pretend to address them all simultaneously, it is likely that the market will suffer some efficiency (allocative and technical) and/or provide bypass mechanisms. On the other hand, renewed attempts at a higher dose of *laissez faire*, (light-handed regulation) have not proved dynamically efficient either. Even if it is widely accepted that it should progressively be up to the market to deal with telecom activities, we still are confronted with the flaws of the actual negotiation processes between firms. Although negation is mentioned as central in

247

various regulatory frameworks (USA, European Union, for instance), it is not yet clear how long it will be before the actors are actually left on their own in reaching reciprocally satisfactory agreements. Interconnection modes and prices are a critical example of this inadequacy.

Industrial considerations are prevalent in telecommunications as well as in software industries. Even if they are present in the media as well, social and cultural considerations are at the forefront of concerns in this area. This is specially true in the European Union and Canada, where a continuous stream of measures has aimed at preserving national (or regional) cultural identities and market shares, mostly through, often complex, systems of quotas and selective support of local media industries. The essential trade-offs here are between local and foreign media companies, their market shares, the cultural content they convey, the supposedly different impacts of national or foreign control, etc.

Communications regulation: specific versus generic, anti-trust, and other regulatory bodies

Two assumptions actually conflict when dealing with communications issues. According to the "normalcy" assumption, communications activities are to fall progressively into the realm of anti-trust policy at large, with market rules concurring with freedom of information principles to bring consumers and citizens the best services at the best price. According to the "cultural exception" assumption, communication is different, and a special regime should apply. As a sign of differences in treatment between two areas, policies, competencies and tools are often, in many countries, segmented among various regulatory bodies. Various modes of segmentation are present, and various agencies can be found dealing with:

- telecommunications
- the media (or even TV and broadcasting on one side and the press on the other)
- frequencies
- anti-trusts at large
- issues pertaining to contents, whatever the conduit.

National, regional (EU for instance), and international (potentially WTO) dimension might interfere, and make the resulting structure even more complex.

Frontiers are now blurring between the previously separated worlds of telecom, the media and computers, as all kinds of information converge into versatile digitized channels. This tendency has until now manifested itself at industry level through joint ventures, strategic alliances, and mergers. Those moves are carefully monitored nationally or regionally by various institutions in charge of uncompetitive practices in general or of the specific cases arising in the communications area in particular. Whether the complex industrial structures which come out of these moves can be handled through the existing anti-trust agencies or the specific communications or media regulators is still an open question, the conceptual basis and aims pursued being somewhat diverse.

Each of those activities and the corresponding bodies build upon a longstanding tradition and practice. Sectoral cultures, conceptions of the aims to be pursued, levels of emergencies and the way to handle them widely differ, giving rise to a host of potential conflicts not to forget conflicts between anti-trust/trade/industrial and innovation policies.

Modes of regulation, of course, should not lose sight of the basic emphasis on lowering prices of all kinds. The other considerations we mentioned often interfere and lead to a more "baroque" set of rules.

A recent proposal at EU level, included in the December 1997 Green Paper on Convergence, would be that the whole organization of regulatory bodies dealing with communications be submitted to a ninety-degree rotation. Instead of "vertical" agencies dealing with specific industries (telecommunications, media, and informatics), the technological convergence would lead progressively to a horizontal organization: networks, services, contents. As concerns networks, access would be the rationale, with a weaker obligation that presently exists, given precisely their number and variety. Services would be mostly considered in an anti-trust perspective. As for contents, Member countries would remain largely free in what they intend to implement in terms of moral values and national culture.

A convergence process on commonly agreed regulation principles, practice and bodies, can only take place as actors, including governments and regulatory bodies themselves, gain an overarching view of the whole picture and become increasingly aware of the issues at stake. No such situation has emerged yet, and whether it will is subject to the redefinition of the EU Commission agenda in a renewed context in 1999. This might entail a lengthy learning process as interested bodies progressively get rid of old patterns and habits.

Conclusion

The nature of competitive and cultural dynamics in communication activities

We have illustrated the particular nature of competitive dynamics in communication. Analysing and forecasting the outcomes of technological change and industrial strategies, and their cultural impact at local and global level, still remains a risky exercise. This holds especially in our area.

Convergence factors interfere with large uncertainties. Potential markets, productivity trends, capital-output ratios and barriers to entry widely differ among the various segments. No intuitive application of the industrial strategist toolbox can easily be made. The reality of the economies of scale and scope, actual synergies, presiding over the recent industrial moves – whether the firms involved are behaving as attackers of defenders – is still hotly debated. Interference with changing customer tastes and aspirations also combine into complex scenarios.

Due to network, critical mass, and standardization effects, competitive dynamics in information and communication activities are of a special kind. They differ from linear, mechanic phenomena, which can be observed in many other manufacturing or service industries. The yields of innovation and marketing efforts in the former are potentially much more dynamic than in the latter. Risks are also very high, as capital-intensive activities are developed in a market characterized by evolving standards and short or unpredictable life cycles for certain kinds of services.

The suspension, then later in 1998, abandonment, of negotiations concerning the "Multilateral Investment Agreement" project, which had been initiated at OECD, is still an example of the perceived potential threats brought in by the freedom granted to large international companies in their investment policy. It is not indifferent that local, cultural, arguments were instrumental in bringing the negotiation to a halt. The problem of "local" and "global" culture we deal with here is still an open one, with new combinations in the process of being invented.

References

Pogorel, G. (Ed.) (1994). *Global Telecommunications Strategies and Technological Changes*. North Holland.

World Trade Organization (1994). *General Agreement on Trade in Services*. Geneva.

World Trade Organization (1997). *Annexes to the 4th Protocol of the GATS*. Geneva.

World Trade Organization (1998). *Trading into the Future*. Geneva.

15

NO CULTURE IS AN ISLAND

An analysis of media protectionism and media openness

Joseph Man Chan

Between restrictive and supportive protection

To adopt trade protection or free trade is the central policy issue in international economics (Krugman and Obstfeld, 1991). The same issue is of even greater importance in the international flow of cultural products because of the ideological effects that they may have, as reflected in the global debate over cultural imperialism and the new information order in the 1970s and 1980s (e.g. MacBride, 1980; Richstad and Anderson, 1981; Lee, 1980). Although the row between blocks of countries such as the advanced Western nations and the developing world has subsided in the 1990s, media protection remains an enduring subject in policy discourse, especially in countries that are experiencing what is to them an asymmetrical cultural flow. The issue is expected to re-surface in the year 2000 for the next round of GATT negotiations (Grainger, 1998).

Protective measures are either restrictive or supportive in nature. Restrictive measures are meant to regulate the inflow and exhibition of cultural products whereas supportive measures aim at promoting the domestic cultural industry. Restrictive cultural protection is analogous to the policy of import-substituting industrialization – a strategy of encouraging domestic industry by limiting imports of goods (Krugman and Obstfeld, 1991). Tariffs and quotas are the most common forms of restrictive protectionism. At the extreme, a country can choose to dissociate from the world by banning all foreign products, as it was once practiced by China during the Cultural Revolution (Chan, 1994a).

Supportive protectionism aims to promote national cultural industry through government sponsorship and subsidy. Economically, supportive protectionism serves to free the domestic industry from market dictates or to enable the domestic cultural industry to survive foreign competition. Restrictive protection and supportive protection may work jointly or independently.

This author agrees that individual nations should have the right to make their own communication policies. Neither media protectionism nor media openness should be imposed on them. However, it is critical for us to be aware of the assumptions, arguments, and empirical bases for and against each policy option. This article attempts to contrast the theoretical and empirical foundations of media protectionism and media openness. It will also assess the relevance of media protectionism to cultural development, especially in this age of global communication.

For protectionism

Media protectionism is premised on the ideological nature of cultural products. Physical goods such as cars, computers, and television sets are often considered to be non-ideological or, to say the least, much less ideological than cultural products, and are therefore less often subject to protective measures. In contrast, cultural products are perceived to be value-laden and ideological. If cultural goods did not have these potential influences, televisual products would receive a much less restrictive treatment.

Media protectionism is deeply rooted in the fear of influence from foreign culture and the loss of cultural integrity. Foreign culture is often viewed with suspicion. Rightly or wrongly, foreign media are accused of causing moral deterioration such as the rise of sexual permissiveness, growing disrespect for authority and even the spread of violence. From the protectionist perspective, foreign culture is on the main socially dysfunctional. For a nation to call itself a nation, it requires a cultural identity of its own. The preservation of a distinct indigenous culture is often considered to be critical for maintaining such a cultural identity. The inflow of a seemingly stronger foreign culture tends to induce fear in the recipient country because of the alternative values and behavioral codes it carries. If the recipient country does find such challenges threatening or alienating, the knee-jerk response is to restrict the proliferation of foreign culture.

The use of protective policy is sometimes tied to the vested interest of the ruling elites who are in a position to make policies. Western culture that advocates, for instance, individualism, freedom, democracy and equality is often estimated to be instrumental in undermining the domination structure of many third-world countries and giving rise to social fragmentation and instability. That explains why some Asian governments, among others, cite "cultural invasion" and "social instability" as reasons for the control of satellite TV (Chan, 1994b). They are afraid that alien values and outside information may erode traditional culture and disrupt racial, religious, and political harmony in their societies.

The governing elites do not act just out of their own concerns, they serve as the articulators of various interests within a nation. For instance, a protective policy may serve to pacify the fears of religious groups over Western decadence and the displacement of domestic religions. It may also serve to ease the teachers' worry over the deterioration of moral standards among the young. The audiovisual industry of a given country may have its own vested interest to protect too. In cases where it enjoys state subsidy and protection, free trade will threaten to change its status quo. For some governments, broadcast television itself is an important source of revenue, as well as an agent of socio-political control. All these interests coalesce to form protective measure against foreign competition.

Asymmetrical cultural exchange is conducive to media protection. The stronger party in such a relationship always favors free trade because of the gains it enjoys. In contrast, the weak tend to resort to protection. This rule applies to both cultural and non-cultural goods such as cars. Known for advocating free trade and viewing international trade as a force not only for prosperity but also for world peace, even the United States tinkered with protectionism when its car exports plunged in face of Japanese competition in the 1980s (Krugman and Obstfeld, 1991).

In the media realm, the United States is undoubtedly the dominating force of the world. Indeed, statistics in the 1990s continue to show that the world's media are American (Turow, 1997): US media products account for 75 percent of broadcast and basic cable TV revenue and 85 percent of pay-TV revenues worldwide.[1] Fifty-five percent of all theatrical film rentals and 55 percent of all home-video billings worldwide are for US products. While the USA reaps about half of global recording revenues, it commands 35 percent of the book sales market. The American domination in the media world is so lopsided that many countries regard such a relationship as a form of cultural imperialism, which is feared to be the major cause of cultural homogenization around the world. Given the huge domestic market and strong transnational media conglomerates that the USA has (Wasko, 1991), few would question the seeming perpetuity of the inequitable international flow of cultural products. Under the perspective of cultural imperialism, free trade is loathed by the developing nations for its role in reinforcing their subordination. Protection is seemingly the logical way to get out of the deadlock.

The fear of American cultural domination is not restricted to just the developing nations, some forms of media protection are practiced even in developed areas such as Canada and Western Europe. To tame the cultural influence from its giant neighbor – the United States – Canada relies heavily on government regulations to strike a balance between freedom of access to international programming and the imperatives necessary for maintaining a national cultural identity (Servaes, 1992). One strategy to help its mass media is to tax the advertising dollars Canadian firms use when they buy advertisements in foreign media outlets that reach Canada (Turow, 1997). Government grants are used to support production by firms which sell programs to Canadian television stations. Western Europe is equally nervous about the penetration of American media fare (Turow, 1997). While some European nations set quotas on how much TV stations can carry foreign programs, the Council of Ministers at the European Parliament funds plans to develop its own audiovisual industry that it can sell to the world. The plan provides seed money for production projects, coproduction, multinational distribution, and the development of audiovisual technologies.[2]

For openness

The policy of free trade is an expression of faith in the effectiveness of the market mechanism in allocating resources around the world. The exporting country of certain goods is one that has comparative advantage over others in producing the goods in question (Krugman and Obstfeld, 1991). In other words, countries will export goods that they have relatively higher productivity. From the vantage of the free trade perspective, the international flow of cultural products resembles the global exchange of regular commodities. Cultural products flow from the industrial countries to less developed countries because their prices are cheaper and the quality is better (Ito, 1990a).

Under this competition model, it is possible for the importing country to change its position in the world map. Japan has been hailed as an outstanding example in this regard (Ito, 1990a; 1990b). Japan was at one time an importer of media and information. However, without resorting to protectionism, Japan finally gained strength and became a media exporter. Hong Kong is an even more telling example because of its small domestic market (Chan and Lee, 1992; Chan, 1997). It is a tiny territory that practices an open cultural policy. Yet it succeeds as a regional media center in the Asia-Pacific region. We shall elaborate on this later.

Media protectionism presupposes an elitist cultural perspective, which does not expect the mass to have a good sense of cultural judgment. In contrast, advocators of cultural openness have greater confidence in and respect for the individual's autonomy in making cultural choices. As consumers, most people around the world prefer an open cultural system and the availability of more choices. From an economic point of view, protection measures not only result in higher costs of production but also lower consumer welfare (Kotler, Jatusripitak, and Maesincee, 1997). A clear demonstration of the damage that can be done to consumer welfare is the undue higher prices that the Japanese and Koreans have to pay for rice caused by their closure to rice imports (Carnahan, 1994). By similar token, the potential loss to audience brought about by cultural protectionism includes higher prices, reduced cultural choice, and undue omission of information.

Unlike protectionism that tends to assume the vulnerability of the domestic culture to foreign influence, free trade policy has a more moderated estimation of the impact of foreign media. It has been increasingly recognized that domestic cultural products have a competitive edge over imports as far as they are comparable in quality (Cantor and Cantor, 1986). Ratings showed that the overwhelming majority of the top twenty television programs in seven Asian nations were locally produced (Wang, 1993). In a country open to foreign satellite TV, the competitiveness of local terrestrial television is observed to be a crucial factor in determining whether people will tune in to satellite television, because of the audience's preference for locally oriented programming (Chan, 1994b). People turn to non-home products only when they find foreign programs to be of higher technical quality, more interesting content, and greater variety.

Local cultural products owe their competitive edge to what Straubhaar (1991) has termed cultural proximity, the audience's familiarity with the language and the cultural context they carry. The local media fare is always easier to understand and culturally resonating. Non-English-speaking countries therefore have linguistic and cultural barriers against American and British media products. Given this

The trend towards globalization gains momentum when democracy and market economy triumph around the world. The downfall of socialism in Soviet Russia and Eastern Europe has lent unprecedented credibility to capitalism and the universal suffrage system. Given its market and social reforms, even socialist China has been losing its status as a source of alternative ideology. China has become much more open to the outside world (Chan, 1994a). Although the entry of foreign culture is still regulated or controlled in some ways, it can get in through different channels, including trade, piracy, and spillover. The movie *Titanic*, for instance, with the personal blessing of Jiang Zeming, the chairman of the Chinese Communist Party, has become a national hit (Wong, Key and Wong, 1998). As China is going to ascend the World Trade Organization, one can expect it to be more open to the world even in the cultural realm.

While globalization is an important trend, it has to be understood in conjunction with the idea of localization: The global and local are relative to one another. This relativity is well captured by the notion of "glocalization" which Robsertson (1995) uses to express the global production of the local and the localization of the global. To be more attractive to the local audience, media operators have to have their programs and content tailor-made for a target area. That is the lesson learned by satellite TV broadcasters such as Star TV in Asia (Chan, 1994b; Lee and Wang, 1995). It discovered that having a country-specific and culture-specific programming is more effective than a Pan-Asian menu.

One fundamental assumption of protectionism is that foreign culture is potentially harmful to indigenous culture. From the open trade perspective, the reverse may be true. Foreign culture is viewed as a national enrichment. It is through the synthesis and hyrbridization of the foreign and domestic cultures that cultural development is achieved. Cultural development is a dynamic process, in which hegemonic powers may be contested and resisted. The culture of a nation is always changing, particularly in this age of globalization when no culture can remain an island. What is considered to be foreign at one time will be considered indigenous if it has been successfully assimilated. The resultant culture, undeniably national, will then serve as a new platform for further development. Given this dynamic view of cultural formation, the need for protective measures is reduced.

A case of extreme media-cultural openness

Hong Kong is a case of extreme media-cultural openness. Hong Kong has been a Chinese society under British rule for about 150 years. Needless to say, it was subject to heavy British influence. Adopting an open cultural policy, Hong Kong is also susceptible to cultural influence from mainland China, USA, Japan, Taiwan, and other parts of the world. Hong Kong therefore serves as a living laboratory for observing the consequences of openness. The observations to be made about Hong Kong are meant to shed light on some of the important issues discussed above.

One significant assumption of media protectionism is that an open policy will result in the radical transformation of an indigenous culture by foreign cultures.

Hong Kong shows that such fear is unwarranted. Hong Kong had all the right conditions to be fully Westernized under British rule and an open environment. Yet the people remain Chinese in many important ways. Anyone who is familiar with Hong Kong and the Western world will agree that the former continues to show, for instance, relatively strong family ties and conservative sexual mores, which constitute some of the characteristics of Chinese societies. Having a distinct identity of their own, the Hong Kong people cannot be mistaken for Americans or British. They do not even hesitate to show their Chinese nationalism when the time calls. During the heat of the 1989 pro-democracy movement in China, as many as one-sixth of Hong Kong's six million residents marched on the streets to render their support. In groups and as individuals, Hong Kong people spontaneously protested against Japan's claim to some disputed islands to the north of Taiwan and Japan's attempts to gloss over its invasion of China during the Second World War. All these illustrate the limit of influence from foreign media and culture on the one hand and the endurance of the Hong Kong Chinese identity on the other. Losing one's cultural identity is simply not as easy as protectionists tend to think. If Hong Kong can survive colonial openness, cultures in a less open environment should more easily hold on to their roots.

Another assumption of media protectionism is that an open cultural policy is conducive to the domination by foreign media. Hong Kong has a small domestic market, which does not favor the growth of indigenous media. However, Hong Kong successfully exploits the overseas market that is scattered in Taiwan and southeast Asia and other Asian societies and turned itself into a regional media center (Chan and Lee, 1990; To and Lau, 1995; Chan, 1996, 1997; Leung and Chan, 1997). All this has been achieved without the help of the government. The case of Hong Kong clearly demonstrates that protectionism is not a necessary condition for domestic media development in developing nations. Given the appropriate conditions and necessary effort, the media-importing countries can transform themselves into exporters. This is not to say that Hong Kong can always maintain its competitive edge. Its market share may fluctuate as the environment changes. While Hong Kong's television industry remains vibrant, its movie industry, for instance, has been suffering from a crisis that is partially precipitated by Hollywood's competition (Einhorn and Grover, 1998). Attested by the outstanding past performance of Hong Kong's movie industry, this should not stop us from concluding that there is at least room for the national media industry to negotiate and compete with its foreign counterparts in an open environment.

Media protectionism tends to assume that policy makers can differentiate the cultural good from the cultural bad. But this is not easy if we, as we should, allow some level of cultural relativism and pluralization. Table 15.1 shows the results of a comparative survey of people's values in Hong Kong, Guangzhou and Beijing in 1998.[3] We can draw several observations: First, Hong Kong citizens are the least likely to resort to illicit means ("backdoor") in achieving their goals, a behavioral tendency that is perhaps cherished by all fair-minded people. We can safely argue that this is tied to the British rule of law in Hong Kong. The point to be stressed

Table 15.1 Comparative values in Hong Kong, Guangzhou and Beijing

Values and cultural practices	Hong Kong % agree	Guangzhou % agree	Beijing % agree
I shall go by the "backdoor" if I have a chance	21.2	50.4	47.5
There is no need to call before visiting a friend	19.4	28.6	26.7
One shouldn't bother when neighbors quarrel	46.1	38.3	40.9
I will definitely not send my parents to the elders' home.	51.2	58.9	50.0
(N)	(504)	(916)	(803)

here is that foreign culture can be socially functional. It is also observed that Hong Kong people are more likely than their mainland counterparts to call before visiting a friend. Whether this cultural practice is good or bad depends on one's vantage: For those who are busy and privacy-respecting, it is "good." The reverse is true for those who have an open schedule and less concern for privacy. Second, the indigenous culture of a nation is not uniform as is often assumed. It varies across regions, cities and social strata *within* the nation. For instance, on the question of whether one should send one's parents to an elders' home, more people in Guangzhou (58.9 percent) readily disagree than Hong Kong (51.2 percent) and Beijing (50.0 percent). In this case, which city better represents the indigenous culture of China Guangzhou or Beijing? Beijing residents are closer to their Hong Kong counterparts rather than Guangzhou's in this regard. In such a case, the exposure to foreign culture is simply an extension of the domestic process of cultural pluralization. The origin of a cultural practice should not be the criterion for judging whether it should be adopted or not. It hinges on whether the practice serves to meet the people's needs.

China provides a strong contrast to Hong Kong. It illustrates what extreme media protectionism could do to a country. Regarding foreign cultural influence as "spiritual pollution," it has been trying to restrict people's access to foreign culture (Chan, 1994a). Such protectionism reached its extremity when China disconnected from the Western world during the Cultural Revolution. Over-protection as such not only gives rise to cultural monotony and sterility, as admitted by many Chinese intellectuals and officials, but also deprives the media of their ability to compete internationally, thus making way for the inroads of foreign media when China reopens. In spite of the huge domestic market and resources that China has in audiovisual production, its media industry pales during competitive encounters with Hong Kong products. Indeed, the popular culture from politically peripheral areas such as Hong Kong and Taiwan has made an immense impact on China, the political center of Chinese societies (Gold, 1993; Tu 1991).

Table 15.2 Comparing media protectionism with media openness

Comparative dimensions	Media protectionism	Media openness
Goals	To protect home media industries. To protect cultural integrity. To protect established interests To maintain social stability and harmony.	To promote home media industries through competition. To favor cultural hybridization. To increase consumer welfare. To open up foreign markets.
Regulatory mechanisms	Administrative restrictive control such as tariffs and quotas. Supportive measures such as state subsidy and sponsorship.	Free trade and market regulation.
Assumptions and arguments	Western cultural domination represents some form of cultural imperialism. Cultural products should be excepted from free trade.	The structure of international communication is a result of differences in comparative advantage. Cultural products can be treated as commodities.
	Cultural integrity or cultural sovereignty is an absolute concept. The challenge of Hollywood is too strong for the home media industry. Competition works only for the advantaged.	Cultural integrity or cultural sovereignty is a relative concept. Given the right conditions, Hollywood can be challenged. Countries can change their relative position in global cultural production.
	Indigenous culture can easily be displaced when exposed. Transborder media have powerful effects. Effective enforcement of restrictive protection is still feasible in this age of globalization.	The genetic base of a culture can hardly be transformed. Transborder media have limited or contingent effects. Restrictive protection is increasingly unfeasible in the age of globalization.
	External causes better account for the underdevelopment of home cultural industry. The masses do not necessarily know what is culturally best for them. Cultural diversity is valued internationally but not necessarily within a nation.	Internal causes better account for the underdevelopment of cultural industry. Consumer choice should be respected. Cultural diversity is valued at both the national and international levels.

Harnessing foreign competition

To open or not to open, that is the question facing many governments. Given that nations vary in their histories and needs, it is foolhardy to recommend a uniform policy for the world. Nations should have the right to make their own choice. However, policy makers should be aware of the goals, assumptions and arguments for and against media protectionism and media openness that are summarized in Table 15.2. Whatever the choice, the policy option should be the result of a rational cost and benefit analysis.

In this age of global communication, no culture can afford being alone. The boundaries between indigenous and foreign cultures are shifting. As evidenced by Hong Kong's case of extreme openness, the fear of foreign culture supplanting a given culture is basically unfounded. Total cultural Westernization is impossible. The home culture of a nation may change on the surface but it is very difficult to transform its genetic base. People's identities are tied more to their blood, soil and religion. Domestic and foreign cultures are not necessarily locked in a zero-sum game. They may interact to form a hybridized culture. Some level of cultural blending and the formation of multiple and hybrid identities are perhaps unavoidable and arguably desirable. At the least, one should not rush to make judgments about the effects of importing foreign cultural products without a more explicit understanding of how cultural borders are constituted, reproduced and modified (Schlesinger, 1987).

Globalization appears to have weakened the capability of nation-states to control the influence of foreign media. However, it is wrong to assume that the nation-state is losing its relevancy in the age of globalization (Schlesinger, 1993). Formal regulation rests mainly in the hands of the national political and commercial elite (Sreberny-Mohammadi, Winseck, McKenna and Boyd-Barrett, 1997). Globalization is not a process that uniformly subverts the national. It may consolidate some nation-states while further weakening the already weak. The idea of cultural sovereignty will continue to run strong in countries that range from Australia, France, Canada to China. Such countries will likely continue to resist the inclusion of cultural products in future GATT agreements (Grainger, 1998). To many nations, cultural products should be excepted from free trade. In addition, the protection rendered by quotas and other controls for the domestic media industry will continue to be valued. The undesirable consequences of foreign culture will be stressed. The nation-state will therefore continue to play a critical role in regulating communication across national boundaries and the development of national cultural industry. It is through a competitive and learning process that nations will eventually discover what best meets their needs.

The adoption of general openness does not require one to have blind faith in the market as the sole mechanism guiding cultural development. On the one hand, the market may fail under some conditions. On the other, it is sometimes necessary to strike a balance between the social need for foreign media and the need to minimize the undesirable changes that they may cause. (What is undesirable, in the last instance, is subject to the interpretation of individual nations.) While media openness is the way to go, one should allow an open policy complemented by a limited form of supportive protection and even restriction on certain potentially harmful content.

The sudden introduction of openness may overwhelm the domestic media industry of a nation, especially in the initial period. It will take a longer time for it to recover, if ever. A good strategy is therefore to open a protected market on a scheduled basis and/or phase by phase. Given a scheduled opening *and* the introduction of domestic competition, the home media industry will have both the drive and the time to get into gear and to develop the power to face up to foreign competition.

Allowing domestic competition is the key to preparing one's media industry for global competition. Without competition among national players, it is impossible for the home industry to develop its strength. Through competition, the home industry can grow and incorporate whatever it can learn from both domestic and foreign players. Indeed, the competitive national environment is crucial for the international competitive success of firms (Porter, 1990). Without open competition, firms – be they car manufacturers or media organizations – lose dynamism and become preoccupied with dealing with regulators and protecting what they have.

In addition to the prerequisite of domestic competition, there are two other conditions for protectionism to work (Porter, 1990). One is the presence of appropriate demand conditions, availability of the essential production factors, and other domestic circumstances which support the development of sustainable advantages.[4] The other requirement for successful protection is that it is limited in duration. Protected industries tend to suffer eventually from the lack of full competition. An undue extended application of protection will keep the infant industry from maturing.

Notes

1 For a more detailed account of the domination of American cultural products, see Barker (1997).
2 The first plan for the said purposes was initiated in 1991. But it was found to be ineffective. A second plan was launched in 1995 whose main concern was to build up the global distributional network for European cultural products.
3 I would like to thank Professor Chen Huailin, Zhu Jianhua and Steve Quo for letting me use their survey data.
4 The development of a domestic media industry requires contingencies such as advertising and economic growth, as in the case of Japan (Ito, 1990b) and Hong Kong (Chan and Lee, 1992), the large size and competitive structure of domestic markets, the availability of a critical mass of competent creative personnel, and the availability of financial services and manufacturers of necessary equipment, as in the case of the United States (Collins, Garnham and Locksley, 1988).

References

Barker, C. (1997). *Global Television: An Introduction*. Oxford: Blackwell Press.

Cantor, M. and Cantor, J. (1986). "The internationalization of TV Entertainment." In S. Thomas (Ed.), *Studies in Communication*. Norwood, NJ: Ablex Publications.

Carnahan, I. (1994). "The new protectionism." *Public Interest*, Spring, 116–21.

Chan, J.M. (1994a). "Media internationalization in China: Processes and tensions." *Journal of Communication*, 44(3), 70–88.

Chan, J.M. (1994b). "National responses and accessibility to Star TV in Asia." *Journal of Communication*, 44(3), 112–33.

Chan, J.M. (1996). "Television in greater China: Structure, exports, and market formation." In J. Sinclair, E. Jacka, and S. Cunningham (Eds), *New Patterns in Global Television: Peripheral Vision*, 127–61. Oxford: Oxford University Press.

Chan, J.M. (1997). "Media internationalization in Hong Kong: Patterns, factors, and tensions." In G. Postiglione and J. Tung (Eds), *Hong Kong's Reunion with China: The Global Dimensions*, 222–38. Armonk, NY: M.E. Sharpe.

Chan, J.M. and Lee, P. (1992). "Communication indicators in Hong Kong: Conceptual issues and findings." In S.K. Lau, Lee Ming-kwan, Wan Po-san and Wong Sin-lan (Eds), *The Development of Social Indicators Research in Chinese Societies*. Hong Kong: The Hong Kong Institute of Asia-Pacific Studies, The Chinese University.

Collins, R., Garnham, N. and Locksley, G. (1988). *The Economics of Television*. London: Sage.

Einhorn, B. and Grover, R. (1998). "What hit Hong Kong's film industry?" *Business Week* (Asian edn), May 4, 24–7.

Featherstone, M. (1990). "Global culture: An introduction." in M. Featherstone (Ed.), *Global Culture: Nationalism, Globalization and Modernity*. London: Sage.

Giddens, A. (1991). *The Consequences of Modernity*. Stanford: Stanford University Press.

Gold, T. (1993). "Go with your feelings: Hong Kong and Taiwan popular culture in greater China." *China Quarterly*, 136, 907–25.

Grainger, G. (1998). "National culutral regimes faced with competition from global media: An Australian perspective." Paper presented to the Conference on the Production and Consumption of National and Local Cultural Products in the Age of Gobal Communication, June 5–7, National Chung Cheng University, Chia-yi, Taiwan.

Hannerz, U. (1997). "Notes on the global ecumene." In A. Sreberny-Mohammadi, D. Winseck, J. McKenna and O. Boyd-Barrett (Eds), *Media in Global Context: A Reader*, 11–18. London: Arnold Press.

Ito, Y. (1990a). "Mass communication theories from a Japanese perspective." *Media, Culture and Society*, 12(1990), 423–64.

Ito, Y (1990b). "The trade winds change: Japan's shift from an information importer to an information exporter, 1965–1985." In J. Anderson (Ed.), *Communication Yearbook* 13, 430–65. Newbury Park, CA: Sage.

Katz, E. and Wedell, G. (1977). *Broadcasting in the Third World*. Cambridge, MA: Harvard University Press.

Kotler, P., Jatusripitak, S. and Maesincee, S. (1997). *The Marketing of Nations: A Strategic Approach to Building National Wealth*. New York: Free Press.

Krugman, P. and Maurice Obstfeld (1991). *International Economics: Theory and Policy*. New York: Harper Collins.

Lee, C.-C. (1980). *Media Imperialism Reconsidered*. Beverly Hills, CA: Sage.

Lee, P. and Wang, G. (1995). "Satellite TV in Asia: Forming a new ecology." *Telecommunications Policy*, 19(2), 135–49.

Leung, G. and Chan, J. (1997). "The Hong Kong cinema and its overseas market: A historical review, 1950–1995." In *Fifty Years of Electric Shadows*, 143–51 (edited by the Urban Council of Hong Kong).

Lull, J. (1991). *China Turned On: Television, Reform, and Resistance*. London: Rouledge.

MacBride, S. (Ed.) (1980). *Many Voices, One World*. Paris: Unesco.

Mowlana, H. (1986). *Global Information and World Communication*. New York: Longman.

Porter, M. (1990). *The Competitive Advantage of Nations*. New York: Free Press.

Richstad, J. and Anderson, M. (Eds) (1981). *Crisis in International News: Policies and Prospects*. New York: Columbia University Press.

Robertson, R. (1995). "Glocalization: Time-space and homogeneity-heterogeneity." In M. Featherstone, S. Lash and R. Robertson (Eds), *Global Modernities*, 25–44. Thousand Oaks, CA: Sage.

Schlesinger, P. (1987). "On national identity: Some conceptions and misconceptions criticized." *Social Science Information*, 26(2), 219–64.

Schlesinger, P. (1993). "Wishful thinking: Cultural politics, media, and collective identities in Europe." *Journal of Communication*, 43(2), 6–17.

Servaes, J. (1992). "'Europe 1992': The audiovisual challenge." *Gazette*, 49, 75–97.

Sinclair, J., Jacka, E. and Cunningham, S. (1996). "Peripheral vision." In J. Sinclair, E. Jacka, and S. Cunningham (Eds), *New Patterns in Global Television: Peripheral Vision*, 1–32. Oxford: Oxford University Press.

Sreberny-Mohammadi, A., Winseck, D., McKenna, J. and Boyd-Barrett, O. (1997). "Editor's introduction: Media in global context." In A. Sreberny-Mohammadi, D. Winseck, J. McKenna and O. Boyd-Barrett (Eds), *Media in Global Context: A Reader*, iv–xxviii. London: Arnold Press.

Straubhaar, J. (1991). "Beyond media imperialism: Asymmetrical interdependence and cultural proximity." *Critical Studies in Mass Communication*, 8(1), 39–59.

Straubhaar, J. (1997). "Distinguishing the global, regional and national levels of world television." In A. Sreberny-Mohammadi, D. Winseck, J. McKenna and O. Boyd-Barrett (Eds), *Media in Global Context: A Reader*, 284–98. London: Arnold Press.

To, Y. and Lau, T. (1995). "Global export of Hong Kong television: Television broadcasts limited." *Asian Journal of Communication*, 5(2), 108–21.

Tu, W.M. (1991). "Cultural China: The periphery as the center." *Daedalus*, 120(2), 1–32.

Turow, J. (1997). *Media Systems in Society: Understanding Industries, Strategies, and Power*. New York: Longman.

Wang, G. (1993). "Satellite television and the future of broadcast television in the Asia-Pacific." *Media Asia*, 20(3), 140–8.

Wang, G. (1996). "Beyond media globalization: A look at cultural integrity from a policy perspective." Paper presented at the Seminar on (Tele)communications Policies in Western Europe and Southeast Asia: Cultural and Historical Perspectives, August 29–September 1, Bruges, Belgium.

Wasko, J. (1991). "Hollywood, new technologies, and Europe 1992." *Telematics and Informatics*, 8(3), 183–94.

Wong, K., Shekming, K. and Lailai, W. (1998). "The Voyage of the *Titanic* into China." *Yazhou Zhoukan*, March 16–22, 19-21.

16

MEDIA IN THE
INFORMATION HIGHWAY

Representing different cultures in the age of global communication[1]

Anura Goonasekera

New communication technologies are creating a new type of community. It is variously referred to as intelligent communities, smart communities, para-social communities, virtual communities, and cyber communities. The social relationships among the members of these communities are not necessarily based on physical proximity. Strategic locations such as transportation crossroads, easy access to raw materials and labor, which were very important for the emergence and sustenance of communities in earlier periods of history, are no longer the deciding criteria for the emergence of intelligent communities. New telecommunication technologies have made it possible for business to produce, consumers to purchase and workers to interact without the need for common physical location.[2]

While an entirely new form of civic organization is emerging, as a result of the impact of new communication technologies, the policies governing these social processes are still influenced by an old mode of thinking. Even the scientific community has not been very helpful in this regard. Social scientists, researchers and popular writers use metaphors borrowed from earlier period of history to describe futuristic developments in the field of communications. We speak of global villages, electronic superhighways, multimedia super-corridors etc. These metaphors are much too simple and commonplace to capture the momentous changes that are taking place in the intelligent communities. However policies continue to be influenced by this thinking. We bring in regulations, deregulation and re-regulation which may be entirely irrelevant to the processes that are going on in the newly emerging communities. There is a vast chasm between the needs of new communication technologies and the policies that are used for its social applications. This is clearly the case in policies that govern the transnational media.

What is significant in the changes that are brought about by new communication technologies is that the traditional centers of control are withering away. Mass communication under the previous modes of production, both capitalist and socialist, used to be controlled by a group of functionaries. It was easy for the owners of the media to design policies to control the media, including its content, at various stages of production. The owners could be media moguls or governments. However, in the intelligent communities, linked to the information superhighway, such direct controls through ownership are becoming increasingly difficult. The service providers of the Internet, for instance, cannot monitor the content of the messages that are transmitted using their online services. Furthermore the traditional distinction between different kinds of media such as print, broadcasting, film are getting blurred. Multimedia is becoming the vehicle of the future. Old-fashioned censorship will now be very difficult to impose. With the advent of new communication technologies the medium, the message and the audience will not be discrete entities. They are interacting and merging to become parts of civil society – an intelligent community. A different morality will emerge. The question is what kind of a morality will this be? Will it support values such as openness, freedom and tolerance that are sorely needed for civil life in any human community? Or will it bring about a hegemony that will be a threat to smaller communities and their cultures?

Modern communication technologies are creating unprecedented opportunities for cultural contacts among individuals and communities living in remote parts of the globe. Transnational television broadcasting is the most conspicuous medium that brings about these cross-cultural contacts. However, apart from television there are other media, both traditional and new, which continue to impact on societies. Electronic networks, e-mail, electronic databases, cellular networks, faxes, telephones are all putting people into contact with each other and cutting down isolation in an historically unprecedented manner.

Transnational media

Spurred on by the opportunities opened up by modern information technology, the media of communication are rapidly getting internationalized. They are looking for far wider markets than those in the countries of production and immediate distribution. Unlike for Hollywood movies, such foreign sales are not a bonus. It is the mainstay. Television is a frontrunner in the quest for global audiences. The newspapers are, however, not far behind. Not only are these media locating correspondents and stringers in a large number of countries, but the management of these media organizations and their modes of production are being diversified. CNN is opening bureaus in Asia. *International Herald Tribune* (IHT) is published from Singapore. *BBC World Service* has commenced program production in India. Rupert Murdoch's StarTV, not being satisfied with Asia-wide audiences for its English-language programs, is now looking for regional-language audiences within Asia. It has commenced programs which cater to communities that speak different Asian languages. Principally these are Chinese-language, Malay-language and Indian-language audiences. While communication technology has created the potential for global media, cultural interests and the logic of the market are fragmenting the global media in Asia into regional, geo-linguistic areas. These geo-linguistic areas cover more than one country. They are supra-national and represent a multiplicity of mores, customs, laws and traditions. This is a situation hitherto unknown in media history of the world.

The internationalization or globalization of media has raised important issues. One such issue is about representing diverse cultures in the programs that these media create. The questions that arise in this respect are: what are the current practices of these global media in recording, reporting and representing the cultures in the different countries that they report on; what are the issues and problems that arise out of such reporting or representation; what ought to be the manner of such reporting by multinational media; how valid are the claims of cultural imperialist theories in the light of experiences in Asia?

These issues raise questions not only of representing cultural diversity in multi-national media but more importantly questions of politics, i.e. power; questions of law – both domestic and international; and questions of international commerce and economics. More often than not politics, law and economics are intertwined in the issues that have so far surfaced in Asia. I will present some specific cases that were given wide publicity in the international media. I will examine the issues of media globalization in Asia as a process of meaning creation necessitated by a clash of interests between leaders in Asian countries and the owners of multinational media. A clash between imperatives of nation building, rapid economic development through authoritarian governance and the ideology of a capitalist, confrontational press of the Western democracies. It is a power struggle principally between the owners of multinational media and the rulers in Asian countries. It will get resolved only after the major contenders agree to a set of international covenants governing the conduct of global communication. We need a Law of the Skies just as much as we need a Law of the Seas. The latter is in place. The former is gradually emerging.

Cases

Let us look at some specific cases. I will look at the gazetting of international publications in Singapore and libel action against *International Herald Tribune* (IHT); allegations of bribery against the Malaysian Prime Minister, Dr Mahathir, in the London *Sunday Times* and its aftermath. (Incidentally the *Sunday Times* is owned by Murdoch.) The Gandhi gaffe in the *Nikki Tonight* program broadcast to India by Star TV, and the case against a television station in Sri Lanka, called Extra Terrestrial Vision (ETV), filed by Star TV, for alleged copyright violations and the implications of the Indian Cable Act (1994) for international satellite broadcasts to India. I believe that knowledge about these cases is a *sine qua non* for an understanding of the role of foreign journalists, reporting on Asian issues in the international press, as perceived by leaders in these countries. The legal principles that emerged through these court decisions and the efforts to create space for coexistence between multinational media and Asian governments is a fascinating study of the emerging culture of transnational communication. It is a sociological study of how communities create meanings in new situations brought about by the introduction of advanced communication technologies.

During the years 1986–87, the Singapore government restricted the circulation of *Time*, *Asian Wall Street Journal* (AWSJ), *Asiaweek* and *Far Eastern Economic Review* (FEER) – all international publications having wide circulation in Singapore. The restrictions were imposed by a Government Gazette notification, under the Newspaper and Printing Act, and hence this procedure is referred to as gazetting. The disputes with *Time*, AWSJ, and *Asiaweek* have been over the right to reply. All three publications had carried stories about events in Singapore which the Singapore government said was factually incorrect. The government wrote to set the facts straight. *Time* and AWSJ refused to publish these corrections. *Asiaweek* published the corrections but without the knowledge of Singapore government edited the reply and attributed the edited version to the Singapore government.

FEER's report, it was alleged, was not only false but was also defamatory of Mr Lee Kuan Yew, the Prime Minister of Singapore at that time. The government wrote to FEER to either substantiate or withdraw the allegations. FEER refused on grounds of editorial prerogative. Its circulation was restricted from 9,000 copies to 500 copies and a libel case was filed in Singapore courts.[3]

A more recent case involved charges of contempt of court and libel against IHT. The article in question was written by an American academic who, at that time, was a senior fellow at the National University of Singapore. It alleged that some intolerant regimes in Asia, which he did not name, rely upon a compliant judiciary to bankrupt opposition politicians. The Singapore courts found the writer, the Asia editor of IHT, IHT publisher and CEO and IHT printer, Singapore Press Holdings, guilty of contempt and libel. Fines were imposed on those convicted.[4] When IHT was criticized for agreeing to pay damages, IHT president, Mr. Richard Simmons, said that the courts have found IHT to have libeled and that it would not contest the High Court decision. It would continue to operate from Singapore. Critics who were demanding that the IHT try to impose American liberal standards abroad were uninformed. (AWSJ, January 18, 1995)

Apart from recourse to legal proceedings, there are also other ways in which Asian leaders make known their displeasure to journalists who publish disparaging articles. Malaysia's Pergau Dam case is instructive in this regard. The London *Sunday Times* of February 24, 1994, in a story headlined "Wimpey offered contract bribes to Malaysian Prime Minister," alleged that the giant construction company, Wimpey, had offered an initial payment of $50,000 through a middle man to the Malaysian Prime Minister, Dr Mahathir Mohammed. The Malaysian Prime Minister was furious at what he alleged were totally false allegations. In retaliation, the Malaysian government decided to shut out British contractors from all infrastructure projects in Malaysia. Announcing the new policy, the Deputy Prime Minister of Malaysia at the same time, Mr Anwar Ibrahim said "the British media may have their own political agendas but we detest their patronizing attitude and innuendoes that the governments of developing countries, particularly a Muslim led nation such as Malaysia, are incompetent and their leaders corrupt" (*Sunday Times* (Singapore), March 13, 1994). Because of these press reports, it was argued that to deal with British companies was to have shady undertones. Therefore, the Malaysian government had decided not to award any new contracts to British companies. This decision affected some big contracts that may have been won by big industries in Britain including General Electric, Balfour Beatty and British Aerospace. Britain lost thousands of jobs. The end result was that the editor of the *Sunday Times* was removed by Murdoch and transferred to another part of his empire. Dr Mahathir said that the editor was sacked.

The Gandhi gaffe involved a Star TV program called *Nikki Tonight* which is beamed to audiences in India. The program features gossip of the Bombay film industry and in one of its programs the host Nikki Bedi egged her guest, Ashok Row Kavi, a gay activist, into repeating scandalous remarks that Mr Kavi had made a long time ago in the press against Mahatma Gandhi, father of modern India. Kavi called Gandhi a bastard Bania. He implied by this that Gandhi was a miser and a sharp dealer. This was a totally false allegation because money meant very little to Gandhi, who lived a very simple life. The allegation went unchallenged in the program. While such a remark may have been tolerated in Western countries it created a roar of angry protests in India. The Indian parliament accused Murdoch of cultural terrorism. Gandhi's grandson complained to the police that Star TV had insulted and defamed Gandhi. The police took action based on the provisions of Indian Law of criminal libel. Warrants were issued for the arrest of Rupert Murdoch and some program officials of Star TV (*The Independent*, July 6, 1995). The program was scrapped and Ms Nikki Bedi lost her job. While incidents such as this one are not common, these nevertheless help to confirm the worst fears of Asian critics of international media who argue that Western media would subvert the values and traditions of their countries.

The fourth case I want to take is from Sri Lanka. A commercial television company in Sri Lanka was taken to court by Star TV for allegedly infringing its copyright. The TV station in Sri Lanka, called Extra Terrestrial Vision (ETV), had been downloading Star TV satellite programs and re-telecasting them on terrestrial transmitters. In addition, it was alleged that the company was blocking Star TV commercials and inserting local commercials for a fee. It was not paying Star TV any royalties for the use of its programs nor had it sought StarTV authority to re-telecast its programs in any form. The Sri Lankan court decided in favor of the defendant. In light of this decision, the current position appears to be that international TV broadcasters cannot complain against unauthorized use of their material once they telecast these programs freely to other countries. Such decisions sit uneasily with World Trade Organization (WTO) agreements on intellectual property rights and copyright. Undoubtedly local laws have to be brought in line with provisions in international agreements once these agreements have been ratified by these countries.

The (Indian) Cable Act 1994 (ICA) is another instance of Indian efforts to regulate the TV broadcasting scene in India. This law clearly applies to transnational TV broadcasts to India when such broadcasts are re-telecast though Indian cable companies. A majority of households in India receive foreign satellite programs through cable services. A dish antennae is too costly for most Indian families to own. ICA stipulates that no program or advertisement can be transmitted in India unless it is in conformity with prescribed program and advertising codes. The program code bans material which offends good taste and decency, criticizes friendly countries, encourage violence or anti-national attitudes, affects the integrity of the nation, encourage superstition or blind belief, denigrates women or children and which contain visuals or words which reflect a slandering, ironical and snobbish attitude in portrayal of certain ethnic, linguistic and regional groups. The Act also limits foreign ownership of local channels to 49 percent. (Banerjee, 1996). It is clear that many a foreign program would fall foul of such a program code.

Many of the areas opened up by transnational communication require or envisage agreements among states in order to gain mutual benefits both in cultural and economic fields. These can take the form of international conventions or bilateral agreements. Such agreements are particularly important in relation to international trade in cultural products. In the absence of such agreements countries have been forced to settle issues of transborder broadcasting on their own and at times in very unconventional ways. The manner in which Hong Kong and Macau settled their differences in transborder broadcasting highlights the different ways in which economic interests could impinge on such decisions (Lee, 1998). At the center of the differences between Macau and Hong Kong was the need for Hong Kong to secure its internal market for Cantonese TV broadcasts. The moment Hong Kong's local Cantonese TV market is adversely affected local program operators such as TVB, ATV and Warf Cable will apply pressure on the Hong Kong government to secure this market.

In 1991, Macau TV (TdM), which is government owned, decided to boost up its signals to cover vast areas of Hong Kong. This would make TdM virtually another free-to-air TV station in Hong Kong without getting a Hong Kong license. Furthermore, one of the TdM channels broadcasts in Cantonese. This would affect adversely the incomes of local program operators. The advertising standards in Macau were freer with few restrictions on cigarette and alcohol commercials. This would result in loss of advertising revenue for local TV stations. Consequently pressure was brought on the Hong Kong government to stop Macau from broadcasting to Hong Kong. In the absence of any covenants, laws or understandings governing transborder broadcasting, the Hong Kong government had no formal way of addressing this problem. It used economic pressure on the Macau government to get them to stop the intended TV expansion. They did this by threatening to legalize casinos in Hong Kong. Legalization of casinos in Hong Kong would affect adversely Macau's most important source of revenue – gambling. People in Hong Kong are the major customers of Macau casinos. If Hong Kong was not a major source of revenue to Macau, probably the Hong Kong government would not have been able to persuade Macau to drop its intention to boost its TV. There was no legal basis on which the two countries could have settled their differences (Lee, 1998).

What conclusions can we draw from these cases? Obviously the main concern of Asian governments is the effect of transnational communication media on their local audiences. These audiences are the political power base of the Asian leaders. It has been argued that the international media which report about events in Singapore and Malaysia are not reporting these for an audience outside of these countries, say people in Britain or the US. In fact, these reports are meant for people in the countries about which the news item is written. English is spoken and read by influentials in these countries and therefore has an impact on an important section of the population. Local-language newspapers pick up these stories and thereby give them wide publicity, even among people who cannot read English. In short, the international press has become an off-shore press to be read and consumed by the people in Asian countries. The AWSJ based in Hong Kong report not to readers in America or Europe but to Singaporeans, Malaysians and other Asians. They are like domestic presses of these countries but based outside of their shores or territorial boundaries. In this situation, the leaders of Asian countries sometimes see the correspondents of the international press as acting like journalists do in America or Europe – taking sides to determine the outcome of events. In other words, Asian leaders see journalists in the off-shore press as interfering in the domestic affairs of their countries. It is even argued that the purpose of such interference is to bring an outcome favorable to the international media organizations for which they work or to the interests of Western countries in general. This they do in many ways: by setting the agenda for influential groups in these countries; by publishing stories that question the honesty and integrity of government leaders, thereby making such leaders fearful of the foreign media. This is a strategy to soften their stand against such media. Freedom of the press is seen as a battle cry to impose Western hegemony in emerging Asian nations. Refusal to publish rebuttals of their stories by international media, which are controlled by companies based in Western countries, is seen as cultural arrogance.

The permission given to international media to operate in an Asian country, it has been argued, is a privilege granted by the government of the Asian country on its own terms. The basic understanding is that these foreign journalists report events in these countries as outsiders for outsiders. In short, they do not become participants in the domestic debates of these countries. These journalists cannot assume a role, say, in Singapore that the American journalists play in America. They cannot become invigilators, adversaries, and inquisitors of the government. No Asian country can withstand such an insidious and irresponsible onslaught from the foreign press. The foreign correspondents are temporary guests in the countries where they are stationed. Most of them have little or no understanding of the language, history, culture or forms of governance in the countries that they try to report on. Some of these journalists approach their subject with a cultural arrogance and superiority which is resented in Asia. In foreign countries these journalists are observers, not participants.

Another point raised by Asian critics of Western media is that the Western capitalist, libertarian ideology of the press is not a universal model that is applicable all over the world and at all times in the same country. In Singapore's encounters with the US State Department over the restriction of the circulation of AWSJ, the State Department said that it deplored the governments restriction of sales. This was despite the fact that AWSJ had refused to publish the Singapore government's reply to an inaccurate report. This was a curious position to be taken by media that champion the freedom of the press and, therefore by implication, freedom of expression. The libertarian view is that the press should be free to publish or not to publish what it chooses, however irresponsible or biased its actions may seem to be. In this model, the audience is seen as freely choosing in the market place of ideas. The "logic" is that where the media are free, the market place of ideas sorts out the irresponsible from the responsible and rewards the latter. But this model cannot be applied to all countries. In different countries, the press has grown out of different historical traditions and political experiences. Consequently, they will play different roles. The free market place of ideas in multicultural, multi-party democracies in Asia can result in the heightening of racial and religious tensions, mobilizing sectional constituencies and arousing emotions. In this situation a partisan media can flood the market place with racially divisive information, confuse and befuddle the people and set the country on a course of racial strife and civil war. In such a media environment, basic issues such as economic growth and equitable distribution are rarely tackled by the press. Instead easy solutions are peddled for complex problems that require hard political decisions. In this situation the free market brings about confusion and violent dissension rather than enlightenment and consensus.

↓ Ethnicity in the global village

While it is true that telecommunications, satellites, computers and transnational media have connected the world together in a manner hitherto unknown in human history and provided unprecedented opportunities for the establishment of closer cultural linkages and identities among nations, this potential for cross-fertilization of cultures has also created apprehensions regarding the erosion of cultural identities of indigenous people. National leaders have voiced fears of the loss of cultural identity due to the intrusion of foreign cultural products and their accompanying values. As such, the communication superhighway is viewed by some Asian leaders more as a threat to cultural identities rather than as an opportunity to create a more consensual culture among neighboring people. Such fears, whether correct or not, has had their influence in creating policy regimes. These policies impinge on foreign journalists working in Asian countries.

Furthermore, upswings in ethnic politics, religious fundamentalism, communalism and nationalism have taken the center stage in the world today. National minorities, in many countries, have become militant activists. For most of these activists, local autonomy and sovereignty take precedence over multicultural co-existence and integration into a global village. Some sociologists and political commentators have described the current spate of ethno-political conflicts in the world as being rooted in the history, culture and traditions of these countries. These conflicts are seen as movements of revivalism or nativistic movements.

The ethno-political conflicts are undoubtedly organized by groups of "elites" who are either defending existing political and financial interests or who perceive political or financial advantages arising from such conflicts. These conflicts are therefore rooted in the mobilization of groups of people on the basis of religion, language, caste, ethnicity or other cultural markers. Claims for legitimacy of such cultural identities are made on the basis of historical or mythological events popular with the groups that are being mobilized. For instance, the extremists sectors of the Bharatiya Janata Party (BJP) of India legitimize the Hindu identity on a national scale and this identity is co-terminus with being an Indian. Minority groups such as Muslims are perceived as "invaders" or "foreigners" who have, through conquest or deceit, forced their way to centers of power. Such "communal consciousness" refuses to accept the plural, culturally differentiated reality of Indian society (Thomas, 1995).

The mobilization of groups on a communal basis easily spills over national boundaries: the training of Sri Lankan Tamil separatist insurgents by the Indian government under Mrs Indira Gandhi, and the haven provided for their military training in Tamil Nadu (Samarajiva and Keerawella, 1988). Both India and Pakistan have accused each other of mobilizing and training insurgents to destabilize their respective governments. Here again, while primordial ethnic and religious loyalties were the bases of such mobilization, these were being used as instruments of state power in a modern context.

While it is true that the mobilization of communal groups by elites is based on identities such as religion, language, caste or ethnicity, these by themselves do not make such groups revivalists of something from their past history or culture. In fact the distinguishing characteristic of modern-day religio-ethnic movements is the weakening of traditional cultural values that bind the individual to the group and insulate them, thereby minimizing the tendency for disorientation. Having weakened and eroded the traditional cultural ties, no alternative ways of binding the individual to his or her community is provided. The basis of social solidarity in the emerging global village is not yet clear.

One important reason for the breakdown of traditional group identities is the suicidal rate of population growth in some countries and the consequent mass migration to the slum cities. Individuals are detached from community, ethnicity, temple/church and caste associations. Their dependency on impersonal channels of communication like mass media are heightened. Large groups of unemployed and floating people are available to be mobilized for innumerable causes, by the "elites" in these countries. Multiparty politics make such mobilization of groups part of political expediency and strategy. In this situation contentious issues proliferate, and the political process gets fragmented with increasing numbers of people advocating various group-related issues. The process leads to the emergence of weak political regimes, leading in turn to political stalemate, public disenchantment, apathy and the rise of extremist groups. The process becomes a vicious circle with political regimes becoming increasingly weaker, and social disorder, riots and assassinations becoming endemic in society.

Ethnic and communal conflicts in the contemporary world are therefore specifically modern phenomena rooted in contemporary socio-economic and political conditions. It is part and parcel of the process of globalization. While such conflicts use metaphors from the past to mobilize groups and communities, these are nothing less than modern political conflicts played on an ethnic, religious or communal plane. The use of such metaphors must be understood as symbols used by the "elites" to manipulate and mobilize the people for their own assent to power.

What we see in the world today are the twin and opposite forces of internationalization and localization playing on each other. Communication has linked up the world in a hitherto unprecedented manner. At the same time it has also created apprehensions about the survival of cultures making communities look inward, become protective and closed. It has not resulted in creating anything like a global village. Nor has it contributed much for consensual understanding or for creating global markets in cultural products. Modern communication technologies have given the opportunity to develop in this direction. However, this requires international understandings, agreements and cooperation based on fairness. This is yet to emerge. What has emerged are deep divisions and perceptions of unfairness.

NICO

The United Nations Educational, Scientific and Cultural Organization (UNESCO) debate on New Information and Communications Order (NICO) is instructive of the concerns and deep division that exist among the principal actors in the emerging global village. It is common ground that there is a profound imbalance between north and south in access to communication and information. Countries in the South depend on communication structures of the developed Western nations for gaining access to information. The debate at times has turned into an ideological denunciation of cultural colonialism and imperialism. The developed countries in turn rejected the cry for a new information order as rhetoric designed to apply political pressure – not a genuine demand.

While the debate on NICO began as a North-South issue and continues to proceed on these lines, it is fact much more than this. It is a question of developing a communication system which would ideally allow every person to express him- or herself freely and choose the information that he or she wishes to have. Viewed in this light NICO addresses a basic question of the Right to Communicate within a global multicultural environment. The opposition to the concept of the right to communicate and the demand for NICO stems from two main ideological stand points. The Western nations distrust the concept of the right to communicate because they see it as part of the New Information and Communication Order of which they are suspicious. They fear that NICO will be used as a lever to impose restrictions on Western particularly US news agencies, on the marketing of Western films and TV programs in third-world countries and on the exploitation of newer markets such as transnational data transfers via satellites.

The countries in the South on the other hand oppose the concept of the right to communicate because they fear that this principle could be used by Western countries to justify the continuation of the present massive imbalance in information flows and unrestricted importation of cultural products and the attendant values from the northern countries.

Therefore, while all sides to the debate accept the concept of the Right to Communicate as valid, there is profound disagreement on the locus of the right. Western countries see it as a right pertaining primarily to the individual and only subsequently and secondarily to the state. On the other hand, developing countries see society and state as the primary locus, with the state having powers to restrict the right in the interest of public good. There is also disagreement as to the content of the right. Some want the definition to include all the rights associated with communication while others prefer a simple statement of the principle. The other aspects of this right such as communication freedom and fairer sharing of resources should be left to a different forum.

The debate on NICO is one instance where global communication has not helped to bring people together. On the contrary it has tended to divide them on the basis of perceived economic gains to be had by exploiting communication resources. Global co-existence has given way to global contentions.

International agreements

Many of the areas opened up by transnational communication require or envisage agreements among states in order to gain mutual benefits such as the potential access it provides to markets. These can take the form of international conventions or bilateral agreements. Such agreements are particularly important in relation to international trade in cultural products. In the absence of such agreements countries have been forced to settle issues of transborder broadcasting, on their own and at times in very unconventional ways. The manner in which Hong Kong and Macao settled their differences in transborder broadcasting described earlier in this paper, highlight the different ways in which economic interests could impinge on such decisions.

Recently some of the issues in this area have been the subject of international debate and negotiations. In the European Community (EC), for instance, trans-border TV is the subject of EC directives. A 1984 EC Green Paper refers to the establishment of a common market for borderless satellite and cable TV operations. Transborder television is also the subject of a 1989 EC Directive. In the European context transborder could mean a common TV culture in Europe. The objective of the 1989 EC Directive was to develop TV cultures in Europe and to establish the identity of a European culture. In February 1996 a reform bill was passed to strengthen the EC Directive and in this endeavor European broadcasters were obliged to observe the European content clause as a result. European-made programs must account for 51 percent or more of the total broadcasts (HBF, 1996). This is obviously a way of restricting the market for cultural products from non-European countries.

In the Asia Pacific region it is difficult to envisage trans-national television or any other type of communication to be the means of establishing a common culture. Unlike in Europe the countries in the Asia-pacific region have different traditions and historical experiences. These countries are far more diverse, suspicious of each other and jealous of their indigenous cultural heritage.

In 1994 the General Assembly of the Asian Broadcasting Union (ABU) met in Kyoto, Japan and adopted a resolution specifying *Guidelines for Transnational Satellite Broadcasters in the Asia-Pacific Region.* The objective of the guidelines was similar to that of the EC Directive but the contents were much different. Unlike the European Directive the ABU guidelines placed emphasis on respecting the cultural diversity in the Asia Pacific region rather than on creating a common transnational culture in this region. In its introduction the guidelines say that the development of satellite television services will undoubtedly foster free flow of information in the Asia Pacific region. At the same time the document asserts that there is serious concern that this situation could have a deleterious effect on the values and cultures of the countries of the region. A series of similar guidelines called *Guidelines on the Program Contents of International Satellite Television Broadcasting in the Asia-Pacific Region* were also adopted at a Tokyo meeting of government policy makers from twenty-one Asian and Pacific countries.

These guidelines reiterated the need:

• to respect the principles of free flow of information and
• to protect the sovereignty and domestic systems of those countries where the satellite signals reach. (HBF, 1996).

It is quite possible that such guidelines would eventually provide a common ground for the development of a pan-Asian TV culture. However, in order to achieve this it would be necessary for the members of ABU and the relevant government agencies to work out a consensus or a common vision among the countries involved. This will require, at some stage, international covenants to bind the countries to a common course of action.

GATT/WTO

In this age of global communication there are many other areas in which trans-border communication has necessitated such international understanding or agreements. Liberalization of trade in cultural products consequent to GATT/WTO[5] decisions is one such area. There was a time when cultural products such as movies, performing arts and music were exempted from trade liberalization. In 1947 when the General Agreement of Trade and Tariff (GATT) was drafted, Article IV of the agreement authorized the imposition of national screen quotas for the "exhibition of cinematographic films of national origin during a specified minimum proportion of the total screen time actually utilized." This was based on a dichotomy between trade and culture – trade liberalization and cultural protection. International trade officials were scarcely involved in issues relating to broadcasting and telecommunications. The recognition of the special character of cultural products is not limited to GATT/WTO. The 1989 Free Trade Agreement between the US and Canada specifically exempted cultural products covering films, videos, TV, radio broadcasting, sound recording and print media. In many countries foreign ownership of media of communication is either prohibited or severely restricted. The reasons are national security and social and cultural considerations. However, under the Uruguay Round of Talks in 1986 the sector of trade in services was brought under GATT commitments to open markets and GATT discipline. The rules of GATT/WTO[6] will now apply to cultural products and services as they would apply to all other services. Traditionally regulatory areas have become market access issues under GATT Uruguay Round Negotiations (Kakabadse, 1995).

The question therefore is whether the rules of trade liberalization could be sensibly applied to cultural products. If trade in cultural products is liberalized, that is cultural protection withdrawn, will it result in the flooding of markets with the products from the more powerful economies, particularly the US? From the point of view of international trade what opportunities do the WTO trade discipline provide for harnessing new markets in cultural services and products?

While it is true that GATT/ WTO rules make no special distinction between cultural products and other goods this by itself does not open up hitherto restricted markets in cultural products. This is because of the GATT/WTO principle of allowing individual countries to make commitments in the market access areas. This mechanism gives all countries considerable flexibility in handling cultural products and services. Each country can decide whether they wish to offer market opening guarantees for any particular cultural product or services. "In addition GATT provide particular flexibility for developing countries wishing to open fewer sectors or liberalize fewer types of transactions in future negotiations, thus making explicit their rights to extend market access in line with their development situations" (Kakabadse, 1995: 76).

TRIPS

From the point of view of international trade in cultural products perhaps what is more significant is the Agreement on Trade-related aspects of Intellectual Property Rights (TRIPS) on intellectual property protection which obliges all member countries that wish to benefit from membership in WTO to apply Berne Convention standards, enforceable through a dispute settlement mechanism. For instance, producers of sound recordings must be granted an exclusive rental right – the right to authorize or prevent the commercial renting of their work. Protection provided for performers and producers will be effective for at least fifty years, and will apply to all signatories to the Agreement. The Agreement also contains detailed obligations on governments to provide effective enforcement including criminal sanctions against copyright piracy. GATT signatories are obliged to provide remedies under their municipal law to guarantee that intellectual property rights can be effectively enforced by foreign nationals who hold such rights. These very detailed and strict provisions, it was expected, would build up investor confidence leading to more trade in cultural products in the international market.

However, intellectual property rights still remain a major concern. This is a particularly sensitive issues in Asia. One reason for this is the relatively weak and ineffective legal and policing mechanisms. It has been claimed that violations of software licenses in Asia-Pacific alone amounted to losses exceeding two billion US dollars in 1994 (Low, 1995). Without protecting intellectual property rights and building inventors' confidence in the protection of their patent rights, Asian countries would be unable to attract business and particularly investments in research and development. Laws and regulations necessary for the enforcement of WTO decisions are still not in place in some of these countries.

Furthermore, decisions of national courts have become quite important in relation to satellite broadcasts in recent times. The Star TV decision in Sri Lanka and the Indian Cable Act are instances where, in the absence of international agreements, local laws were used in the determination of issues relating to international broadcasting.

The important point is that a body of legal decisions, customs, conventions and treaties are continually evolving. Transnational communication is being regulated in one form or another. It is important to elucidate the principles based on which such regulations are being made or attempted. Cultural considerations and commercial considerations seem to be competing with each other in the evolution of these principles. Flow of information at present depends much more on national policies than on international agreements. Systematic research is needed to elucidate the processes involved.

Another concern which impinges on international trade is the proliferation of international electronic networks. The Internet, for instance, is fast becoming a household word in South-East Asia, particularly in the more affluent countries in this region. This has opened a vast area of contentious issues ranging from cyber-trade, cyberdollars, cyberporn to censorship. Many governments in Asia assumed it as their moral duty to preserve core cultural values and protect society as a whole from what these governments perceive as corrupting foreign influences. This fear of foreign cultural domination is fueled by the historical antagonism between the colonized, subordinated countries of Asia and the colonizing and hegemonic imperial powers. It has been reinforced by the popular discourse of media imperialism which became a powerful intellectual theme in the 1960s. Western media products were perceived as culturally and morally harmful to the wellbeing of Asian countries.

There is little or no contention regarding pornography on the Internet. Very few, if any, would argue in favor of it. But in other areas there is much room for contention. For instance, it often happens that what is legal in one country may be illegal in another. And cyberspace being seamlessly global, it has been argued that cyberspace censorship requires stricter laws (*The Straits Times*, April 12, 1995). Application of such laws becomes very difficult, particularly when it comes to electronic mail. Furthermore, it is clear that the existing laws are not in step with developments in cyberspace. It is difficult to frame laws to control and censor information considered offensive and also, at the same time, allow a free flow of information.

Market competition

Cyber trade is another area of concern. According to one report there were an estimated 100,000 websites in early 1996 and their number is doubling every three months. Business activity has begun to grow on the Web. It has been estimated that commercial websites numbered 50,000 in 1996 (Ang, 1996). Business deals through the Internet are said to account for around 4.1 percent of purchases in the US in 1994 and are expected to grow up to 16 percent by the year 2000 (*The Straits Times*, August 14, 1994). Such activities of electronic purses could lead to the building up of currency and credit beyond the control of national governments and could create problems in the implementation of monetary policies. Imposing import duties and sales taxes could become increasingly difficult leading to losses in government revenue (Low, 1995).

As this trend towards transborder satellite multi-channels in the Asia-Pacific region increase, the competition for market shares is likely to intensify. Most of the current satellite programs are in English, Chinese and Indian languages. Japan and Korea are also likely to enter this market. In addition to the current commercial transborder broadcasting services by private companies, several governments in the region have also launched international services or are planning such services. Notable among these services are CCTV International of China, Korea Channel and the Japanese international TV broadcasts. These telecasts are for the nationals of these countries living abroad.

The main characteristics of Asian satellite services at present can be summarized as follows:

- Singapore and Hong Kong have become the centers of Asian satellite TV services
- Satellite sub-regions have been formed based on cultural similarities; for instance, the Chines- language region and the Indian-language region
- An ASEAN sub-region has been formed as a result of the ten member countries of ASEAN and neighboring countries launching broadcast satellites for domestic services.

I think it is not an exaggeration to say that there is a scramble for the domination of the skies. Large numbers of satellites are being placed in orbit by governments and multinational corporations (see Table 16.1). For as little as US$25,000, China could uplink a communication satellite using its long-march rocketry. The skies have become open territory. This is looked on with apprehension by many countries in Asia. Organizations and individuals are now examining ways and means by

Table 16.1 Geostationary satellites in the Asia-Pacific region

Country	Number of satellites	Launch dates	Coverage
Australia	4	1985, '87, '92, '94	Australia/New Zealand, Papua New Guinea
Hong Kong	4	1990, '94(2), '95	Regional
India	5	1990, '92, '93, '95	Indian sub-continent
Indonesia	6	1983, '87, '90, '92, '95, '96,	Regional/ASEAN
Japan	12	1988(2), '89, '90(3), '91, '92(2), '94, '95(2), '97	Japan/Asia Pacific International
Korea	2	1995, '96	Korea
Malaysia	1	1995	South-East Asia
China	4	1988, '90, '94, '95	South-East Asia
Thailand	2	1993, '94	ASEAN/Europe
Tonga	6	1983, '94, '95(2), '96, '97	Asia Pacific, Eurasia

Source: Asian Communications, June 1995, 9(6), 29–32

which the international community could bring some order into this situation before it spins out of control. The Kuala Lumpur-based ABU has already formulated a series of guidelines to be followed by transnational broadcasters. This, however, is not binding to any of the members of ABU. They remain simply guidelines for voluntary compliance. International agreements are required to bind countries to such rules.

Generic cultural products

We are also seeing changes in the very concept of foreign media programs. Earlier we could identify such programs on the basis of the countries of origin. The US was identified as providing the bulk of these media programs. It could be argued that in the future the world will see "generic entertainment software," created by the confluence of capital from the US, Japan, Europe and other nations, servicing the newly deregulated and privatized media systems in Asia and elsewhere. In the future, it may not make much of a difference if an increasingly "generic" cultural product is owned and produced by companies in America, Japan, Europe or Asia. The challenge is: how could one identify a path towards autonomous national cultural productions in a system that is increasingly catering to the marketing imperatives of transnational companies. Perhaps encouraging independent producers for small media for niche audiences in local languages is the answer. The emergence of regional markets for cultural products is a fair indication that despite these overarching developments in global media room has been left for autonomous, national cultural productions.

The loud and clear message of globalization is that we live in the same world. But different groups see different meanings in this world. Communication across cultures facilitated through advanced technologies makes for more informed, more aware persons with, possibly, a less parochial outlook. It can promote unity among diverse people and contribute to the emergence of a more tolerant, consensual culture crossing national borders. Trying to shut oneself off from the "intrusion" of foreign cultural influences may, perhaps, be like blinding oneself in the hope that one may walk with more safety in a jungle of pits and precipices. The global spread of media is here to stay. It cannot be wished away. We must learn to live with it. In order to harness its potential for good, one should look at it as an opportunity to open one's eyes through education and experience and not to blind them in fear and ignorance.

However, in a world that is divided on the basis of wealth and power we need international agreements and common understandings if fairness is to prevail in the way we share opportunities created by advanced technologies. The formulation of international agreements relating to the common use of the skies will be the first step in this direction. Many would agree that it is no longer desirable to allow only those with technological capability to harness the skies either for transborder communication or for any other use. This would obviously require an examination of both international and municipal laws, conventions and customs that apply to the use of the skies at present. This requires both legal and social scientific research, preferably by an international community of scholars. The findings of this research will form the basis to initiate discussions among nations in order to agree on the ways in which the resources in the sky are to be used. We already have a Law of the Sea. Perhaps this could provide a model, though not an exact one, that could be a starting point for an examination of the emerging Law of the Sky. Principles enshrined in the Law of the Sea such as the recognition of certain areas of the sea as the "common heritage of mankind" perhaps will find parallels in the skies.[7]

In such an inquiry the international community should also consider the rights and responsibilities of governments and countries that receive unsolicited TV broadcasts from foreign commercial companies. Already international conventions exist in areas such as civil aviation, activities on celestial bodies, exploration and the use of outer space and the allocation of the radio spectrum. It can be argued that cultural products in the form of TV programs beamed to one's territorial skies are as important as any other object in the sky. Therefore, in fairness to both the senders and the receivers, the international community should agree on rules and regulations governing such conduct.

Theoretical implications

Human beings are meaning-searching and meaning-creating animals. They act on the interpretation of meanings. Events that they encounter must be meaningful to them. Human beings interact with each other on the basis of understanding of each others' expectations. We interact with others in the expectation that the other would behave in a "predictable" manner. When people do not act on the basis of our predicted expectations we even say that these people are crazy. Such predictability is required not only for social relations among individuals but also for relations

281

among individual countries. The law is one of the principal ways in which these expectations are crystallized among members of a community. International law is the crystallization of these expectations among members of the international community. In this sense the law is one of the finest cultural contributions of human kind. It is the basis for cultural advancement and civilized living. However, history has shown us that laws can also be used to dominate and victimize. It is necessary that laws are recognized as fair, just and legitimate by all those who live by it. Amidst the clash of interests between multinational media and Asian governments we see a search for such meaningfulness. In other words a process of meaning creation is taking place. We could interpret this as the emergence of a new set of meanings to which both contending groups could subscribe. Legal decisions have crystallized these meanings as principles or regulations. When the IHT president told his critics, who were demanding that IHT try to impose American liberal standards abroad, that they were uninformed, he was agreeing to a different role for the multinational media that would allow it to co-exist in countries with press ideologies different to that of the US. The dismissal of the London *Sunday Times* editor, Andrew Neil, removal of Nikki Bedi from Star TV, and the withdrawal of the BBC World Service programs from Star TV's telecasts to China carry the same message. If multinational media want to do business in Asia, they must learn to co-exist with the forms of governance in these countries. Perhaps there is no profit to be made in cultural imperialism. A new set of meaningful relations is emerging in Asia between the multinational media and the governments in these countries.

Modern communication technologies have created social situations where the traditional and older systems of conducting business will not do. It has created new situations which require new modes of response. As it is, some countries that have to decide on such a response to new situations have no option but to use the prevailing municipal law. India's response to the Gandhi gaffe, Sri Lanka's response to Star TV's complaint of using unauthorized commercials and India's supreme court decision regarding the use of the airwaves are interpretations of legal principles applicable in the countries that decided these cases.

How best can communication researchers examine this situation where there are cogent arguments for pursuing different communication policies by different countries? Max Weber, the eminent German sociologist, used a theoretical construct called "ideal type" to understand social structures and social processes form a sociological perspective. An ideal type is a model constructed by the social scientist or researcher. It is based on empirical and historical observations but an ideal type is not found in its "pure" form in empirical reality. It is a theoretical construct – a tool to observe, interpret and understand empirical reality. For instance, Weber described an ideal typical bureaucracy. It is not found in its ideal typical form anywhere in the world. However, the description of its principles, logical connections, outcomes and its structure (hierarchy) are illuminating. Perhaps Asian communication scholars should begin to construct historically informed ideal typical models of media structures. The Western model or the capitalist press model is one such type. Libertarian press freedom is its sheet anchor. Its driving force is profit. It is risk-taking capitalist enterprise. The US press is perhaps the archetypical example. In the words of Peter Hamilton, former publisher of the *Wall Street Journal*, "a news paper is private enterprise owing nothing whatsoever to the public, which grants it no franchise. It is therefore affected with no public interest. It is emphatically the property of the owner who is selling a manufactured product at his own risk" (quoted by Mahathir, 1989: 114). Nobody could have described the parameters of an ideal typical Western capitalist press better. In contrast to this we have the communist model of the press which is basically an instrument of state policy. It is state owned, party operated and Marxist-Leninist in ideology. An annual subsidy from the government is its main source of revenue. A third model is the communitarian model. Perhaps this model approximates the Asian press. It has similarities with the capitalist press. Profit is high on its agenda of priorities. Advertising is a prime source of revenue. Working in tandem with the government of the day for the general wellbeing of society is another priority. It is therefore not an adversarial or confrontational press like that of the Western model. Maintaining high journalistic standards is important in this model. An overriding feature is the predominance of the collective over the individual. This is in consonance with the national ideologies in some Asian countries such as Pancasila (five principles) in Indonesia, Ruknegara (Framework of the Nation) in Malaysia and Shared Values in Singapore. In all three models, censorship is a fact of life. In the capitalist free-enterprise press, one would be very foolish to publish stories critical of the owners of the press or go against the owners' commercial and political interests. Advertisers are another powerful group that keep journalistic freedom in the capitalist press in check. In the Communist press profit is not a concern. Newspapers are even distributed free. They are displayed on notice boards for anyone to read. In the emerging Asian model of the press governments are key players and one would be very foolish to go against important government policies. In all three systems an overarching ideology has developed. In the capitalist press it is press freedom. In the communist press the ideology is one of serving the proletariat by propagating the communist party line. In the Asian model it is freedom and responsibility.

What we see in all three types of ideology is a process of meaning creation, or making the activities of the press meaningful to the people who are its audience. Each type of policy clearly serves a dominant group in society. It may be the owners of the media, or the communist party bosses, or the leaders of the government in power. What is more interesting is that when we examine press systems as ideal types we see changes that are taking place within each system. As we saw earlier, the capitalist model is adapting to the situations in Asian countries where it is looking for markets. Murdoch, who wants to do business in Asia, would not hesitate to drop programs from Star TV that offend governments of Asian countries. His removal of the editor of the London *Sunday Times*, his dropping of the program Nikki Tonight and removal of BBC World Service from Star TV's telecast to China are all examples of the adaptation of the Western free press/free enterprise model to realities in the media scene in Asia. Equally momentous changes are taking place in the Communist press. The tortuous road to press freedom in China is well documented in Yu Xu's study of the birth and demise of the *World Economic Herald* (1992). What is interesting in this account is that the struggle for openness, freedom and democracy came from the ranks of the journalists within the Chinese Communist Party itself. Although the *Herald* waged an unprecedented struggle against the Communist Party's tight control of journalists it could not change this. It perished in the effort. The *Herald*'s experience in testing the limits of an outmoded political system toying with new entrepreneurial spirit has implications far outside the *Herald* or the press in China. It reflects the vulnerability of the media in most countries under the tight control of political ideologies both from the Left and the Right. The values and meaning-creating processes in these countries are far more complex and faces intense competition from ideologues who have a vested interest in maintaining the status quo in relation to media systems.

There are no easy formulae that journalists could follow in reporting other cultures. Perhaps knowledge about the background to the cases filed against foreign media would help. It would at least make them aware of the thinking of the other side on these issues. Freedom of the press will not be accepted as a defence as easily as in the Western countries. Perhaps sincerity and honesty will be more appreciated. Foreign journalists working in other cultures need to be as free of value judgments as is humanly possible. They should be able to step out of their role as journalists and examine their own agendas and those of the organizations for which they work. It is dangerous to get involved in the issues being reported. They should never appear to take sides to bring a desired outcome. Knowledge of the history and culture of the country which is being reported on is always useful. However, this is not easy to acquire in a short time. Intellectual honesty is a good principle to follow in the search for truth. However, one should also be aware that truth is often a question of conformity with the conventions of the epistemic community to which one belongs. It is that which conforms to the relevant criteria accepted in the social circle of one's "knowers." Very often these are understandings that are in harmony with the conventions of the culture to which one belongs. One needs to transcend this idea of truth. And herein lies the greatest difficulty of reporting events in Asian cultures by foreign journ   .s.

Conclusions

It is clear that transnational communication engendered by modern communication technologies requires a consensually agreed set of rules and expectations. The WTO provides a broad framework in relation to both trade in goods and services. The principle of free trade has been enthroned in WTO decisions.[8] In the absence of covenants or agreements among countries as to the use of the skies for transborder communication, trade in cultural products still works on different expectations by different countries. This is compounded by violent social movements based on ethnic, linguistic and other social identities. Fears of cultural annihilation by the powerless countries and the division of the world into cultural markets by the powerful countries need to be reconciled on an agreed basis. The international convention on transborder communication is therefore a pressing need at the moment. This is particularly so in Asia.

No doubt any move to convene an international convention to bring about a law of the skies will be controversial. Those who benefit from the present unregulated situation will presumably not want any such law. There will necessarily have to be compromises. It is necessary for us to step back and look at issues from a broader philosophical perspective. We should begin by recognizing the enormous diversities in culture and the ethical considerations that arise out of this diversity among nations. Communications technology has brought vast cultural contacts among people of different nations. It has provided unprecedented opportunities for the establishment of closer cultural linkages and identities. It has also raised fears of cultural domination and obliteration of ethnic identities. History has shown us that traditional indigenous cultures are strong and adaptable and is at times strengthened in the face of challenges. History has also shown that there is danger of a destructive backlash against all foreign influences – good and bad – when countries are faced with foreign cultural intrusions. Perhaps what is required most at the present stage of development of global communication is to provide systematic education, both formal and informal, as to the nature of this phenomena. This requires continuing research. We need an informed public discourse through the media, through the schools and through public debate. If the enormous possibilities for commerce across cultures, opened up by modern technology, are to be harnessed for human freedom, betterment, tolerance and understanding it is necessary for the international community to have a shared vision of the future. An international convention is the first step in the development of this vision.

Notes

1 Some of the material in this chapter was presented at the 28th Annual Conference of the International Institute of Communication (IIC), Sydney, Australia, in October 1977 and at the conference on Internationalizing Communities at the University of Southern Queensland, Toowoomba in November 1996.

2 Building Smart Communities: How California's Communities can thrive in a digital age. San Diego State University, 1997. It was published by the International Center for Communications, San Diego State University in 1997 with a foreword by John M. Eger, Executive Director.

3 The article in question was about a Marxist conspiracy revealed by the government in which some members of the Catholic Church were implicated. The report was about a meeting held between Mr Lee and Catholic leaders led by Archbishop Yong. In his suit Mr Lee alleged that the article depicted Mr Lee as being intolerant of Roman Catholic Church and that he set out to victimize Catholic priests and workers (*The Straits Times*, January 1988). The Singapore courts found all four defendants guilty of ill-will, spite or wrong or improper motive. It awarded Mr Lee $230,000 in damages. Eight years after this incident FEER remain gazetted under the newspaper and Printing Act. However, after many years, the permitted circulation has been increased to 4,000 copies.

4 IHT was ordered to pay Mr Lee Kuan Yew $300,000 in damages, $350,000 to Prime Minister Mr Goh Chok Tong and $300,000 to Deputy Prime Minister, Mr Lee Hsien Loong.
5 General Agreement of Trade and Tariff or GATT. World Trade Organization (WTO). GATT was replaced by WTO in 1995.
6 There are twenty-seven separate legal agreements and 25,000 pages of liberalizing commitments on market access for goods and services which entered into force in January 1995 together with the creation of WTO.
7 Convention on the Law of the Sea: article 1(1) and article 136, 140
8 The Uruguay Round has been described as the biggest and most difficult trade negotiation in history. It produced results that no one thought would be possible when the Round commenced in 1986. It is said that there has been no comparable achievement since the creation of Bretton Woods institution in 1944.

References

"Asia's slice of space." *Asian Communications*, 1995, 9(6), 29–32. Hong Kong: ABS Business Press.

Banerjee, I. (1995). *Media ownership and Convergence in the age of Convergence.* London: International Institute of Communication (IIC) (Global Report Series).

Clarke, A.C. (1996). "New communication technologies and the developing world." In A. Goonasekera, *et al.* (Eds), *Opening Windows: Issues in Communication.* Singapore: AMIC.

Galtung, J. (1977). "The new economic order in world politics." In A.W Singham (Ed.), *The Non-Aligned Movement in World Politics*, Westport, CT: Lawrence Hill.

HBF (1996). *Asia Speaks Out: Towards Greater Program Diversity in Asia.* Tokyo: Hoso-Bunka Foundation.

Horton, D. and Whol, R. (1956). "Mass communication and para-social interaction: Observation of intimacy at distance." *Psychiatry*, 19, 215–29.

Ito, Y.(1994). "Why information now." in G. Wang (Ed.), *Treading Different Paths: Informatization in Asian Nations*, New Jersey: Ablex.

Jussawalla, M. (1994). "Access to information in a world without borders." In G. Wang (Ed.) *Treading Different Paths: Informatization in Asian Nations*, New Jersey: Ablex.

Kakabadse, M.A. (1995). "The WTO and the commodification of cultural products: Implications for Asia." *Media Asia*, 2(2), 71–7.

Kohayama (1968). Quoted by Y. Ito in "Why information now," in G. Wang (Ed.) *Treading Different Paths: Informatization in Asian Nations*, New Jersey: Ablex.

Lee, K.C. (1994). "Britain learns the high cost of press freedom." *The Sunday Times*, March 13. Singapore: Singapore Press Holdings.

Lee, P.S.N. (1998). "Foreign television in Hong Kong: Little watched but favourably received." In A. Goonasekera and P.S.N. Lee (Eds), *TV Without Borders: Asia Speaks Out.* Singapore: AMIC.

Low, L. (1995). "Social and economic issues in information society: A South East Asian perspective." Paper submitted at the Workshop on Chances and Risks of the Information Society: Its Social and Economic Effects in Europe and South East Asia, September 18–20, 1995, organized by the School of Communication Studies, NTU, and FES, Singapore.

McLuhan, M. (1964). *Understanding Media: The Extensions of Man.* New York: McGraw-Hill.

Mahathir Mohamad (1989). "The social responsibility of the press." In A. Mehra (Ed.) *Press Systems in Asean States*, 107–16.

Samarajiva, R. and Keerawella, G. (1988). "Sri Lanka: Mass communication in a civil regional conflict." *Canadian Journal of Communication*, Special Issue, December, 103–9. Montreal: McGill University.

Schiller, H.I. (1976). *Communication and Cultural Domination*, White Plain, NY: International Arts and Science.

Thomas, P. (1992). "Media and politics of revivalism in India." *Media Development*, 3, xxxix.

Waterman, D. (1994). "The Economics of Television Program Production and Trade in Far East Asia," *Journal of Communication*, 44(3), 89–111.

Yu, Xu (1992). "The press and political continuity in China: The case of the world economic herald." *Asian Journal of Communication*, 2(2), 40–63.

Weber, M. (1949). *The Methodology of The Social Sciences*. In E.A. Shils and H.A. Finch. Illinois: Glencoe.

17

RECONCILIATION BETWEEN OPENNESS AND RESISTANCE

Media globalization and new policies of China's television in the 1990s

Junhao Hong

From the late 1980s throughout the 1990s, television worldwide has been under-going a new wave of tremendous changes. These changes in television, a medium which acts as the world's common cultural ground (Dizard, 1994), have resulted from the evolution of the world's political environment, economic structure, technological advancement, and cultural ecology; meanwhile, unprecedented transformation in the media has also profoundly altered the global scene (Sepstrup, 1989; Hamelink, 1994; Maney, 1995; Downing, 1996; Mosco, 1996; Mowlana, 1997). Although the emphasis and degree of the changes in television in different regions/countries have been various, and have focused either on institutional and structural changes or on ideological changes (Blumler, 1993), several general traits have been reflected in the alterations. Among them, one major trend is deregulation and another one is globalization (Steinbock, 1995). As the pace of these trends becomes more vigorous, so does the need to address the impact which these trends can have on the cultures and societies of individual countries (Mohammadi, 1997).

While deregulation means change in degrees of "being regulated," globalization refers to a process of structuration that encompasses homogenization and hetero-genization (Mowlana, 1996). Both deregulation and globalization have yielded global transformations of environment (Steinbock, 1995). However, in different countries or regions, deregulation and globalization have manifested themselves in different phenomena, such as privatization, commercialization, and marketiza-tion (Blumler, 1993; Rowland, 1993; Vedel and Bourdon, 1993). Together, these phenomena have promoted a rapid growth of television. In return, again the proliferation of television has given great impetus to the trends of deregulation and globalization. Deregulation and globalization of the media have been so strong that no country's media has been able to evade them. Even in countries such as

Russia and China, where the media were treated as part of the chief ideological state apparatuses ever since the media were put in use (Althusser, 1971), substantial institutional and structural changes, and even to a certain degree evolution in the ideological concept, have all occurred (Pei, 1994; Johnson, 1995; Chaudhary and Chen, 1995).

Accompanying the tendency towards deregulation and globalization has been the trend of adjusting and redesigning media policies in countries ranging from Western industrialized nations to communist/former communist nations and third-world nations (McDowell, 1997). To most countries across the world, globalization has posed more of a dilemma than an opportunity, and thus setting new media policies has been a urgent task (Winseck, 1997). The rationale for doing so was out of each country's political, economic, and cultural concerns: as McAnany and Wilkinson (1996) point out, despite the variations of the considerations, most countries adjust and redesign media policies mainly in order to resist Western or American – depending on the individual cases – influences, whether they are political, economic, cultural, or ideological.

The past ten years have been a critical period in China's television both in terms of its growth and policy remaking. The drastic development of television has made Chinese television one of the world's largest, most sophisticated and powerful broadcasting systems. The largely adjusted new policies have enabled the country's television to have become one of the global major media players – buyers, sellers, competitors, etc.

Since the Chinese Communist Party (CCP) established its media system half a century ago, mass media in China has always been part of the CCP's political machine. The fate of the media has always been bound to the fluctuation in the political climate. In the late 1980s, Chinese television suffered a serious setback after the pro-democracy Tiananmen Square event in 1989. But during the 1990s, especially after the late paramount leader Deng Xiaoping in 1992 called for a continuous reform and openness, the media have not only quickly recovered but also, along with a more rigorous economic transition, a few new situations have emerged. Confronting the dilemma between continuing the open-door policy and resisting the Western influence, in the 1990s the CCP has adjusted most of its media policies.

This chapter examines China's position – a newly opened television giant with the world's largest viewership under a tightly controlled political system – which is under siege from worldwide trends of deregulation and globalization. In a centralized communication system such China's, central policies are the most critical factor for any changes. Therefore, this study attempts to analyze the motivations, implications, and impacts of China's television import and export policies in the 1990s. The purpose of this research is to explore how countries such as China were affected by the worldwide tendency of deregulation and globalization, how the country has reacted to and counteracted those trends, how new policies were shaped and contested in an age of globalization, what factors and motivations caused the CCP to reconcile between openness and resistance, and what the implications of the new policies have been.

289

This research was mainly based on primary sources obtained by the author in China. Most of the documents and other data were collected from interviews with Chinese officials, researchers, and media practitioners.

New situations of China's television in the 1990s

Three years after the Tiananmen Square event, in 1992 Deng Xiaoping made an inspection tour to southern China during which he called the country for a further openness and deeper reform. Soon after this, economic reform was not only put back on the CCP's agenda but was also carried out at a faster speed and on a broader scale. Reforms in other spheres which were curtailed due to the Tiananmen Square event, including the media, were also resumed. The continuous open-door direction and further reform have brought about new situations of mass media in general, and television in particular.

The new explosion of television

Deregulation in China was realized through the decentralization of television. Similar to cases in many other countries, the direct and most evident consequence of the decentralization – the Chinese version of deregulation – was a new explosion of television stations.

For many years, the central government restricted television stations only at the regional and above regional levels. Beginning in the early 1990s, many new provincial, regional and local television stations became incorporated. In 1992 alone, fifty new television stations were established, making a 22.8-percent increase from 1989. In each of the three years of 1994, 1995 and 1996, the increase rate kept a percentage similar to that of 1992. As a result, the total number of television stations established in the first five years of the 1990s was nearly equal to the total number of television stations that had been established over the three decades between the 1950s and the 1980s. This swift proliferation of television continued until 1997, when experts warned the government that China had more television stations than most Western industrialized nations and that the number of the country's television stations was disproportional to its economic ability (*China Radio and Television Yearbook 1996*, 1997).

But what was more phenomenal was the even quicker growth of cable television stations. Program-generating cable television stations were rare in the 1980s. Even by 1990, there were no more than 100 cable stations in the country (*China Radio and Television Yearbook 1992*, 1993). In May 1991, China's first major program-generating cable television, Beijing Cable Television, was on the air. In subsequent months, cable stations at different levels were seen everywhere. By the end of 1991, there were a total of more than 400 cable television stations (Zhou, Ren and Yang, 1993). In 1992, Shanghai Cable Television (SCTV), China's largest and most advanced cable station, was established. According to an interview with Wu (1997), President of SCTV, in 1996 SCTV alone had two million household subscribers and the station has became one of the world's largest cable networks.

290

This nearly out-of-control growth of television has generated an unanticipated high demand for programming. As is the case with many other countries, the explosion of television stations in China did not arrive with a correspondingly fast development of program production. Despite the fact that production did increase during the same period, the speed of the increase of production was far behind the speed of television station's growth. Thus, the supply was far beyond the demand, resulting in a serious nationwide shortage of television programs. Subsequently, the swift development of broadcasting infrastructure has substantially widened the gap between the needs for programming and its capability for production.

In order to resolve the problem, many television stations, especially local ones, inevitably have looked to import programs. According to Gong Xueping (1997), former president of STV and presently deputy mayor of Shanghai in charge of culture and media, many television stations' heavy dependence on imports has made the government decide not to license any new television stations; instead, the government has been cancelling unqualified television stations, defining "unqualified" as those stations which totally relied on imports.

The marketization and corporatization of television

While privatization and commercialization have been sweeping over television systems in many countries, what has happened in China's television has been marketization and corporatization. Media privatization has always been a forbidden issue in China. Therefore, there have not been any changes in media ownership. All media institutions are government owned. Likewise, media commercialization has not been a favorable idea to communist authorities because commercialization has been perceived as something that will eventually alter the fundamental nature and the primary function of the communist media.

However, under the influence and pressure of the changing international environment as well as the country's domestic transition from a state economy to a state-controlled market economy (or, as some call it, a Leninist market economy), the CCP has allowed television to move toward marketization and corporatization. What marketization and corporatization in the Chinese context really mean is that, despite the fact that by nature television stations are still government agencies, stations must be operated like a corporation in order to join the market competition and to seek revenues for their survival; television stations will either no longer receive or will be provided with less government subsidy. Regardless of what it should be called – an alternative version of commercialization or "commercialization with Chinese characteristics" – marketization and corporatization have been phenomenal in China's television since the early 1990s.

The government has implemented a series of directives on reforming the media's financial structure. With increasingly reduced government subsidies, television stations have unavoidably become more and more dependent on advertising revenues and other profit-seeking activities. By 1993, at least one-third of the operating cost of televisions had been derived from advertising and other business sources (J. Yu, 1990; Jiang, 1993; Chan, 1994a). By 1996, more than half of the operating cost of television had come from the market (Ma, 1997). In more developed areas such as Shanghai, Beijing, Guangzhou, Tianjing, and Wuhan, commercial revenues have made up the bulk of television stations' financial resources. As for Shanghai-based OTV, China's first non-government subsidized television, according to its president Mu (1997), since the first day of operation in 1993, 100 percent of the station's finance has come from market activities. As Lee (1994) points out, in the short period of the early 1990s commercial support has become the financial backbone of television stations' survival. The severance of state subsidies to the media has "unleashed their vital energy to meet intense market competition, causing them to cater to the growing needs and tastes of a diverse audience" (Lee, 1994: 15).

As market competition has brought additional flexibility and opportunities to television stations, it also has pressured them into seeking more appealing programs in order to be competitive. Until most recently, independent production companies were not allowed in China. All television stations had to produce programs on their own. But producing market-competitive programs not only requires advanced skills, but more importantly, also necessitates large investment. Most television stations, especially local ones, not only lacked production ability but also lacked investment and financial resources. Then, a short cut in order to maintain market competitiveness was the purchase of programs from abroad. On average, producing a one-hour quality teledrama in China costs more than purchasing a one-hour foreign teledrama. Thus, structural changes in television – marketization and corporatization – have again generated a high demand for appealing, quality programs, which has further led to an excess of imported programs on television screens. For a period of several years, television stations' market competition was more like just a competition for importing foreign programs. Until recently, after the government took some actions to re-regulate imports, television program imports were out of control and very chaotic.

The increasingly fierce competition between Chinese television and foreign television

Prior to the 1980s, foreign programs entering China had to go through official procedures and channels, which meant that they had to be imported by government-owned media institutions. Any unofficial import was illegal. Very few foreign programs entered China unofficially or illegally – through smuggling and available only on the black market. But now, the majority of foreign programs enter the country unofficially: they arrive through the sky and can be obtained by any household with a satellite antenna. In the past few years, a batch of major transnational television programmers have poured into Asia with a particular interest in China's potentially huge market. Several American and European broadcasting companies have been looking for ways to tap into the newly-discovered world consuming power. CNN, BBC, MTV Asia, and Prime Sports have all entered the Asia/China market either by setting up their Asian operation branches in Hong Kong or by opening an office in Beijing, "all vying for a share of the great market" (Hachtan, 1996: 55). While ESPN has begun its pan-Asian satellite transmission, HBO has been considering the Asia/China market for a pay-movie channel as well as a free general entertainment channel. In the meantime, Japan's NHK has also been looking at regional distribution via satellite. There even has been an idea of creating an NHK-led Global News Network (GNN) to counter and compete with American and European transnational media organizations. Even the world media mogul Rupert Murdock, in order to obtain a slice of the "China pie," has attempted to get the approval from the Chinese government to let his Star TV enter the country (Geddes, 1991; Tanzer, 1991; Westlake, 1991; Tan, 1993; Dizard, 1994; Hachten, 1996; Ma, 1997; Zhou, 1997; Roberts, 1998).

Although, thus far, transnational television services have not been permitted a "direct operation" in China, abundant foreign programming is now hovering over China's sky day and night via satellite. This programming is watched by dozens of millions of Chinese audiences. According to Ma (1997), in the 1990s, each year about two million satellite dishes have been bought by Chinese individuals. And, according to an interview with Yun (1997), professor of the Beijing Broadcasting Institute, in Guangzou, Shanghai, Beijing and other major cities there were millions of satellite receiver owners. These satellite dish owners now watch Star TV, CNN, and NHK everyday, especially the Hong Kong-based Star TV, which has five specialized Chinese-language-speaking channels broadcasting twenty-four hours a day (Poon, 1997). In 1996, a Chinese government survey admitted that forty-eight million households – about 20 percent of China's total households – receive Star TV (Zhou, 1997).

Foreign television services have grabbed a considerable portion of Chinese viewers away from the country's own channels. Because of what we may call the availability, intrusion, or competition of transnational satellite television programs, China's television has lost a great deal of audience share. Moreover, because most foreign programs carries an "exotic flavor," advanced production skill, and appealing plots, transnational television services have put Chinese television in a weaker and disadvantageous position to compete with them. In order to find a way out and to compete for the audience share, many Chinese television stations unfortunately have again turned to relying more heavily on foreign programs: they are using foreign programs to compete with foreign programming. Although this strategy allows some television stations to survive, as remarked by Chi (1997), a senior official of the Ministry of Radio, Film and Television, it has also been a form of suicide for the nation's television.

The changes of the social structure and the audiences' tastes

Economic reform and political opening have inevitably had a strong impact on the social structure. Among them, one was the change in the workday system and another one was the change in audience's tastes.

In the early 1990s, the six-workday per week system, which had been used for decades, was changed to a five-workday per week system. The new workday system has doubled the people's leisure time; but even more importantly, it has altered people's life styles. For more than four decades from the beginning of Communist China in 1949 to the early 1990s, the country used a six-workday system. Accordingly, television stations just needed to prepare better programs for Saturday evenings and Sundays. But the new workday system has again resulted in a demand for more and better television programs.

In order to be compatible with international standards, one of the steps towards China's openness, around 1992 Beijing, Shanghai, Guangzou, and some other large cities started a five-workday system. Overnight, this change meant that hundreds of millions of people's leisure time doubled. For most people, the easiest and most economical solution has been to watch more television. Thus, the change in the workday system has provided television stations with an opportunity and a challenge. Television stations need more appealing programs, and the battles for better programs among television stations has further escalated. During an interview, vice president of Oriental Television (OTV) Liu (1997) admitted that because a great hunger for appealing programs remains unfilled among television stations, importing foreign programs has been considered an effective "one stone, two birds" weapon: it simultaneously eases the lack of programs and the lack of *appealing* programs.

While the change in the social structure and people's lifestyles has generated an even further demand for more appealing programs, changes in audiences' tastes have also generated a similar demand. In the 1990s, television audiences have become increasingly harder to hold on to. There have been two main reasons. One is that the audiences' tastes have become more sophisticated, and the other is that people are now able to be more selective about their leisure activities.

Since the opening of television imports in the late 1970s, audiences have had opportunities to view programs of various themes and styles. Their tastes have been "trained" to be much more sophisticated and their standards and expectations much higher. Specifically, with access to a variety of choices of programs provided by both domestic television services as well as the "uninvited" foreign television services, viewers were no longer as "loyal" as they were to their own country's program providers; they have become "difficult customers." The former situation where viewers had only one or two channels to watch has vanished forever. According to Wang (1997), vice director of the General Office of Radio, Film, and Television Ministry, even in mid-size cities (cities with a population of one-half to one million people), there are approximately seven broadcasting television channels, plus dozens of cable channels and several satellite channels, and in large cities (cities with a population of over one million people), the audiences have access to at least ten broadcasting television channels, about thirty cable channels, and a number of foreign satellite television channels.

The more choices audiences have, the more pressures television stations receive, and the winners of the battles for audiences are always those who can provide "better" programs. While the term "better" can hardly be defined objectively, to the audiences "better" simply means more appealing. As Bishop (1989) claims, when it comes to catering to audiences' tastes, television programs can be categorized at two levels. After basic needs for something to watch are fulfilled, television programs will move to fill the "higher" needs such as curiosity, sex and love, as well as self-esteem, competence, and achievement. Regardless of judgment on value system or ideological preference overall, Western television often provides this second level of programming, whereas Chinese television seldom does so. To the audiences, inevitably, imported programs have seemed more appealing than domestic programs. Once again, the change in the audiences' tastes has pushed television stations for more imports.

In the 1990s, Chinese audiences have had more selection regarding their leisure activities. As economic reform has enabled people to become richer than they previously were, the political opening has brought them relatively relaxed social and cultural environments. Many Western-style leisure activities and facilities have emerged in the country, such as Karaoke, KTV, dance clubs, video-tape rental services, and even night clubs. Accordingly, if television programs were not appealing, viewers no longer needed to stay home with their television sets as they had done earlier. Even further, around the mid-1990s, VCR sets became common in most mid-income families. For instance, in 1997 there were 500,000 VCR sets in Shanghai alone, which means that about 20 percent of households owned VCRs. As Hachten (1996) posits, VCRs can have profound effects not only on viewers but also on broadcasting and other media. Thus, this poses a challenge to the latter. As Parsons (1993) observes, the change in the audiences' selection for leisure activities also reflects a social transformation, and this social transformation has also created a serious challenge to television. Now, more than ever, Chinese television has to learn to be audience centered and market driven, because the "relative affluence and freedom to choose will mean that products the government deems to be good for people will be swamped by products people want to buy" (Bishop, 1989: 180). Looking for an escape hatch, many television stations were again forced to rely on importing more foreign programs in order to hold onto the audiences.

Although the aforementioned situation in the 1990s represent discrepant aspects and reflect discrepant dimensions, they all have pushed television stations to struggle for a higher quantity of programming, for more appealing programs, and for more diverse thematic and stylistic programs. However, due to the fact that production capability was still at a relatively low level, willing or unwilling, an easier solution for most television stations was to expand foreign-program imports in order to fill airtime, to hold onto audiences and to get more advertising revenues.

Television's increasingly heavy and even excessive or entire dependence on importation was not something the CCP liked to see. Foreign television programs' dominance of China's television, or more precisely, Western programs' dominance of the communist television, has made the CCP feel uneasy. The CCP has never-theless sensed urgent needs for reevaluating and redesigning its media and cultural product importation policies.

New policies on media and cultural product imports

Facing a reshaped international environment and attempting to compromise between maintaining the open-door direction and resisting the Western influence, the CCP has redesigned its media and cultural product import policies in the 1990s.

The new policies were based on somewhat contradictory or conflicting factors. First, the CCP no longer dared to cut off media and cultural product imports as it did before. The consensus was that the opening in media and cultural product imports must be maintained, otherwise the people would be unhappy with the CCP, which would ultimately endanger the Communist Party's ruling position. Second, the authorities knew that in fact they were no longer able to curtail media and cultural product importation: due to the increasingly advanced technology and due to the fact that overly rigid restrictions will only backfire and force audiences to seek foreign programs through transnational satellite broadcasting, the black market or smuggling. Third, the CCP did not have the intention to cut off media and cultural product importation. Since the 1990s, not only has China's television industry benefited from importing foreign programming, but the country's economy and society has benefited as well. Fourth, on the other hand, however, the CCP was also by no means intending to relinquish control over the cultural and ideological sphere. As always, the CCP was very concerned about the political, ideological and cultural consequences of the Western influence in the country. According to an interview with Chen (1997), a research fellow at the Media and Communication Institute of China Social Science Academy, to the CCP, in confrontation with the worldwide trend of globalization, opening China to the outside world both economically and culturally is not only unavoidable, but also necessary; nevertheless, the CCP's definition of opening has never meant being Westernized. Therefore, the new policies were a mixed product of the CCP's intention to continue the open-door direction and maintain its "fundamental principles," which were buttressed by nationalism and Marx-Lenin-Maoism (Scalapino, 1963). As claimed by Li Tieying, the CCP's Politburo member in charge of media, culture, and education, two fundamental principles were the cornerstone of the new policies. First, China will continue to open its door to the world not only economically but also culturally. Second, China's cultural exchanges with other countries should keep two things balanced: the country's media and cultural product imports must resist Western dominance, and as a long-term goal China must also make substantial efforts to expand its cultural exports, to create a balanced cultural trade with other countries, and to enter the global cultural arena as an equally important player. Li reminded China's media practitioners of being careful about "the inferior spiritual products of the Western culture" while maintaining the open-door direction (*People's Daily*, June 10, 1993).

Promoting domestic production

Unlike before, when the major concern of the media and cultural import policies was how to effectively prohibit or control, a new emphasis has been placed on promoting domestic production and encouraging television stations to compete with foreign programs. The CCP was aware that the attempts to sanitize foreign influence have already been severely undermined by the presence of too many broadcasting satellite dishes, too many shortwave radio sets, too many foreign journalists in the country, too many open telephone lines, too many fax machines, and too many Internet users. All these, although necessary for modernization, have been perceived by the CCP as a threat.

To reduce the degree of this Westernization, or "cultural deficit," China made plans to double its domestic production in the 1990s. For major television stations, the target was to be able to produce ten hours of their daily programs; for others, the target was four hours (Chan, 1994a). In addition, the CCP also launched a massive counter-Western-influence campaign among media and cultural institutions, which included a huge project of producing 100 patriotic theme teleplays and the "Five Ones Project." The former were assigned to the nation's television industry by the central government and the latter required that every year, every province produce one quality teleplay, one quality stage drama, one quality movie, one quality ethnic or local opera, and one quality musical. They should be "domestic" both in the content and format, not just "the local version of Hollywood style" (Kleinsteuber, 1992). The CCP's Central Propaganda Ministry allocated a special fund for these projects (*People's Daily*, August 25, 1993). Each of the thirty provinces has also set specific plans to echo the campaign and allocated a budget to support producing quality programs. As a result of this policy, in the past several years, domestic production has grown steadily. Table 17.1 provides an illustration of the growth of China's domestic television production during the first half 1990s.

Expanding exports

Efforts to expand exports of China-produced programs to the global television market have also been encouraged by the CCP. Under this new policy, the government has subsidized a series of specially designed productions which are aimed at overseas markets. This approach was part of the CCP's ultimate goal of gradually improving the world's overwhelmingly unidirectional flow of media and cultural products and making China's television more internationally competitive.

According to an interview with Ma (1997), a senior official of the Radio, Film, and Television Ministry, four main methods were used to expand the exports. The first method was to boost direct international sales; the second was to provide programs to overseas Chinese television stations or channels at no cost or low cost; the third was to run video rental services overseas; and the last was to launch regional satellite television services.

The government established a specialized company, China International Television Inc., to undertake the task of promoting sales. In the past few years,

297

Table 17.1 Hours of domestic programming shown on television per week

Year	Hours of domestic programming (per week)	Increase over previous year (percentage)
1990	8,274	n.a.
1991	9,593	15.9
1992	11,913	24.4
1993	17,902	38.9
1994	24,187	35.1
1995	31,067	28.4

Source: Ministry of Radio, Film, and Television, 1997.

television program exports have been increasing steadily. According to the statistics provided by China Television International Inc., in Hong Kong, Taiwan, Singapore, Thailand, Japan, Korea, and other southeast Asian countries – even including Vietnam, China's most recent war enemy – China has become one of the region's major television program suppliers. Despite the fact that China's television exports to other areas of the world still were limited due to linguistic, cultural and/or ideological differences, in recent years exports to Western European countries have been increasing, especially once several countries such as Germany and France redesigned their Far East/China policies. China has also expanded its television exports to the United States (Yu, 1997).

In addition, recent efforts included the incorporation of CCTV's Fourth Channel, the network's international channel dedicated to overseas Chinese and transmitted via satellite; the launching of another satellite channel based in a Fujian province over Taiwan, Hong Kong, and Southeast Asia; and the purchase and operation of Hong Kong's Phoenix Television, one of Star TV's major channels, which is now used by the communist regime as a global channel targeting half of the globe (Wang, 1997). Not only has the export volume been greatly expanded, but also the themes and styles of the exported programs have become much more diversified.

Setting the quota system

Another new policy was setting the quota system. For the first time in China's television history, in the early 1990s, the CCP issued an explicit quota policy regarding percentages of broadcasting hours of imported programs. This policy mandates that in principle the percentage of broadcasting hours of foreign programs cannot exceed 15 percent of a television station's total broadcasting time. Regardless of whether one perceives this percentage as low or high, this new policy should be viewed as a positive step because there had never been such an explicit quota policy before.

Quotas have been criticized for being paternalistic and inefficient, and for reducing the audience's freedom of choice. However, as Renaud (1993) argues, a quota system also can be seen as fulfilling distributive aims; it becomes a means, however imperfect, of improving the country's ability to restore competition in the international market. Therefore, while the new policy, criteria, and regulations still appear to be quite restrictive, they can also be interpreted quite positively if we consider China's political system and its formerly ambiguous policies.

Certainly, the fundamental concern of the quota system was to limit Western cultural influences. But adopting a quota system has legitimized the CCP's resistance of Western influences rather than simply prohibiting or restricting imports. Because of this quota policy, on the Chinese television screen the dominance of Western programs, particularly the dominance of US programs, has nevertheless begun to diminish, albeit slowly.

Balancing the import source

In the 1990s, another new step in China's media and cultural exchange activities was parallel to the CCP's adjusted foreign policy. China's foreign policy during the late 1970s and the 1980s was criticized by some third-world nations for being "too soft to the West" because China needs Western capital and technology (Zhi, 1997). Although the CCP did not admit that tendency, since the late 1980s – particularly after the Tiananmen Square event in 1989 – China nevertheless adjusted its policy towards the West. The CCP wanted to establish a balanced relationship with both third-world nations and Western countries. To the CCP, cultural exchanges were not just part of foreign relationships, but they were always an important indication of the degree of foreign relationships.

During the post-Cold War era, balancing the import source functions as one of China's major diplomatic strategies rather than merely acting as a media policy. While continuing to import television programs from Western countries, the CCP has given import priority to programs from non-Western countries, especially those countries that maintain good political relationships with China. As for Western countries, they have also been singled out: priority has purposely been given to European countries, Canada, Japan, and Australia, not the United States. According to an interview with Xu (1997), president of China International Television Inc., at the present time, programs from non-Western countries is particularly welcome and often assigned a better spot in the television stations' programming schedule than Western programs are, although in reality non-Western countries do not have much programs to offer. This new policy has nevertheless been somewhat effective. As Chen (1997) observes, as a result of this new policy, in the last few years the dominance of Western programs on Chinese television screens – especially the dominance of US programs – has begun to alter, although not very visibly. Presently, programs from other countries, such as Central European nations, Asian states, former Eastern European bloc countries, and Latin- and South-American nations, are more welcome and often get a good spot in the programming schedule (Zhou, 1997).

Further decentralizing and depoliticalizing television

As these new policies basically reflected the CCP's prudence toward globalization and its resistance to the Western influence, the policies of further decentralizing and depoliticalizing television reflected the CCP's willingness for a continuous openness.

A new policy began during the 1990s, which was intended to distinguish networks and major stations from local, small or specialized television stations, such as educational stations. As Chan (1994a) observes, the CCP now attaches discrepant political status and functions to discrepant media institutions. While the central media organizations are still considered to be nothing but the CCP's mouthpieces, such strict requirements will no longer apply to media institutions at lower levels. This new step, as Baum (1991) indicates, was part of a global tendency throughout the communist world whereby the pattern of centralized political control has been greatly, although not uniformly, attenuated. The difference between this new approach and the former policy is that, unlike previously when all television stations were equally tightly controlled, now networks and major television stations still receive tight control whereas local, small or specialized stations are given a bit more freedom or flexibility. Thus, to a certain extent, this new policy has reflected the CCP's limited openness to the outside world or tolerance of the Western influence. This new practice of setting various control criteria for television stations at various levels should be viewed as a meaningful symbol. Although it is unrealistic to expect the Party to relinquish its control on media and culture, this change has symbolized that the CCP nevertheless still wants to continue its open-door direction when confronting globalization.

Besides further decentralizing television, the CCP's intention to continue the open-door direction was also demonstrated through its efforts to further depoliticize television. Television in China was always treated as a purely political and ideological instrument. A new policy now claimed that television is a multi-functional tool which serves both the needs of the Communist Party and the needs of the people. Because of this depoliticization, television's entertainment and social-service functions have been recognized. Despite the fact that politics and ideology are still the dominant function, efforts to make television useful both to economic development and to people's daily lives have also become evident. Moreover, in recent years, by and large, television's political and ideological functions have been gradually reduced, and in the meantime its entertainment and social-service functions have been increasingly emphasized. This tendency to become more depoliticized was crucial in alleviating the clashes ensuring from the process where communist television merges with the so-called global television – Western television.

Implications

China's new media and cultural product importation policies in the 1990s contain contradictory or conflicting intentions and elements. On the surface, the country's media were facing a dilemma. In fact, it was not the media but the CCP itself that was facing the dilemma (Su, 1994). Changes in China's media always have had a close connection to changes in the country's political and economic spheres: when the country's political climate and economic development became more open and diverse, the media also headed towards an open, plural, marketized, and entertainment- oriented direction; and *vice versa*.

However, in fact, the contradictions or conflicts that have been seen in China in recent years have also precisely reflected the dilemmas and challenges which many other countries had been confronting and how they have compromised between the opposing choices. Unable to avoid media globalization, the CCP has chosen a balanced, but contradictory and conflicting, model for the country's media. The reasons behind the motivations of the new policies are located between the two ends of a spectrum: the one end is to continue the open-door policy, and the other end is to resist Western influence. According to Chan (1994b), few countries are at either of the two ends of the spectrum, i.e., virtual suppression and total openness. The majority of countries are located in between the poles. Depending on whether they are closer to "total openness" or to "virtual suppressiveness," they roughly fall into three categories: regulated openness, illegal openness (open not legally, but in practice), and suppressive openness (heavily restricted or very limited openness). During the last few years, China has evolved from a virtual suppression to a suppressive openness.

Apparently, there remain many restrictive components to the new policies. Yet, despite this, the new policies have still basically reflected an open-door intention. There are a number of factors that have kept China on the track of openness. As the last communist stronghold, China faces growing international challenges and pressures to be open. As Baum (1991) notes, globalized markets, information flows, and cries for popular empowerment have already conspired to render autarky, self-reliance, and neo-Maoist ideological mobilization obsolescent as developmental strategies and have radically altered the political environments of Eastern Europe and the former Soviet Union. China's chaos-fearing leaders have discovered that they cannot achieve their goals without openness and pluralism. For China, it is now impossible to shut the door without exacting a huge price (Lee, 1994). Therefore, the CCP has been proclaiming that China will never change its open-door direction. And the adoption of the open-door direction was the most crucial fact for the changes in media and cultural product imports, which has to some extent signified a relaxation of ideology and social control.

In fact, China's television has already departed substantially from the classic Soviet model. As Sparks and Reading (1994) point out, two important categories can be used to measure the degree of departure. The first is in the nature of the programs shown, and the second is the readiness to carry advertising. Contrary to the image of a tightly controlled and wholly propagandistic output, a considerably high percentage of programming shown on China's television was purchased on the world market. The percentage of China's imported television programs is now even higher than that in many Asian countries, third-world nations, and former communist countries. As for carrying advertising, the amount of television advertising has reached a historical high.

Nevertheless, the fundamental concern and the overall goal of the new policies is still to resist Western influence. The CCP has learned that, in the post-Cold War world, fast-moving political and social changes are being strongly influenced, shaped, and accelerated by transnational communication. To the Chinese communist leaders, high among the various factors contributing to the worldwide collapse of communist regimes was certainly the impact of Western influence. Fearing this kind of threat, the CCP launched the "anti-spiritual pollution campaign" in 1983, the "anti-bourgeois liberalization campaign" in 1987, and the "anti-peaceful evolution campaign" in 1989. In each case, the perceived threat was the influence of Western media and culture (Chan, 1994b).

These new policies have reflected little change in the CCP's concept of media and culture as a purely political tool and ideological state apparatus. The introduction of marketization and corporatization into the media has been a controlled process in which political factors have played and still play a decisive part because of the assumptions that free-market competition should not be totally adopted into the Chinese system. This system continues to subscribe to Marxist and Maoist thoughts and has a communist party which shows no intention of relinquishing its grip over the media. Accordingly, in recent years, while media marketization and corporatization have emerged, the mass media, as a whole, have yet to demonstrate their independence as genuine social institutions and purely independent market forces; instead, politically the media still insist on the dictatorial rule of the Communist Party (Chan, 1994a). As Sparks and Reading (1994) observe, overall the continuities are much more than the discontinuities between communism's past and communism's present in terms of political structure and media nature.

However, there are indeed significant differences between the old policies and the new policies. The main difference between the new policies and old policies was not the overall principle, but the approach: the previous form of resistance to Western influence was to isolate China from the outside world or to sever the country's contact with the West, but the new resistant approach was to open China to the outside world and then to compete with the Western countries in the global arena. In short, a revolutionary-type approach has been replaced by a cooperative-type approach. It should be noted that the new approach is of great significance because it corresponds to a global characteristic in the transition of the world political structure from the Cold War era to the post-Cold War era. In Polumbaum's view, for China these new policies are a good signal because they have shown that the country's "fluid and manipulatable" system has been becoming "increasingly formalized and regularized," and overall the new policies have suggested "a subtle, graduate, and still-evolving institutionalization of media management" (1994: 118). At any rate, according to Zhang (1997), director of the Policy and Regulation Office of the Ministry of Radio, Film, and Television, these new policies so far have generally proven effective. That is, they serve the CCP's two intentions: to continue its openness in media and cultural product imports and to minimize the Western influence.

Conclusion

Changes in the global media in the 1990s have had a profound impact on countries across the world. The growing global cultural exchanges among countries have become among the most important of international activities. However, thus far, media globalization is virtually a media Westernization. Therefore, to most countries, changes in global media have posed a dilemma.

Facing the global environmental changes, most countries' media have undergone various changes, including structural, institutional, and policy changes. Among them, setting, adjusting, or redesigning media policies have been one urgent and difficult task. Although the motivations for policy changes in different countries resulted from various concerns, the fundemantal concern was: while openness has become unavoidable, how does a country protect its own political, ideological, economic, and cultural interests, and how does it resist foreign influence (McAnany and Wilkinson, 1996)?

These and other concerns have urged the CCP to reconsider its media and cultural product import policies. The CCP has adopted a series of new policies in an attempt to both maintain the open-door direction and to resist Western influence. These new policies have vividly reflected the CCP's ambivalent attitude: under siege from globalization, the CCP has neither wanted to lose the opportunity to become an active part of the global village nor has it wanted to give up its control on culture and ideology. In fact, the compromise is a result of the high demand and the shortage of supply, the need for openness and the fear of Western influence, and the willingness to accept globalization and reluctance to give up control.

There interpretations can be made of China's new policies. First, in recent years reconciling openness with resistance has become a common trend in many countries across the world. Second, there was more "old stuff" than "new stuff" in those policies, or, that is to say, there was more continuity than discontinuity in those policies. Third, the major concern of the new policies was still to resist Western influence.

In general, three trends for the future of China's media and television may be identified. First, the open-door direction will be maintained and the policies in the 1990s will continue to be the basic guidance for media and cultural product imports in the next few years. Second, even though those policies may be altered slightly in the future due to new factors, essentially the media will still be an ideological apparatus of the Party and the fundamental elements of those policies will remain untouched. Lastly, despite the fact that the CCP's two efforts – openness and resistance – are contradictory or conflicting and represent two opposite directions, the CCP will still attempt to reconcile these two opposing directions until they have no choice at all.

Overall, the post-Deng era has reflected a drifting course or a compromise between openness/acceptance of globalization/Westernization and self-protection/resistance to globalization/Westernization. Ironically, as Huang (1994) sees it, "socialist" or "communist" are now understood as maintaining monopoly control of political power by the Communist Party, while the "market system" is understood as using whatever capitalist means are necessary to keep things moving. Time is needed to know whether these two different strategies can work well together or not. Frequent clashes between these two strategies have already often been seen both in China as well as in other countries. Therefore, what can be expected would still be a twisted course because, as Chan (1994a) observes, the tension between the CCP's desires to deflect the Western influence and to continue the open-door direction has been growing in recent years.

The present Chinese communist regime in the post-Deng era will certainly continue to prevail. Thus, two predictions may be more certain than others. First, China's media in the foreseeable future will not be total replicas of the Western model. Second, however, the media, especially television, will be more marketized and corporatized. That is because in both so doing the state can license the media organizations but also grant a degree of autonomy in exchange for the media observing certain controls. As a result, the CCP ultimately may be able to remain hegemonic in the political and ideological sector, while at the same time it may further relax a measure of control in the areas of media administration, management, financial resources and, to some extent, program import policies.

References

Althusser, L. (1971). *Lenin and Philosophy and Other Essays*. New York: Monthly Review Press.

Baum, R. (Ed.). (1991). *Reform and Reactions in Post-Mao China: The Road to Tiananmen*. London: Routledge.

Bishop, R. (1989). *Qi Lai! – Mobilizing One Billion Chinese: The Chinese Communication System*. Ames, IO: Iowa State University Press.

Blumler, J. (1993). "The British approach to Public Service Broadcasting: From confidence to uncertainty." In R. Avery (Ed.), *Public Service Broadcasting in A Multichannel Environment*, 1–28. New York: Longman.

Chan, J. (1994a). "Media internationalization in China: Process and tensions." *Journal of Communication*, 44(3), 70–88.

Chan, J. (1994b). "National responses and accessibility of Star TV in Asia." *Journal of Communication*, 44(3), 112–31.

Chaudhary, A. and Chen, A. (1995). "Asia and the Pacific." In J. Merrill (Ed.), *Global Journalism: Survey of International Communication* (3rd edn), 269–329. New York: Longman.

Chen, L. (1997). Interview with Chen, research fellow of the Media and Communication Institute of China Social Science Academy.

Chi, P. (1997) Interview with Chi, senior official of China's Ministry of Radio, Film, and Television.

China Radio and Television Yearbook 1992. (1993). Beijing: China Radio and Television Press.

China Radio and Television Yearbook 1996. (1997). Beijing: China Radio and Television Press.

Dizard, W. (1994). *Old Media, New Media*. New York: Longman.

Downing, J. (1996). *Internationalizing Media Theory: Transition, Power, Culture Reflections on Media in Russia, Poland, and Hungary, 1980–1995.* Thousand Oaks, CA: Sage.

Geddes, A. (1991). "Asian satellite television blasts off." *Advertising Age*, October 28, 5.

Gong, X. (1997). Interview with Gong, deputy mayor of Shanghai.

Hachten, W. (1996). *The World News Prism: Changing Media of International Communication* (4th edn). Ames, IO: Iowa State University Press.

Hamelink, C. (1994). *The Politics of World Communication.* Thousand Oaks, CA: Sage.

Huang, Y. (1994). "Peaceful evolution: the case of television reform in post-Mao China." *Media Culture, and Society*, 16, 217–41.

Jiang, O. (1993). "Development of China's radio and television in 1991." In *China Radio and Television Yearbook 1992*, 10–11. Beijing: China Radio and Television Press.

Johnson, O. (1995). "East central and southeastern Europe, Russia, and the newly independent states." In J. Merrill (Ed.), *Global Journalism: Survey of International Communication* (3rd edn), 153–87. New York: Longman.

Lee, C. (1994). "Ambiguities and contradictions: Issues in China's changing political communication." In C. Lee (Ed.), *China's Media, Media's China*, 3–20. Boulder, CO: Westview Press.

Liu, W. (1997). Interview with Liu, vice president of Oriental Television.

Kleinsteuber, H. (1992). "The global village stays local." In K. Siune and J. Truetzschlers (Eds), *Dynamic of Media Politics.* London: Sage.

Ma, Y. (1997). Interview with Ma, senior official of the Ministry of Radio, Film, and Television.

Maney, K. (1995). *Megamedia Shakeout: The Inside Storey of the Leaders and the Losers in the Exploding Communications Industry.* New York: John Wiley and Sons.

McAnany, E. and Wilkinson, K. (Eds) (1996). *Mass Media and Free Trade: NAFTA and the Cultural Industries.* Austin, TX: University of Texas Press.

McDowell, S. (1997). Globalization and Policy Choice: Television and Audiovisual Services Policies in India. *Media, Culture, and Society*, 2, 151–72.

Mohammadi, A. (Ed.) (1997). *International Communication and Globalization.* Thousand Oaks, CA: Sage.

Mosco, V. (1996). *The Political Economy of Communication: Rethinking and Renewal.* Thousand Oaks, CA: Sage.

Mowlana, H. (1996). *Global Communication in Transition: The End of Diversity?* Thousand Oaks, CA: Sage.

Mowlana, H. (1997). *Global Information and World Communication: New Frontiers in International Relations.* Thousand Oaks, CA: Sage.

Mu, D. (1997). Interview with Mu, president of Oriental Television.

Parsons, P. (1993). "Marketing revolution hits staid giant, while in China advertising blooms like a thousand flowers." *Advertising Age*, July 19, 25–38.

People's Daily. (1993). "100 dramas of patriotic themes assigned to television stations," August 25, 1.

People's Daily. (1993). Li on China's culture policy," June 10, 3.

Pei, M. (1994). *From Reform to Revolution.* Cambridge, MA: Harvard University Press.

Polumbaum, J. (1994). "Striving for predictability: The bureaucratization of media management in China." In C. Lee (Ed.), *China's Media, Media's China*, 113–28. Boulder, CO: Westview Press.

Poon, J. (1997). Interview with Poon, corporate affairs manager of Star TV.

Renaud, J. (1993). "International trade in television programs: Quota policies and consumer choice revisited." In E. Noam and J. Millonzi (Eds), *The International Market in Film and Television Programs*. Norwood, NJ: Ablex.

Roberts, J. (1998). "Rupert's black eye: Contrite HarperCollins settles with an author." *Newsweek*, March 16, 44.

Rowland, W. (1993). "Public Service Broadcasting in the United States: Its mandate, institutions, and conflicts." In R. Avery (Ed.), *Public Service Broadcasting in A Multichannel Environment*, 157–94. New York: Longman.

Scalapino, R. (1963). "Communist China – the first fourteen years." In W. Petersen (Ed.), *The Realities of World Communism*, 123–63. Englewood Cliffs, NJ: Prentice-Hall.

Sepstrup, P. (1989). "Implications of current developments in West European broadcasting." *Media, Culture and Society*, 11, 29–54.

Sparks, C. and Reading, A. (1994). "Understanding media change in East Central Europe." *Media, Culture and Society*, 16, 243–70.

Steinbock, D. (1995). *Triumph and Erosion in the American Media and Entertainment Industries*. London: Quorum Books.

Su, S. (1994). "Chinese communist ideology and media control." In C. Lee (Ed.), *China's Media, Media's China*, 75–88. Boulder, CO: Westview Press.

Tan, Y. (1993). Interview with Tan, Asian marketing coordinator of Turner Broadcasting Company.

Tanzer, A. (1991). "The Asian village." *Forbes*, November 11, 32.

Vedel, T. and Bourdon, J. (1993). "French Public Service Broacasting: From monopoly to marginalization." In R. Avery (Ed.), *Public Service Broadcasting in A Multichannel Environment*, 29–51. New York: Longman.

Wang, J. (1997). Interview with Wang, president of Phoenix Chinese Channel of Star TV.

Wang, Y. (1997). Interview with Wang, vice director of the General Office of the Radio, Film, and Television Ministry.

Westlake, M. (1991). "Asia's telecoms market attracts foreign equipment suppliers: Busy signals." *Far Eastern Economic Review*, March 7, 43–4.

Winseck, D. (1997). "Contradictions in the democratization of international communication." *Media, Culture, and Society*, 2, 219–46.

Wu, Y. (1997). Interview with Wu, President of Shanghai Cable Television.

Xu, X. (1997). Interview with Xu, President of China International Television Inc.

Yu, C. (1997). Interview with Yu, vice director of Foreign Affairs, China's Ministry of Radio, Film, and Television.

Yu, J. (1990). "The structure and function of Chinese television, 1979–1989." In C. Lee (Ed.), *Voices of China: The Interplay of Politics and Journalism*, 69–87. New York: The Guilford Press.

Yun, P. (1997). Interview with Yun, professor of the Beijing Broadcasting Institute.

Zhang, H. (1997). Interview with Zhang, director of the Policy and Regulation Office of Ministry of Radio, Film, and Television.

Zhi, L. (1997). Interview with Zhi, research fellow of Sichua Social Science Academy.

Zhou, C., Ren, Q. and Yang, P. (1993). "Development of China's cable television." In *China Radio and Television Yearbook 1992*, 32–34. Beijing: China Radio and Television Press.

Zhou, J. (1997). Interview with Zhou, director of the General Editorial Office of China Central Television.

18

GLOBALIZATION: CONSUMPTION AND IDENTITY

Towards researching nodal points

Rico Lie and Jan Servaes

The goal of this concluding chapter is to explore aspects of the relation between (a) cultural globalization, (b) consumption and (c) identity, and identify areas of research. In the current age of globalization, consumption is increasingly becoming cross-cultural. All kinds of flows – like those of people and all kinds of products – are increasing in quantity and changing in quality. The more specific question that will be addressed is therefore: "How does this process of changed and changing cross-cultural consumption of products, people, information, knowledge and inter-pretations relate to culture and local-global identities?" The possible answers to this question seem to be heading in two opposite directions. The first line of answers points us in the direction of cultural homogenization and the emergence of uniform identities. The second line of answers addresses the emergence of hybrid identities and points us in the direction of diversity. The first line of answers builds on dependency thinking and early modernization theories. The second line of answers builds on what we have termed the multiplicity paradigm (Servaes, 1998). In the process of changing from modernization-dependency thinking to thinking in terms of multiplicity, several shifts in emphasis have occurred. The first shift is that the emphasis in communication processes has been changed from the emphasis on the producer/sender to the emphasis on the *consumer/receiver*. A second shift is towards an emphasis on *culture* and on cultural identity. People speak of the "cultural turn." A third shift that can be identified is a shift from an emphasis on similarities (What makes people the same?) towards an emphasis on *differences* (What makes people different?). These three sub-paradigmatic shifts will be addressed throughout this chapter.

It is assumed that the two basic concepts underlying processes related to globalization and identity are *communication* and *culture*. Communication is of course closely related to consumption. All communication includes consumption. Though globalizing identities (globalization) and the linked process of localizing identities (localization) are the result of communication/consumption in its widest possible forms, it is through communication that culture is made public and shared, and, secondly, it is through culture that the forms of communication are shaped. Moreover, the content of communication is culture, and culture itself can incorporate different modes of communication. Culture and communication seem to be two linked and inseparable processes. Communication is regarded to be all (inter)action between people (P), between people and institutions (I), and between people and products (P) (PIPs). Although this (inter)action is in form and content highly influenced by culture, communication can also have changing cultures/identities as a result.

Globalization/localization is such a process of changing cultures/identities. All communication can lead to intended or unintended globalizing or localizing change. As a result of the centrality of culture and communication, a theoretical basis for the study of globalization/localization, consumption and identity needs to have a comprehensive and integrated view on these concepts. From the perspective of communication scholars this would mean that the ultimate goal is to embed communication in culture. For the communication specialist the entry to the relation between culture and communication will be communication. From an anthropological perspective, this would mean that in the study of cultural processes, more emphasis would be put on issues specifically concerned with communications. In order to explore the basic concepts of communication and culture let us first take a look at how these concepts are approached in the disciplines of *symbolic anthropology*, *communication studies* and *cultural studies*. In the second part of this chapter we will then shift attention towards globalization/localization, consumption and identity and present a model on researching nodal points.

Culture and communication

Symbolic anthropology

In the beginning of the 1960s a new field of study emerged within social anthropology: symbolic anthropology. With the coming of symbolic anthropology it was the concept of culture that was specified. Previously there was little interest in the concept of culture, but with the introduction of the concept of symbol, a handle was offered to put the concept of culture into operation. Where Malinowski and Radcliffe-Brown – as founding fathers of British social anthropology – were debating about the centrality of either function or structure, the symbolic anthropologists centralized the concept of culture. The symbolic anthropologists see culture as the concept that is responsible for being a human being, namely "the ability to symbolize." As we intend to show here, this "new" symbolic perspective on culture has opened ways for seeing culture *as* communication.

Symbolic anthropology has its roots in British social anthropology, but does not exist without explanation. There seems to be only little agreement on what symbolic anthropology actually stands for: "During the 1960s and 1970s, discussions of culture theory showed a preoccupation with the idea that cultures are systems of symbols and meaning" (Singer, 1984: 32). Ever since, different anthropologists have given different names to this new perspective on culture. A few are: "comparative symbology" (Victor Turner/Mary Douglas), "interpretative anthropology" (Clifford Geertz), "structural (intellectual) anthropology" (Claude Lévi-Strauss/ Edmund Leach), Singer pleaded for a "semiotic anthropology" and Peacock claimed to have introduced the term "symbolic anthropology" in 1965. All these different names refer to a specific theoretical perspective. A perspective that positions symbols, their appearance, their operation and their use in the center of culture.

Ortner, in an excellent compressed account of theory in anthropology since the 1960s, argues that "symbolic anthropology" as a label was never used by any of its main proponents in the formative period – say, 1963–66. Rather, it was a shorthand tag (probably invented by the opposition), an umbrella for a number of rather diverse trends" (Ortner, 1984: 128). According to Ortner there were two major trends in symbolic anthropology: (a) Clifford Geertz, David Schneider and the Chicago School (influenced by Max Weber), and (b) Victor Turner at Cornell University (influenced by Emile Durkheim). The most prominent difference is that the Geertzians's focus is on "culture" (how do symbols operate as vehicles of "culture?" – from the actor's point of view), whereas the Turnerians's focus is on "society" (symbols as *operators* in the social process; more concerned with how symbols actually do what all symbolic anthropologists claim they do: operate as active forces in social processes).

Although Tennekes (1982), a Dutch anthropologist, agrees with the above-mentioned theoretical perspective, he warns for a too broad symbolic anthropology. He sees symbolic anthropology as a thematic specialism within the total field of anthropology. According to Tennekes, symbolic anthropology has four objects of study: *myths, rituals, symbolic classifications* and *collective representations*. We, building on Tennekes, see symbolic anthropology not in the first place as a thematic specialism (it has a too arbitrary character), but as a symbolic perspective on human processes in society. The particularity of this perspective is stressed by seeing cultures represented or classified by the use of symbols.

In sum: symbolic anthropology is perceived as a symbolic perspective on processes which take place within structures. Such a perspective seems useful for the following reasons: first, its concern with how signs become symbols; second, its concern with how symbols operate as vehicles of culture, and how culture itself can be seen as a system of symbols; third, its concern with how symbols actually operate in processes, and how they represent and classify a particular culture, and fourth, as a result, its concern with how symbols are consumed and in more general terms operate in the processes of cultural globalization and cultural localization.

There are two basic works underlying the development of this "new" symbolic perspective on culture. The first is *Philosophy in a New Key* by Susanne Langer (1948) and the second is Ernst Cassirer's *The Philosophy of Symbolic Forms* (1929). Langer showed that what makes a human being a human being is his/her ability to symbolize. This ability is the key to understanding all forms of interaction and communication. In communication studies one often refers to Langer as one of the central persons in developing symbolic theory. One can also trace its development by referring to the biologist Johannes von Uexküll and Ernst Cassirer's adjustments to his functional circle. Uexküll developed a scheme for the biological world:

> Every organism, even the lowest, is not only in a vague sense adapted to (*angepasst*) but entirely fitted into (*eingepasst*) its environment. According to its anatomical structure it possesses a certain *Merknetz* and a certain *Wirknetz* – a receptor system and an effector system. Without the cooperation and equilibrium of these two systems the organism could not survive. The receptor system by which a biological species receives outward stimuli and the effector system by which it reacts to them are in all cases closely interwoven.
>
> (Cassirer, 1944: 24)

In the human world, the functional circle (receptor system – effector system) is quantitatively enlarged and qualitatively changed. Between the receptor system and the effector system we find in human beings a symbolic system. The answers in human beings toward outward stimuli are not direct as in the animal world, but delayed by the symbolic system (Cassirer, 1944). This symbolic system is a key to understanding the differences in human culture. Differences in human culture are made up by differences in symbolic systems. A symbolic system is culture-bound and a medium or any product is not only communicating through a symbolic system, but entirely made up by it. Within the centrality of human being's capacity to symbolize many different theories developed based on either Ferdinand de Saussure (1857–1913) or Charles Sanders Peirce (1839–1914). Many different perspectives emerged, and theories on signals and indices, signs, images, symbols and so forth developed. Here, to keep it simple and to the point, symbols will include connotations (subjective meanings) and signs will not include connotation. Therefore, symbols are culture-bound, because meaning is culture-bound, and signs are not. Signs are a construct of the researcher/outsider and do not exist in real life. In real life, and from an interpretative perspective, signs without culture do not exist.

As mentioned, symbolic anthropology as it developed since the 1960s has two important representatives: Clifford Geertz and Victor Turner. Also these two anthropologists have had and still have their influence on the development of interpretative communication studies. Turner is mainly known through the introduction of his concepts "liminality" and "communitas." Furthermore, he has linked these concepts with the study of rites. "Liminality" refers to the middle phase of rites, which Van Gennep distinguishes in his classic book Les *Rites de Passage* from 1909. Van Gennep distinguishes three phases in all *rites de passage*: separation, margin (or *limen*, signifying "threshold" in Latin) (transition) and reaggregation (reintegration). Particular in initiation rites (e.g., initiation from boy to man, marriage or dying) these phases can be distinguished quite clearly. In the phase of transformation one does not belong to society and one is not a member of normal daily structure.

One is located in a time and space that has no social definition. The identity of the person or group is unclear. Such a liminal position offers a possibility of reflection and critique, but also of idealizing, equality and intense comradeship: "communitas" (Turner, 1969). It is in liminality that communitas emerges. Turner sees social structure as the opposite of communitas (Turner, 1974: 231) as communitas exists outside structured time.

Turner's theory has been very influential in the anthropological studies of socio-cultural rites. But also within communication studies, Turner's ideas with regard to liminality and communitas have been used for the study of television (e.g. Martin, 1981; Newcomb and Alley, 1983; Hoover, 1988). The act of watching television is regarded as a liminal experience; a phase in which the viewer experiences a transformation. The viewer leaves behind his daily life and enters the ideal utopian world of "communitas." This is a basic way to denote that there is a fundamental difference between watching "the world of television" and being in the real world. It is rather strange that the interest from communication scholars in Turner's theories doesn't go further than the concepts of "liminality" and "communitas," and shows no interest in Turner's ideas on an anthropology of performance or experience. Turner wrote, especially in the period before his death in 1983, about how to consider symbols within different fields of social action. In other words, he theorized about how cultural symbols are producing meaning in different situations of social action, including all kinds of acts of consumption. For instance, watching a soccer match in a pub differs from watching the same match in a domestic situation. Not only can one speak of a different ritual, and consequently of a different kind of liminality, but all the cultural symbols belonging to the ritual get a different connotation, because of the difference in the social situations. This kind of contextual socializing of cultural symbols is something Turner saw as an important aspect of the way symbols work. In a study on Turner, Moore states: "...the important point is that symbols, condensed and multi-vocal, may speak to different people in different ways; the construction and reconstruction of meaning occurs with specific, dynamic contexts of social process" (Moore, 1997: 234).

This is a very important point, because if the same symbols connote different things in different situations, how do they relate to social structure? If the same cultural symbols or symbolic forms (like a documentary on killing whales or on bull fights) are interpreted in different or even contradictory ways, the relation between symbolic forms and social structure becomes multi-interpretable. There is no clear connection because of the dynamic character of the symbols. Therefore, as Moore goes on:

> Culture exists as experience; it only occurs insofar as it is practiced. This leads to an anthropology of performance and a concern with praxis (literally, "action" or "practice," as in the performance of an art or skill), rather than an anthropology of social structure
>
> (Moore, 1997: 234)

For many, especially those who are working in the interpretative interdisciplinary field of the human sciences, the symbolic story of culture begins with Clifford Geertz. Geertz was probably for many non-anthropological scholars a first in-depth theoretical contact with anthropological thought. Somewhere in the 1960s he gave a lecture for *The Voice of America* under the title "The Transition to Humanity". He ended with:

> We are going, in the next few decades, to look at culture patterns less and less in terms of the way in which they constrain human nature and more and more in the way in which, for better or for worse, they actualize it; less and less as an accumulation of ingenious devices to extend pre-existing innate capacities and more and more as part and parcel of those capacities themselves; less and less as a super organic cake of custom, and more and more as, in a vivid phrase of the late Clyde Kluckhohn's, designs for living.
>
> (Geertz, no date: 8)

Geertz didn't know then what we know now: he himself was one of the key persons who formulated this change in thinking about culture (Geertz, 1973: 1983).

When communication scholars refer to theories on symbols they more often point to Geertz than to Turner. Geertz has studied the concept of culture more in-depth than Turner did. As Turner was more interested in how symbols operate in social life, Geertz was more concerned with the concept of culture itself. It was James Carey who, by way of reviewing *The Interpretations of Cultures* in 1975, introduced Geertz and his ideas concerning culture in communication studies: "To read the essays chronologically, though they are not so laid out in the book, is to witness the development of an increasingly precise and powerful theory of culture and one that progressively becomes a theory of communication as well" (Carey, 1975: 174). For an analysis of Geertzian theory with regard to its relevance for communication studies we refer to two earlier works (Lie, 1997a; Servaes and Lie, 1996).

From communication studies to cultural studies

The history of communication as a concept and the history of communication studies as a discipline is worth a study of its own. Communication is the main object of study in communication studies and much has been written on the concept. The history of communication studies, theories and ideas is in the process of becoming quite well documented and the field can identify its own founders and key scholars (see, for instance, Hardt, 1979; Rogers and Balle, 1985; Lent, 1995; Schramm (Chaffee and Rogers (eds), 1997). However, much of the available history or overviews of communication thoughts focuses almost solely on the development of mass media studies as a specialized area within the broader frame of communication studies. This media centrism has long been the dominant perspective and reduced the issue of culture to be only context.

The emphasis in both – communication studies and media studies – is mainly on the English-speaking world and especially on the United States of America. European development of communication studies or the Asian, African or Latin American development of communication studies and theory is less documented. This is true at least for the English language. In Europe, communication studies and theory developed as a separate discipline as late as the post Second World War period. In its early days, it simply followed the American-based communication studies that already flourished in the United States before the Second World War. This is also the case in Asia (see, for instance, Dissanayake and Said, 1983). It emerged simultaneously with the inventions of the new mass media. It is therefore no surprise that communication studies were media centered. In the early American and European days, the social and political study of communication equalled the study of the (impact of these) new mass media. One could say that, on the one hand, there was a *technological fascination* with the new media like radio, film and television and, on the other hand, an *instrumental fascination* with propaganda, persuasion and effects. The media were seen as important instruments in shaping people's behavior and attitudes

Things have changed since these early days. Communication studies itself has undergone several paradigm shifts and is now in a process of evolving towards a "culture centered paradigm," taking anthropological ideas into account and leaning towards a fusion with cultural studies (see, for instance, Baran and Davis, 1995; Renckstorf and Wester, 1997). In the early days, the concept of culture seemed of little relevance to the development of communication studies in general. It was common place to see communication as communicating culture. The content of the messages was culture (M = culture). As the emphasis in this time in the history of communication research was on the sender side, culture could be seen as an intention of the sender (S = M = culture). The sender was seen as putting culture into the message. Because of the dominant influential perspective, it seems also logical to assume that communication was regarded as having a direct influence on culture (R). The culture of the receiver (R) changed according to the culture "transmitted" ([S = M] = [R]) One could term this perspective on the relation between communication and culture the old mainstream/dominant perspective. Culture was directly transmitted from sender to receiver.

In the last twenty or thirty years we have seen, within the human sciences in general, and within communication study in particular, a shift away from the above perspective. The paradigm shift in communication studies refers to two related developments. First, we have witnessed a shift from media centrism to audience

$$\{[S \quad \Rightarrow \quad M]\} \quad \Rightarrow \quad [R]$$

S = Sender; M = Message; R = Receiver; [] = culture; {} = emphasis in theory and studies

Figure 18.1 Media centrism: the old mainstream perspective on the communication process and culture

$$[S] \qquad \Leftrightarrow \qquad \{[M \qquad \Leftrightarrow \qquad R]\}$$

S = Sender; M = Message; R = Receiver; [] = culture; {} = emphasis in theory and studies

Figure 18.2 Audience centrism: the new perspective on the communication process and culture

centrism (from production to consumption). Audience centrism centers the audience in the study of the communication process. This shift is often summarized in the following two sentences; in stead of asking "What do the media do to people?" ($M \Rightarrow R$), one should ask "What do people do with media?" ($M \Leftarrow R$) (Katz, 1959; 1980). This basic idea of reversal marked the change in focus of theory development and studies which started in the 1960s. The shift was not only a reversal of perspective, but included a changed perspective on culture. It was with the shift to audience activity in communication theory and studies that culture came into the picture in a *contextual* way. The message and the receiver were not separately placed in a context of culture, but together, as a process of decoding ($[M \Leftrightarrow R]$) (see Figure 18.2). Studies had undermined the direct influence of messages on changing cultures and the linear transmitting of cultures. This was especially felt in the field of intercultural communication. It became clear that American culture was not simply transmitted through for instance television programs to other countries. Scholars recognized that the receiver was decoding the programs in his or her own cultural context. So, with the shift towards an emphasis on the audience, a more contextual perspective on culture was introduced.

Within this "new" audience-centered perspective, Frissen and Nelissen (1993) distinguished and addressed four theoretical approaches: the uses and gratification approach, the information-seeking approach, media use as social action and cultural studies (for a review see Frissen and Nelissen, 1993). Characteristic for these four approaches is that the process of decoding is studied in a socio-cultural or individual framework. In this new perspective, the emphasis is no longer on culture as being transmitted through messages. Instead the emphasis is on the cultural context of the acts of reception/consumption. Furthermore, several nuances are being made with regard to culture. The culture transmitted is not simply the same as the culture of the receiver and the contextual culture of the receiving acts. This again differs from the contextual culture of the production process (the sender side).

All four approaches mentioned above emphasize that media consumption is not an isolated activity, though, cultural studies seems to differ from the other three approaches in several ways. Cultural studies cannot be seen as either media centered or audience centered. It tends to study the whole process of communication, or processes of communication, as *cultural processes* (see Figure 18.3). This means that culture is not only seen as *context*, but as *text*. Cultural studies expresses an integrated view on culture and communication and in many cases uses the symbolic anthropological notion of the concept of culture. Furthermore, following Hall, "culture" is the site of convergence (Hall, 1980: 59) and not

$$\{[S \quad \Leftrightarrow \quad M \quad \Leftrightarrow \quad R]\}$$

S = Sender; M = Message; R = Receiver; [] = culture; {} = emphasis in theory and studies

Figure 18.3 A cultural studies perspective on communication and culture

communications (Carey, 1975: 175) (see also Ang, 1990; Martin-Barbero, 1993; Silverstone, 1994; and others). In theorizing the concepts of culture and communication, cultural studies contributes substantially to a more fundamental embedding of the concept of communication in the concept of culture.

As far as the reception acts are addressed within cultural studies, scholars tend to talk about *consumption*, instead of reception. Consumption is a broader concept than reception and includes not only the reception of media content, but also the reception of countrysides, food, cities, neighborhoods, tourists, migrants, drinks, social festivals, rituals, consumption goods and so on. Furthermore, consumption has a more active connotation than reception and stresses the activity of actors. Consumption is seen in this chapter as an active process of symbolic communication. Consumption can be seen as a conglomerate of moments of cultural interpretations within the local level. As such these are crucial moments for identity spin-off processes, like globalization and localization.

The moment of consumption seems to be a crucial moment, but still needs to be embedded in a broader cultural frame. Such an idea of grasping the whole "circuit of culture" is very well illustrated by the Sage series on *Culture, Media and Identities* (Hall, 1997a). The whole series studies the "circuit of culture" which consists of five major cultural processes: representation (RP), identity (ID), production (PR), consumption (C) and regulation (RG). "Taken together, they complete a sort of circuit – what we have termed the "circuit of culture" – through which any analysis of a cultural text or artefact must pass if it is to be adequately studied" (Du Gay, 1997: 3). S ⟺ M ⟺ R is no longer an isolated process of communication, but includes the whole wealth of the circuit (see Figure 18.4).

Underlying the shift in emphasis in communication studies is a more general shift in the philosophy of communication studies which is generally associated with a turn towards interpretative and qualitative research. This concerns a shift in epistemology (assumptions regarding knowing) and ontology (assumptions regarding reality). Especially in (inter)cultural contexts we can witness a shift from a passive epistemology (knowledge arises out of discovery) towards an active

$$< \ \{[RP, ID, PR, C, RG]\} \ >$$

RP = representation; ID = identity; PR = production; C = consumption; RG = regulation; [] = culture; {} = emphasis in theory and studies; <> = culture of the researcher

Figure 18.4 A new cultural studies perspective and the position of the researcher in the process of communication and culture

epistemology (knowledge arises out of interaction between knower and known; knowledge is interpreting) and from a non-actional ontology (people as factors) towards an actional ontology (people as actors) (see, for instance, Littlejohn, 1983: 18–23; Dervin and Huesca, 1999). It is in this philosophical context that we touch upon issues such as (inter)subjectivity, normative theories, inner perspectives, etic-emic distinctions, participatory theories, etc. Therefore, it is also in this context that we need to problematize the *position of the researcher/outsider* in studying or guiding/interfering the cultural process. Especially in an intercultural context, the researcher is often an outsider to the cultural process. But even if the researcher shares the same culture, his or her position remains problematic. Figure 18.4 shows that, although the researcher is recognised as a subject in the process of communication and culture, he or she is not always problematized within the emphasis in theory and studies.

Emphasizing the wholeness in a specific perspective, cultural studies has in a sense created the meeting of symbolic anthropology and communication studies. The new field has evolved towards a distinct discipline with its own representatives, its own paradigm and object of study.

Cultural globalization, consumption and research

Globalization and localization

In recent years, the disciplines of anthropology, communication studies and cultural studies have shifted their attention towards using the process of (cultural) globalization/localization as an umbrella for sheltering their theoretical and practical enterprises. Anthropology shifted interest from classical ethnographic studies in search of authenticity to an interest in global-local connections (see for instance, the Routledge series on *The Uses of Knowledge: Global and Local Relations* (Strathern, 1996)). It also shifted attention towards current issues of consumption in general (see for instance Miller, 1995: 289), cross-cultural consumption (see, for instance, Howes, 1996) and the sociological/anthropological study of the consumption of places and cities (see, for instance, Urry, 1995; Eade, 1996). Communication scholars also shifted from isolated media studies towards more embedded cultural studies as they are moving towards the "culture centered" paradigm in communication studies. Interdisciplinary cultural studies had already taken up the theme in 1990 with a special issue of *Theory, Culture and Society* on global culture (Featherstone, 1990). More recently, the already mentioned book series *Culture, Media and Identities* (Hall, 1997a) discusses all aspects of globalization and localization. Disciplinary boundaries within the study of globalization/localization seem to be fading.

Within this interdisciplinary field of studying culture, much has been written on the process of globalization/localization. Globalization is often said to refer to the process of the world becoming a single place. The increased flows of knowledge – especially on the Internet – will cause a homogenized world culture. Such a political-economic and top-down perspective on development and change disregards that most people first of all live locally, in the sense of geographically, bounded lives. From within these localities people incorporate elements from other cultures. A homogenization in the supply of products and in the production processes themselves, does not implicitly mean that consumption is also homogenizing. This is one of the central aspects in the above discussed paradigm shift. Globalization/localization can also be approached as a(n) (inter)subjective/interpretative process. In this case it articulates changing identities.

Identity and consumption are two closely related terms. In a sense it can be said that consumption defines identities or even that identity is consumption; "you are what you consume." In the current age, collective and individual identities seem to be fragmented (see Servaes, 1997). With this we mean that identities are composed by interpreted fragments that originate from multiple levels. These levels range from the global to the local. A global identity and a local identity are therefore "ideal" forms, not existing in real life. All identities are a mixture of global and local aspects. People in local settings constantly reshape their own individual and collective identities by consuming cultural elements originating from a variety of levels. Within such a more people-centered perspective on globalizing and localizing identities (globalization/localization), and building on earlier research (Lie, 1997b and 1997c), we can distinguish several aspects in the process of defining cultural globalization/localization:

(aspect a)

Globalization and localization refer to a process of changes taking place in people's perceptions of time and space. On the one hand it refers to a broadening/widening of all kinds of boundaries... On the other hand it refers to a strengthening or a firmer articulation of existing boundaries...

Globalization/localization is in essence about changing perceptions of time and space. Giddens defined globalization for instance as "the intensification of world-wide social relations which link distant localities in such a way that local happenings are shaped by events occurring many miles away and vice versa" (Giddens, 1990: 64). By this definition he emphasises that local happenings can be interpreted in a broadening frame of time and space ("at distance"). Though, people's perceptions/interpretations within this frame of time and space tend to go in two opposite directions. First, we can identify the globalizing direction of homogeneity, synchronization, integration, unity and universalism (*scale enlargement*) and second, we address the direction of heterogeneity, differentiation, disintegration, diversity, variety and particularism (*scale reduction*). Although the different directions are often recognized, little is known about how the two are related and interconnected. Is the second direction a process of resistance to the globalizing process? Is localization a process of counteraction? Is it to be seen as an effort to counterbalance the international flow of alien cultural products? Does a macro culture globalizing process exist or can it only be found in the local?

317

All the ethnic and cultural movements around the world are not global in perspective. They are not about homogenization, they are about *differentiation*. Differences can only exist if there are others, and if there are others, there are boundaries. Locality, community, Gemeinschaft (Tönnies), neighborhood (Appadurai) all exist because of small-scale *boundaries*, which are either symbolic (Cohen, 1985), structural (political, economic, social, cultural), territorial/ geographical or virtual (Jones, 1995). Cultures have always tried to distinguish themselves from other cultures, emphasizing differences rather than similarities. The only way in which these movements can be termed global is in their use of new communication technology. Now, different groups, especially in the fourth world, can communicate with each other through e-mail, fax and visuals. This of course only means that their *means* of communication are global, not their *goals*.

Maybe we can actually pinpoint a process of broadening/widening of all kinds of boundaries, but cultural homogenization seems to be a myth. It does not exist as an actual process in its purest form. It is a mythical idea we probably need in order to be able to confront and emphasise the idea of cultural diversity.

> Television with its packaged imagery may sometimes suggest the vision and evoke the veneer of cultural globalism, but we must not confuse an essentially illusory effect with the continuing reality of ethnic and national divisions. It is not in the power of television, or any other media, to undermine these underlying realities.
>
> (Smith, 1992: 12; see for related discussion also Ferguson, 1992)

(aspect b)

Globalization and localization, as far as they refer to culture, are interpretative processes...This means they are not objective processes, but defined differently by different subjects, belonging to different communities, in different times and different spaces...

What is emphasised with this aspect is that globalization and localization not only refer to abstract changes taking place at a macro level; they also refer to how people, situated at local levels, perceive these changes. This aspect also points at what Braman (1996) has termed "interpenetrated globalization." With this she means that the relationship between the parts and the whole may be understood as mutually constitutive; the global never exists except in the local. In fact, this seems to be one of the new fundamental issues in thinking about globalization. Thinking about cultural globalization is not something completely new, but simply building on already existing theories and ideas such as "the global village," dependency thinking, Americanization/Westernization, cultural imperialism, media imperialism and cultural synchronization. But linking it in an intrinsic way to a process of localization seems to be a breakthrough. We now recognize that globalization and localization are two polar points on a continuum and that studying globalization from a people centered local perspective is not the exclusive domain of fieldwork anthropologists.

(aspect c)

Globalization and localization are in fact one process, because they are two sides of the same coin...The same (inter)cultural domains of origin (e.g. watching international television programs, encounters with international tourists, business contacts within the global economy...) can lead to both; a global interpreting process or a local interpreting process...This can even take place in the same interpretative community. Therefore, the processes are intrinsically linked to each other...

The main issue here is that we can identify different *domains of origin* to the process of globalization/localization. Domains of origin – causes or sources to the process – contribute in one way or the other to the process of globalization and localization. Globalization/localization as a process of change, is a result of acts and interactions. It originates from communication because all interaction is communication. We can distinguish between three different domains of origin: "personal communication," "institutional communication" and "product communication." These domains refer to communication between "people living in a particular local setting" on the one side, and, respectively, "people from other local settings" (P), "institutions" (I) and "products" (P) on the other side. It is these domains or communication processes that we can focus on in order to grasp the globalization/localization process (see Table 18.1).

Personal communication (P) between members of a cultural "in-group" and members of a cultural "out-group" is the first major domain of origin. All kinds of long-term or permanent intercultural migration (labor migration, student exchange, volunteers in development aid, military presence, etc.), and all kinds of short-term intercultural encounters, like those in "international" tourism (leisure migration) are major elements of concern. Especially in many "countries in development," tourism is regarded as an important factor in the globalization/localization process. This is mainly caused by the fact that the encounters are short-term. Because there is no time to get to know each other, people on both sides presume a lot. Therefore, the short-term encounters within the tourism industry have a major influence on the interpretative processes of globalization and localization.

Institutional communication (I) is the second domain of origin that is distinguished. In the field of communication and culture, it is important to realize that not only international television (as an institution) adds to the globalization/localization process. Other forms of *institutional communication*, like film, radio, telecommunications, the Internet, etc. are also responsible. Moreover, it is not only the media industry that is a major player in changing cultures. Other – sometimes overlapping – institutions like the cultural industry in general, religion(s), global politics, art, science, the economy and commercial trade, tourism, capitalism and production, etc., add to these changing processes.

What we mean by "institutional communication" might need some additional explanation. First of all, institutional communication refers to communication that is institutionalized. It refers to practices that are regularly and continuously repeated, legitimized and maintained by social norms. For instance a "flow of power" in a particular society is accepted by most of the people living in that society. Therefore, this accepted power has been institutionalized. The same can

Table 18.1 Domains of origin of globalization and localization

Domains of origin	Inclusion	Possible cases	Case examples
Personal communication (P)	– verbal and non-verbal communication between people	– communication between people from different cultures	– communication with tourists from another culture
Institutional communication (I)	– communication with institutions (bottom-up interpretations of institutions as a whole)	– the cultural/ media industry	– perceptions of mass media/ television as institutions
		– the consumption industry	– perceptions of industries such as Nike, McDonald's
		– the tourism industry (as an example of people migrations)	– perceptions of the tourist industry and the flow of migrants
Product communication (P)	– cultural/media products	– television programs	– watching *Baywatch*, *Neighbours*
	– consumer goods	– tourists artefacts	– buying and possessing masks, pottery
		– luxury goods	– drinking Coca-Cola
		– clothes	– wearing Nikes, Benetton
		– public products	– watching ads, cars, people in public places

be true for a "flow of television programs" or a "flow of people." The flow itself has been institutionalized. Being institutionalized does by no means mean that there is no change. Change occurs within an institution. The television programs or people that flow from one country to another change over time, but the institution remains. So, on the one hand, "institutional communication" can be regarded as "flows that are institutionalized." This however is not what we are aiming at here.

The aim is "communication with institutions" (=institutional communication as interaction). This refers to communication between persons and institutions in society (e.g. general perceptions and opinions about the institutions; e.g. "Television stimulates the fantasy and creativity of my children," "I think tourism is good for our society," "All those advertisements in our street are very ugly... They are all in English."). In this case "institutional communication" consists of general ideas and statements about institutions. Here the *interpretations/perceptions* of institutions by people living in local settings are emphasised. The difference between "institutionalized communication" and "communication with institutions" is that the first is a top-down communication flow; the latter is solely a process of interpretation and thus consumption. "Institutionalized communication" is a prerequisite for the bottom-up interpreting process of "communication with institutions," but of no further interest to a people-centered perspective on globalization/localization.

One of the major institutions that need to be addressed within the domain of institutional communication is the institution of "mass media" as part of the cultural industry. As a domain of origin this institution can be studied as a form of institutionalized communication. In this case one can study the top-down flow of communication or media products (television programs, films, newspapers, etc.) and the top-down flow of power (mass media policy). The study of these flows will be addressed later under (aspect d). In the case of "communication with institutions," which is at issue here, one's focus is on the communication between persons and the institution of mass media, in other words, the perceptions of the institutions. Within existing mass-media landscapes, television is one of the key issues because of its communication through talk and moving pictures, its widespread availability, and its (possible) content from/for other cultures. Therefore, a main focus can be on the perceptions of television as an institution (an example of the cultural industry). Other forms of "communication with institutions" concern the other two domains of origin: tourism as an institution (the tourism industry) and consumer goods as an institution (the production side of the consumption industry).

Product communication (P) is the third domain of origin. Communication *with* all kinds of ("international") products (consumption) and communication *about* all kinds of ("international") products (e.g. advertising) contribute to the process of globalization and localization. This field of study has come to be known as material culture and consumer culture. Within this field of study, products can be divided in two major groups. On the one hand we have *cultural/media products*, like "international" television programs, action movies, video clips, books, theater plays, etc. On the other hand we have *consumer goods* like food, Nike sports clothes, baseball caps, Benetton clothes and (street) advertisements for these, and other, consumer goods and cultural/media products. Communication with these goods/products (consumption/"things or objects in use") is regarded as a third domain of origin.

The above-distinguished three domains can be regarded as the most important sources of the processes of globalization and localization. Describing these domains of origin "internally as institutions," and "as interaction or in interaction with local people" gives us a fair indication of the process of globalization/localization.

(aspect d)

Globalization and localization as one linked process refers to the adoption/integration and dissociation/disintegration of cultural elements belonging to an "out-group" or to another socio-cultural level...

The PIPs originate from different societal levels, like the global, national and local level. The above-distinguished domains of origin can therefore be ascribed to different levels of origin. Coca-Cola and *Baywatch* are, for instance, global products. National products are, for instance, national television programs or national symbols such as national flags and national anthems. Local products, like local foods, originate from local settings. Although the above examples seem clear enough, the important question to ask is, of course, "What criteria do we use to ascribe people, institutions and products to what levels?" In our opinion this is a fundamental research design problem. We seem to have two options here. Either we, as researchers/outsiders, ascribe the PIPs to levels or we let local people/the researched do it. Using the origin of the production as a determining factor here is not an option. A product can be domestic in production, but global in use. It seems to be in the process of consumption that we will have to look for criteria on determining the level of origin. We will return to this later when discussing research design issues.

The three domains of origin (personal communication, institutional communication and product communication) and the three societal levels of origin (global, national and local) can be framed within four flows. The different kinds of flows can than be seen as responsible for the upward/outward process of globalization and the downward/inward process of localization. Approaching the process of globalization/localization from the angle of flows is overlapping the earlier discussed approach to the same process from the angle of communication. (For a short history of flow research, see Lie, 1997c.) The following flows can be distinguished: the communication flow, the power flow, the cultural interpretation flow, and the participatory flow. The first two are top-down flows. The latter two are bottom-up flows. It is important to note here that the communication flow and the power flow can in themselves be regarded as institutions in the sense as mentioned earlier (top-down institutionalized communication).

The communication flow is the top-down flow of people and products (cultural/media products as well as consumption goods). Institutions cannot be studied as flowing from the top downwards, because the flows themselves are the institutions. The communication flow, in the case of the flow of cultural products, starts with the producer of the product and ends with the watcher, listener or reader in a local setting. The actual consumption by the consumer is not included in the communication flow. In other words, the sending part of communication is under study here and this sending part is seen as an institution (see for instance, Servaes and Malikhao, 1998). *The power flow* is the top-down flow of policy and power with regard to the flow of people and products (regulation).

The cultural interpretation flow is the bottom-up flow of interpretations of people living in a geographical defined setting. People give meaning by interpreting the PIPs. *The participatory flow* is the bottom-up flow of action. This action refers to active participation in the cultural industry, the tourist industry and/or the consumption industry. This flow can for instance include counter movements, alternative tourist actions or the production of local reproductions or variants of foreign products, etc. However, it does not necessarily have to involve *counter* action. It can also mean working in the McDonald's or in a Coca-Cola plant. *Local discourse*, talk or as we named it elsewhere "the horizontal intra-level shared spiral flow" is the last "flow" under study. People talk about phenomena of globalization and localization. The local and national mass media report about issues related to globalization and localization. This local discourse is important as it discusses the integration or rejection of aspects of the domains. It therefore needs to be studied as local, but not cross-cultural communication. (For more information on levels and flows see Lie, 1997c.)

Researching nodal points

The situation with regard to the relations between globalization, consumption and identity is complex and intricate. Therefore, it seems necessary to adopt a convergence approach and an integrated approach to its study. Such an approach lets problems converge at key crossings or nodal points and approaches these crossings from the same perspective. This means that one does not study linear processes of for instance the long road from the production to the consumption of "global" products, the historical processes of the rise and fall of nations, or the cultural changes within subgroups. With a convergence and integrated approach we mean that one does not study these processes in totality – not underestimating the fruitfulness of such an enterprise – but instead, focuses on the nodal points where several processes intersect. In this way, problems/processes are not primarily approached in their own terms, but mainly in their interrelation with other problems/processes. In this way one can also speak of an integrated approach, because the problems are approached by stressing their links in an integrated manner; with the same underlying theoretical arsenal.

Building on the above, we have distinguished several nodal points of research. These points are deduced from the new cultural studies perspective that has been mentioned earlier, and are situated within intersecting processes of flows, levels and globalizing and localizing identities. The nodal points are: production (PR), regulation (RG), the local entry point of the communication flow (E), representation (RP), consumption (C) and action (A). Identity (ID) is articulated in the globalization/localization process itself, and is not a nodal point for research.

(nodal point PR)

Nodal point PR is a moment of *production*. What is produced at this point is either *people* ("production" is used here in the sense of "originating form") or *products and goods* (in the sense of actual production and "originating from"). It is the crossing point of, on the one hand, the communication flow and on the other hand the level of origin. The level of origin (global, national or local) is variable as is shown by the varying diagonal directions of the process of globalization/localization. The smaller the angle gets between "globalization/localization" and the "local level," the nearer – more visible – the moment of production will be for people at the local level. The nearer the moment of production gets, the better people can probably associate with the communication flow. This is assumed to be the case, because the communication flow is getting shorter and smaller. When a product is produced in a nearby village (within the intra-national level), the flow itself is more transparent to the people. When a product is instead produced in a far-away country, the flow is less visible. The products are just there in the local stores or on the local screens. In the area of mass media, an example would be that local television as an institution is closer to the people's homes than MTV or CNN as institutions. This has consequences for the institutional communication in general. When the process of "institutionalized communication" (the top-down flow) changes in length, there will also be changes in what we have called "communication with institutions" (general ideas, perceptions, opinions and statements about institutions). How these changes relate to each other remains to be seen. We will return to this case in point when we discuss the nodal point of consumption.

(nodal point E/RP)

E is the moment of *entry*. People and products/goods enter the local level. It is the point where the "communication flow" and the "local level" meet. As such it is also an entry point for institutionalized communication. The most important point to stress here is that the entry point is not a moment of consumption. The reason for a distinction between entry (E) and consumption (C) is that consumption is approached from an actor perspective and not a political economy perspective. Approached from this angle, the communication flow does not include consumption. Consumption is by definition horizontal and bottom-up and surely not top-down. *Reception* would therefore be the better word here, because it only connotes the moment of receipt. E is simply the end station of the top-down flow. From here the PIPs enter local discourse and the processes of consumption, interpretation and identity articulation start.

RP stands for *representation*. Representation (e.g. advertising) is seen here as being without local discourse. Representation is regarded as a product, yet to be interpreted by people living in local settings. However, this does not mean that representation is by definition completely without local content or local relevance. "...in order to sell, it must first appeal; and in order to appeal, it must engage with the *meanings* which the product has accumulated and it must try to construct an *identification* between us – the consumers – and those meanings" (Du Gay *et al.*, 1997: 25). These meanings are at this point only offered and have yet to go into a process of decoding, local discourse, consumption and bottom-up flows. Content analysis is an example of possible strategies to research the issue of representation. It can, however, never draw conclusions about actual consumption. It can of course produce hypotheses.

(nodal point RG)

RG means *regulation* and is also a moment of production. What's being produced here is power. The "highest" form of power is located at a macro regional level.

There is no power source at the global level. We have no world government. The closest regulating body to a world government is the United Nations. One of the most important levels of power is still the national level, although there seems to be a trend towards regulation at macro-regional levels, such as the European Union (EU) and the Association of South East Asian Nations (ASEAN). However, on the other hand, we can also identify a process of deregulation. Despite these tendencies, national governments are still major producers of power and thus regulation. Regulation has a two-way relation with production. Production influences regulation, but regulation also influences production. In the second case, regulation is on the globalization/localization continuum located at a higher level than production. For instance, when a product is produced at the national level (ascribed as originating from the national level), macro-regional policy does regulate the flow of this product. European audiovisual policy, for instance, does apply to national audio-visual products. The same national audio-visual product can also encounter intra-national policy/power. This is, for instance, the case when national programs are rebroadcasted by regional television stations, or, to give another example, when foreign cultural products are censored, or when migrants are denied the right to vote in local elections.

In the moments of power production that are situated at the local level, the vertical power flow is reduced to zero. Institutional power does not exist any more. This does not mean that within local discourse the issue of power is of no relevance. Power within the local level does exist, but has a horizontal character, like the ones based on kinship, age and local land rights. Every human relation and interaction has an intrinsic element of power and regulation is located within the community.

(nodal point C)

Nodal point C is the key moment of *consumption*. It is located at the local level. This is in fact the moment where *personal communication, communication with institutions* and *product communication* are made concrete (see the earlier discussed "aspect c" of globalization/localization). At this nodal point we can study people's interpretations of products, institutions and people (PIPs) and describe the bottom-up cultural interpretation flow. These interpretations are fundamental to identity processes. As such they are also regarded as the domain of origin for the process of globalization/localization as far as it is approached from a people centered perspective. In Table 18.1 we have already indicated some case examples for study, like perceptions of television as an institution, watching the television program *Neighbours*, buying souvenirs, drinking Coca-Cola, wearing Nike sports clothes and watching advertisements.

Research into the moment of consumption can take different shapes. In line with the paradigm shift, as explained in the first part of this chapter, it seems logical to use qualitative and interpretative research methods and techniques. These are suitable for research into interpretations. Techniques can vary from surveys, over focus groups to participant observation.

(nodal point A)

Point A is the moment of origin for *action*. This is the moment that we have called elsewhere *the action-oriented dimension of communication for localization* (see Lie, 1997b). This dimension of communication for localization refers, for instance, to the activities of grassroots social movements concerned with cultural and ethnic issues, but also issues related to processes of democratization. It is these activities that try to counterbalance "global" cultural flows and express concern with local cultural identities. The first concern is with localization and not with globalization, because the emphasis lies on *differences*. As an active concept "communication for localization" refers to supporting the voice of the local (which in some cases can also mean national or even macro-regional) or disadvantaged groups (either in a global, macro-regional, national, regional or local arena), in order to counterbalance the global communication flow and to positively favor "the right to culture" from the inside out.

In Figure 18.5, the nodal points of research are brought together with the process of globalizing and localizing identities.

What can we conclude from the scheme for research into globalization and localization?

- The most obvious conclusion is that researching the nodal points might lead to a *manageable* research project into the process of globalization/localization. The nodal points of production (PR), entry/representation (E/RP), regulation (RG), consumption (C) and action (A), can be studied in an integrated project. Studying these points within a frame of flows and local discourse can forward more grounded statements on the globalization/localization processes of identities.

- Within such a study, *consumption* seems to be the key moment as it is the center of rotation for globalization/localization processes. It is the moment where people's use of symbols and their interpretations are located. The interpreting processes of consumption are seen as the domains of origin for the processes of globalizing and localizing identities. It is here that identities are either starting to lean towards globalization or towards localization.

- There are *multiple globalization/localization processes* at work. We can identify different globalization/localization continuums. Two diagonal continuums have been explicitly drawn in Figure 18.5. On every continuum we can situate a moment of *production*. (It is also possible to locate several moments of production; e.g. in the case of Coca-Cola: the product itself is produced at the global level, but advertising (representation) is for instance produced at the different national or intra-national levels. This has not been explicitly drawn in the scheme.) *Regulation* can be situated in at least three different nodal points on every globalization/localization continuum. The points are the intersections with the macro-regional level, the national level and the intra-national level. The third point of *consumption* is in every continuum located in the center.

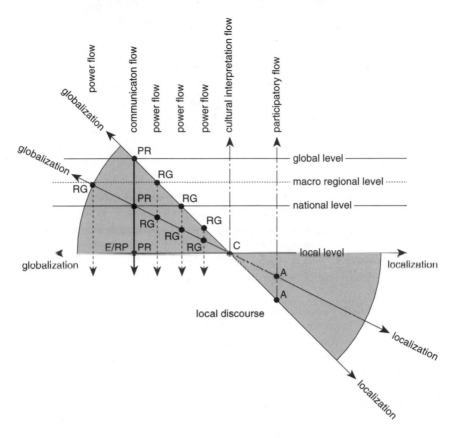

PR = production, E=entry, RP=representation, RG=regulation, C=consumption, A=action

Figure 18.5 Nodal points of research in a people-centered perspective on globalization/
localization

This connotes the people-centered perspective. If applicable, the nodal point of *action* is the fourth point to be found on every globalization/localization continuum.

• The nodal point of *entry* and *representation* (E/RP) is the only nodal point that is not located on a globalization/localization continuum. This is because the moment has a special status. The moment is either the end station of the communication flow (including representation) or the point of departure for decoding, local discourse, consumption and the bottom-up flow of interpretations. These latter are associated with the nodal point of consumption. It is however included as a nodal point because of the relevance of content analysis for research into globalizing and localizing identities. One could indeed argue that the issue of representation is the real "hardware" source.

- In a people-centered perspective on the process of globalization/localization, the domains of origin of the process (consumptions) are situated exactly in the middle of the polar points of localization and globalization. The nodal points of production (PR), regulation (RG) and representation (RP) are systematically located nearer to the polar points of globalization (left to the polar point of consumption). Only the nodal point of action (A) is located nearer to the polar point of localization (right to the nodal point of consumption). This indicates that production (PR), regulation (RG) – and representation (RP) – have implicit *globalizing tendencies*, whereas local action has *localizing tendencies* by, for instance, counteracting the globalizing tendencies.
- Every product is produced locally. As already mentioned earlier, this causes problems for *ascribing products and people to levels*. However, it needs to be done in order to be able to research globalization and localization issues. It is assumed in this model that the researcher/outsider decides that something is produced at a global, national or local level. Let us illustrate this with two examples.

Example 1: Coca-Cola is a global product. Why? With Coca-Cola being a global product, we mean that the production of Coca-Cola can be located at the global level. The product is globally distributed and known in almost all countries in the world. Furthermore, the product/company uses a global strategy in the communication flow. Coca-Cola is not specifically or only aiming at national or local entities. It is global in its outlook and approach. A global strategy can however insist on approaching nations and localities in its own terms. This does not make the product less global. Coca-Cola's strategy is sometimes referred to as a "multi-local" global marketing strategy. Moreover, consumers in their outlook towards the product (the cultural interpretation flow) can reach all the way up to the global level. People in local settings can see a product as being a global product. This is certainly true for Coca-Cola (see, for instance, Gillespie, 1995: 191–7, although here the global aspects are often mixed with the "American way of life"). It might also be clear from this example that the issue of *representation* (the way Coca-Cola is promoted and presented to the consumer) is very useful in helping the researcher/outsider ascribe a product to a level.

Example 2: The second example is situated in the field of tourism. The question that needs to be answered here is when to denote a tourist as a global tourist, or as a national tourist. The question is how to ascribe people to the different levels? When Germans visit the Netherlands, their neighboring country, they are not called global tourists. When Japanese go for their honeymoon to Guam, they are referred to as national Japanese tourists, not global tourists. The same is true for mainland Americans visiting Hawaii. What seems to be the case is that most tourists are ascribed as being of national origin. National tourists bring their national societal background as the primary frame for interpreting "the other." Global tourists are rare, because they are defined as *not* using another single national framework as the main frame of reference for interpreting "the other." International tourists are therefore mainly ascribed as originating from the national level. The tourist industry itself is a global industry, because it transcends national boundaries and is dominated by transnational companies.

- Only at the local level itself, globalization/localization is a *horizontal* process. The communication and power flows do not exist anymore. Nothing is institutionalized. This means that all the products, consumption goods and people originate from within the local level, without hierarchical structuring. There is no contact, whatsoever, with higher societal levels. There is no contact with foreign people and products. Everything is produced within the local level and communicated through local discourse. Regulation also exists only within the local level. Hierarchical regulation does not exist. Social community power is the only regulating source. It is horizontally distributed. It is an ideal situation in which globalizing and localizing identities seem to have no meaning anymore.

Conclusions

After having addressed the basic concepts of communication and culture within the disciplines of symbolic anthropology, communication studies and cultural studies, we have distinguished four different aspects in the process of defining cultural globalization/localization. These four aspects emphasised that globalization/localization is a linked process, an interpretative process and a process of changes taking place in people's perceptions of time and space. By stressing these aspects, globalization/localization articulates changing identities. It has explicitly been emphasised that globalization can be researched as a local process of changing identities. Globalization is seen as originating from local consumption and local discourse. Situated at the local level, globalization has an outlook towards national and global levels. On the other hand, the same moments of consumption can lead to inward processes of localizing identities. In this way this concluding chapter has also addressed the three sub-paradigmatic shifts towards culture, consumption and differences.

We lack insights into how the processes of cultural globalization and localization actually operate in locally defined public spheres. We consequently also lack insights in how the global is linked to the local and in how new perceptions of the global and the local lead to adjusted (cultural) identities. This chapter has therefore proposed – in line with the new cultural studies perspective – to do research into the selected nodal points of production (PR), regulation (RG), representation (RP), consumption (C) and action (A). It has been argued that there are in fact multiple globalization/localization processes at work and that consumption seems to be the key moment. Researching these nodal points might lead to a manageable research project and might provide us with more specific answers to the otherwise complex issue of globalization.

References

Ang, I. (1990). "Culture and communication: Towards an ethnographic critique of media consumption in the transnational media system." *European Journal of Communication*, 5, 239–60.

Baran, S.J. and Davis, D.K. (1995). *Mass Communication Theory. Foundations, Ferment, and Future.* Belmont, CA: Wadsworth Publishing Company.

Braman, S. (1996). "Interpenetrated globalization: Scaling, power, and the public sphere." In S. Braman and A. Sreberny-Mohammadi (Eds), *Globalization, Communication and Transnational Civil Society*, 21–36. Cresskill: Hampton Press.

Carey, J.W. (1975). "Communication and culture" [Review of "The interpretation of cultures"]. *Communication Research*, 173–91.

Cassirer, E. (1944). *An Essay on Man: An Introduction to a Philosophy of Human Culture.* New Haven, CT: Yale University Press.

Cassirer, E. and Manheim, R. (1929, 1965). *The Philosophy of Symbolic Forms.* London: Yale University Press.

Cohen, A.P. (1989, 1985). *The Symbolic Construction of Community.* London: Routledge.

Dervin, B. and Huesca, R. (1999). "The participatory communication for development narrative: An examination of meta-theoretic assumptions and their impacts." In T. Jacobson and J. Servaes (Eds), *Theoretical Approaches to Participatory Communication*, 169–210. Creskill, NJ: Hampton Press.

Dissanayake, W. and Said, A.R. (Eds) (1983). *Communications Research and Cultural Values.* Singapore: AMIC.

Du Gay, P. (1997). Introduction. In P. Du Gay, S. Hall, L. Janes, H. Mackay and K. Negus (Eds), *Doing Cultural Studies. The Story of the Sony Walkman.* London: Sage/The Open University (book 1 in the series *Culture, Media and Identities*).

Du Gay, P. (Ed.) (1997). *Production of Cultures/Cultures of Production.* London: Sage/The Open University (book 4 in the series *Culture, Media and Identities*).

Du Gay, P., Hall, S., Janes, L., Mackay, H. and Negus, K. (1997). *Doing Cultural Studies. The Story of the Sony Walkman.* London: Sage/The Open University (book 1 in the series *Culture, Media and Identities*).

Eade, J. (1996). *Living the Global City: Globalization as Local Process.* London: Routledge.

Featherstone, M. (Ed.) (1990). "Theory, Culture and Society." *Explorations in Critical Social Science*, 7(2–3), June (special issue on global culture).

Ferguson, M. (1992). "The mythology about globalization." *European Journal of Communication*, 7, 69–93.

Frissen, V. and Nelissen, P. (1993). "De kijker bekeken; Een overzicht van mediagebruik en publieksonderzoek." In Bardoel, J. and Bierhoff, J. (Eds), *Communicatie. Werking, Invloed.* Groningen: Wolters-Noordhoff.

Gillespie, M. (1995). *Television, Ethnicity and Cultural Change.* London: Routledge.

Giddens, A. (1990). *The Consequences of Modernity.* Cambridge: Polity Press.

Geertz, C. (1983). *Local Knowledge*. New York: Basic Books.

Geertz, C. (1973). *The Interpretation of Cultures*. New York: Basic Books.

Geertz, C. (no date). "The transition to humanity." *The Voice of America Lectures*, Anthropology Series 3.

Gennep, A. van (1981, 1909), *Les Rites de Passage*. Paris: Édition A. et J. Picard. (translated in German by Klaus Schomburg and Sylvia M. Schomburg-Scherff, 1986, Frankfurt/ Main: Campus Verlag GmbH)

Hall, S. (1980). "Cultural studies: Two paradigms." *Media, Culture and Society*, 2(1), 57–72.

Hall, S. (Series Ed.) (1997). *Culture, Media and Identities*. London: Sage/The Open University (series of 6 books).

Hall, S. (Ed.) (1997). *Representations: Cultural Representations and Signifying Practices*. London: Sage/The Open University (book 2 in the series *Culture, Media and Identities*).

Hardt, H. (1979). *Social Theories of the Press. Early German and American Perspectives*. Berverly Hills, CA: Sage.

Hoover, S.M. (1988). *Mass Media Religion: The Social Sources of the Electronic Church*. Newbury Park: Sage.

Howes, D. (Ed.) (1996). *Cross-Cultural Consumption. Global Markets, Local Realities*. London: Routledge.

Jones, S.G. (1995). "Understanding community in the information age." In S.G. Jones (Ed.), *CyberSociety: Computer-mediated Communication and Community*. London: Sage.

Katz, E. (1980). "On conceptualizing media effects." *Studies in Communications*, 1, 119–41.

Katz, E. (1959). "Mass communications research and the study of popular culture." *Studies in Public Communication*, 2, 1–6.

Lent, J.A. (Ed.) (1995). *A Different Road Taken; Profiles in Critical Communication*, CO: Westview Press.

Lie, R. (1997a). "Een antropologische vluchtroute uit het mediacentrisme." In J. Servaes and W. Fissen (Eds), *De Interpretatieve Benadering in de Communicatiewetenschap: Theorie, Methodologie en Case-studies*, 135–56. Leuven: ACCO.

Lie, R. (1997b). "What's new about cultural globalization?...Linking the global from within the local." In J. Servaes and R. Lie (Eds), *Media and Politics in Transition: Cultural Identity in the Age of Globalization*, 141–55. Leuven: ACCO.

Lie, R. (1997c). "Levelization and de-levelization. Researching the global in the local in a participatory way: Toward a qualitative multi-level flow analysis." *Culturelink*, August 22, 1997, 131–48. Dossier on Networking in Third World Environments, Zagreb, Croatia: Culturelink/IRMO, Network of Networks for Research and Co-operation in Cultural Development, Institute for Development and International Relations (IRMO).

Littlejohn, S. (1983). *Theories of Human Communication*. USA: Wadsworth Inc.

Mackay, H. (Ed.) (1997). *Consumption and Everyday Life*. London: Sage/The Open University (book 5 in the series *Culture, Media and Identities*).

Martín-Barbero, J. (1993). *Communication, Culture and Hegemony: From the Media to Mediations*. Newbury Park: Sage.

Martin, B. (1981). *A Sociology of Contemporary Cultural Change*. Oxford: Basil Blackwell.

Miller, D. (1995). "Consumption studies as the transformation of anthropology." In D. Miller (Ed.), *Acknowledging Consumption. A Review of New Studies*, 264–95. London: Routledge.

Moore, J.D. (1997). *Visions of Culture. An Introduction to Anthropological Theories and Theorists*. London: Sage.

331

Newcomb, H. and Alley, R.S. (1983). *The Producer's Medium: Conversations with Creators of American TV*. New York: Oxford University Press.

Ortner, S.B. (1984). "Theory in anthropology since the sixties." *Comparative Studies in Society and History*, 26(1), 126–66.

Renckstorf, K. and Wester, F. (1997). "Mediagebruik als sociaal handelen. Theoretische uitgangspunten, methodologische implicaties en enkele consequenties voor onderzoek." In J. Servaes and V. Frissen (Eds), *De Interpretatieve Benadering in de Communicatiewetenschap. Theorie, Methodologie en Case-studies*, 39–65. Leuven: ACCO.

Rogers, E.M. and Balle, F. (Eds) (1985). *The Media Revolution in America and Western Europe*. Norwood: Ablex.

Schramm, W. (Chaffee, S.H. and Rogers, E.M. (Eds)) (1997). *The Beginnings of Communication Study in America: A Personal Memoir*. London: Sage.

Servaes, J. (1997). "Mass media and fragmented identities." In J. Servaes and R. Lie (Eds), *Media and Politics in Transition. Cultural Identity in the Age of Globalization*, 77–88. Leuven: ACCO.

Servaes, J. (1999). *Communication for Development. One World, Multiple Cultures* (Foreword by Jan Pronk). Creskill, NJ: Hampton Press.

Servaes, J. and Lie, R. (1996). "Toward a more interpretative communication research 'framework': Television as a cultural system; An interpretation of Clifford Geertz." *Communicatio*, 22(1), 42–9.

Servaes, J. and Malikhao, P. (1998). "A critical examination of a UNESCO study on television flows in Europe and Asia." Paper presented at the conference The Production and Consumption of National and Local Cultural Products in the Age of Global Communication, June 5–7, 1998. National Chung Cheng University, Chia-Yi, Taiwan.

Silverstone, R. (1994). *Television and the Everyday Life*. London: Routledge.

Singer, M. (1984). *Man's Glassy Essence; Explorations in Semiotic Anthropology*. Bloomington: Indiana University Press.

Smith, A.D. (1992). "Is there a global culture?" *Intermedia*, 20(4–5), 11–12.

Strathern, M. (Series Ed.) (1996). *The Uses of Knowledge: Global and Local Relations*. London: Routledge (6 books).

Tennekes, J. (1982). *Symbolen en hun Boodschap*. Assen: Van Gorcum.

Thompson, K. (Ed.) (1997). *Media and Cultural Regulation*. London: Sage/The Open University (book 6 in the series *Culture, Media and Identities*).

Turner, V.W. (1969). *The Ritual Process; Structure and Anti-structure*. Chicago: Aldine Publishing Company.

Turner, V.W. (1974). *Dramas, Fields, and Metaphors. Symbolic Action in Human Society*. Ithaca: Cornell University.

Urry, J. (1995). *Consuming Places*. London: Routledge.

Woodward, K. (ed.) (1997). *Identity and Difference*. London: Sage/The Open University (book 3 in the series *Culture, Media and Identities*).

INDEX